D1169781

ENVISIONING
Human Geographies

ENVISIONING
Human Geographies

EDITED BY Paul Cloke • Philip Crang • Mark Goodwin

A member of the Hodder Headline Group
LONDON

Distributed in the United States of America by Oxford
University Press Inc., New York

ARNOLD

First published in Great Britain in 2004 by
Arnold, a member of the Hodder Headline Groups,
338 Euston Road, London NW1 3BH

http://www.arnoldpublishers.com

Distributed in the United States of America by
Oxford University Press Inc.
198 Madison Avenue, New York, NY 10016

© 2004 Edward Arnold (Publishers)

All rights reserved. No part of this publication may be reproduced or
transmitted in any form or by any means, electronically or mechanically,
including photocopying, recording or any information storage or retrieval
system, without either prior permission in writing from the publisher or a
licence permitting restricted copying. In the United Kingdom such licences
are issued by the Copyright Licensing Agency: 90 Tottenham Court Road,
London W1T 4LP.

The advice and information in this book are believed to be true and
accurate at the date of going to press, but neither the editors nor the publisher
can accept any legal responsibility or liability for any errors of omissions.

British Library Cataloguing in Publication Data
A catalogue record for this book is available from the British Library

Library of Congress Cataloging-in-Publication Data
A catalog record for this book is available from the Library of Congress

ISBN 0 340 72012 3

1 2 3 4 5 6 7 8 9 10

Typeset in 10/14 GillSans by Charon Tec Pvt. Ltd, Chennai, India
Printed and bound in Malta

What do you think about this book? Or any other Arnold title?
Please send your comments to feedback.arnold@hodder.co.uk

CONTENTS

Introduction

Paul Cloke

Personal vision?

This book presents a series of personal visions for the future of human geography. Before introducing each chapter, I want to dwell briefly on this interconnection between the personal, the subject and the visionary agenda, because it seems important to recognise that the 'subject' of human geography is very much to be found at the interstices of individual human geographers and the collectivity of their and others' work. To identify stimulating futures for human geography, then, will at least in part entail a recognition of the kinds of intellectual, ideological, aesthetic and everyday prompts which fire the personal human geographical imagination. An understanding of why we are interested in particular subjects/objects/modes of human geographical study will not solely be found in the quality and persuasiveness of the canon of study which already exists, important though that is. Such an understanding will also demand some scrutiny of the subjectivities, identities, positionalities and situated knowledges that we as individuals bring to the collectivity of that canon.

The iteration of individuality and collectivity is, I suspect, a fundamental but sometimes taken-for-granted aspect of the academic profession of human geography. In the every-day events of seminars, tutorials, presentations, reading groups and the like, *choice* is exercised over the focus of the event; *politics* are worked out in its conduct and inter-relations; *experience* is deployed in order to ground, illustrate, compare or contrast; *position* is expressed (and sometimes shifted) in critical engagement with text and discussion; *knowledge* is displayed in the structuring or destabilisation of understanding; and deep-seated but sometimes difficult-to-define aspects of *opinion* – like and dislike – surface in the seemingly instinctive reaction to particular ideas and expressions. For years now, many human geographers have reacted vehemently against the notion that they should operate as some kind of white-coated automaton, carrying out their work in the tyranny of supposed neutrality and objectivity. It seems important, however, to avoid the opposite essentialism – the idea of caring, sharing human geographers totally in touch with their identities and thoroughly able to recognise and control the reflexive prompting of their subjectivities. No, these expressions of individuality seem much less certain than such an image might suggest. They emerge fitfully and inconsistently, as capable of being swayed by fashion or prejudice as being developed with intellectual or emotional certainty. They also bear the marks of unspoken but plainly evident agendas, such as the pursuit of personal or professional reputation, the external structuring of suitable 'deliverables' of research and scholarship, and differential levels of ease with arenas of power – where exploration, subjugation and demand of respect are both presenced and performed.

Individuality in human geography, then, is a somewhat difficult-to-grasp series of prompts, often hidden behind and justified by a liaison with the existing collective canon. Nevertheless, further scrutiny of what we as individuals bring to the table seems to me to be both necessary and fruitful if we are to proceed to a discussion of what it is to envision the future. There are many ways of approaching such a task, some of which focus autoethnographically on the self, and others which analyse the reflexive principles (ideologies, theories, spiritualities and so on) around which the self is thought to be fashioned. Yet another approach, and one which I have found to be both informative and fun in teaching, is to use a sense of like and dislike of texts (books, papers, films) as a mirror of the particularity of an individual approach to the subject. The task here is to fashion an opportunity to choose texts which appeal, and to present an account of that choice – a kind of *Desert Island Disc(ourse)s* – allowing others to offer an interpretation or deciphering of what emerges with reference to the interface between the individual and the texts. There are obvious dangers here, notably the risk of a deliberate fashioning of choice to present a persona which is knowledgeable/fashionable/tasteful/intellectually right-on. However, suspend your scepticism and give it a go. Here, for example, is a summary of a recent exercise in which I chose ten books with links to human geography for my desert island. They were as follows (in no particular order, and bearing in mind that the Bible and the complete works of Shakespeare are already in the bag).

1.   *David Korten (1995) When Corporations Rule The World*

David Korten is the founder of The People-Centred Development Forum, an organisation concerned with the creation of just, inclusive and sustainable societies through voluntary action. His populist book charts the concentration of economic and political power in a small number of financial institutions and corporations, which are largely blind to human interests and focussed increasingly on short-term financial gain. Although Korten's 'establishment' approach sometimes grates (I think that I really would rather hear commentaries on these issues from the perspective of idealistic, supposedly old-fashioned, left-wing politics), his critical exposure of globalisation necessitates some kind of personal response. It chimes loudly and harmoniously with the issues of practical justice that I share with my wife Viv, who is a champion for ethical trading, and runs a local Traidcraft network in Bristol.

2.   *John Rawls (1971; 1999) A Theory Of Justice*

This is a book that, to my shame, I have only recently discovered and read. Rawls expounds a theorisation of justice which encompasses both liberty and socio-economic benefit. I don't find it user-friendly (I'm worried that this exposes an intellectual shallowness on my part), but I do find it provocative in terms of appropriate political and ethical futures. I am struck by potential parallels with biblical philosophies of agape, caritas and justice. It is a book that I want to go deeper into.

3. Cynthia Duncan (1999) Worlds Apart

Mil Duncan's account of rural poverty in Appalachia, the Mississippi Delta and New England presents powerful ethnographic evidence of the connections between place, community, politics and inequality. She contrasts the downward spiral of persistent poverty which erodes community and political will in Appalachia and the South, with the strong civic culture in her New England case study, where a rather different community fabric seems to offer pathways for the escape from poverty. This book scratches where I itch in its concerns for the political and ethical spaces of rurality, and in its methods of encountering its subject.

4. Joanne Passaro (1996) The Unequal Homeless

A painstaking ethnography of homelessness in New York, Joanne Passaro's book underscores, for me, the continuing importance of social geographies. Not only does she emphasise the cultural and moral locations of homelessness, but her perspectives on gender and race demonstrate how the preferential treatment given to homeless women both keep (predominantly black) men on the streets, and endow women escapees from the streets with embodied and traditional ideals of womanhood.

5. Tim Cresswell (1996) In Place Out Of Place

Jim Duncan's cover note sums up this book more eloquently than I ever could:

> 'Through a close reading of that which is considered to be "out of place" in our society, Cresswell casts a brilliant light on the role of space and place in the practices of everyday life and the maintenance of ideological belief … This is new cultural geography at its best.'

More particularly, Tim Cresswell's study presents ideas and understandings which seem to me to work when applied to knowledges arising from research into rural poverty and rural homelessness.

6. David Syring (2000) Places In The World A Person Could Walk

Syring's evocative and memory-laden anthropological study of the Texas Hill Country explores the notion of belonging to a place. His family histories of 'homeplace' interweave graciously with the adoption of the town of Fredericksburg as a virtual home for German Americans attracted by the heritage tourism industry. His recognition of the importance of the local church, both as social nexus and as container of memory, adds important dimensions to the wider discussion of what it is to recognise a place as a spiritual home.

7. Iain Borden (2001) Skateboarding, Space And The City

My 18-year-old son, Will, is a skateboarding fanatic. Through his eyes I have learned to rethink the city of Bristol and beyond. His eye for the architecture of place relies on embodied knowledges of surfaces and edges which had previously evaded my perview. His sense of resistance to the conventions and authority of the city is vital to the embodied expression of energy and emotion through skateboarding. Iain Borden's book charts the subculture through which skateboarders experience and understand the city. For me, this is Will's human geography.

8. Jane Desmond (1999) Staging Tourism

I am fascinated by nature–society relations, and in particular have become interested in relational agency, which notably involves the co-constitution of place by non-human and human agency. Jane Desmond's study of the role of bodies and performance in tourism is an excellent analysis of the cultural and the natural. It also demonstrates how the bodily presences and performances of animals (in her case the killer whales and dolphins of the animal theme park) become invested with meaning. Her book prompts me to think through rather more carefully the political and ethical ramifications of taking non-human agency seriously.

9. Charles Villa-Vicencio and John de Gruchy (eds) (1994) Doing Ethics In Context

This is a book I picked up in the University of Cape Town bookshop during a trip to Khayelitsha, where I have an involvement in a community partnership scheme. The book both evokes and speaks into the grounded ethical issues of practical involvement in a South African township. It is written by South African theologians from a wide range of traditions and perspectives, applying the ethics in African, feminist and liberation theologies to everyday South African issues such as violence, human rights, economic justice and reparation. Its pitch as an introductory text is a salutory reminder of the complexity and depth of understanding required even to introduce yourself in a post-colonial framework to situations such as those encountered in Khayelitsha.

10. Ryszard Kapuscinski (2001) The Shadow Of The Sun

Africa again – this time seen autobiographically by a legendary Polish journalist who presents compelling accounts of the changing politics of Africa over half a century. Describing the starving people of war-torn Sudan, he writes:

> 'we are here among a people who do not contemplate transcendence and the existence of the soul, the meaning of life and the nature of being. We are in a world in which man, crawling on the earth, tries to dig a few grains of wheat out of the mud, just to survive another day'.

The poetics of his reflection stand in memorable contrast to the betrayed humanity of his subject.

So, what does such an exercise reveal? First, I acknowledge that this simple device will itself always involve partial and sometimes fleeting revelations about the individualism(s) concerned. The choice of texts will be indicative; last year – even last week – it would have been different. Equally, the process of choice and presentation is itself culturally political. Even if I am not overtly trying to persuade you to adopt these books as your own, or to approve of my choice, I am, of course, aware of the opportunities and vulnerabilities involved in disclosure. Inevitably I have been careful about what is included in and omitted from the annotations, and thereby I have imposed a sense of structured reflexivity onto the proceedings. However, (and my experience with this kind of device is that it tells others more about your self than you know yourself) some salient reflections do emerge.

First, I am interested to discover just how few of the chosen authors are human geographers by discipline. Here I am not suggesting any lack of quality or impact in the work of human geographers, who themselves speak to audiences both within and beyond their disciplines. No, I would simply point to the increasingly interdisciplinary nature of the work we do and the texts we read. Although there is a clear disciplinary politics at work to ensure the survival and ongoing health of human geography, our interests and passions cannot and should not be contained within such strict boundaries. Envisioning an intellectual future for human geography will inevitably reflect both the recognition of suitably centripetal tendencies in order to offer an account, and perhaps even a defence, of our core concerns, and a grasping of interdisciplinary opportunities for being in the world alongside others with different ways of knowing that world.

Second, I would want to propose that for me there is an inevitable liaison between my human geography and the practices and concerns of my everyday life. This is not to espouse some sentimental type of heart-on-the-sleeve liberalism, nor to attempt to guilt-trip anyone for whom the liaison with the everyday is different. It is simply to suggest that for me, the boundaries between research and practice are sometimes permeable, with research interests flowing into everyday action and vice versa. Interestingly, the everyday interests of family and friends also conspire to break through the barrier into everyday human geography interests (note Will and his skateboarding, for example).

Finally, there does appear to be at least a loose structuring of the concerns and interests expressed in the exercise. For example, there is a strong political passion relating to issues of justice and injustice, which finds expression in research interests in poverty and homelessness. Such passion perhaps lacks an obvious theoretical cohesion, drawing as it does on a range of knowledges, but it does serve to position my human geography within a terrain of politicised concern. It also sponsors a lively interest in human geographies of ethics. Moreover, there is also evidence of particular geographical terrains of interest, most obviously relating to rural areas, but with other territorial emphases, notably the homeless city and the township. Another commonality is a respect for ethnographic ways of encountering the people of these terrains and territories. Such structured positions and knowledges, however, are made complex by other cross-cutting influences. An adherence to Christian spirituality complicates standard adoption of secular social theory or ideological precept, whilst also offering a capacity to raise awkward ethical questions. And quite how the emphases on embodiment and nature–society relations fit with these other positionings I find difficult to explain, at least without admitting to the allure of some theory for its own sake, and of tourist places with their own capacity for pleasure.

Now, your reactions to the books which I chose, and more importantly your choices and rationales if asked to undertake a similar activity, will inevitably be different from mine, and that surely is the point. It is the differences of individual human geographers nudging up against the commonalities of human geographies which create the environment of dynamic positions and knowledges and, when applied to space, place and nature present fundamental sites for claims about the intellectual distinctiveness of human geography.

And it is the experience and expression of discontent with these positions, knowledges and sites, along with the recognition of unresolved itches to scratch, which can bring vision for the future of these human geographies.

Envisioning human geographies

It is with this matter of vision that this book is principally concerned. What follows is a series of visions for the future of human geography, and the hope of we, the editors, is that these visions will provide a vigorous and far-sighted debate about what human geography could and should be concerned with at the beginning of this new century. Our authors have been asked to think forwards, taking a line of enquiry into the nature of human geographies which might fruitfully be translated into such forward thinking. They have been asked to map out important new territories of enquiry, and to facilitate a wider envisioning of the subject. Accordingly, we have not attempted to present a systematic coverage of different aspects of the subject, but rather the book consists of a series of personal manifestoes for the future of the subject. We have wanted to give space here for the individualities of the authors to nudge up against the wider commonalities of human geography.

Taking full account of the importance of the individuality expressed in each chapter, we have nevertheless provided authors with a structured space within which they can work. This structure stems from four broad concerns which have already been mentioned here and which will run through, though with differing relative emphases, all the chapters. These are: *position, knowledge, nature, space*.

- By **position**, we mean the location of the discipline, institutionally, geographically and personally.
- **Knowledge** refers more to the character of human geographical thought.
- **Nature** and **space** address the two fundamental sites for claims about the intellectual distinctiveness of human geography.

In **Chapter 1**, **Neil Smith** examines one of these fundamental sites in more detail when he reflects on some of the key emerging problematics in the treatment of space within social theory. He argues that space is increasingly the language of the most innovative social and cultural theory, before drawing on the work of Lefebvre to examine why this might be the case. He then provides a critique of the treatment of space by both Lefebvre and Soja, before concluding with a discussion of the continued practical and political significance of the active 'production of space'. He argues that an insistence on the connections between space and nature – 'between space and the substance that fills it' – can help to fulfill the promise of a respatialisation of social theory. His own vision of the future is one where practical geographical knowledges are simultaneously spatial, natural and social, and where an understanding of lived experience can help overcome the conceptual limits of spatial abstraction.

Margaret Fitzsimmons addresses another of the fundamental sites for human geographers in **Chapter 2**, where she argues for a human geography which fully engages with questions of nature. Fitzsimmons' core concern is about how to 'know about nature' in ways that support conscious socio-ecological projects which address both nature and difference, and in ways that aid people to construct a better future. She focusses on the science of ecology and its implications for knowing and acting in a human geography which is utterly concerned with nature. Here, she sees ecology as modelling certain ethical commitments: a respect for life, and a concern about using the world as a laboratory without carefully designed and controlled experiments in which creatures are not harmed. Such ethical commitments, she argues, will put ecologists and human geographers into the front line of the science wars, refuting the idea that science offers the only useful knowledge about the world, and suggesting that the deployment of this scientific knowledge outside the laboratory represents the principal source of unintended consequences in the site of nature. These visible questions and engagements in ecology, she argues, point very clearly to unexamined questions and engagements in human geography.

These key sites of space and nature are brought together in **Chapter 3** by **Michael Watts**, who questions what it might mean to envision a spatiality of nature appropriate to the twenty-first century. In order to address this question, Watts deploys the idea of *enclosure* as a way of exploring some fundamental aspects of nature–society dialetics. He shows how the territory of nature is reconstituted through boundaries, property lines and markets, and how enclosure entails loss of rights, obligations and responsibilities. Watts deploys the metaphor of the zoo to show how nature presents a living monument to its own external demise, but he also shows how animals and places have been transformed, so to speak, from within, through conversion into sites of accumulation. By focusing on the broiler chicken industry, he shows how the chicken genome project marks a late-twentieth-century process of Frankensteinian enclosure, with animals confined to broiler houses, and the chicken contractor enclosed within a highly oppressive industrial broiler complex. Watts' warning is that new forms of confinement, dispossession and loss of rights are already at work, backed both by the forces of the state and by the mythos of science and technology. His response is to point towards an informed, legitimised and sharpened class politics.

The next six chapters tackle questions of position and geographical knowledge. In **Chapter 4**, **Mark Goodwin** argues for a continued engagement between political economy and human geography. However, he also emphasises that this should take place from a 'post-disciplinary' perspective – one where a sensitivity to issues of uneven development and geographical difference is not confined to that small piece of the intellectual world we continue to label as 'geography', but which is commonplace across the social sciences. Paradoxically perhaps, he maintains that such a perspective will enhance the influence of geographical knowledges on political economy. However, this political economy must be renewed, not only to take on board matters of space and spatiality, but also to address a range of new concerns which stem from the continued upheavals of contemporary capitalism. He outlines the framework for this renewed political economy, and sets out what this might mean for an enhanced engagement with geographical ideas.

A very different agenda is asserted by **Nigel Thrift** in **Chapter 5**, who sets out a manifesto for non-representational human geography, which he sees as a machine for multiplying questions and thereby inventing new relations between thought and life. Thrift's agenda is to emphasise the many solutions rather than the one, to create 'differents' and 'manyness' rather than being content with sameness. His is a 'multi-verse', not a 'uni-verse', in which intersection, transfer, emergence and paradox are core ideas. His is also a political programme. Non-representational theory, he argues, gives a chance to those encounters and interactions that are partly invisible in the hegemonic regime, and are thereby excluded from the definition of what counts as knowledge. It presents human geographers with new emphases on how and what it is to think. Representation can only cover so much of the world. Non-representational spaces are a kaleidoscopic mix of space times, constantly being built up and torn down. These space times are embodied, shot through by bearers of unconscious thought, and politicised by an ethics which works on the faculty of judgement as it is actually exercised, that is in the immediate present. And these non-representational space times offer potentials for greater grace, hope, joy, respect, dignity and fun – thus presenting an alternative politics for human geography.

Catherine Nash, in **Chapter 6**, offers a postcolonial take on human geography, asking whether the discipline can move from its position of colonial complicity, and producing a positive answer. She argues that the work of colonial discourse theorists and postcolonial critics does provide an agenda by which human geographers can address the complexity of colonial relations, the cultures of domination, resistance and hybridity, and the classed and gendered differences of privilege and power in the post-independence state. Perhaps most of all, postcolonial geographies can operate in the present climate of both globalising and separatist impulses to enrol both history and geography to creatively and critically rethink identity and belonging, rather than simply deconstructing them.

The question of position is also tackled by **Geraldine Pratt** in **Chapter 7**, whose essay on feminist human geographies first problematises the notion of a feminist politics at a time when the emphasis of human geographies is on the wider geographical production of difference, and then offers an agenda for the unravelling of these politics. A feminist politics, she argues, needs to be alert to the suspicion that women are not fully included in the universalisms of this day and age. Feminist geographies represent a persuasive resource for alliance-building between women and other marginalised groups. Such a resource can be used to highlight the particularity that dwells within universalist claims in human geography and politics, and to insist on the difference that differences can make.

In **Chapter 8**, **Marcus Doel** explores the contours of a poststructuralist geography by setting out his own top forty essential selections, liberally spinkled with and illustrated by exerts from literary fiction. Through these he initially explores the position of poststructuralism *vis-à-vis* structuralism, before taking up similar concerns to those of Nigel Thrift in discussing the impossibility of representation. He argues against the reduction of human activity to either labour power or a force of consumption, instead preferring to stress the experiential and experimental. He then moves on in his essential selection to focus not on form or function, not on objects or subjects, but on sets of relations and differential powers. Geography enters not as a found object, but as something which has to be assembled and 'lent a transient consistency' in contexts which are, as yet, barely discernible. Indeed, he cautions against any attempt to envision a future for the discipline, before emphasising the dangers of forcing too restrictive a view of geographical practice. There is no conclusion to this chapter – only a plea to recognise that everything is always in constant motion and perpetual circulation, and that through this movement space 'takes place'.

Finally in this group of chapters, **John Pickles** reflects in **Chapter 9** both on the role of digital information and imaging systems in constructing new worlds, and on the limits of these computational representations. He seeks to broaden the discussion of 'the world in the wires' to formulate an appreciation of 'the wires in the world'. In the chapter he details five examples of large-scale cyber engineering projects, at the heart of which are significant new conceptions of space, bodies and subject. He sets an agenda which not only seeks to understand the shifting boundaries of the everyday cyborg world, but also traces the social systems that arise in the phantasmic spaces that are co-constituted through information and communication technologies. These spaces, argues Pickles, are contestable, but they will be strongly contested by forces of monopoly power, and totalisation logic against which human geographies of resistance may have to be mobilised.

The final three chapters represent a range of specific responses to the warnings raised earlier in the book. In **Chapter 10**, **David Smith** reviews the recent explorations of moral geographies, and the contemporary engagement of human geography with ethics, considering the implications of these perspectives for the analysis and practice of social justice. In his account, Smith advances a conception of social and environmental justice which transcends undeserved geographical differences in life chances. However, he argues that if human geographers are to make claims about helping to create a better world, they should take considerable care to ensure that such claims are built on a firm moral foundation. The establishment of new institutions and social arrangements in order to equalise human life projects is ultimately a political project which is only conceivable if driven by the most powerful moral argument. Smith argues that it is to a postmarket morality that such a vision needs to be directed.

Chapter 11 might usefully be read alongside the first part of this introduction, in order to marry the individualisms there disclosed with a subsequent vision for an agenda for human geography in which different strands – the justice of political economy, the intense engagement with judgement in cultural studies and the potential contribution of faith and spirituality – have a place in the acknowledgement of appropriate ethical frames, imaginations and practices. In the chapter, I suggest that if radical ideas and radical practices are to go hand in hand, we need to address the apparent inability to retain a critical political edge in human geography. Noting Marc Augé's distinction between a sense of the other and a sense *for* the other, I argue that any goal in human geography for developing an emotional, connected and committed sense for the other may necessitate a prompting of the moral imagination, which includes political/ethical/spiritual constellations of issues such as charity, agape and evil. Drawing on the work of Hannah Arendt and Melissa Orlie, the chapter emphasises imaginations of power that recognise 'evil', the crisis of the citizen-subject, and the recovery of political enthusiasms for 'invisible powers'.

In the final chapter, **Chapter 12**, **Sue Ruddick** discusses an agenda for activist human geographies. Her approach is not to sound a clarion call for greater political engagement, for the response to such calls is often only momentary. Rather, she seeks from human geographers a sustained personal connection to committed political and intellectual engagement with the possibility and necessity for making things better for people. Such activism sits uneasily with the professional human geography tyranny, which expects continuous winning of research grants and continuous fresh conceptual contributions. It reflects the need for collaborative political activity rather than individual intellectual production. Perhaps most of all, such activism requires academics to cross the boundaries of privilege and to confront their personal stake in an issue. Words alone will not cross these boundaries. Human geographers cannot simply write themselves as activists. Ruddick's call is not only for a permeable boundary between research and everyday life, but also for a highly connected political existence which flattens that boundary and allows actions to speak at least as loudly as words.

We, as editors of this book, asked our authors to be predictive and provocative. They have variously obliged. We now ask our readers to take this collection of essays and reflect on it individually. What is your vision for the future of human geography, and what is prompting it? How will you go beyond the geographies of warning to the geographies of response, and beyond the writing of action to becoming active?

Bibliography

Borden, I (2001) *Skateboarding, Space and the City: Architecture and the Body*, Oxford: Berg.

Cresswell, T (1996) *In Place Out of Place: Geography, Ideology and Transgression*, Minneapolis: University of Minnesota Press.

Desmond, J (1999) *Staging Tourism: Bodies on Display from Waikiki to Sea World*, Chicago: University of Chicago Press.

Duncan, C (1999) *Worlds Apart: Why Poverty Persists in Rural America*, New Haven: Yale University Press.

Kapuscinski, R (2001) *The Shadow Of The Sun: My African Life*, London: Allen Lane.

Korten, D (1995) *When Corporations Rule The World*, London: Earthscan.

Passaro, J (1996) *The Unequal Homeless: Men on the Streets, Women in their Place*, New York: Routledge.

Rawls, J (1999) *A Theory of Justice (Revised Edition)*, Oxford: Oxford University Press.

Syring, D (2000) *Places in the World a Person Could Walk*, Austin: University of Texas Press.

Villa-Vicencio, C and De Gruchy, J (eds) (1994) *Doing Ethics In Context*, Cape Town: David Philip.

1
Space and substance in geography

Neil Smith

'The "fetishism of space,"' wrote James Anderson (1973, p3) in a highly influential argument, 'is the geographer's particular conceit'. The critique was aimed at a scientific geographical tradition that drew increasingly sophisticated and abstract depictions of spatial forms and relationships, but that often confused spatial form for social cause. It explicitly adapted Marx's critique of ideology embodied in the notion of the fetishism of commodities. According to Marx, the substantive social relations between different groups of people working under different conditions to make specific commodities is obscured in the purely quantitative relationship between the different prices of the commodities; the relationship between people comes to appear as a relationship between the things themselves. That is, the commodities themselves, material or otherwise, are fetishised. According to the spatial corollary, the social relations between people come to be represented as the relations between places; here, the places become fetishised. A popular illustration might involve poverty: to the extent that social analysts explain poverty as resulting from where people live – ghettoes reproduce poverty – rather than focusing on its social causes in terms of class, race, gender and other social and political relations, spatial fetishism disguises social causes. A related if more contemporary example is the so-called spatial mismatch thesis. According to this argument, concentrations of unemployment are explained in terms of a 'spatial mismatch' between the location of jobs and the location of able workers, rather than as a result of social differences. Not least because of Anderson's critique, emerging radical geographies have long conceived their task as an exploration of the dialectics of space and society in a way that would simultaneously respatialise social theory (and in the process reveal much about social and political relations) and, at the same time, socialise the spatial discourse of geography. The point was to recentre geographical space politically without, at the same time, falling foul of the fetishism of space.

In this chapter I want to reflect on the success of that project and, by so doing, to think about the direction spatial theory has taken in recent decades, and to reflect on some key emerging problematics in the treatment of space. In part, the argument will be historical: it is important to understand the origins of the so-called spatial turn wherein the entire language of social theory has been spatialised, but it is also vital to understand the limits to that shift. This will involve some reflection on different philosophical conceptions of space, but will also lead to a consideration of the seminal work of French social theorist Henri Lefebvre, who stands as a central figure in the spatial turn. A critical take on one aspect of Lefebvre's treatment of space, and especially a treatment of space *vis-à-vis* nature, will highlight the incompleteness of the spatial turn and suggest directions for future analysis by geographers. In particular, it strikes me that some deployments of spatial concepts in recent social and cultural theory risk replicating a certain spatial fetishism, and that an insistence on the connections between space and nature – space and the substance that fills it – will help to fulfil the promise of a respatialisation of social theory.

There is little doubt, in retrospect, that the respatialisation of social theory has enjoyed tremendous success in the last three decades. True, the mainstream discipline of geography at the beginning of the twenty-first century seems oddly drawn into a self-fulfilling spiral of mutually re-enforcing conservatism and self-doubt: while British geographers have reclaimed the 'royal' as part of their professional identity, in the United States, the purported 'shame' of 'being a geographer' dominates the century's earliest presidential pronouncements about the prospects for geography (Golledge, 2000). The much vaunted successes of Geographical Information Systems (GIS) in helping to realise the dream of a positivist revolution in geography seems to have exacerbated more than abated the disciplinary angst, especially in US geography. Yet all of this takes place light years away from the pursuit of social theory in geography. Our various concerns with space as socially produced have become a pervasive and powerful theme throughout the social sciences and humanities. The success of social theory and the disorienting angst of mainstream geography are not unconnected, of course, and this is well illustrated in signs of an emerging backlash against social theory. By contrast, however, the sense of optimism among social theorists in geography – and, it has to be said, among many physical geographers too – is quite divergent from any institutional malaise and is rooted in real successes. *Our* intellectual experience with geography and space comes from a dramatically different world from the one that re-echoes disciplinary insecurities of past decades. When Oxford literary critic Terry Eagleton (1997) argues that geography 'now looks set to become the sexiest academic subject of all', he is referring to social and cultural theory and the effects that 30 years of vibrant theoretical exploration *vis-à-vis* space have had in the social sciences and humanities. More to the point, Eagleton seems more in touch with the discipline's place in the intellectual world than many of the discipline's own institutional leaders.

The situation today is remarkably similar to that of a century ago. Then, too, expressions of angst about the imminent 'end of geography' mixed with signs of its recrudescence. The end of geography was thought by many to follow logically from the results of economic expansion – the supposed closure of colonial and polar exploration, along with continental frontiers – while the subsequent conflagration of World War I and the remaking of the world map that ensued gave geography considerable urgency and topicality. Fears of the end of geography today are usually linked with a more abstract, if equally real, 'globalisation', this time financial rather than immediately territorial. But they come at a time when, in social and cultural theory circles at least, geography is increasingly fashionable (Smith, 2003).

Spatial concepts increasingly provide the grammar of the most innovative social and cultural theory today, from many threads of historical research to French social theory, postmodernism to literary criticism, and there are many interconnected reasons for this. Deep-seated critiques of historicism (the belief that history is the unchallenged determinant of social form), the shattering of a twentieth-century geo-economic order and its constitutive geographical assumptions, the restructuring of spatial scale, the promise of a new globalism and local responses to it, a rediscovery of spatial language as a highly fertile source domain for metaphor and a distinctly spatial interpretation of newly fashionable issues of representation have all contributed to this recrudescence of a spatialised reading of social change and form. The renaissance in critical geography is a part of this dramatic shift, both fuelling and fuelled by it. The pervasiveness and wide public appeal of GIS is traditionally explained as resulting from the enhanced possibilities for representing spatial data attendant upon widespread computerisation technologies, and important as this technical revolution has been, the public embrace of GIS is aesthetic and cultural as well as instrumental, equally an expression of this new spatial imaginary.

While geographers have an obvious self-interest in promoting space as a vital language of social and political power, the spatialisation of social theory nevertheless provokes a number of questions. In the first place, while fashionability is obviously preferable to obscurity, the new focus on space is not without its own dangers. There is a crucial question of the extent to which this 'spatial turn' has been more than skin deep. How thoroughly has the spatial turn ploughed up the roots of a centuries-old historicism? How firmly is the new spatialism implanted? Put most crudely, perhaps, why space? Why *should* our analysis of social difference and political possibility be rewritten in the language of space? It is time, in short, to re-examine with a critical eye the history of the spatialisation of social theory, and perhaps to do so while keeping in mind the possibility that despite the roots of this project in an explicit critique of fetishism, we may yet have reached a point where that same social theory tempts its own, more sophisticated spatial fetish. These are questions that centrally involve those of us trained as geographers, but they are also, as I want to argue here, of such profound significance that they cannot be boxed in by narrow disciplinary interests and claims.

A spatial turn?

In 1973, the prospect that a so-called spatial turn would take hold of late-century social and cultural theory would have been dismissed as idle disciplinary fantasy or simply treated with derisive laughter (see Soja, 1989). Such a shift has taken place nonetheless, and it is nothing short of remarkable. The influence of spatial and geographical ideas throughout wide spectra of the intellectual landscape is unmistakable. Eagleton's exuberant assessment is one expression of this. More broadly, scholars are recasting their work in explicitly spatial terms. From numerous disciplines – anthropology and architecture, comparative literature and communications, environmental science and art history, diplomatic history and music, sociology and international relations – young scholars especially are retooling their projects in more explicitly spatial terms. It may not be too much of an exaggeration to suggest that in many fields space has become the 'next big thing'.

It is tempting to see this as part of a larger intellectual movement; certainly it is contributing to the institutional restructuring of various disciplines (even as institutionalised geography itself remains strangely impervious or deliberately resistant). But it is not simply an academic phenomenon either. Just as campus feminism and identity politics, to take two obvious examples, have significantly affected popular culture since the 1980s – even as they themselves were products of the revolts of earlier decades – the spatialisation of popular cultural discourse also expresses a much more thoroughgoing shift. There are many signs of this. The debates on the public sphere and cosmopolitanism that have galvanised the public intellectual wing of the humanities since the 1990s are heavily undergirded by a renewed spatial vision of the world, although this is not always made explicit. The journals *Public Culture* and *Social Text* increasingly mobilise a geographical nitty-gritty as the fabric of theory. Andrew Ross, one of the most prominent of a new generation of public intellectuals in the 1990s, has published a series of books rooted in a highly geographical if not always acknowledged sensibility: *Strange Weather* (1991), *The Chicago Gangster Theory of Life: Nature's Debt to Society* (1994) and *No Sweat: Fashion, Free Trade, and the Rights of Garment Workers* (1997). David Harvey's (1989) *Condition of Postmodernity* was nominated as one of the top 25 books of 1989 by the *Village Voice*, and a few years later listed by the British magazine *New Statesman and New Society*, as one of the top 100 books of the second half of the twentieth century.

The point here is not to rehearse the historical fact, or contribute to some self-satisfied celebration of the emerging success of a broadly geographical vision of the world. Rather, we are now at the point where a little critical reflection on the success of the spatial turn is important. In some ways, the importance of this critical distance from our own success is placed in sharpest relief by certain popular books that mobilise this new geographical sensibility. David Landes' *The Wealth and Poverty of Nations* (1998) and Jared Diamond's *Guns, Germs and Steel* (1998) have been two of the most prominent bestsellers in this genre. Each book in its own way gives a wide historical explanation to geographical difference, the reasons why different societies experience such different economic fates, why some places grow rich while others stagnate. Their answers are couched very much in terms of geography, to the point where they indulge a certain geographical determinism – old-style spatial fetishism. To these works we might also add the rather ill-informed work of economist Paul Krugman (1997), who at least deserves credit, in the context of his chosen profession, for recognising however dimly that the spatiality of markets may actually have some relevance in terms of how they work.[1]

Thirty years ago, such books would not have been written, or if they were they would not have received notice. Geography was dead: progressive US global leadership had eliminated geography (except as expressed in the aberrant, trivial binaries of cold war geopolitics) as a determinant of global fates; world geography was the product of markets and markets know no geography. Arguments such as Landes' and Diamond's would have been written off as un-modern. To be modern *was* to be beyond geography. But to paraphrase historian of science Bruno Latour from a quite different context, if aspatiality is modernity, we are not and have never been modern. Geography today is very much alive, and the resurgence of geographical sensibilities has opened the door not just for the more sophisticated analyses of geographical space, but for more deterministic readings that hark back to absolutist notions of space.

If the popularity of these and other books bespeaks a 'geography redux', it also expresses a potentially more troubling development. One can imagine, for example, that as the spatial turn becomes established, a new generation of critics will use the gaping logical and conceptual holes in such determinist works to challenge not only the veracity of specific texts but the advisability of the whole spatial turn itself. Geographers will be held up as having become inexplicably influential if dramatically wrongheaded, while the carousel of fashionable academic topics moves rapidly on to the next 'next big thing'.

There are already signs of this. Literary critic Kristin Ross (1996) has argued that the spatial turn is already, to all intents and purposes, over. Been there done that. Further, she warns, for all that a new spatiality heralded a progressive critique of social and literary theory in the 1980s and 1990s, and was instrumental in the establishment of a broadly left-oriented academic culture in this period, there is no necessary link between a spatial language and progressive politics. She cites the case of late nineteenth-century France where, following ignominious defeat to the Prussian army in 1870, a revanchist nationalism instantiated a geographical grammar for reconstructing a sense of French national pride and superiority. This was, not coincidentally, a period of major institution building for geography, an era in which the modern university discipline of geography was largely established, not just in vanquished France but in Bismarckian Germany, where the utility of geography for the new imperial ambition was all too obvious.

Ross is correct to remind us about the easy affiliation of a spatialised lexicon with quite varied political positions, and the case of late nineteenth-century France is an important corrective to some contemporary assumptions about the politics of space. More generally, whether in their modern disciplinary form or otherwise, geographical knowledges, whatever else they have been, have generally operated as handmaidens of state power. Viewed this way, therefore, the assumption of a broadly progressive shift allied with a turn to spatial concerns is an historical oddity to say the least, and we might do well to appreciate Ross's scepticism.

And yet there is more to the question than that. Current declarations of the end of the spatial turn can hardly be referring to a successful rewriting of all social science to incorporate a hitherto missing spatial purview. That project has only just begun, and whole continents of academic and non-academic knowledge remain closed to anything other than trivial spatial interpretation. Political science, for example, is rooted in a largely fixed vision of different territorial states which divide the world, but this basic spatial structure to the discipline and its objects of analysis does not then guarantee a sophisticated spatial approach. Quite the opposite: the fixing of space in the form of the taken-for-grantedness of national states is a means of assuming space away; spatial relations are reduced to relatively obvious questions of a 'geopolitics' that is not only conceptually trivial but historically superceded. New departures in international relations theory seek to renovate this elementary conceptual framework, but the fierce resistance from within political science suggests precisely how far the spatial turn has yet to go. Likewise, the spatialised language of much urban sociology is under institutional attack on the one hand, and on the other rests on a too simple assumption of spatiality into the notion of community.

Rather, it seems that declarations of the end of the spatial turn are responding to the pervasiveness of the *language* of space and, with a keen eye on the short life of fashionable ideas in cultural theory today, and an equally keen sense of the 'endism' (the end of everything) that accompanies it, they may simply be getting a jump on the 'next new thing'. If we leave aside the more euphoric and hubristic claims for the spatial turn, and especially those that confuse spatial metaphor and materiality, it is surely evident that while this turn has been greeted with far greater support and success than could have been dreamed of in the 1970s, it has only just begun to scratch the conceptual surface of how we think about the world. Yet such overblown claims for the spatial turn, if taken seriously, have the self-defeating effect of suggesting that 'everything is over before it has hardly begun' (Agnew, 1995, p380).

There is also a disciplinary dimension to the question of the spatial turn. It is perhaps not surprising that initial signs of disquiet over claims for the spatial turn are coming from literary criticism, comparative literature, humanities programs and English scholars, as well as geographers themselves. Having launched a highly successful campaign in the 1970s and 1980s to possess rights to the theorisation of culture in academia and the public sphere – a battle lost first and foremost by anthropology – the disciplines grouped around literature and English are now fighting to retain an intellectual hegemony that many progressive humanities scholars arrogate as part of their disciplinary birthright with all the presumption displayed by the traditional Western civilisation canon they so ardently oppose. Much as globalisation appears from a different perspective as the construction of empire, interdisciplinarity here can become the cover for a certain disciplinary imperialism.

This was perhaps best illustrated in the so-called 'Sokal affair', in which the otherwise excellent journal *Social Text* published an article advocating a postmodern approach to physics. The journal did not have the article assessed by a physicist or by anyone knowledgeable in the field, and as the editors soon discovered to their chagrin, the piece was a deliberate hoax (Sokal, 1996).[2] A highly publicised ridicule of radical social theory in its various forms quickly followed in the public press. The following syllogism seems, however implicitly, to have guided *Social Text*'s editorial decision: culture comprises a web of meanings and representations; it is the peculiar expertise of English and the literary disciplines to explain textual representations to us; whether physics or poetry, the substance of an article makes little difference as regards the prerogative of textual critics to arbitrate the fate of a piece of writing. Space and its theorisation was not the point of the Sokal affair, but the crucial point is that the same disciplinary imperialism manifested there is quite capable of setting its sights on questions of space which can, after all, also be treated as 'representations' susceptible to the prerogatives of the literary disciplines: all writing is literature. A heavy price is potentially paid for treating the world as a text.

The issue here is not to establish 'ownership' of questions of space, and even less to assert geography's disciplinary claims; no discipline 'owns' space – the idea is absurd. From mathematics to architecture, physics to poetry, space is amenable to many kinds of treatment. Rather, the point is to insist that the perfectly legitimate literary critique of spatial concept is only a part of the story, that at the very least in the flush of the new fashionability of spatial concepts such literary treatments need to be sensitive to already existing spatial theory, such as that on offer from geographers, and that under no circumstances does a literary *hegemony* over spatial concepts enhance our analysis of space. Such a narrow disciplinary presumption, on the contrary, narrows the field of intellectual and political possibilities.

The comprehension of spatiality is not exhausted by representational analysis – space has a reality beyond its representations, however problematic access is to that reality – and at the very least, the spatial turn demands that alternative modes of conceptualising space be uncovered. The literary embrace of space, largely organised around the rediscovery and deployment of space as source domain for metaphor, not only depends on a singular notion of space but obscures as much as it reveals. As Gerry Pratt (1992, p241) has commented, many spatial metaphors currently in vogue 'dress up and potentially reproduce some very conventional intellectual subject positions … underwrite new sets of dividing practices, and promote a remarkable arrogance or naivety towards the construction and destruction of and caring for places' (see also Smith and Katz, 1993). More generally, a naive social constructionism which, suspicious of materiality, treats space first and foremost as representational or conceptual, turns out to be paradoxically conservative; it fails to unearth conceptions of space that differ significantly from traditional Enlightenment treatments of space bequeathed by Kant, Newton, Descartes and others, which in many respects represented an elaboration and universalisation of the presumptions of Euclid's geometry. What emerges from these latter thinkers is the conception of space as *absolute*: events, objects and processes occur within a pre-existing space (*a priori*, for Kant) and occupy specific locations within space conceived as a co-ordinate system. The point of the spatial turn is precisely to get beyond such straightforward, almost instinctive, notions of space. The theorist who has, arguably, done most to propel us in this direction is the French writer Henri Lefebvre, and we now turn to his work as the focus of a more philosophical discussion about space.

Why space? Henri Lefebvre and the malcongruence of ontology and history

The post-1960s insistence from within geography that 'space matters' was premised on a three-part claim:

- first, different societies create different geographies as an expression of their social structures and social relations;
- second, the ways in which these geographies are traditionally understood (up to and including the naturalisation of space, the denial that space is socially made) comprise an ideology of spatial form, difference and process;
- third, socially produced spaces themselves help to structure, mold and reinforce certain kinds of social behaviours, assumptions and relationships that in turn have profound political effects.

The specific connections and relationships rendering the spatial as social and vice versa were recognised to embrace a much more complicated swath of questions. This dialectic of space and society was at once starkly obvious, therefore, yet to a considerable extent it still represented a conceptual *terra nova*. As late as the 1970s, the politics of space represented a yawning intellectual frontier that had rarely been broached and which promised many adventures.

In the English-speaking world, the argument was resolutely historical. The privileging of time over space could be traced philosophically in the intellectual history of European thought since perhaps the seventeenth century, but the political point was much more rooted in the here and now: how does a geographical reframing of uneven development, ghetto construction, nationalism, regional development and underdevelopment and suburbanisation, alter or sharpen a politics opposed to imperialism, capitalism, race and gender oppression? The importance of Henri Lefebvre in this period was not just the flurry of conceptual and political insights that affirmed the profundity of space, but the fact that he provided a philosophical rationale for positing space at the centre of the political project, and that this reaffirmation came from outside geography. His arguments gave powerful independent support to the claims of geographers that the political importance of space transcended such disciplinary concerns. Lefebvre's work was quickly read in much of continental Europe and Latin America, but infused much more slowly into the English-language debates. Beginning in the 1970s, on the basis of several translated articles, various secondary translations and (at the time) one book, his work on the politics of space became a vital philosophical flagstone for the unfolding spatial turn. So much so that by the time his 1974 tome, *The Production of Space*, was translated into English 17 years later, its audience was widely convinced already of what it took the message to be, the book's difficulties notwithstanding.

Responding viscerally to the urban uprisings of the 1960s and the urban movements these threw up, Lefebvre came to argue that politics was first and foremost a question of the politics of space. The pivotal thing that societies do, he argued, is to produce space, and spatial practice is perforce the crown jewel of politics. 'Capitalism has found itself able to attenuate (if not resolve) its internal contradictions for a century', Lefebvre (1973, p21) famously wrote. 'We cannot calculate at what price, but we do know the means: *by occupying space, by producing a space.*' In the wake of both the extraordinary hegemony of capitalism and the failures of Stalinism, a reconstruction of revolutionary politics as a politics of space was the primary task. Politics, he argued, was now a spatial more than a historical practice. This argument significantly upped the ante for a spatial politics, giving it a fundamental justification that has suffused the spatial turn well beyond those who were immediately influenced by Lefebvre's work. The brilliance of his argument about the 'production of space' is difficult to understate, especially when one remembers that it came a full decade earlier than the social constructionism that became *de rigeur* in 1980s and 1990s cultural and social theory, and indeed paved the way for it. Apart from anything else, Lefebvre's conceptualisation of space obliges geographers and others to move beyond the sense of space as given, *a priori*, absolute, and to treat space instead as in the first place relative. The contours and contents of space and spaces, for Lefebvre, are not pre-given, but are produced *relative* to the social and natural processes, objects and events that comprise space.

The shift that Lefebvre signals from the priority of absolute to the priority of relative space was being independently explored in English-language geography in the early 1970s and is now widely accepted, at least in principle. Far from the only conceptualisation of space, absolute Newtonian or Cartesian conceptions of space are increasingly seen as exceptions rather than the norm. In consort with a range of other shifts in cultural and social theory, Lefebvre's work is increasingly conceived as anchoring a new 'spatial ontology' for politics. If ontology provides a knowledge of what exists, spatial ontologies suggest the specific and inherent spatialities of the world. Edward W. Soja (1989, 1996) has made some of the most explicit arguments in this regard, and his influential reading of *The Production of Space* in particular has helped establish an emerging tendency, rooted in Lefebvre, to assert or assume the priority of space in distinctly ontological terms. But we need to be careful because there are really two arguments here. The argument that relative space philosophically precedes absolute space – that absolute space is a special case in a wider sea of possible (i.e. relative) conceptualisations of space – cannot be accepted wholesale without also accepting the priority of space *per se*. The importance of making this distinction is that certain dangers may obtain in the resort to a spatialised ontology, that rather than forging a new amalgam of spatial *cum* historical knowledge, an equally opaque spatialism may simply replace historicist ontology. This is not in any way Lefebvre's position, but that has not prevented others from moving in this direction, and it should prompt us to ask some basic questions about the supposed priority of space. Why space? What precisely is Lefebvre's argument for the priority of space? Why does a reconstruction of politics now require a spatial practice? Does the pursuit of politics as spatial practice imply that we cease to think of politics as equally an historical practice (see Smith, 1997, 2001).

In *The Production of Space* (Lefebvre, 1991) two kinds of answers are continually given to this kind of question. The first is indeed ontological and emerges from the work of Lefebvre as philosopher. Hegel is the centrepiece here – quite literally insofar as Lefebvre hails Hegel and Hegelianism as 'a sort of Place de l'Etoile with a monument to politics and philosophy at its centre'. For Hegel, he concludes, 'historical time gives birth to that space which the state occupies and rules over'. Against this, Marx's reinstatement of revolutionary time, Bergson's idealisation of time, Husserl's phenomenology and Lukacs' imprisonment of space as the jailer of false consciousness, all represented in very different ways a restoration of time against Hegel's dramatic acclamation of space – his affirmative 'fetishisation of space in the service of the state', as Lefebvre puts it (pp21–22). If Nietzsche stands out for his prescient resistance to this philosophical back-tow, his embrace of the simple positivism and dramatic force of absolute space is an easy target for Lefebvre's critique.

Lefebvre can be seen as doing for space in Marxist theory what Lukacs (1971) did for time. Both Lukacs and Lefebvre strain their marxism through Hegel, but while Lukacs grasps from Hegel the historical process of the argument and emphasises the acute temporality of social change, Lefebvre locates himself at the conclusion of Hegel's argument, taking the 'end of history' very literally: 'space' is the 'product and residue of historical time' (see Lefebvre, 1970). *The Production of Space* is fundamentally about the spatiality of everyday life, its practice and conceptualisation, and the succession of spatial regimens that carries us to the political present. History is in the process of disappearing as time comes to be 'dominated by repetition and circularity, overwhelmed by the establishment of an immobile space which is the locus and environment of all Reason', and thereby 'loses all meaning' (p22). Geography in the broadest sense, not history, is the crucial result of this Hegelian movement, for Lefebvre.

The victory of space over time may be philosophically ordained, but it is equally an historical process, and history provides the second answer for Lefebvre – the proof of philosophy, one might say – to the question of the priority of space. The second half of the twentieth century, he suggests, has witnessed three vital shifts that establish the priority of space. First, 'the state is consolidating on a world scale', and this means that

> '[s]pace in its Hegelian form comes back into its own. The modern state promotes and imposes itself as the stable centre – definitively – of (national) societies and spaces. As both the end and the meaning of history – just as Hegel had forecast – it flattens the social and "cultural" spheres' (Lefebvre, 1991, p23).

Second, the unprecedented violence of the twentieth century – the wars, revolutions, victories and defeats – bespeaks an inevitable opposition to the imposed rationality of the state, a new negativity that 'corresponds precisely to Nietzsche's vision'. As Andy Merrifield (1995, p296) says, 'Lefebvre never recanted a certain nihilistic sensibility that he culled from Nietzschian thought'. Third, and more specifically, Lefebvre concludes that 'the working class' has not by any means 'said its last word' (p23).

Just as Lefebvre seems to be bringing some of his more abstract philosophical arguments to earth, he relaunches his historical explanation of the priority of space into a
more symbolic domain. An 'epoch-making event' that is 'generally ignored' – namely,
the smashing of the traditional spatial codes that had dominated Western societies since
the sixteenth century – took place in the early years of the twentieth century, he says.
Cribbing from Virginia Wolf's famous quip of the same ilk, he explains that 'around 1910
a certain space was shattered. It was the space of common sense, of knowledge (*savoir*),
of social practice, of political power', the space alike of Euclidean geometry, Renaissance
perspectivism, Newtonian physics and descriptive geographies. The artistic revolution
initiated by cubism announced most vividly the advent of the new space, and Picasso's
1907 painting, *Le Demoisseles d'Avignon*, marks this shift precisely. 'Picasso's space *heralded*
the space of modernity.' For Lefebvre, Picasso 'glimpsed the coming dialectical transformation of space and prepared the ground for it …, discovering and disclosing the contradictions of a fragmented space' (pp25, 300–4).[3]

Although geographers are obviously drawn to Lefebvre's spatial vision of politics and
convinced by the power of his proposal of the 'production of space', this simultaneous
ontological and historical justification for recentering space is, by comparison, unconvin-
cing. Hegel's ontology, which Lefebvre struggles to strip of its barest teleology, is presented alongside Picasso, the global consolidation of the state and the negativity of
violence and resistance. But these shards of an empirical history, only sketchily and very
unevenly elaborated in ensuing chapters, sit very awkwardly with Hegel's ontology.
Hegelian space 'comes back into its own' only insofar as history is made the proof of
ontology, yet the precise connections between correlated ontologies and histories are
barely explored. They are presented as parallel, but they are not coherently connected;
they are at best 'malcongruous'.

Soja has implicitly recognised this dilemma. Backing away from an earlier spatial ontology that defined itself in opposition to historicism, and even to some extent history, his
more recent argument about an 'ontological trialectic', posits a three-way relationship
between what he calls 'historicality', 'sociality' and 'spatiality' (Soja, 1996). Also labelled
the 'trialectics of being', this triad rehabilitates history, but it does so at the expense of
subordinating space, time and society to ontology. That may well be sympathetic with
Lefebvre's intent, indeed I expect it is, but this does not resolve the problem of malcongruence, rather it highlights and compounds it. Ontology now explicitly encapsulates history and is expressed through it. Ontology drives historical as well as geographical
change. Philosophy makes space and time more than the other way round.

There are several problems with this formulation. In the first place, whereas Marx
famously argued that philosophers had only interpreted the world and the point was to
change it, Lefebvre's prioritisation of space and Soja's 'trialectics' unduly posit philosophy
itself as the crucible of social change. Second, the intent of Marx's argument is to collapse
the philosophical distinction between ontology and epistemology. Lefebvre is not
unaware of this, deliberately beginning *The Production of Space* with a strategic discussion

aimed at highlighting the isolated abstractions and fetishised concepts of space that 'philosophico-epistemological' thought has produced, divorced from a sense of social and physical space. It provides him with a critical lever *vis-à-vis* the contemporary French social theory of Foucault, Althusser, Lacan, Kristeva and others. Yet even as the discussion becomes more historical in later chapters of *The Production of Space*, the philosophical attitude remains and the traditional distinction between ontology and epistemology is never successfully countered. Lefebvre's is an anti-philosophical philosophy. Third, and more concretely as regards the question of space, the affinity of space and ontology represented by assertions of a refound spatial ontology risks providing an attractive philosophical foundation not just for a certain spatial exceptionalism but for a new, more sophisticated kind of spatial fetishism. The question remains: why space?

Much as with his philosophy, Lefebvre's history is an anti-history. Insofar as ontology and history struggle with each other throughout the text, his philosophy reaffirms his anti-history, and vice versa, while his history and anti-philosophy are equally reaffirming of each other. This is perhaps clearest in Lefebvre's history of space. Substituting for Engels' schema, which identified a historical evolution from primitive communism through slavery and feudalism to capitalism, socialism and communism, Lefebvre identifies a broad historical evolution from absolute space through historical to abstract space, which he identifies with modern capitalism. If this movement represents a definite historical evolution for Lefebvre, the optimistic 'logic' of a subsequent differential space seems to invite a particularly teleological side of Hegel back into the history. Philosophy re-emerges as the expression of human self-consciousness, 'producing' the results of history. In obvious contrast to Marx, it is never clear in Lefebvre what the specific social relations are that nudge this logical evolution of spatiality forward. How does real social activity by real people in structured social relations make this history move? Lefebvre's answer is again ambiguous. He periodically cites class struggle in a broad, all encompassing sense that we would now frame in terms of struggles rooted in diverse social differences and movements, but more often than not it is a conceptual shift that moves history along. Philosophy already and always encapsulates real histories. The question of how changing philosophical conceptualisation garners historical change is elided, and the malcongruence of history and ontology is itself raised to an ontological principle.

So why is Soja's 'ontological trialectic', combining history, spatiality and society (in the broadest senses), not the solution that rescues Lefebvre's ontology? It can surely accommodate such a malcongruence, indeed a good argument could be made that malcongruence is a premise of the dialectic. The answer goes back to the status of ontology. Ontology in western social thought in the last two centuries has generally been conceived as (in the words of *Chambers Twentieth-Century Dictionary*) 'part of metaphysics', an investigation of 'the principles of pure being', a study of 'the nature and essence of things'. The very idea of ontology embodies an extreme foundationalism anchoring liberal philosophical modernism, whereas the critique that emerges from, among other places, marxism, feminism and postmodernism, suggests something quite different. The impulse toward ontology today does not necessarily imply such a simple foundationalism, but it does come in response to the intense relationality via which social and spatial realities are generally conceived; fixity denied in one arena resurfaces in another, re-introduced via the back door (and with all the authority) of philosophy. But what passes as 'ontological' in one place, one society or one time is surely highly variable, and cannot be abstracted from the coordinates of space, time and social difference. Yet the power of the so-called 'trialectic' is premised on precisely this abstraction, which allows ontology to stand apart from place, moment and society. Historicality, spatiality and sociality are philosophical ingredients of the ontological trialectic, otherwise labeled 'the trialectics of being' (Soja, 1996).

I have dwelt on Lefebvre because his arguments about the necessary spatiality of politics have not only been influential, but have helped to broadcast and legitimate a sense of the foundational spatiality of politics. In the process, however, many of the creative intellectual and political struggles that got us to the point of 'seeing' the production of space have become flattened into an ontological presumption in which the power of space is increasingly accepted while, ironically, the rationale for such a position recedes from critical view. The assumptions that radical geographers fought so hard to render into common sense may now be in danger of becoming their own ideology, a new fetishism of space. An explicit recombination of the intellectual pillars of Lefebvre's mal-congruence – philosophy and history – may offer a way out of this dilemma.

Space after spatiality

The intensified scrutiny of spatiality in the late twentieth and early twenty-first century may well represent the culmination of two projects. The first is an intellectual project aimed at the conceptual ordering of space. It was hatched in seventeenth- and eighteenth-century Europe, and engaged people such as Descartes, Newton, Kant and, in a different vein, Leibniz, but follows through to Hegel, Nietzsche, Einstein and others. The second, and intimately related, is a practical project aimed at ordering space 'on the ground'. It was hatched about the same time and is intimately tied to the privatisation and nationalisation of space as an expression of emerging capitalist social relations.

Descartes' announcement of space as an infinite and homogeneous *res extensa* established an unprecedented dichotomy between space *per se* and the social and natural objects and events that populate space. That which was glimpsed in the pioneering abstractions of Euclidian geometry was, by the twentieth century, taken for granted with little sense of how revolutionary a proposal it was in the seventeenth. The social generalisation of this distinction on the one hand freed space from erstwhile theocratic authority and merely local constructions, and on the other gave rise to a whole new (cartesian) system of spatial coordination. Such an audacious abstraction of space from its substantive dimensions raised the possibility of a universal 'science of space', a project pursued energetically by Newton and given absolute sway by Kant for whom, in an early wedding of space and ontology, space comprised an *a priori*, always already given. There followed a new and dramatic abstraction of space by mathematicians and physicists – from

Gauss (number theory) and Riemann (n-dimensional spatiality) to Einstein (relativity theory) and the apparently continuous regress in physicists' efforts to identify elementary particles (quarks, nuons, etc.). The explanation and description of the 'shape' of space, and later space–time, became the primary goal of science. At the same time, and not entirely unrelated, the conceptual abstraction of space led to the exploration of social space, mental space and conceptual space more generally, alongside the abstractions of physical and mathematical spaces.

In the early Enlightenment world, not only was space for the first time radically separated from the material world of nature, but an unprecedented asymmetry was introduced between them. In their abstractness, Newtonian (absolute), Cartesian (conceptual) and especially Kantian (*a priori*) space also contributed to an evolving priority of space over nature. Nature itself was a given, unless somehow obliterated, but the obliteration of space was much harder to conceive. Social and natural events took place in a world already delineated in terms of space and time rather than the other way round. If this sense of spatial priority still remains common sense in most western societies, it was also fundamentally challenged by relativity theory and quantum mechanics, which were premised on a much denser relationality between space, time and materiality.

In retrospect, then, Lefebvre seems as much a product of this history as a departure from it. The insistence on ontology and on the priority of space, and the weaving of both arguments together into a spatial ontology, stretches back not just to Hegel but equally, if less obviously, to Kant and – for good or bad – the early Enlightenment. More importantly, whereas the notion of 'the production of space' brilliantly theorises the relativity and relationality of social space, it does so at the cost of returning nature to a pre-Einsteinian state. In part, the philosophical importance of relativity theory was precisely that the materiality of the universe was potentially recentred in relation to space and time; no longer homogeneous, the curvature of space–time could only be conceived in terms of the mobility of matter. If part of this shift is captured in 'the production of space', there is no equivalent argument in Lefebvre concerning the 'production of nature', which would seem to be a corollary implied by relativity theory. Indeed, quite the opposite; nature, he says, is 'murdered by anti-nature' (capitalism) (Lefebvre, 1991, p71) and the priority of space, dating back to Kant's *a priori*, is protected.

Philosophically, while Lefebvre recognises acutely the evisceration of space that this western philosophical tradition both expresses and extolls, and recognises too, much as Einstein did, the possibility of a revolutionised relationship between nature and space, there is no sense that the priority of space and nature might be reversed – that space may be the product of nature rather than nature the supplicant of produced space. This is especially surprising given Lefebvre's evident appreciation of Leibniz, whose 'relational space', insisting against Descartes that space was nothing if not occupied, provides a partial precursor to the kind of reconnection of space and matter glimpsed in relativity theory.

In all fairness, it should be pointed out that the radical reprioritisation of nature *vis-à-vis* space has not yet been accomplished in the physical or mathematical sciences either.

The Austrian physicist Ernst Mach may have expressed this ambition most forcefully, and Einstein's relativity theory was among other things an explicit attempt to prove Mach correct – to prove the priority of materiality over spatiality – but despite the success of relativity theory, Einstein himself pulled back in the 1930s to a conservative resort: the distinction between ontology and epistemology. Frustrated by his inability to prove what he called 'Mach's Principle' (the priority of matter), Einstein retreated to the argument that while the material world had to be seen as epistemologically prior, there was no final proof of ontological priority (see Jammer, 1969; Smith, 1984).

This argument is important for several reasons. First, it provides some kind of context for Lefebvre's malcongruence of history and philosophy, drawing the two sides of this dichotomy into a closer relationship with each other, historicising his ontological claims, while also demonstrating the difficulties involved. Second, it points towards a rather different direction for geography, and we shall return to this point shortly. Third, this contextualisation puts into sharp focus the progressive as well as the more traditional assumptions that mark Lefebvre's argument. Lefebvre brilliantly intimates the culmination of the Enlightenment while remaining one of its most faithful thinkers. He insists on the recovery of a spatiality that already lies at the core of that tradition. If his uncritical insistence on the primacy of space makes him more the child of Leibniz *and* Newton than of Einstein, the brilliant exposure of 'the production of space' is nonetheless a prescient statement of the culmination of the modern ordering of space.

A second, more practical spatial project is peaking simultaneously. It is no accident that the ordering of space in terms of conceptual categories coincided with its ordering on the ground. The proliferation of capitalist relations of production in Europe after the seventeenth century also called for some quite practical answers to vital social and economic questions. If inherited collectivisms and communalisms, full or partial, provided no effective basis for capital accumulation, what were the specific alternatives? What forms would the privatisation of the means of production take? There was nothing predetermined about the answers to these questions, although in retrospect the answers did prove to be highly geographical. Not only were fields and factories privatised as the property of 'owners' (rather than possessors), but all manner of possessions became 'real property' in an unprecedented way – from clothes and bodies to homes and tools. Of course, this endowment of bourgeois rights was dramatically uneven in terms of class and race, gender and sexuality, but the important point here is that the territorialisation of rights after the seventeenth century was a significant part of the answer to the social problem of facilitating capital accumulation. At the scale of the body and the home, the territorialisation of rights established the juridical individual as a social reality and part of the field of social reproduction *vis-à-vis* production.

A parallel argument pertains at the national scale. Premised on economic competition between discrete capitals, these same capitals also required advanced levels of cooperation, whether concerning the formation of standing armies for sake of defence, the provision of transportation infrastructure, or the adoption of effective forms of labour control.

How were these contrasting requirements of competition and cooperation to be rationalised, arbitrated? The system of national states was in many ways the centrepiece to the political solution that emerged. The Peace of Westphalia in 1648 not only consigned the Roman Empire to history and rang the death knell for theocracies of all stripes, but it established a system of nation states as the basis for European economic growth. A core social and economic problem in the genesis of capitalism found its solution in the production of a specific kind of geography, which had its heyday in the two centuries from the French and American revolutions to the break-up of the Soviet Union after 1989 (for a good statement of the history leading up to this transition, see Arrighi, 1994).

From the scales of the body and home to the national and the global, therefore, produced geographies have been imposed and contested as solutions to social and economic conundrums. It is no different today. 'Globalisation' is touted as the appropriate (spatial) solution to the problems posed by the increasing obsolescence of national-scale markets in the context of the expanded scale of social production and increased integration of financial markets and communications infrastructure. Ideologists of globalisation, guided largely by the interests of finance capital, proclaim that the new globalism means the end of geography and the withering away of state regulation – a nice capitalist appropriation of Lenin who, much earlier, pined for the withering away of the state – whereas, of course, globalisation is itself another highly geographical response to the contradictions of capitalist profitability which, in the wake of the Asian economic crisis of 1997–99, have come to seem as acute as they are uneven. If the spacelessness of the global capitalist system is a self-serving utopian myth expressing a sharp class vision of the world, there is nonetheless a reality to the loss of at least *economic* power experienced by some national entities in the global economy. Globalisation no more heralds the end of nations and nation states than nation states implied the end of cities in the seventeenth century Mediterranean, but for all the fact that capitalism has always been global, we are currently witnessing the culmination of the nation-state system as a conveyance of capital accumulation. The power of national states is being dramatically restructured in relation to the global economy, while the role of national as well as global state entities is being challenged from below. However much states may assert themselves politically, militarily or culturally, the usefulness of the system of national states *as political economic organising blocks for capital accumulation* is definitively waning. That some states may reinvent themselves as successful corporate entities would prove rather than disprove the point.

The abstraction of space in late twentieth-century geography responds in quite specific ways to the evolution of these two projects. It has led to a certain desocialisation of geography, most evident in the equations and algorithms of positivist geography and in the abstractions of GIS technologies that blur the always-contested translations linking representation and reality. Not unlike Einstein, proponents of the power of GIS defend its epistemological value while backing away from ontological claims: the resulting maps are 'only as good as the data that made them', 'the error coefficients are as important as the maps, if not more so', and so on. How we know is here radically separated from what we know – except, of course, that in reality it is not. The representational power and splendour of the maps filling the computer screen shrivel any and all quibbling caveats.

But the abstraction of space was also a hallmark of the post-positivist intellectual trends that saw themselves as the 'social' alternatives to positivism. There, too, the crucial distinction is not between representation and reality, but between those representations that retain a connection with the realities they supposedly represent and those which do not. The latter become free-floating; the purview of the social narrows dramatically in favour of abstracted spaces of conceptualisation, whether postmodernist dissonance, marxist analytics of value, or poststructuralist spatialisations of representation.

After Lefebvre's announcement of the production of space, and with scientific analyses of space–nature locked into an infinite ontological regress in search of the elementary forms of physical existence – a regress increasingly driven by abstract mathematical logic rather than any material impulse – it may be that the spatialisation of the material world has reached some sort of zenith. On the one hand it is difficult to see where further spatial abstractions of the mathematical sort could lead without reconnecting more seriously (than in the infinite regress of elementary particles) to the material world. On the other, the 'production of space' gives the lie to the very same abstraction of space that even Lefebvre himself could not quite escape.

In this context, it may be that the spatialisation of geography has also reached its zenith. As Marx knew well, abstraction invites fetishism. A new and more explicit resocialisation of geographic practice and discourse may now be necessary. Ironically, if the argument here has any validity, this may take the form, in part, of a refocusing on the substance of space rather than its form. Philosophically, this might imply a focus on what we are abstracting from rather than the abstractions themselves, that is a focus on the natural and social processes and events that for Newton occurred 'in space' but that for Leibniz or Einstein gave space its form. Somewhat prosaically, it may be possible to see the global upsurge of an environmental movement since the 1970s as precisely the expression of this historical conjuncture – a political insistence on the priority of the substance of space–time over its abstraction. Of course, by the late 1980s western environmental politics was thoroughly co-opted into an establishment politics (Katz, 1998) to the extent that even George Bush Sr. could, however ludicrously, call himself the 'environmental president'. But this is precisely the point: environmental politics were too powerful to be ignored or deflected but had to be embraced. *Sustainability* used to be a radical environmental demand pertaining to the physical and biological conditions of social and environmental reproduction, whereas today it pertains first and foremost as a question of profit rates. The issue, therefore, is not support for a comfortably establishment environmentalism in the US or Europe, but rather the political movements from rural Asia, Africa and Latin America (as well as North America and Europe) that have retained a powerful sense of the connection between vastly different productions of nature and a *socially* sustainable future. Whether the Chipko movement in India, the Ogoni of the Niger delta, or the anti-colonisation movements of Amazonia – whatever their well-rehearsed limitations – or, indeed, the maquila workers movement in Mexico/US or the anti-WTO movement from Seattle to Prague, Bangkok to Genoa, it seems likely that the impulse for social change in the future will focus on the material conditions of life, including questions of spatiality. They will connect work and nature, unions and environmentalism, in pleasantly new and different combinations. There is no guarantee that non-western movements will escape the co-option that captured post-1980s environmentalism in the west, but then the movement in the west is also itself reconstructing. The spatial differentiation of daily life will necessarily be a crucial ingredient, but not the organising principle, of this politics *per se*. The history of space becomes integral to the history of nature rather than the other way round.

The relationality of space, an intellectual and political project hatched in the sciences of the late nineteenth and early twentieth century, has been socialised five or six decades later. Today the limits to spatial abstraction seem increasingly clear and the dangers of an unintended fetishism of space equally so. They point beyond such an emphasis on an abstracted space toward a geography that is post-spatiality yet which remains inherently spatial. The production of (social) nature is no less elemental than the production of space. Space matters, of course, but even more so the processes and events that make nature and space, and the new resocialised geographies of the early twenty-first century will reverse the priority of form over substance. Practical geographical knowledges are simultaneously spatial, natural and social; they are lived and abstractable at the same time, giving no priority to the latter.

Notes

1. Krugman concludes quite erroneously not only that Jacques Derrida is a marxist, but that this French post-structuralist is the primary inspiration behind economic geography in the last three decades.
2. As one who joined the editorial board of *Social Text* shortly after this fiasco, I am not, it should be clear, dismissing the journal *tout court*. In fact, if Sokal's target was some kind of undifferentiated postmodernism/post-structuralism, *Social Text* was an irresponsible target to choose insofar as it had always mixed social scientists and political activists with literary scholars.
3. Notice that for Lefebvre, *contra* Foucault, Bergson's era witnesses the demise of one set of spatial codes rather than the origins of a privileged time, *de novo*. For a longer discussion of this transformation – better on time than on space and thus still a symptom of the privileging – see Stephen Kern (1983).

Bibiography

Agnew, John (1995) 'The hidden geographies of social science and the myth of the geographical turn', *Environment and Planning D: Society and Space*, 13.4, 380.

Anderson, James (1973) 'Introduction', *Antipode*, 5.3.

Arrighi, Giovanni (1994) *The Long Twentieth Century*, London: Verso.

Diamond, Jared (1998) *Guns, Germs and Steel*, New York: WW Norton.

Eagleton, Terry (1997) 'International Books of the Year', *Times Literary Supplement*, 5 December.

Golledge, Reginald D (2000) 'NEVER be Ashamed of Being a Geographer', *AAG Newsletter*, June.

Harvey, David (1989) *The Condition of Postmodernity: an Enquiry in to the Origins of Cultural Change*, Oxford: Blackwell.

Jammer, Max (1969) *Concepts of Space*, Cambridge, MA: Harvard University Press.

Katz, Cindi (1998) 'Whose Nature, Whose Culture?: Private Productions of Space and the "Preservation" of Nature'. In Bruce Braun and Noel Castree (eds) *Remaking Reality: Nature at the Millenium*, London: Routledge, 3–41.

Katz, Cindi and Smith, Neil (1993) 'Grounding Metaphor: Towards a Spatialized Politics' in Michael Keith and Steve Pile (eds) *Place and the Politics of Identity*, London: Routledge, 67–83.

Kern, Stephen (1983) *The Culture of Time and Space 1880–1918*, London: Weidenfield and Nicholson.

Krugman, Paul (1997) *Development, Geography, and Economic Theory*, Cambridge, MA: MIT Press.

Landes, David (1998) *The Wealth and Poverty of Nations: Why Some are So Rich and Some So Poor*. New York: WW Norton.

Lefebvre, Henri (1970) *La fin de l'histoire*, Paris: Editions de Minuit.

Lefebvre, Henri (1973) *La survie du capitalisme, la reproduction des rapports de production*, Paris: Anthropos. Translated as *The Survival of Capitalism*, London: Allison and Busby, 1974.

Lefebvre (1991) *The Production of Space*, Oxford: Blackwell.

Lukacs, Georg (1967) *History and Class Consciousness*, Cambridge, MA: MIT Press.

Merrifield, A (1995) 'Lefebvre, Anti-Logos and Nietzsche: An Alternative Reading of "The Production of Space"' *Antipode*, 27.

Pratt, G (1992) 'Spatial metaphors and speaking positions', *Environment and Planning D: Society and Space*, 10, 241.

Ross, Andrew (1991) *Strange Weather: Culture, Science and Technology in the Age of Limits*, London: Verso.

Ross, Andrew (1994) *The Chicago Gangster Theory of Life: Nature's Debt to Society*, London: Verso.

Ross, Andrew (1997) *No Sweat: Fashion, Free Trade, and the Rights of Garment Workers*, New York: Verso.

Ross, Kristin (1996) lecture at the Conference on Invisible Cities, Cooper Union, New York, October 3–5.

Smith, Neil (1984) *Uneven Development. Nature, Capital and the Production of Space*. Oxford: Basil Blackwell, 71–73.

Smith, Neil (1997) 'Antinomies of Space and Nature in Henri Lefebvre's "The Production of Space,"' *Philosophy and Geography*, 2, 49–69.

Smith, Neil (2001) New Geographies, Old Ontologies, *Radical Philosophy*, 106, 21–30.

Smith, Neil (2003) *American Empire: Roosevelt's Geographer and the Prelude to Globalization*, Berkeley: University of California Press.

Soja, Edward S (1989) *Postmodern Geographies*, London: Verso.

Soja, Edward S (1996) *Thirdspace*, Oxford: Basil Blackwell.

Sokal, Alan D (1996) 'Transgressing the boundaries: Toward a transformative hermeneutics of quantum gravity', *Social Text*, 46–47, 217–252.

2
Engaging ecologies

Margaret Fitzsimmons

Human geography has a long tradition of engagement with the relationships between people and nature. From the nineteenth-century contribution of Ratzel's *Anthropogeographie*, human geography moved through environmental determinism and possibilism to a focus on anthropogenic change – the manners and circumstances within which people 'opposed themselves to Nature as one of her own forces', creating livelihoods embedded in landscapes of human learning, innovation and history. Geographers studied the past and present lifeways and landscapes of their own and other places, reporting on the diverse and intricate arrangements through which people lived within and changed the world. But as we have studied the world, the world has changed. The last 200 years have been a time of massive ecological change, driven by the political and economic expansion of one way of life – industrial capitalism – writing over the landscapes and lifeways of other human cultures. Attention to 'our place in nature', must thus engage the institutions by which we organise our own lives and livelihoods if we intend our work to contribute to a human geography that values ourselves and others (human and non-human) now and in the future.

Encountering the scope and scale of the construction of new landscapes of and by industrial capitalism, human geographers warned of their consequences. In his 1938 paper 'Plant and Animal Destruction in Economic History' (Sauer, 1938; reprinted in Leighly, 1963) Carl Sauer reviewed the destructive impact of recent human activities on ecological processes.

> 'In the late eighteenth century the progressively and rapidly cumulative destructive effects of European exploitation become marked. They are indeed an important and integral part of the industrial and commercial revolution. In the space of a century and a half – only two full lifetimes – more damage has been done to the productive capacity of the world than all of human history proceeding.' (Leighly, 1963, p147)

Sauer emphasised three areas of loss for particular attention: the extinction of species and varietal forms; the restriction of useful species through loss of habitat and range; and the destruction of the soil's function as a location of essential ecological and hydrogeological processes. He placed responsibility for attention to these issues firmly within the role of the social scientist:

> 'To this summary review of some of the suicidal qualities of our current commercial economy the retort may be made that these are problems of the physical rather than the social scientist. But the causative element is economic; only the pathologic processes released or involved are physical. The interaction of physical and social processes illustrates that the social scientist cannot restrict himself to social data alone' (Leighly, 1963, p152)

More recently, contributors to critical human geography have taken up the implications of human (economic and social) institutions that set the rules about what we do with nature. In multiple sites, geographers have studied the relentless circulation of capital and accumulation through the bodies and spaces of humans and others, a circulation that creates the landscapes of capitalism, the thrusts and withdrawals of 'uneven development', new geographies of wealth and poverty and new dimensions and scales of ecological change. I cannot attempt a thorough review of this literature here, but I will mention a few personal landmarks: Neil Smith's *Uneven Development* (1984); David Harvey's essay 'Population, Resources, and the Ideology of Science' (1974) and also, of course, *Justice, Nature and the Geography of Difference* (1996) and *Spaces of Hope* (2000); contributions to edited volumes, such as Dick Peet and Michael Watts' *Liberation Ecologies* (1996), Bruce Braun and Noel Castree's *Remaking Reality* (1998), and Jennifer Wolch and Jody Emel's *Animal Geographies* (1998); Ken Olwig's *Nature's Ideological Landscape* (1984); and the continuing work of Diana Liverman, Lucky Yapa, Richard Munton, Piers Blaikie, Sarah Whatmore, Terry Marsden, Cindi Katz, David Demeritt, Rebecca Roberts, Jacquie Burgess and Carolyn Harrison, Diane Rocheleau, Karl Zimmerer and other colleagues and friends.

In this new literature, contributors have also warned of the danger of uncritical acceptance of knowledge about nature as proposed by the natural sciences, as ontologically prior to knowledge of and political choices about ourselves and our intentions. Harvey's 1974 essay remains a masterful example of this danger. Many geographers have been active in challenging popular conceptions of social reality, whose authority rests on their metaphorical resonance with theories of 'natural hierarchy' from the sciences, where these arguments have been deployed to support social relations of domination based on naturalised categories: gender, race, sexual orientation. We must continue to confront the uncritical assertions made by those whose academic authority is not complemented by insight into the situated and contingent complexities of human social life, the core concerns of critical human geography. However, resentment of these occasional abuses should not lead us to overlook what natural scientists, in certain disciplines, are telling us about their own practices, concerns and commitments.

My charge in this chapter, to identify the key conceptual components that should shape a human geography engaged with questions of nature in the coming decades, is much too grand to realise. Many people will shape this new geography, from many positions and standpoints. My contribution here is founded in my own history of engagement – in my encounters with cultural geographers, biogeographers and ecologists, political economists, political theorists and planners and philosophers and historians of science – in my years of teaching and research about how people build institutions that structure the way we work with nature. So, from within this particular and personal standpoint, in this essay I will ask: 'what does it mean "to know about nature" in ways that support conscious socio-ecological projects that address both justice and difference, in ways that aid people to construct a better future?' To ground and illustrate my argument, I will focus on one kind of 'knowing about nature' – the science of ecology – and its implications for knowing and acting in a human geography concerned with the question of nature.[1]

Geography and ecology

Ecology is the study of the interactions of myriad kinds of creatures that have effects on each other and their world. We can say about life (as the philosopher Roy Bhaskar (1989) suggests we must say about reality) that it is 'structured, differentiated, and changing'. Life is also an *emergent* phenomenon – that is, living organisms, though they must comply with the laws of physics and chemistry, also manifest their own higher-order processes of self-organisation, as individuals, species and communities of interaction in space and time.

Life, and the evolution of life, has made our world and ourselves; life is what we share with others (human and non-human). Though geophysical processes do matter inde-pendently, the consequences of the appearance and evolution of life are present in all that we inhabit; the oxygen/nitrogen atmosphere, the breakdown and reconstruction of min-erals and landforms, the incorporation of sunlight and nutrients into living tissues and the metabolism of these through networks of composition and decomposition in the bodies of ourselves and others.

In focusing on interactions among organisms and, for some ecologists at least, the impact of these interactions on evolution and the geophysical environment, ecology offers us a distinctive perspective into nature. Nature, as Raymond Williams (1977, 1980, 1989) showed us so clearly, can mean many things. Concepts of nature are constituted both in the ordinary activities of everyday life and in grand cultural productions and metanarratives (a point Michel Foucault (1970) made eloquently in *The Order of Things*). In our time, they are also strongly constituted in science. Other scientific disciplines claim to produce knowledge of nature. Most of them work by taking nature apart, taking nature into the laboratory, disassembling and decomposing nature and then trying, like 'all the king's men', to put nature back together again in their minds, their laboratories and their factories. This strategy yields powerful kinds of manipulative knowledge and new technologies, but the laboratory does not lead us to understand how things work in the world. It may, in fact, be destructive, as the 'unintended consequences' of techno-science, modern science let out into the world, proliferate outside the safeguards of the laboratory. Moreover, laboratory work suffers when compared with field observation as a way of knowing the world, substituting a meticulously disciplined and ordered environ-ment for engagement with the real and contingent aspects of temporal scale, spatial scale, scope, realism and generality (Diamond, 1986). All of these real and contingent issues are of great interest to geographers. They are also of interest to ecologists.

In *Justice, Nature and the Geography of Difference* (1996), David Harvey draws our attention to four facets of the interactions among living organisms that create the complexity of the world. These are:

1. Competition and the struggle for existence (the production of hierarchy and homogeneity).
2. Adaptation and diversification into environmental niches (the production of diversity).
3. Collaboration, cooperation and mutual aid (the production of social forms).
4. Environmental transformation (the production of nature).
   (Harvey, 1996, p190)

Harvey is careful to warn us that these facets are to be understood (and used) as 'relational categories, not mutually exclusive processes'. They engage each other dialectically; each incorporates the others. Harvey's purpose is to:

> 'depict the fundamental physical and biological conditions and processes that work through all social, cultural, economic projects … in such a way as not to render those physical and biological elements as a banal and passive background … [so that] … somehow the artificial break between "society" and "nature" [may] be eroded, rendered porous, and eventually dissolved.' (Harvey, 1996, p192)

Human geographers will recognise how these facets have been used to frame the distinct and bounding assumptions of other social science disciplines: in a broad sense, economics focuses on competition; anthropology and cultural studies focus on the production of diversity; and sociology focuses on social interactions and social forms. Though we are likely to retain our disciplinary attachments, many critical social scientists will welcome the possibility of a constructive conversation that this schema implies. At the same time, for many of us, it is difficult to think about 'social evolution' without being reminded of the naturalisation of concepts of hierarchy and difference which uncritical appropriations of evolutionary arguments have led to in the past. But Harvey's purpose is to lay the foundation for social change based on human agency and the desire for social justice, not to subordinate and discipline people's desires by invoking 'laws of nature'. Harvey sees people as capable of making their own worlds, though they may not begin in circumstances of their own choosing. In fact, Harvey's arguments in his work of the past ten years bring the question of nature back into the core of human geography. As Harvey argues, all human geographies engage specific socio-ecological projects and the distinctive social relations they presuppose; social relationships with nature are present in those projects, whether or not they are brought into view.

This idea of an agency also underlies some biologists' vision of the agency of organisms. In *The Dialectical Biologist*, Levies and Landon (1985) write, 'Natural selection is not a consequence of how well the organism solves a set of fixed problems posed by the environment; on the contrary, the environment and the organism actively codetermine each other.' (p89) Though some evolutionary biologists portray evolution as the working out of a set of deterministic rules, others recognise that evolutionary biology is a histor-ical science in which chance and contingency must be recognised and accommodated (Gould, 1984). Human geographers should be aware that evolutionary theory in biology is a much richer, more heterogeneous and more contested terrain than could be suspected from the popular writings of sociobiologists (see, for example, Fox Keller and Lloyd, 1992).

In arguing for the centrality of a critical reconciliation of our understanding of society and nature, David Harvey (1996) states:

> 'We badly need a much more unified language than we currently possess for exercising the joint responsibility toward nature that resides with the social and biological/physical sciences. … This is, however, dangerous territory – an open field for organicist or holistic rather than dialectical modes of thinking – and it may require deep shifts in ontological and epistemo-logical stances on both the social and natural scientific sides, if it is to succeed.' (p190)

This is, in fact, dangerous territory, as others have also warned us. To begin, it is important, as we cross the apparent boundary between human geography and ecology, to keep in mind the distinction between *analogy* and *homology*. Analogies draw our attention to simi-larities in process in our comparisons of phenomena whose origins are distinct from each other ('this is like that', in that it is similar in form or process); homologies refer to phe-nomena that arise out of a process of common descent ('this and that' are related through a common point of origin'). Conceptions of nature in human geography and of human society in ecology have at times blurred this distinction.

Initially, ecology and geography were closely related explorations. In the US, the founders of the Association of American Geographers included several prominent plant ecologists, and Ellsworth Huntington was the third president of the Ecological Society of America. However, as the modern disciplines have developed, their intersections (and interchanges) have been attenuated: biogeographers form the primary bridge between geography and ecology; and ecologists looking for allies among the social sciences have looked primarily to economics. Though cultural ecology, and now political ecology, look to ecology to provide both knowl-edge about nature and theoretical analogies (and homologies) that can be applied to the study of culture and society, this has not yet led to much conversation between the disci-plines. If we are to encourage this conversation, it may be useful to look further into ecology.

Looking into ecology

As we look into ecology as a source of knowledge that can help us know about nature, we can now employ new tools. Both the emerging field of science studies and recent contri-butions in the history of science offer help in viewing ecology not just as a body of accu-mulated knowledge, but as a community of science practice.[2] Science studies focuses on the practices of scientists in laboratories, disciplinary communities and institutions such as refereed journals and research institutes, in constructing networks of articulated knowledge that enrol humans and non-humans into new ways of making a difference in the world.

Science is performed and situated as particular ranges of social practice. Ecology, as a science discipline, must construct itself to survive and prosper in a social and institutional world in which the value of social investment in science must be regularly reaffirmed. Increasingly, for the last century and more, the industrial democracies have invested in science to reap the rewards of new knowledge that helps them compete in economic and military arenas. It is difficult to estimate the magnitude of this investment, since much of it occurs as tax-deductible or subsidised research within the private research and development activities of firms, but research and development (R&D) receives annual commitments of billions of dollars. Though national investment in research has been growing rapidly in the US, private investment has been growing much more rapidly: 'The federal government provided 60% of R&D support in 1967, 46.3% in 1987, and 30.5% in 1997' (Matthews, 2000).[3]

For most of the natural science disciplines, this means that the activities of scientists (within firms and even in universities) are increasingly directed to the development of what will become *proprietary* knowledge, eventually to appear in the world embedded in new commodities. This activity connects those disciplines closely with their related industries, for which they produce both knowledge and knowers — scientific and technical workers (for example, about 80% of chemistry Ph.D.s in the US go into industrial jobs). Though ecology has a long tradition of engaging with applied questions (such as biological control of insect pests), the science practices of ecologists rarely lead to the development of patentable knowledge. Therefore, ecology has needed to rely on other justifications for its support. The first of these was the presentation of ecology as a science of *public interest* — both in the sense that the benefits of ecological knowledge could be widely shared (for example, in improved agricultural practices, in pest control or the effective management of forests or fisheries of economic interest), and in the sense that people are curious about and want to know about the living world. The second justification for social investment in ecology, particularly since the ecological effects of a globalising economy and of new chemically based industrial practices have been appearing, is the value of ecology as a *precautionary* science. It is in this sense that David Harvey (1996) writes:

> 'It is precisely the task of ecological analysis to try and identify unintended consequences (both short and long term, positive and negative) and to indicate what the major effects of actions are.' (p195)

Each of these two alternative roles — *public interest* and *precaution* — can create conflict for ecology with those other sciences involved in the development and valorisation of proprietary forms of knowledge.

The practice of ecology links natural history explorations, field observation, field and laboratory manipulation, mathematical modelling and narrative theoretical statements, and intense theoretical debates within the discipline to outputs such as documentary films, popular books, textbooks, refereed journals, administrative reports, strategies of environmental management and court testimony. Ecologists are active in universities, public agencies and non-profit advocacy organisations, and even in some industries. Ecological arguments erupt locally, nationally and internationally. Ecologists design and test agricultural systems, seek out rare species, measure energy flows and nutrient cycles and restore abandoned land. They can be found working in every part of the world. In all of these positions and sites, ecologists circulate actively, transmitting and circulating the arguments of their community.

When we ask 'What is ecology?' we find that it is many things simultaneously:

- The science that studies the interrelationships of organisms, including humans, and their living and physical environments.
- A changing discipline, with multiple points of view into the world.
- A lively and engaged community of scientists actively involved in development of their networks and linkages into everyday life.
- A structure of engagements for translating knowledge into practical action and political power, using the arguments of *precaution* and *public interest.*

We can organise and investigate these multiple modes and moments of action by deploying the concept of *vascularisation* offered in *Pandora's Hope* by Bruno Latour (1999), who states:

> 'There are five types of activities that science studies needs to describe first if it seeks to understand in any sort of realistic way what a given scientific discipline is up to: instruments, colleagues, allies, public, and finally, what I will call *links* or *knots* so as to avoid the historical baggage that comes with the phrase "conceptual content".' (p99)

Latour depicts these as overlapping circuits of action: mobilisation, autonimisation, alliances and public representation surrounding, supporting and contextualising the central heart of links and knots. Figure 2.1 depicts this circulatory system as it applies to the vascularisation of the discipline of ecology in the United States (with the content of the central 'links and knots' not specified within the figure but discussed below).

Mobilisation of the world 'deals with expeditions and surveys, with instruments and equipment, but also with the *sites* in which all the objects of the world thus mobilised are assembled and contained' (Latour, 1999, p101). For ecologists, this mobilisation includes the species concept as it is materially mobilised through taxonomic collections and now gene sequences. It also includes methods of field observation (mapping and sampling practices such as transects and quadrats, and devices for extracting, abstracting and refining what is found in the field) and places protected for field observation. Latour traces the practices of 'circulating reference' that connect each moment of observation to its conceptual referent, enabling the next moment of observation and eventually linking the activities of people, plants, soil particles and earthworms from the Amazon to the professional journal and beyond. Within ecology, subdisciplinary communities can be distinguished by their tools and sites: population ecology, community ecology and ecosystem ecology mobilise and enrol the world through different objects of analysis, methods of measurement and concepts. Ecologists regularly deploy new means of mobilisation, such as remote sensing. Latour (1999) points out that, 'An ecologist whom nobody used to take seriously can now intervene in a debate with beautiful satellite photographs that

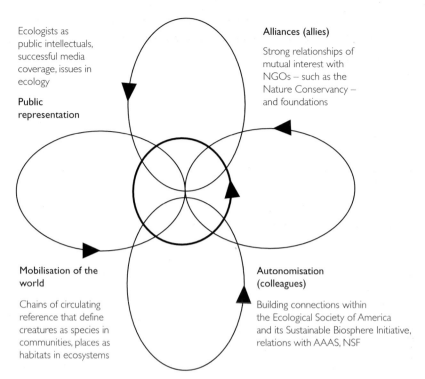

Ecologists as
public intellectuals,
successful media
coverage, issues in
ecology

**Public
representation**

Alliances (allies)

Strong relationships of
mutual interest with
NGOs – such as the
Nature Conservancy –
and foundations

**Mobilisation of the
world**

Chains of circulating
reference that define
creatures as species in
communities, places as
habitats in ecosystems

**Autonomisation
(colleagues)**

Building connections within
the Ecological Society of America
and its Sustainable Biosphere Initiative,
relations with AAAS, NSF

Figure 2.1   *The vascularisation of ecology*

allow her, without budging from her Paris laboratory, to observe the advance of the forest in Boa Vista' (p101).

Autonomisation refers to 'the ways in which a discipline, a profession, a clique, or an "invisible college" becomes independent and forms its own criteria of evaluation and reference' (Latour, 1999, p102). For ecologists in the United States, an important aspect of this has been their efforts in developing the institutional structure and activities of the Ecological Society of America (ESA), and strengthening the presence of ecology in the National Science Foundation (NSF), the American Association for the Advancement of Science (AAAS) and other institutions.

The Ecological Society of America, founded in 1915, now has approximately 7,600 members. Its members work in the academy and the schools, in government and NGOs, and in industry. Fifteen sections represent the range of current research interests. The ESA publishes three journals (*Ecology, Ecological Applications* and *Ecological Monographs*); it also publishes issues papers for the general public, in hard copy and on the Internet. At its annual meeting, the ESA convenes sessions on current research but also on teaching and public communication of ecological knowledge. The society thus takes an active role in setting an agenda for the discipline and in communicating the importance of ecology to students and citizens.

In 1988, the Ecological Society of America formally began a process of 'research planning', recognising that it was crucial for their discipline to define and communicate a research agenda that would explain and justify the importance of continuing public funding of ecological research. The eight years of the Reagan presidency and the Republican ascendency in Congress had shifted the balance of Federal funding of science (through the National Science Foundation, agency budgets and tax initiatives for private proprietary research and development) toward the proprietary and away from the precautionary and public interest forms of scientific work. The work of the members of the ESA's Committee for a Research Agenda for the 1990s led to the publication, in early 1991, of 'The Sustainable Biosphere Initiative: An Ecological Research Agenda' (Lubchenco et al, 1991). The Initiative called for '(1) basic research for the acquisition of ecological knowledge, (2) communication of that knowledge to citizens, and (3) incorporation of that knowledge into policy and management decisions'. The sequence of these goals is significant. The document identifies three priority areas:

1. **Global change**, including the ecological causes and consequences of changes in climate; in atmospheric, soil and water chemistry (including pollutants); and in land-and water-use patterns.
2. **Biological diversity**, including natural and anthropogenic changes in patterns of genetic, species and habitat diversity; ecological determinants and consequences of diversity; the conservation of rare and declining species; and the effects of global and regional change on biological diversity.
3. **Sustainable ecological systems**, including the definition and detection of stress in natural and managed ecological systems; the restoration of damaged systems; the management of sustainable ecological systems; the role of pests, pathogens, and disease; and the interface between ecological processes and human social systems.

The first two of these initiatives are tied to already well-established institutional networks within and without science; the third (within which is embedded 'the management of sustainable ecological systems') offers to return ecologists to their historical roles as architects of alternative human practices in agriculture, restoration and the management and conservation of biodiversity. Here, we see the ESA recognising that technologies are enabled by social institutions. In 1995, the ESA further recognised the importance of speaking to both the community of scientists and other communities in separating the Vice Presidency of the Association into two roles, Science and Public Affairs.

Ecology has been successful in building and maintaining important alliances. These have independently come to Latour's conclusion that:

> 'Immense groups, rich and well-endowed, must be mobilised for scientific work to develop on any scale, for expeditions to multiply and go farther afield, for institutions to grow, for professions to develop, for professorial chairs and other positions to open up. … [I]t is not a question of historians finding a contextual explanation for a scientific discipline, but of the scientists themselves *placing the discipline in a context* sufficiently large and secure to enable it to exist and endure.' (Latour, 1999, p104)

Given the social investments in the structures of natural science, the first context within which ecology has succeeded in placing and maintaining itself is the institutional framework of natural science itself. Ecology is considered a biological science, and the biological sciences are growing in importance and power. In the National Science Foundation in the United States, ecology is located in the Division of Biological Sciences and has prospered with the fortunes of this division. In the fiscal year 2001 budget request for NSF,[4] the Biological Sciences were to receive $511 million in support of research activities (12.6% of the requested NSF research and training budget), where the Social, Behavioral and Economic Sciences (which include Geography and Regional Science) were targeted for $175 million – less than 5%. Within the Division of Biological Sciences, Environmental Biology (which includes Ecology and Systematics) was budgeted for $119 million – 23% of the Division's funds, and an increase from the previous year of 32.7%. The continuing availability of NSF funding for research in ecology protects its legitimacy as a scientific activity of national interest, and at the same time enables ecologists to claim the attention of their university administrators and to feed and clothe their graduate students. Programs that support research and training in ecology include the Long-Term Ecological Reserve program (which supports a series of ecological research sites), the umbrella program in Ecological Studies and its subsidiaries in Ecosystem Studies (ecosystem ecology) and Ecology. Table 2.1 shows the active grants listed in these programs (and in Geography/Regional Science and Science and Technology Studies) for fiscal year 2000.

Thus, fiscal year 2000 active funding for ecology-related programs totalled about $170 million. Since NSF pays universities indirect overhead for this research, about two-thirds of the funds go directly to the research project. On the University of California formula, where the remainder is divided between state budgets and the discretionary funds of university administrators, this would mean approximately $28 million in discretionary funds distributed to university administrators across the country. Assuming that most of these grants are funded for the usual three-year period, the funds to an average successful investigator may not be that large – about $60,00 a year for the program in Ecology – but this still represents a substantial underwriting of faculty research and graduate student support. Transfers of government funds through this process to manufacturers of

Table 2.1 *National Science Foundation Funding for Ecology, Geography and Science Studies, 2000*

Program	LTER	Ecosystem	EcolStud	Ecol	Geog/RS	STS
Number of awards	29	154	7	212	201	171
Doctoral dissertation grants	NA	15	1	29	74	40
Total $	62,909,912	72,066,218	1,118,363	54,594,888	18,605,320	10,280,801
Mean $	2,169,307	439,428	159,766	257,523	92,564	60,122

scientific equipment are much less for these fields than for the biomedical fields, chemistry, or physics, of course.

The ESA has developed strong alliances with major foundations, with particular non-government organizations (NGOs) such as the Nature Conservancy, and with scientists working in US government agencies with responsibility for ecological management. Foundation interest in ecology is important to the support of the discipline, both financially and politically. This interest is related both to the construction of successful alliances that underwrite the work of ecologists and, as cause and consequence, to public representation of ecology as the discipline that speaks for the environmental commons, and for the millions of other species with which humans share it. Ecologists working in public interest organisations are closely tied in to the activities of the society, as are many in the Forest Service, the Fish and Wildlife Service and other agencies.

The public representation of ecology has been crucial to its successful vascularisation and its expanding influence. Ecology has entered the public imagination through a number of routes – popular books like Rachel Carson's *Silent Spring* (1962) and Paul and Anne Ehrlich's work; natural history documentaries in film and television (Mitman, 1999); the organising activities of environmental groups, the lessons of teachers in elementary schools and many others. Many of the most prominent ecologists write regularly for popular audiences while maintaining their reputation as leading scientists. In this era of 'unintended consequences' of the expansion of industry and the deployment of new forms of science and technology, ecology's two claims of *public interest* and *precaution* have made it the scientific foundation of resistance to science-as-usual in the employ of accumulation.

Though popular presentations of ecology – the old canons such as Aldo Leopold's *A Sand County Almanac* (1949), *Silent Spring*, or classic introductory textbooks like Eugene Odum's *Principles of Ecology* (1953) – may not represent the research frontiers of modern ecology, the discipline does not repudiate them nor challenge the popular understanding of the field. Instead, some senior ecologists continue to write for, and speak to, popular audiences, encouraging a sense of citizen participation in the discipline. They also speak to other scientists and to legislators about the central importance of their field, serving as 'public intellectuals' for their discipline.

One such recent statement is Jane Lubchenco's 1997 Presidential Address to the American Association for the Advancement of Science (Lubchenco, 1998).[5] In this address, titled 'Entering the Century of the Environment: A New Social Contract for Science', Lubchenco begins:

> 'As the magnitude of human impacts on the ecological systems of the planet becomes apparent, there is increased realisation of the intimate connections between these systems and human health, the economy, social justice, and national security. Urgent and unprecedented environmental and social changes challenge scientists to define a new social contract. This contract represents a commitment on the part of all scientists to devote their energies and talents to the most pressing problems of the day, in proportion

> to their importance, in exchange for public funding. The new and unmet needs of society include more comprehensive information, understanding, and technologies for society to move toward a more sustainable biosphere – one which is *ecologically sound, economically feasible, and socially just.*' (p491, emphasis added)

She continues:

> 'National security, social justice, the economy, and human health are appropriately considered to be environmental issues because each is dependent to some degree on the structure, functioning, and resiliency of ecological systems. Linkages among the social, political, economic, physical, biological, chemical and geological systems present new challenges to scientists. What is the role of science in meeting these challenges?' (p494)

It is in this context of assertions of urgent application, of scientific centrality, and of great social significance that ecology forms its 'links and knots', its 'pumping heart', its core conceptual content.

The core concepts of ecology are well depicted as a network of links and knots. For many social scientists in the past, ecology has provided a metaphor for order and stability in the social, as well as the natural, world. We are now warned that scientific ecology will no longer serve this purpose (Demeritt, 1994; see also Scoones, 1999). Equilibrium models of ecosystem functioning have been set aside by many ecologists, though some still assert the possibility of a connection between species (or functional) diversity, or biodiversity, and dynamic stability in the ecological regulation of earth systems. For many ecologists, disturbance has become a more interesting focus – a change that opens up ecological research to anthropogenic disturbance as well as to the impinging impacts of a dynamic physical world. The importance of this to ecology, and its initial vascularisation, is visible in the new NSF Biocomplexity Initiative, a cross-cutting research program that (according to its web page) promises to articulate scientific understanding of

> 'the dynamic interactions that occur within biological systems, including humans, and between these systems and the physical environment. From individual cells to ecosystems, these systems exhibit properties that depend not only on the individual actions of their components, but also on the interactions among these components and between these components and the environment.' (www.nsf.gov)

Though ecologists appear as a disciplinary community in these various articulations, there are clearly subcommunities within the discipline. These groups make use of different tools, and different imaginaries, to engage with the world in quite different ways. The first dimension of difference reflects the tensions between field ecology and ecological modelling. Theoretical statements in ecology are now often made in mathematical form, which tends to segregate 'theoreticians' from experimentalists/observers (though collaboration, and some polymath individuals, can help to cross this divide). Ecologists, like geographers, have suffered from tensions between nomothetic and ideographic commitments. The second dimension is that patterns of engagement among the various subfields of ecology reflect differences in research practices and in the unit of analysis.

For example, population ecologists tend to imagine the world through the frame of individuals within species, and connect intellectually and politically with the commitments of conservation biology. Community ecologists are more interested in interactions among species, and their 'activists' are likely to turn to agroecology and other designs for sustainable management of communities such as forests. Finally, ecosystem ecologists view the world in terms of flows of chemicals and energy, and have taken up the banner of 'ecosystem services'. However, despite these differences most ecologists share certain conceptual and moral commitments. Core concepts shared by most ecologists include:

- That organisms are more than the sum of their parts, and that forms of interaction among organisms (communities, ecosystems) have emergent properties.
- That variation and diversity are significant.
- That there are scale effects in ecological relationships that need to be recognised and understood.
- That both disturbance and resilience are important to ecological interactions.
- That we know little about much of the world.
- That biocomplexity – the complex interactions that occur among the myriad organisms of the world – is a fascinating and difficult terrain to explore.

Ecologists are also likely to share certain ethical commitments: a respect for life; and a concern about using the world as a laboratory without strong results, from carefully designed and controlled experiments or systematic observations, that indicate that kinds of creatures will not be irreparably harmed.

Through these activities of mobilisation, autonomisation and the formation of alliances, the ESA has created the conditions for a powerful public representation of the importance of ecology. One arena for this has been the production and dissemination of the ESA publication *Issues in Ecology*. This series, which began publication in 1997, is 'designed to report, in language understandable by non-scientists, the consensus of a panel of scientific experts on issues relevant to the environment' (this quotation is taken from the boilerplate that identifies the purpose of the series in each issue). To date, nine issues have been published on topics including the changing nitrogen cycle (with attention to anthropogenic changes and the role of nitrogen as a pollutant in various ecosystems); biodiversity, environmental services and ecosystem functioning; biological invasions; ecological principles and forest management; the environmental and ecological implications of growth in aquaculture and the problem of increasing demand for water.

These *Issues* present an (unexamined) geography of ecological concern that is at once globalising and particularising: illustrations include abstract and universal diagrams of ecological processes and flows, maps of global distributions of ecological impact, graphs of increasing problem magnitude over time and many photographs of the victims – species and landscapes. Ecological problems are described as urgent, but also as requiring further research. The tone of these publications is designed to invoke both public interest and precaution.

The authority of the *Issues* papers is supported by:

- The standing of their authors, including eminent scientists who also appear as 'public intellectuals' and disciplinary leaders.
- The identification with and situation of their authors in prominent research universities, government agencies and NGOs.
- The process of their production, which includes the consensus of an appointed panel of scientists 'chosen to include a broad array of expertise in this area', peer review, and approval by the Board of Editors of Issues in Ecology, themselves eminent scientists.
- Reference to support of the research and publication by prominent foundations and agencies.
- Parallel publication of more technical reports (in many but not all cases) in the ESA journal *Ecological Applications* (with mention in the *Issues* paper of the number of references cited in the more academic version).

For the most part, this vascularisation appears uncontested. However, as Latour suggests, scientific controversies (where they appear) often illuminate the process of construction of scientific knowledge. One such controversy erupted in regard to *Issues in Ecology* #4, 'Biodiversity and Ecosystem Functioning: Maintaining Natural Life Support Processes'. The authors of this issue left unquestioned the popular vision of biodiversity – based on the number of species – which had been constructed in prior public representations of the meaning of biodiversity but which was not universally accepted among ecologists. In response, eight ecologists published a letter in the July 2000 *Bulletin of the Ecological Society of America* challenging the argument of this *Issue* – that higher levels of biodiversity (defined as numbers of species) had been shown to be related to higher levels of ecosystem function (defined by measures such as net biomass accumulation). They said that this overlooked the importance of their research findings. The editors of the *Bulletin* also published responses from the *Issues* series editor (himself one of the authors of the report) and from the lead author of the report in question. This exchange illustrates some of the contradictions that can appear within the ecological project. This is both a scientific controversy (in that the published results of different research projects have not fully resolved the relative importance of numerical diversity and functional diversity in terms of ecosystem function in the short and long term) and a political controversy (in that the two groups in disagreement with each other have different external alliances). The opponents accused the *Issues* authors of giving in to the 'conservation lobby'; at least several of the opponents themselves work within range management departments or institutions where they are held accountable to agricultural or forestry interests. There is therefore a material opposition in the circumstances of their work which may fuel the heat of this confrontation.

However, it is remarkable that the complex vascularisation through which the ESA has progressed, since the initiation of this research planning process in the late 1980s, has thrown only this one controversy into public view. As a discipline and a community, ecologists have successfully extended their networks into the multiple worlds of creatures, colleagues, allies and public discourse, nourishing and strengthening the nodes and knots of their own engagements with each other in the process, and making a difference in the world.

What geographers can make and do

What does this mean to human geographers who study nature society with the intent of conscious socio-ecological projects of human liberation and responsibility towards nature? My purpose in offering this long exploration of the successful vascularisation of ecology is to suggest three possibilities.

1. That we, as geographers, can use this understanding of the on-going construction of ecological knowledge in our own contributions to the discussion of nature and society. To say that ecology is constructed as an embedded social process is *not* to say that the world that ecologists seek to know is somehow not real. We must be aware of the distinction between analogy and homology in our own theoretical contributions, framed by metaphors like cultural or political ecology, and develop these carefully, avoiding the assumptions of organicism and holism which ecologists have relinquished. Harvey's suggestion that we can find a common language in recognising competition, adaptation, the production of social forms and environmental transformation as points of shared insight should be pursued. We need to attempt a common language to begin a conversation.

2. That we, as geographers, can engage with ecologists as potential allies in a wide range of conscious socio-ecological projects. This alliance is possible because of our common disciplinary goals of *public interest* and *precaution*. It is possible because the circumstances and practices of the work of ecologists are very like ours. At first, this engagement may need to take place in the sites to which ecologists themselves are addressing their attention: in conservation, agriculture and land management. Many ecologists have abandoned the imaginary world in which humans are not found. We can help them move beyond the convention that biodiversity is *there* and not *here*. Together, we can recognise that biodiversity is a process, not a state, and that to protect and maintain that process will require substantial changes in the practices and rules that structure human life. We can engage with ecologists because some of them now understand that social justice is essential to the success of their project, as well as ours.

3. That we, as geographers, must seek to vascularise our own communities, strengthening our relationships with our subjects (human and other), our colleagues (including ecologists), our allies and our contribution to the construction of a public discourse. We must do so affirmatively but with a goal of mutual aid. We must seek to avoid militant particularism and global ambition in our own discipline, and we must join with allies to recognise and challenge it in others. Our goal is not a totallising of theory, but a shared engagement for social change to the benefit of the world – and we must trust each other, as we can, to achieve that goal. We must recognise that successful vascularisation includes discovery, integration, teaching and service, and commit to support those among us who make contributions in any of these areas.

We must reject the idea that the most important role of those of us within the university is the generation of proprietary knowledge for the powerful without.

What roles and opportunities are there for human geographers?

In the academy, we must move beyond critique. We must recognise and affirm those who are finding better ways to construct their lives. Globalisation has its evident discontents; accumulation mobilises those who resist its commodification of social relationships and choices. People are finding ways to share responsibility for the natural world, in city and countryside. Explore the world, discover those places, and write home about them. Enrol in the 'foreign service'. We must spend time in the spaces of other disciplines, translating, negotiating, observing, learning. This means learning to treat with respect people whose customs and conceptions may differ from our own. Work in the world as a laboratory. Work with people to create new networks of alliances of humans and others. Help people understand, and learn from them, how expectations and institutions limit what they can see within the world. Map larger spaces. Remember that our work has a purpose, not just to understand the world but to change it. Keep that purpose in mind and share it with others. As Harvey (2000) suggests,

> 'To construe ourselves as "architects of our own fates and fortunes" is to adopt the figure of the architect as a metaphor for our own agency as we go about our daily practices and through them effectively preserve, construct, and reconstruct our life-world.' (p200)

Acknowledgments

I have made two long visits to the territories of ecology and biogeography, first in graduate school and now at UC Santa Cruz. In that time, many teachers, colleagues, friends and students have guided me along the paths and shown me the landmarks of their disciplines. Of this many, two stand out: Walt Westman and Laurel Fox. Each worked generously to help me see – where I may still err, they are in no way to blame. I would like to thank Laurel Fox and Diana Liverman for helpful comments on this paper, with the usual disclaimers fully in effect.

Notes

1. I focus this chapter on ecology because I work at the interface between ecology and human geography. Other geographers (particularly Diana Liverman and David Demeritt) have worked with and drawn our attention to the global change community, which is based in the physical earth sciences (particularly climatology). Their engagements with that community of natural sciences (and their comments on that engagement) inform my analysis in this chapter and provide a model for the ways in which human geographers can participate critically and constructively in these explorations and debates.

2. Four recent books on the history of ecology provide a rich resource. Sharon Kingsland, in *Modeling Nature: Episodes in the History of Population Ecology* (1995), traces the rise

of mathematical modelling in population ecology, relating this to the need to support practical applications of ecological knowledge, to the attraction of mathematicians to the discipline, and to the belief that ecology could only become a modern science by freeing itself from historical reasoning and specific, ungeneralised engagement with species and places. Gregg Mitman, in *The State of Nature: Ecology, Community, and American Society 1900–1950* (1992), reviews the debates within community ecology about the priority of competition or of collaboration and mutual aid as most central to ecological theory; he connects these debates to their analogues within the social and political debates of the time. Frank Golley, in *A History of the Ecosystem Concept in Ecology: More Than the Sum of the Parts* (1993), and Joel Hagen, in *An Entangled Bank: The Origins of Ecosystem Ecology* (1992), provide different views of the development of ecosystem ecology and address the connections of this approach to Cold War concerns of agencies such as the US Atomic Energy Commission.

3. The National Science Foundation had a R&D budget in 1999 of $2,654.8 million. This made up 52.5% of all federally funded basic research conducted at the nation's colleges and universities, with the exclusion of biomedical research sponsored by the National Institutes of Health. Also, NSF provides almost 30% of the total federal support for science and mathematics education.

4. This is the proposed budget released in 2000. The actual budget, with the Bush administration in power and the ongoing struggles in Congress, differs.

5. Note that Lubchenco was the lead author of the Ecological Society's *Sustainable Biosphere Initiative* and subsequently President of the ESA, before being elected to the presidency of the AAAS.

Bibliography

Bhaskar, R (1989) *Reclaiming Reality: A Critical Introduction to Contemporary Philosophy*, London: Verso.

Braun, B and Castree, N (eds) (1998) *Remaking Reality: Nature at the Millennium*, New York: Routledge.

Carson, R (1962) *Silent Spring*, Boston: Houghton Mifflin.

Demeritt, D (1994) 'Ecology, objectivity and critique in writings on nature and human societies', *Journal of Historical Geography*, 20: 22–37.

Diamond, J (1986) 'Laboratory Experiments, Field Experiments, and Natural Experiments', in Diamond, J (ed.), *Community Ecology*, New York: Harper & Row.

Foucault, M (1970) *The Order of Things: An Archaeology of the Human Sciences*, London: Tavistock.

Fox Keller, Evelyn and Lloyd, Elisabeth A (1992) *Keywords in Evolutionary Biology*, Cambridge, MA: Harvard University Press.

Golley, F (1993) *A History of the Ecosystem Concept in Ecology: More Than the Sum of the Parts*, New Haven: Yale University Press.

Gould, Stephen Jay (1984) 'Balzan Prize to Ernst Mayr', *Science*, 223, 255–257.

Hagen, J (1992) *An Entangled Bank: The Origins of Ecosystem Ecology*, Piscutaway: Rutgers University Press.

Harvey, D (1974) 'Population, resources and the ideology of science', *Economic Geography*, republished in Harvey, D (2001) *Spaces of Capital: Towards a Critical Geography*, New York: Routledge, 38–67.

Harvey, D (1996) *Justice, Nature and the Geography of Difference*, Oxford: Blackwell.

Harvey, D (2000) *Spaces of Hope*, Berkeley: University of California Press.

Kingsland, S (1995) *Modeling Nature: Episodes in the History of Population Ecology*, Chicago: Chicago University Press.

Latour, B (1999) *Pandora's Hope: Essays on the Reality of Science Studies*, Cambridge, MA: Harvard University Press.

Leighley, J (ed.) (1963) *Land and Life: A Selection from the Writings of Carl Ortwin Sauer*, Berkeley: University of California Press.

Leopold, A (1949) *A Sand County Almanac*, New York: Oxford.

Levins, R and Lewontin, R (1985) *The Dialectical Biologist*, Cambridge, MA: Harvard University Press.

Lubchenco, J (1998) 'Entering the Century of the Environment: A New Social Contract for Science', *Science, 279*: 491–497.

Lubchenco, J, Brubaker, Linda B, Carpenter, Stephen R, *et al*. (1991) 'The Sustainable Biosphere Initiative: An Ecological Research Agenda: A Report from the Ecological Society of America' *Ecology*, 72 (2): 371–412.

Matthews, C M (2000) 'U.S. National Science Foundation: An Overview', Congressional Research Service Report for Congress, 95–307.

Mitman, G (1992) *The State of Nature: Ecology, Community, and American Society 1900–1950*, Chicago: Chicago University Press.

Mitman, G (1999) *Reel Nature: America's Romance with Wildlife on Film*, Cambridge, MA: Harvard University Press.

Odum, E (1953) *Fundamentals of Ecology*, Philadelphia: Saunders.

Olwig, K (1984) *Nature's Ideological Landscape*, London: Allen and Unwin.

Peet, R and Watts, M J (eds) (1996) *Liberation Ecologies*, London: Routledge.

Sauer, C O (1938) 'Plant and animal destruction in economic history', *Journal of Farm Economics*, 20: 765–775.

Scoones, I (1999) 'New Ecology and the Social Sciences: What prospects for a fruitful engagement?', *Annual Review of Anthropology*, 28: 479–507.

Smith, N (1984) *Uneven Development: Nature, Capital, and the Production of Space*, New York: Blackwells.

Williams, R (1977) *Marxism and Literature*, Oxford: Oxford University Press.

Williams, R (1980) 'Ideas of Nature' in *Problems of Materialism and Nature*, London: New Left Books.

Williams, R (1989) *What I Came to Say*, London: Hutchinson.

Wolch, J and Emel, J (1998) *Animal Geographies*, New York: Verso.

3
Enclosure: a modern spatiality of nature

Michael J Watts

'What happens when mechanisation encounters organic substance?'
(Seigfreid Giedion (1948) *Mechanization Takes Command*, p6)

'From the fifteenth century to the nineteenth, evaluations of common right were inseparable from the larger question of enclosure and the engrossment of small farms. For
enclosure meant the extinction of common right, and the extinction of common right
meant the decline of small farms.' (J M Neeson (1993) *Commoners*, p15)

In his magisterial study, *Traces on the Rhodian Shore* (1967), Berkeley geographer Clarence
Glacken charted, over the period between the ancients and the end of the eighteenth century, the parallel histories in Western thought of three foundational ideas through which
nature and culture came to be interpreted: the idea of a designed earth, the influence of the
environment on society and the role of humans as modifiers of the natural world. Glacken
began with the Hellenistic age – the affinity of theology and geography, Xenophon's treatise
on design, Aristotle's teleology of nature – and, for each epoch, explored the ways in which
a panoply of great thinkers wrestled with the idea of the earth as a planned abode, of environmental influence and determinism within a divinely created world, and of the capacity of
humans to control nature through technology, labour power and science. Schooled in intellectual history, Glacken sought to emphasise the historical continuities of ideas and how
foundational notions were typically modified and enriched by other theories relating to culture, history and the nature of the earth. Plenitude, the organic analogy, the role of human
institutions such as religion and government, for example, all figured prominently in the ways
in which a designed earth or human-induced transformation of nature was articulated in different places and at different times. His account stopped, however, at the very birth of
industrial modernity in the late eighteenth century when, as he put it:

'[T]here ends in Western civilisation an epoch in the history of man's relationship to nature.
What follows is of an entirely different order, influenced by the theory of evolution, special-
isation in the attainment of knowledge, acceleration in the transformation of nature' (p705).

The Industrial Revolution, a term Glacken disliked, marked a watershed after which the ideas of design, influence and modification carried entirely new meanings. Much of the sense of rupture – ideological, scientific, political, economic, cultural – wrought by industrial capitalism was foreseen in the ideas of Malthus, Godwin and Buffon, three figures selected by Glacken to close out his encomium. *Traces* was seen by Glacken as a prelude for a subsequent treatment of such towering figures as Marx, Darwin, Weber, Durkheim and Einstein as he brought his story up to the arrival of the nuclear age – and in so doing to return to the very old idea of apocalypse and extermination in Western thought. A sequel to *Traces* was in fact completed in the early 1980s, continuing Glacken's extraordinary intellectual history up through the nineteenth and twentieth centuries, but the manuscript was mysteriously destroyed.[1]

Glacken's challenge, to chart the vast complexity and the dense intellectual traffic between nature and modernity, has not been taken up, at least not in the encyclopedic way he depicted in *Traces*. 'Nature', 'culture' and 'modern', Raymond Williams (1976) famously said, are some of the most complex and difficult words in the English language, always unstable and polyvalent, their meanings shaped by and bound up with the problems they are being used to discuss. Glacken brought to this semantic difficulty an abiding concern with 'great ideas' and intellectual biography. Yet, in spite of his historical range and depth, he was less sensitive both to the ways in which particular knowledges and ideas were produced and to the material conditions of their production – what we would now call discourse and discursive practice – and to the ways in which space, and forms of spatiality, enter into the history of ideas of nature and culture. Glacken was, of course, concerned with space in the sense of different landscapes and environments, and the ways in which certain environments (climate and forests, for example) were deemed to be more or less influential on human character or settlement. But he was less attuned to what geographers would now call the spatialities of nature: that is to say, how notions of territory, place, boundary, inclusion, confinement and so on – the spatial lexicon, in short – are central to the ways in which the foundational ideas he identified are constituted, negotiated and fought over.

What, then, might it mean to envision a spatiality of nature appropriate to the twenty-first century? This is a wholly unmanageable question put in such stark terms, but I want to pose it at least in order to think about the sort of project that Glacken envisaged, even if I depart from his own history of ideas approach. More precisely, I want to deploy another keyword to think about the spatialities of nature and the modern: to use the idea of *enclosure* as a way of exploring some fundamental aspects of nature–society dialectics, of what Glacken saw as design, environmental influence and human modification of the earth.

Enclosure

> The gipsey's camp was not affraid
> I made his dwelling free
> Till vile enclosure came and made
> A parish slave of me
> John Clare, *The Lament of Swordy Well*, 1822, (reprinted 1967)

Michael J Watts

Enclosure, according to the *Webster's Dictionary*, means to surround on all sides, to place within a container and to shelter or hide. But in the English language the word has a strong historical referent, namely the English Parliamentary enclosures of the eighteenth and nineteenth centuries. To understand enclosure in all of its complexity – a process which began in England in the fifteenth century – is to begin with the idea of a commons and what Neeson (1993) calls 'commoning economies'. English villages, certainly up until the eighteenth century, were distinguished by the fact that land – for cultivation and grazing – was shared in some way. To read John Clare's poetry on the village of Helpston, published almost 200 years ago, is to experience a natural world that was known to him by virtue of its openness. The sharing, the common access, the possession without ownership of common lands, provided a social integument to village life:

> Love hearken the skylarks
> Right up in the sky
> The suns on the hedges
> The bushes are dry
> The slippers unsullied
> May wander abroad
> Grass up to the ancles
> Is dry as the road
>
> There's the path if you chuse it
> That wanders between
> The wheat in the ear
> And the blossoming bean
> Where the wheat tyed across
> By some mischevous clown
> Made you laugh though you tumbled
> And stained your new gown
> (Clare, 1967, p39)

Commoning economies involved common *right* – that is to say, access to pasture, to waste and to other village lands through customary (and *de facto* legal) forms of usufructory right. These rights provided for the commoner – for the English peasantry who still existed in the eighteenth century – some measure of independence from the labour market (having to work as labourers) and the cash economy (having to purchase the means of subsistence). Much of England was still 'open' in 1700, and the commons were intact; by 1840 most land was enclosed and the commons virtually obsolete. In Helpston, where Clare wrote his poetry, the wheat and beans still grew, but they were now fenced and railed; in more pastoral areas, the rights to graze were abrogated. Enclosure meant the closing of the countryside, a sort of confinement.

> These paths are stopt – the rude philistines thrall
> Is laid upon them and destroyed them all
> Each little tyrant with his little sign

> Shows where man claims earth no more divine
> But paths to freedom and to childhood dear
> Aboard sticks up to the notice 'no road here'
> And on the tree with ivy overhung
> The hated sign by vulgar taste is hung
> As tho the very birds should learn to know
> When they go there they must no further go
> This with the poor scared freedom bade goodbye
> And much they feel it in the smothered sign
> And the birds and trees and flowers without a name
> All sighed when lawless law's enclosure came
> (Clare, 1982, p415)

The controversial enclosure acts, which gained momentum from the 1740s onward, had devastating effects on commoners: 'strip the small farms of the benefit of the commons', wrote an observer, 'and they are all at one stroke levelled to the ground'. Clare's nature was transformed physically (and ecologically), but enclosure also meant the loss of particular customs, rights, forms of livelihood. When Clare says enclosure made people a slave of the parish, he meant that commoners lost land and use rights, which threw them at the mercy of the rural labour market and of parish charity. The land, and the landscape, no longer looked the same; its boundaries and borders restricted movements and hence altered the experience of the landscape, and these juridical and economic derelictions hastened the end of a certain sort of moral economy, of a particular sort of sociability, of a sense of community. None of this is to wax nostalgic nor to mythologise the relations of exploitation and of subordination in the seventeenth-century English village. It is rather to grasp a process of simultaneous natural, physical and socio-cultural transformation: a particular spatiality of nature.

Enclosure is a powerful historical fact and the carrier of a dense 'cluster' of meanings (the language is from Williams again) that refers to a spatial process: land formerly open is now enclosed (the hedgerows and fences are its markers). Place and territory is reconstituted through boundaries, property lines and markets. But enclosure was simultaneously a loss of rights, obligations and responsibilities. Enclosure involved a loss of the 'open' commons; it wrought a sort of confinement, dispossession, incarceration, privatisation and social transformation all at once. Describing a part of this process, Karl Polanyi (1947) referred to it as the Great Transformation. Enclosure marked two epochal moments: a deepening of the market as common rights were displaced by private property and land ownership and by wage work; and the efforts of the state (through parliamentary enclosure) to both simplify and make more visible the rural world. Polanyi referred to the former in terms rise of the self-regulating market, as a process of 'disembedding' and as the 'discovery of society': enclosure took human practices out of the realm of the social (local custom) and embedded them in the commodity economy overseen by a new form of liberal governance. James Scott (1998) has described the latter as state legibility, that is to say, a process by which nature and society is simplified and ordered, what he calls 'abridged maps'. A state cadastral map is paradigmatic of the ways in which the state is central to the process by which 'exceptionally complex, illegible, and local social practices' – for example, the commons – are substituted by a 'standard grid whereby it could be centrally recorded and monitored' (p2).

So, enclosure comes to speak for the social, the spatial, the cultural, the political economic and the natural all at once. It is a stunning example of what Doreen Massey (1994) calls the power-geometry of space–time compression. Place and community are refigured by new flows of accumulation, investment and a deepening of market relations. It is a contradictory process too, because as it closes it also opens, it excludes but also confines. Not everyone experiences the dislocations in the same way; it is, as Massey says, a complex and socially differentiated process. Enclosure was born at the ground zero of a particular sort of modernity and, insofar as it is geographical, makes space and space-making (like the census, the map, the factory) central to the idea of the modern. But how can enclosure – as one way of thinking about the spatiality of nature – be made to speak to a mature industrial capitalism, a world in which, unlike John Clare's universe, the market and the commodity has come to dominate virtually all aspects of social life?

Zoo

In the zoo, as John Berger (1980) famously put it, animals constitute a living monument to their own demise: 'everywhere', he says, 'animals disappear' (p24). In posing the question, 'Why look at animals?', Berger sought to show that there is a central paradox residing in our experience of the zoo and its inhabitants. It is a source of popular appeal and considerable attraction – 'millions visited the zoos each year out of a curiosity which was both so large, so vague and so personal that it is hard to express' (Berger, 1980, p20) – and yet in the zoo 'the view is always wrong ... like an image out of focus' (p21). Inevitably zoos disappoint. The excitement of the wild is replaced by alienation, lethargy, isolation, incarceration and boredom. The spark which has historically linked man and animal has been extinguished. At the heart of the zoo's paradoxical status is a sort of double alienation. On the one hand the zoo is a sort of prison – a space of confinement and a site of enforced marginalisation, like the penitentiary or the concentration camp, and on the other it cannot subvert the awful reality that the animals, from whatever vantage point they are viewed, are 'rendered absolutely marginal' (*ibid.*, p22). The inescapable fact is that the zoo recapitulates the relations between humans and animals, between nature and modernity. It *demonstrates*, as Berger says, a basic ecological fact of loss and exclusion – the disappearance and extinction of animals – through an act of incarceration.

Berger was at pains to connect the zoo as a monument to loss, as a space of confinement to a human crisis, specifically to the disposal, or perhaps more appropriately the enclosure, of the peasantry. In quick succession, the emergence of the zoo – that is to say, the marginalisation of the animal – is followed by the marginalisation of a class – the peasantry – for whom familiarity with, and a wise understanding of, animals is a distinguishing trait. The second half of the twentieth century, as Eric Hobsbawm (1994) noted in his magisterial book *The Age of Extremes*, contained 'the most dramatic and far-reaching social change … which cut us off for ever from the world of the past, [namely] the death of the peasantry' (p289). If the world-renowned San Diego zoo memorialises wildlife extinction and animal loss, perhaps the monument to the death of the peasantry is the folk museum replete with its artifacts and arcana of rural life. As Malamud (1995) says, the zoo is a locus of pain and loss. Both historical losses are, in Berger's vision, 'irredeemable for the culture of capitalism' (Berger, 1980, p26).

Berger offers, I think, a productive way of thinking about nature. To put the matter starkly, one might say that the relation between animals (or more properly nature) and modernity can be construed as a gigantic act of enclosure – necessitating, of course, loss and displacement – which contains a double movement. The first, of which the zoo is the exemplary modern instance, is to accomplish what Stephen Greenblatt, in *Marvelous Possessions* (1991), calls 'the assimilation of the other' (p3). By putting Marx to the service of the assimilation process, Greenblatt suggests that the zoo, for example, is part of the 'reproduction and circulation of mimetic capital' (p6). Containing animals, the zoo is what he calls a cultural storehouse, part of the proliferation and circulation of representations that become for Greenblatt:

> 'a set of images and image-making devices that are accumulated, "banked" as it were, in books, archives, collections, cultural storehouses, until such time as new representations are called upon to generate new representations' (p6).

This mimetic quality of capitalism suggests that the representations – of animals, of ecosystems, of nature – are social relations of production. The representation is both the product of the social relations of capitalism and is a social relation itself 'linked to the group understandings, status hierarchies, resistances and conflicts that exist in other spheres of the culture in which it circulates' (*ibid.*, p6). The zoo is, then, product and producer (Malamud, 1995). The zoo places animals in captivity ('preservation', 'salvage ecology') as a response to – the product of – the devastating ecological consequences of modernisation. Equally, the zoo culture serves as an institutionalised means, a scientific means no less, to represent animals in quite specific ways and generate culturally mimetic portrayals of itself.

The zoo 'matters' to the extent that its images and representations of animals achieve a reproductive power – by speaking to our humanity or the philanthropy of capitalists, by enhancing environmental sustainability, by perpetrating the distinctions between the wild chaos of nature and the order of a rational capitalist world. The fact that zoos disappoint, to return to Berger, is simply to assert that the hegemony of representations is never complete or fully secured, and that the zoo cannot possibly cover its tracks. The zoo is unequivocally about loss and captivity, and the very antithesis of the fecundity and freedom that nature purportedly signifies. Not simply a product, the zoo is an unwitting producer, 'capable of decisively altering the very forces that brought it into being' (Greenblatt, 1991, p6).

In this sense then, the zoo is a sort of metaphor for thinking about nature and capitalism.

There is, however, a second vectoring in the double movement of animals and modernity. Berger gestures to it in his invocation of the relation between the animal and the historic demise of the peasantry. Properly speaking, the historical reference point here is the agrarian question of the mid- and late-nineteenth century in Europe (Kautsky, 1899). What, asked Karl Kautsky in his classic book *Die Agrarfrage* (1906), is happening to the peasantry? In his still relevant account of the German agricultural sector in the last quarter of the nineteenth century, the agrarian question encompassed accumulation (How were surpluses extracted from the peasant-dominated agricultural sector?), science (How were the forces of production being revolutionised?) and politics (What were the political implications for the German Social Democratic Workers Party of the disintegration and differentiation of the peasantry?). Of course, Kautsky was at pains to point out that the 'disappearance' of the peasantry was a more complex and uneven process than the orthodox Marxist predictions might suggest. Nevertheless, his book illustrates clearly that Berger's concern with the historic loss of the peasantry was, at the same time, the process by which land-based and livestock activities were *industrialised*:

> 'The transformation of agricultural production into industrial production is still in its infancy. [But] bold prophets, namely those chemists gifted with an imagination, already are dreaming of the day when bread will be made from stones and when all requirements of the human diet will be assembled in chemical factories ... But one thing is certain. Agricultural production has already been transformed into industrial production in a large number of fields.... This does not mean that ... one can reasonably speak of the demise of agriculture ... but [it] is now caught up in the constant revolution which is the hallmark of the capitalist mode of production.' (Kautsky, 1899, p297)

In the current parlance, peasant agriculture was subject to the twin processes of appropriation and substitution (Goodman, Sorj and Wilkinson, 1987). The former spoke to the process by which more of the production process (including the inputs) were provided by off-farm industry, while the latter identified the increasing trend to produce food and fibres in factories as a fully industrial process comparable to non-agricultural forms of manufacture. On one side stood drip irrigation and genetically modified crops, and on the other the feedlot or the industrial manufacture of artificial sugars.

To return to Berger, the demise of the peasantry as a social class with certain rights is homologous to the industrial and scientific assault on animals and nature (also with rights) within the food provisioning system. What Kautsky saw in its infancy was the process by which science was harnessed to the problem of the industrialisation of livestock and crop production. Genetics lay the groundwork for the application of new technology – and the drive for mechanisation – to the plant and the animal directly. To quote Seigfreid Geidion's magisterial book, *Mechanization Takes Command* (1948), 'what happens when mechanization encounters organic substance? (p6) He properly addressed the question of the mechanisation of agriculture from the eighteenth century, and the means by which bread and meat were mechanised, displacing the artisan crafts of butchery and bread making, and of course transforming popular taste. Even in 1948 when the book was published he could, however, observe: 'Still of unmeasured significance is mechanization's intervention in the procreation of plants and animals' (p7).

Giedion was, of course, charting the process by which the high-yielding corn variety or the milk cow laced with BST had been converted into sites of accumulation. In so doing, the animal and the plants had been, as it were, transformed from *within*. The zoo represents the transformation from *without*, the extinction of species that attended the ecological devastation wrought by industrialisation. One might say, then, that the alienated, lethargic elephant in Berger's description of the zoo and the genetically modified sheep are both monuments to the historic losses of capitalism. One memorialises the ecological (biodiversity) crisis of modernity; the other the scientific and industrial reconstitution of nature (Haraway, 1991). I wish to make the point that both elements of this double movement can be understood as a form of enclosure – and by definition confinement, incarceration, discipline and subjection. Both necessitate some sort of assimilation of the other, but unlike the zoo in which it is the reproduction and circulation of mimetic capital that predominates, the industrial milk cow or battery hen *is* productive capital, though livestock too, and in the name of all commodity production, has its own stock of images, representations and fetishistic qualities.

Feathered friends

According to the latest Agricultural Census, 8.2 billion chickens were produced in the United States in 2000 (roughly 30 per person). In 1991, chicken consumption per capita exceeded beef, for the first time, in a country which has something of an obsession with red meat. The fact that each American man, woman and child currently consumes roughly 1.5 pounds of chicken each week reflects a complex vectoring of social forces in post-war America: first, a change in taste driven by a heightened sensitivity to health matters, especially the heart-related illnesses associated with red meat consumption. Second, the fantastically low cost of chicken meat, which has in real terms *fallen* since the 1930s (a century ago Americans would eat steak and lobster when they could not afford chicken). And, not least, the growing extent to which chicken is consumed in a panoply of forms (Chicken MacNuggets, say) which did not exist 20 years ago and which are now delivered to us by the massive fast-food industry – a fact which itself points to the reality that Americans eat more and more food outside of the home (food consumption 'away from home' is, by dollar value, 40% of the average US household food budget).

Broilers are overwhelmingly produced by family farmers in the US, but this turns out to be a deceptive statistic. They are grown by farmers under contract to enormous transnational enterprises – referred to as 'integrators' in the chicken business – who provide the chicks and feed; the growers (who are not organised into unions and who have almost no bargaining power) must borrow heavily in order to build the broiler houses and the infrastructure necessary to meet contractual requirements. Growers are not independent farmers at all; they are little more that underpaid workers – what we might call 'propertied labourers' – of the corporate producers who also dominate the processing industry. Working in the poultry processing industry, in which the broilers are slaughtered and dressed and packaged into literally hundreds of different products, is one of the most underpaid and dangerous in the country (a new US Government report cites almost two-thirds of all poultry processing plants as in violation of overtime payment procedures!). Immigrant labour – Vietnamese, Laotian, Hispanic – now represents a substantial proportion of workers (almost wholly non-union) in the industry. The largest ten companies account for almost two-thirds of broiler production in the US. Tyson Foods, Inc., the largest broiler producer, accounts for 124 million pounds of chicken meat per week, and it controls 21% of the US market with sales of over $5 billion, two-thirds of which go to the fast-food industry. According to Don Tyson, the CEO of Tyson's, his aim is to 'control the center of the plate for the American people'.

The vast majority of chickens sold and consumed are broilers (young chickens) which, it turns out, are rather extraordinary creatures. In the 1880s there were only 100 million chickens. In spite of the rise of commercial hatcheries early in the century, the industry remained a sideline business run by farmers' wives until the 1920s. Since the first commercial sales (by a Mrs Wilmer Steele, in 1923 in Delmarva, who sold 357 in one batch at prices five times higher than today), the industry has been transformed by the feed companies, which began to promote integration and the careful genetic control and reproduction of bird flocks, and by the impact of big science, often with government support. The heart of the US chicken industries is in the ex-slave holding and cotton growing South. Until the Second World War, the chicken industry was located primarily in the Delmarva peninsula in the mid Atlantic states (near Washington, DC). During the 1940s and 1950s the industry moved south – it was restructured and relocated – and with it emerged the large integrated broiler complexes – what in current parlance is now called flexible or post-Fordist capitalist organisation. The largest producing region is Arkansas – the home state of ex-President Clinton – and the chicken industry has been heavily involved in presidential political finance and lobbying, including a recent case in which the Secretary of Agriculture was compelled to resign. The lowly chicken, in other words, reaches into the White House.

The post-war history of the national and global chicken, or 'broiler', industry is one of mind-boggling dynamism and growth. Advances in breeding, disease control, nutrition, housing and processing have conferred upon US integrators some of the lowest production costs in the world. Since 1940, the industry's feed conversion rate has declined precipitously from three pounds of feed per pound of liveweight to under two pounds. Over the same period the average broiler live weight has increased from 2.89 lbs to 4.63 lbs and the maturation period – the time required for a bird to reach market weight – has plummeted from over 70 days to less than 50. The result is what was called in the 1940s, the 'perfect broiler'. Avian science has now permitted the mind boggling rates at which the birds add weight (almost five pounds in as many weeks!). The average live bird weight has almost *doubled* in the last 50 years; over the same period the labour input in broiler production has fallen by 80%. The broiler is the product of a truly massive R&D

Table 3.1 *The Chicken Revolution: US Broiler Production and Consumption 1934–2000*

Year	US Production (million heads)	Increase Over Previous Period (per cent)	Maturation (days)	Feed Conversion Rate*	Labour Input (hours)**	Price Per Pound (dollars) live	Price Per Pound (dollars) r-t-c[1]	Average Liveweight (pounds)	Per Capita Consumption (pounds) r-t-c
1934	34	–	112	4.30	5.1	0.193	–	2.84	0.7
1940	143	321	–	–	–	0.173	–	2.89	2.0
1945	366	156	–	–	–	0.295	–	3.03	5.0
1950	631	72	–	–	–	0.274	–	3.08	8.7
1955	1,092	73	–	–	–	0.252	–	3.07	13.8
1960	7,795	63	–	–	–	0.169	–	3.35	23.6
1965	2,334	30	–	–	–	0.150[2]	26.5	3.48	29.9
1970	2,987	28	–	–	–	0.135	26.4	3.62	36.8
1975	2,950	–1	–	–	–	0.262	45.1	3.76	36.8
1980	3,963	34	–	–	–	0.279	49.1	3.93	46.6
1985	4,470	13	–	–	–	0.302	50.8[3]	4.19	52.0
1990	5,864	31	–	–	–	0.324	54.8	4.37	61.0
1994	7,018	20	–	–	–	0.350	55.7	4.63	69.9
2000	8,262	18	45	1.75	0.12	0.336	58.14	5.00	89.6

* Pounds of feed per pound of live broiler.
** Hours per 100 lbs. of broiler meat.
[1] ready-to-cook.
[2] live price changed to live weight equivalent price in mid 60s.
[3] 9-city wholesale price changed to 12-city composite wholesale price in 1983.

Source: Poultry Tribune, September 1995, p15, United States Department of Agriculture Statistics 1994–2000.

campaign; disease control and regulation of physiological development has fully industrialised the broiler to the point where it is really a cyborg: part nature, part machine. Our understanding of chicken nutrition now exceeds that of any other animal, *including* humans! High technology and industrial production methods have also been the key to the egg industry. A state-of-the art hen house holds 100,000 birds in minuscule cages stretching the length of two football fields; it resembles a late twentieth-century high-technology torture chamber. The birds are fed by robot in carefully controlled amounts every two hours around the clock. In order to reduce stress, anxiety and aggression (which increases markedly with confinement and increased egg laying), the birds are housed in low-intensity light or wear red contact lenses which, for reasons that are not clear, reduces feed consumption and increases egg production.

All of this has been driven by a small number of large integrators who dominate the chicken *filiere*. Tyson Foods – the largest broiler integrator – currently accounts for 21.6% of the US ready-to-cook market, and in 1995 claimed total sales of $5.5 billion. The integrators are increasingly global actors who supply some of the most aggressively transnational companies, namely the fast-food industry, who often represent the leading edge of capitalist expansion as markets open up under the pressure of neo-liberal reforms. The US is the largest producer and exporter of broilers, with a sizable market share in Hong Kong, Russia and Japan. Facing intense competition from Brazil, China and Thailand, the global chicken industry is driven by the lure of the massive Chinese market, and by the newly emerging and unprotected markets of Eastern Europe and the post-Soviet states. However, the world chicken market is highly segmented: Americans prefer breast meat (and most production of such is for the home market), while US exporters take advantage of foreign preference for leg quarters, feet and wings to fulfill the large demand from Asia. The chicken is a thoroughly global creature – in its own way not unlike the global car or global finance.

I wish to focus here on the role of big science and the productivity revolution (see Boyd and Watts, 1996). Two forces were central to the radical increases in biological and labour productivity, and in the reconstitution of the broiler itself. First, the move to year-round confinement, made possible by the discovery of vitamin D in 1926, facilitated the shift to *industrial* broiler production. Second, the federal government stepped in during the depression years to lay the foundations for the post-war productivity increases and the application of what one might call 'big science' to the industry. Although chicken breeding experiments had been established by the USDA as early as 1912, it was not until 1933, with the establishment of the National Poultry Improvement Plan (NPIP), that the government emerged as a major force in facilitating the development of new techniques in disease control, breeding and husbandry. Gradually, mortality rates were reduced – approximately 30% by the end of the 1930s – which permitted the move to more intensive confinement operations.

What proved to be decisive during the war and immediate post-war years, however, was the revolution in primary breeding. Until the 1940s, farmers had relied on pure breeds that had been developed for egg production, with little concern for meat qualities. With increased demand for chicken meat during the war, breeders began to focus their attention on the development of specialised breeds for meat production. In 1944, the search for the broad-breasted chicken began in earnest as the A&P food chain launched a series of national breeding contests. Striking illustrations of early retailer power in product design, the two 'Chicken of Tomorrow Contests' in 1946 and 1951, which greatly accelerated the development of the modern broiler industry by establishing cross-breeds or hybrids as the standard throughout the industry, ushered in the age of the 'designer chicken'. Employing principles pioneered in the hybridisation of corn and other crops, primary breeders developed standard pedigrees of male and female lines that combined to pro-duce a superior bird. By the 1950s, such cross-breeds provided the genetic basis of the modern broiler industry, and breeders focused on fine tuning their pedigrees to meet the ever more exacting demands for genetic uniformity and quality assurance. On the eve of integration in the broiler industry, moreover, the 'biological lock' of hybridisation strengthened the boundary between the primary breeders and the rest of the industry – a boundary that has persisted to this day.

Complementing these dramatic advances in breeding were substantial public investments in nutrition, disease control and *confinement* technologies during the immediate post-war period, much of which was sponsored by the land grant universities and the federal government. The development of high-performance rations combined with the use of vit-amin B-12 and antibiotics in feed dramatically reduced mortality and increased feed con-version efficiency. At the same time, the completion of rural electrification facilitated substantial improvements in environmental control and labour productivity within confine-ment operations. Whereas in 1940, an average 250 man-hours were required to raise 1000 birds to maturity, by 1955, the required time had dropped to 48 hours.

William Boyd's excellent research (2001) has shown that in terms of biological prod-uctivity, mechanisation and industrialisation, the chicken has no peer in contemporary food provisioning. The prosaic chicken has been made over in such a way that it can only be thought of as bionic. In 1935 the average weight of the broiler was 2.8 lbs, it took 112 days to reach market weight and had a feed conversion ratio (lbs feed/lbs broiler) of 4.4; 50 years later the figures are respectively 4.6 lbs, 43 days and 1.9. It is the leading edge of just-in-time flexible production, and in the designing of nature to meet the industrial labour process. The chicken, moreover, is quickly becoming *the* global meat. It was the combin-ation of confinement, nutrition and growth research, and genetic improvement that pro-duced, by the 1950s, a chicken which was '*made to order to meet the needs of the meat industry*' (Warren, 1958, p16, emphasis added). By the 1980s the new biotechnologies entered the broiler industry, specifically the life sciences companies intent on genetic engineering to develop breeds keyed to the sale of proprietary health products. Furthermore, with the famous Chakrabarty ruling in 1980, substantial interest was aroused in the possibility of transgenic chickens subject to patent protection. The possi-bility of a full genetic map of the chicken – assisted by the fact that DNA can be isolated from nucleated red blood cells, unlike most mammalian species – is well under way,[2] which would 'allow selective improvement to proceed on the basis of genotype rather than phenotype, representing a very significant expansion in breeding power' (Boyd, 2001, p659).

The chicken-genome project, then, marks an archetypal late twentieth-century process of enclosure with, it needs to be said, Frankensteinian qualities. First, confinement which marks both the shift from open range to broiler houses, but also a process of industrial integration within a highly oppressive broiler complex, and which has as its counterpoint the enclosure of the chicken contractor (Boyd and Watts, 1996). Second, the 'designer chicken' establishes the extent to which nutritional and genetic sciences have produced a 'man-made' broiler to fit the needs of the industry. It is, then, a classical cyborg (Haraway, 1991). There is, of course, something grotesque about the creation of a creature which is a sort of growth machine, steroidally enhanced, producing in unprecedentedly short periods of time, enormous quantities of flesh and muscle around a sort of Frankenstein-like skeleton. Third, the chicken is transformed into a site of accumulation; this is reflected, of course, in its curious physiognomy and anatomy ('all breast and no wings'). Harvey's (1998) important account of the body as an accumulation strategy focuses on three moments: productive consumption of the working body, exchange and individual consumption. What is striking about the chicken – indeed the meat industry more generally – is the extent to which the 'working body' has not simply been 'Taylorised' in some way, but actually constructed physically to meet the needs of the industrial labour process. The poultry industry in this sense combines the worst of productive consumption of the human body (the appalling working conditions and health deficits associated with working on the line) with the most horrifying forms of reconstituted nature. Nineteenth-century working conditions meet up with twenty-first century science.

Harvey spends less time, however, on the dialectics of nature itself, namely the fact that the effort to convert the body into a site of accumulation runs up against the ethical, social and biological limits of commodification (see Polanyi, 1944). This is, of course, nowhere clearer than in the broiler industry. It is perfectly obvious that the chicken industry is on the verge of a major biological and, specifically, health crisis. On the one hand, the dangers of disease – the Hong Kong derived avian flu in 1998 is a case in point – are enormous, driven in part by the susceptibility of fragile and vulnerable chickens to new pathogens which are able to destroy flocks very quickly. One part of this crisis is driven by resistance to antibiotics – the R-plasmid problem – and another part by emergent diseases. Furthermore, efforts to increase breast meat yields have created a high propensity for musculo-skeletal problems, metabolic disease, immuno-deficiency and male infertility (Boyd, 2001), which is to say higher bird mortalities. At the social level, the health problems of the industry are legion. In the US, for example – where the salmonella problem and chicken are virtually synonymous – the human health effects from resistant bacteria of animal origin due to antibiotics used as feed additives, has remained largely unregulated. In June of 1999 (*Le Monde*, June 13 1999, p210) frightening news of dioxin contaminated chickens in Belgium exposed once again the trade-off between cost-driven growth promotion and long-term vulnerability associated with increased antibiotic resistant pathogens and feeding additives. Here, the popular concern with labelling and moving back to free-range chicken sharpens the contradictions of the industrial and productivist model of agriculture. And finally, there are the ethical questions raised by confinement, battery hens and the suffering imposed by mass production (see, for example, the activities of United Poultry Concerns and the work of Davis, 1995). Peter Singer, who once sat in a cage in the middle of Melbourne to publicise the plight of battery hens, specifically argues that the 'simple' chicken deserves to be protected from unnecessary pain (see *New Yorker*, September 6 1999). Animal welfare questions are, in this regard, no longer local or parochial concerns; indeed, they have reached the bargaining table of the World Trade Organisation. The European Union has been concerned to pressure trade partners to meet its own animal welfare standards since, throughout the 1990s, the EU has been concerned to limit animal rights considerations against the 'competitive position of EU producers in a market liberalised under WTO agreements' (Fisher, 1999, p13). Nonetheless, on June 15 1999, the EU Agriculture Council finally decided to prohibit the use of battery cages by 2012 (and Britain has recently banned battery hen production – *Daily Mail*, June 25 2002).

If my prosaic chicken story reveals anything, it is that the monuments to animals which John Berger invokes are on shaky foundations, and in their different ways cracked and pitted with the contradictions of the modernist impulse to commoditise and industrialise nature. One response to the crisis of nature modernised has, of course, been articulated in terms of animal rights and social justice (see Coetzee 1999; Wolch and Emel, 1998). On the US side of the Atlantic, at least, it is clear that the animal rights movement has considerable popular and academic credibility and legitimacy. The fact that courses on Animal Liberation are offered at the Harvard Law School, and that the *New York Times* can run a leader on the Great Ape Legal Project (part of the Animal Legal Defense Fund) which is now widely understood to have compelling grounds for bringing a suit to trial that is 'the inevitable culmination of challenges [the legal profession is] … starting to make to the principle that animals are property without legal rights' (*New York Times*, August 22 1999, p2) are cases in point. Enclosure and confinement, space–time compression and a new power geometry will always generate, as John Clare's poetry revealed, the most profound dissent.

Captain Chromosome

However, one group (operating in East Anglia under the sign of Captain Chromosome) refuses the strategically and epistemologically fatal 'nature/artifice' fork, and by implicitly claiming Captain Swing and the agricultural luddites (of the sixteenth century) as ancestors, intuitively grasps the nub of the new developments down on the farm, and their historical continuity, namely that genetically engineered crops and patents represent a further seizure of the commons, and will bring a new round of enclosures and global proletar-ianisation (Boal, 2001, p156).

In early March 1998, the US Department of Agriculture and the Delta and Pine Land Company were granted US patent number 5,723,765. It involves a method of producing sterile seeds in second-generation plants by the transfection of a so-called lethal gene that produces seeds incapable of germination. As the inventor pointed out, the patent prevents the escape of a plant by natural seed dispersal; it is a way of 'self-policing the unauthorised use of American technology' (*New Scientist*, 1998, p22). The terminator gene condenses the novel essence of the so-called molecular or rDNA revolution: namely, the capacity to vastly expand the taxonomic range available for gene transfer, and the ability to target specific processes in plants and animals. The fact that the genome of humans or fruitflies or tomatoes or chickens can now be mapped presents the possibility that the new frontier of accumulation and profitability has opened up: namely, the building blocks of human, plant and animal life. To return to Polanyi, the very stuff of life has now been embedded in the marketplace – and disembedded from nature.

The centrality of the gene as the distinctively modern map of nature reaffirms the power of the enclosure as a way of exploring the contemporary landscape of what Glacken called interpretations of nature and culture. To return to the terminator gene, the rDNA revolution has provided the technocratic capacity to enhance precision, control and goal specificity within the agricultural and indeed the entire biological realm. Molecular biology can now make use of a complex legal and juridical apparatus – the patenting industry – by which the genes or germplasm may itself be subject to the dull compulsion of the market place. The debate over the trade in germplasm (a prerequisite for the life science companies like Norvartis and Monsanto) is being subject to a genetic enclosure. All manner of germplasm is now owned privately and traded through the marketplace; bio-prospecting for using genetic material is now at the forefront of life science accumulation. There is a profound sense in which communities in Ethiopia or New Guinea have lost their common rights to their own genetic and plant material.

In the same ways that the eighteenth-century English enclosures were an object of popular scorn and resistance, so it is to be expected that the appearance of genetically modified crops and animals has generated their own 'luddites'. During 1997, a number of actions against the 300 or so field trial sites for GE crops in the British Isles were undertaken by the likes of the Lincolnshire Loppers, Captain Chromosome, the Kenilworth Croppers and Superheroes Against Genetics. In the autumn of 1997, Galelic Earth Liberation trampled Monsanto's modified maize field in County Carlow; in West Sussex a genetically engineered rapeseed was uprooted, and there has been significant sabotage – eliciting much popular sympathy – in France and Germany, most memorably against the Norvartis drying plant in Nerca, France. At least 36 field sites were 'visited' by these luddites in the UK during the 1998 growing season. As Iain Boal (2001) has shown, the surfacing of someone like Captain Chromosome in Norfolk cannot be understood outside of the fact that the region has a long history of both resistance to enclosures and an association with agricultural innovation. Furthermore, he properly notes that this resistance cannot turn on the reclamation of a pristine nature for the good reason that the East Anglian landscape is not a natural landscape but is, to return to Glacken, a humanly modified locality, a relic of open-cast peat mines. Captain Chromosome gestures to an earlier history of enclosure but cannot claim to return to an uncontaminated or natural landscape of the past either.

Captain Chromosome and the terminator gene confront us with the twenty-first century enclosure as the forces of the market and of capital are now massing on the frontiers of the building blocks of life itself. New forms of confinement, dispossession, loss of right are already at work backed, as in John Clare's time, by the forces of the state but now armed with what Boal (2001, p154) calls 'the promethean mythos of science and technics'. The sort of legibility, simplification and control invoked by James Scott (1998) is in the process of generating a new power geometry whose borders, vectors and alignments are far from clear.

Recombinant DNA and genetically modified organisms also returns us to Glacken's triad of historical ideas of culture/nature: design, influence and modification. Of course, the capacity to transform is now incomparably vast in relation to Glacken's account of the Hellenistic world or early modern Europe. Indeed, the very idea of design has now scaled heights that even some of the early nineteenth-century scientific boosters like Saint Simon could not possibly have anticipated. But curiously, this has made Glacken's reference to environmental influence even more compelling. There is no simple Promethean victory for science for the very good reason that the likes of the Aral Sea, or the global resurgence of malaria, or the possibility of a genetically modified apocalypse cast a long shadow over the enhanced powers of human modification of nature. In confirming the salience of Glacken's analysis for the twenty-first century, amidst the hype and hubris of the human genome project and the life science transnationals, I have sought – through the deployment of enclosure as one sort of spatiality of nature – to ground his foundational ideas in the 'great transformation' of contemporary global capitalism. Enclosure was the final blow to peasants in the commoning economy of England. But the result was a landscape that, to cite Neeson (1993), informed, legitimised and sharpened class politics. Perhaps there is a moral in the story for the new millennium.

Note

1. Glacken's psychological health deteriorated in the latter years of his life, a condition that can be traced back to the Vietnam War and the protests on the Berkeley campus (when he served, to his chagrin, as Chair of the Department of Geography). His sequel to *Traces* was completed in the early 1980s, but was not well received by the University of California Press, which distressed Glacken greatly. While it appears that Glacken destroyed the manuscript as his condition deteriorated in the 1980s, substantial portions of chapters have been located and are currently housed with the Glacken papers in the Bancroft Library on the Berkley campus.
2. Israeli geneticist Avigdor Cahaner has recently engineered a featherless fowl, which is heralded as the 'high-speed future of chicken farming' (see www.theage.com.au/articles/2002/05/211021882051923.html).

Bibliography

Benton, T (1995) *Natural Relations*, London: Verso.

Berger, J (1980) *About Looking*, New York: Pantheon.

Boal, I (2001), 'Damaging Crops', in N Peluso and M Watts (eds), *Violent Environments*, Ithaca: Cornell University Press, pp.146–154.

Boyd, W (2001), 'Making Meat' in *Technology and Culture*, 42, pp.631–663.

Boyd, W and Watts, M (1996) 'Agro-industrial Just-in-Time', in Goodman, D and Watts, M (eds), *Globalizing Food*, London: Routledge.

Clare, J (1967) 'Love Hearken the skylarks', in Robinson, E and Summerfield, S (eds), *Selected Poems and Prose of John Clare*, Oxford: Oxford University Press.

Clare, J (1982) 'The Mores', in Barrell, J and Bull, J (eds), *The Penguin Book of English Pastoral Verse*, London: Penguin.

Coetzee, J (1999) *The Lives of Animals*, Princeton: Princeton University Press.

Davis, K (1995) 'Thinking Like a Chicken', in Adams, C and Donovan, J (eds), *Animals and Women* Durham: Duke University Press.

Fisher, C (1999) 'Animal Welfare Likely to be on the WTO Menu', *Bridges*, 3/6, 13.

Giedion, S (1948) *Mechanization Takes Command*, New York: Oxford University Press.

Glacken, C (1967) *Traces on the Rhodian Shore*, Berkeley: University of California Press.

Goodman, D, Sorj, B and Wilkinson, J (1987) *From Farming to Biotechnology*, Oxford: Blackwell.

Greenblatt, S (1991) *Marvelous Possessions*, Chicago: University of Chicago Press.

Haraway, D (1991) *Simians, Cyborgs and Women*, London: Routledge.

Harvey, D (1998) 'The body as an accumulation strategy', *Society and Space*, 16, 401–421.

Hobsbawm, E (1994) *The Age of Extremes*, New York: Pantheon.

Kautsky, K (1899) *La Question Agraire*, Paris: Maspero.

Kautsky, K (1899/1988) *The Agrarian Question*, London: Zwan Press.

Malamud, R (1995) *Reading Zoos*, New York: New York University Press.

Massey, D (1984) *Space, Place, Gender*, Minneapolis: University of Minnesota Press.

Neeson, J (1993) *Commoners*, Cambridge: Cambridge University Press.

Polanyi, K (1944) *The Great Transformation*, Beacon: Boston.

Scott, J (1998) *Seeing Like a State*, New Haven: Yale University Press.

Singer, P (1975) *Animal Liberation*, New York: Pantheon.

Warren, D (1958) 'A half century of advances in the genetics and breeding improvement of poultry', *Poultry Science*, 37/1, 4–20.

Williams, R (1976) *Keywords*, Oxford: Oxford University Press.

Wolch, J and Emel, J (eds), (1998) *Animal Geographies*. London: Verso.

4
Recovering the future: a post-disciplinary perspective on geography and political economy

Mark Goodwin

'What is needed is a new political economy which combines the breadth of vision of the classical political economy of the nineteenth century with the analytical advances of twentieth-century social science.' (Gamble et al, 1996, p5)

Introduction

I want to begin this chapter by exploring the apparent paradox in its title – that my vision for the future of human geography should entail a post-disciplinary perspective that encompasses the breakdown of traditional disciplinary boundaries. This does not mean that I see no role for issues of geography and the study of spatial dynamics within a renewed political economy. Quite the reverse, I want to make the claim that these concerns should be central to the exploration of a whole range of contemporary themes within political economy. In this sense, I want to explore both the influence of political economy on geography, but also the arguably more important influence of geography on political economy. More important because the day-to-day practices that are the focus of political economy – the dynamics and conflicts involved in the production, accumulation, division and distribution of wealth – are intrinsically spatial. Any account of these which lacks an appreciation of geographical form and substance will inevitably be partial. As Thrift (2001) puts it, 'the new political economy is being constructed through new spatial forms that are not just incidental to some supposed overlaying capitalist dynamic, *but are what capitalism is*' (p378, my emphasis).

This means that my vision for human geography is not one driven by disciplinary imperialism, or by a desire for geographers to stake claim to a small part of the intellectual world as theirs to study. Instead, I look forward to an academic practice, at least in the social sciences, where a sensitivity to issues of uneven development and geographical difference is commonplace. According to Lee (2002), such a sensitivity will always be disruptive of disciplinary ways of thinking by forcing on to the agenda the geographical 'complexities of practice and instance'. He goes on to make the critical point that:

> 'what these disruptions do to spaceless concepts and theories is less to establish a separate sphere of intellectual endeavour than to illustrate the more general principle that practice and instance are always and everywhere disruptive' (p334).

I am arguing in this chapter that political economy should take on board this 'general principle' by acknowledging the ways in which social and economic relations are spatially constructed and spatially constituted. I begin by charting the development of political economy, as what we might term a pre-disciplinary field of enquiry (see Jessop and Sum, 2001), before examining the key ways in which a political economy approach influenced human geography. Finally, I will set out the parameters of a new political economy by looking at recent developments across the social sciences. An extended conclusion then considers the role that matters of space and spatiality might play in this renewed political economy.

Political economy and geography – a pre-disciplinary legacy in a disciplinary world?

The 'science' of political economy emerged in seventeenth-century France, when attempts were first made to understand the operation of the economy from the point of view of the nation state, rather than from the perspective of a single household. This in turn was closely linked to the desire to promote the management of the entire national economy as opposed to the economics of the household. In this sense its origins lie in analysing the relationship between the public and private spheres, around key issues such as the production and accumulation of wealth, the nature of property rights, state formation and the distribution and disposition of economic surplus. As Barnes (2000) notes, 'questions of apportioning the surplus among social classes necessarily pushed inquiry beyond the purely economic and into the social and political spheres' (p593). In other words, the connection between the political and the economic was provided not just by a stress on the accumulation of wealth, but also through a concern with the ways in which that wealth was distributed, and with an analysis of the social conditions under which it was produced. Moreover, the breadth of classical political economy meant that the writings of those who contributed to it – authors such as Ferguson, Hegel, Hulme, Locke, Smith and Ricardo – ranged across politics, philosophy, economics and law. It is also interesting to note that much of this early work had a deep concern with morality, and with social and moral order. Adam Smith, for instance criticised the ways in which measures of individual 'worth' tended to be based on income or wealth rather than on what a person is or does, and he also expressed concern over the effects of an increasing division of labour on job satisfaction and public service (see Sayer, 2001).

It is not surprising that the foremost critique of these early political economists was provided by Marx, who possessed a unique intellectual capacity to engage with, and indeed move beyond, all these concerns. One of the great strengths of Marx's work is its ability to provide connections between the economic, the political and the social. It is not accidental that two of his most important works, *The Grundrisse* and *Capital* are subtitled *Foundations of the Critique of Political Economy* and *A Critique of Political Economy* respectively. In these, Marx reformulated the concepts of classical political economy to develop a much broader theory of economic development, historical change, social formation and political revolution. Thus, throughout much of the eighteenth and nineteenth centuries, the study of political economy was pre-disciplinary – it would have made no sense to Marx, or Smith, or Hegel to label them as economists or political scientists or philosophers. They were all three and much more besides.

The richness of these early studies of political economy was soon lost as the disciplinary ventures of economics and sociology were established during the late nineteenth century. Where Marx had revealed how economic relations between commodities were in fact based on social relations established in the processes of production, exchange and consumption, the disciplinary era divorced the analysis of economic relations from their social and political foundations. Gough (1979) notes how economics in particular 'developed by abstracting its analysis from social relations and specific social structures. Its basic postulates were seen to be as applicable to Robinson Crusoe on his desert island as to the activities of General Motors' (p6). Sociology established itself as the domain of study concerned with social relations, and political science emerged to deal with politics and political relations – but in each case they were largely divorced from an analysis of the economic relations of production (masked to some degree by sociology's abiding concern with definitions of social class). By the start of the twentieth century, the integrative elements of political economy had been jettisoned in favour of tightly drawn disciplinary practices. Political economy became identified with, and to a certain extent displaced by, economics. Its moral, cultural, social and political concerns were overwhelmingly discarded. This is a situation which has still not been fully remedied a century later, and one which is responsible for the continued, but fundamentally misplaced, elision of political economy with economism, functionalism and structuralism.

Geography, meanwhile, was carving out its own disciplinary niche by focusing on matters of human–environment interrelationships, and their regional expression. The displacement and the narrowing of political economy had few immediate repercussions for the discipline, which for the first half of the twentieth century pursued links with the physical sciences and the humanities rather than the social sciences. Geography's first full engagement with the social sciences came via spatial science. Somewhat ironically, by constructing a series of models based on the assumptions of neo-classical economics this engagement actually ended up downplaying geography and uneven development. As Gregory (1989) has noted, these models assumed a 'world of perfect competition, … a world without history and geography, and once those "imperfections" or "distortions" were introduced the assumptions of neo-classical economics became untenable' (p72). Unease over the abstract models and technocratic output which resulted from this encounter with neo-classical economics did much to promote a turn towards political economy within geography (Smith, 1984). Gregory records how, 'as late twentieth-century capitalism was plunged into a profound crisis, ...so the *historical geography* of capitalism became ever more visible and the credibility of the neo-classical calculus ever more precarious' (*ibid.*). Put simply, as the discipline entered the 1970s, many geographers came to the conclusion that they lacked the theoretical and conceptual tools to analyse and understand the huge economic restructurings and social transformations that were increasingly its object of study.

David Harvey was among the first to identify the problem – and enter a plea for political economy as the solution. In *Social Justice and the City*, Harvey (1973) explained that he turned away from positivist spatial science and towards a Marxist-inspired political economy because he could find no other way of 'accomplishing what I set out to do, or of understanding what has to be understood' (p17). In contrast to the fragmented analysis of positivism, with its

> 'tendency to regard facts as separate from values, objects as independent of subjects, "things" as possessing an identity independent of human perception and action, and the "private" process of discovery as separate from the "public" process of communicating the results' (p11–12).

Marxism offered a 'reconciliation among disparate topics and the collapse of dualisms' (p17). This meant in turn that it held out the hope of uniting the intellectual breach between geography and the social sciences, and of remedying the fact that 'social processes and spatial forms are, for the most part, distinct in our minds if not in reality' (p10). Here, Harvey is drawing attention to the holistic possibilities offered by political economy, which were lost in the disciplinary turn a century before.

To these academic concerns underpinning the shift towards political economy, Harvey also added moral and ethical imperatives. As he wrote in *Social Justice and the City* (1973):

> 'There is an ecological problem, an urban problem, an international trade problem, and yet we seem incapable of saying anything of depth or profundity about any of them. When we do say something it appears trite and rather ludicrous. In short, our paradigm is not coping well. It is ripe for overthrow. The objective social conditions demand that we say something sensible or coherent, or else forever ... remain silent. It is the emerging objective social conditions and our patent inability to cope with them which essentially explains the necessity for a revolution in geographic thought. [Our task] does not entail ... mapping even more evidence of man's patent inhumanity to man ... the immediate task is nothing more nor less than the self-conscious and aware construction of a new paradigm for social geographic thought' (pp129 and 144–5).

The search, then, was on for the concepts and categories that could help construct the new paradigm in geographic thought and explanation.

Approaches inspired by both the political and academic understandings of political economy played a key role in this search. Very soon they became highly influential, if not dominant, within the discipline. Only twenty-two years after the publication of the original

Models in Geography (Chorley and Haggett, 1967) celebrated spatial science it was possible for Richard Peet and Nigel Thrift (1989) to edit a definitive two-volume collection of essays entitled *New Models in Human Geography: The Political-economy Perspective.* They claimed that human geography had undergone a transformation – theoretically, socially and politically – which 'can be traced to the emergence, and the widespread acceptance, of a new set of models which have a common root in the notion that society is best understood as a political economy' (p3). According to the *Foreword*, written by Doreen Massey (1989), one of the intentions of the collection is to bear witness 'to the richness and range of work which has developed over this relatively short period within the political-economy approach' (pix). One of the remarkable aspects of these two volumes is the sheer breadth of work which was fitted under the rubric of political economy. Defining political economy as a 'social economy, or a way of life, founded in production' (*ibid.*) allowed the authors to include work under the broad headings of environment and resources, uneven development and regional change, the state and politics, the city, civil society and social theory, and thus shift the emphasis beyond economic change and restructuring. Among the 25 chapters, stretching over 750 pages, are those covering the geography of law, the local state, gender, race and racism, culture and landscape, social reproduction, environmentalism and locality.

Here we are almost back to the breadth of concerns studied by early political economy in its pre-disciplinary era, when it sought to analyse the relationship between state and economy, or the public and the private. A focus on the economic is joined by one on politics, social change and culture. Although issues of morality and ethics are absent (see Chapters 10 and 11 in this collection) the range of ideas present still gives some idea of the sheer scope of work within geography which could be confidently contained under the label of political economy. With the considerable benefit of hindsight this publication can be said to represent the apogee of Marxist-inspired political economy within geography. The next decade witnessed a series of stringent critiques of Marxism, and its influence within geography, from a number of different perspectives. Some of these have been attacks on the very concepts employed within political economy – Sayer (1995) and Gibson-Graham (1996, 1997), for example, have both questioned the ontological and epistemological use of the twin categories of class and capitalism. Others have questioned the empirical validity of a Marxist political economy that finds it difficult to encompass a diversity of social struggles, including those centred around gender, race, ethnicity, sexuality and environmentalism (see, for instance, Deutsche, 1991; Massey, 1991; Morris, 1992). More than this, some have made the accusation that Marxist geographers have not just ignored other critical perspectives, but have also been complicit in actively marginalising them 'by virtue of [their] patriarchal, ethnocentric and other unacknowledged assumptions' (see Castree, 1999 for an extended review of these critiques – the citation is from p138). Many of these critiques have come together under the umbrella of the 'cultural turn'.

The 'cultural turn' is the catch-all description given to a set of intellectual shifts which took place from the mid 1980s. These were not confined to geography, but were felt across the humanities and the social sciences, and even influenced debate within the natural sciences about the social and discursive construction of scientific knowledge (see Demeritt, 1996, 1998). Taken as a whole, these shifts went some way to establishing an inter-disciplinary field of enquiry which became labelled as cultural studies. Within geography, the notion of a cultural turn has been used to signify three interrelated shifts (Crang, 1997, 2000). The first signals the growth, and growing influence, of cultural geography as a sub-discipline. The second refers to the preoccupation with matters of culture that has been felt across all areas of human geography. In this sense a concern with issues such as discourse, representation, identity and imagination was increasingly found, for instance, within economic, political, urban, social and historical geography, and was not merely confined to cultural geography. In many ways this shift mirrored the growth of a political economy perspective across these sub-disciplinary areas (as documented in *New Models in Human Geography*) which had taken place in the 1970s and 1980s. Third, these shifts within geography were related to a growing concern with issues of culture outside the academy. In particular the 1990s witnessed the growth of the so-called 'cultural industries', the pervasive influence of new digital medias, and the gradual move towards identity-based representational politics. In overall terms, this led to a situation where Sayer (1994) could claim that 'one of the most striking features of the last decade of radical academic literature has been the shift from economy to culture' (p635). He later noted (1997) that 'the flip-side of this has been a decline in interest in political economy' (p16).

One major reason for this decline has been the continued elision between political economy and the economic. In many ways the cultural turn was based on a rather oppositional definition of culture, as a separate sphere of intellectual endeavour, counterposed to the economic as another distinct sphere. These separate arenas were (rather falsely) set up to represent two alternative ways of looking at the world. Within this dichotomous approach, to be labelled as belonging to one camp was to be excluded from the other. Hence the 'cultural turn' was (again rather falsely) viewed as an event which happened in opposition to political economy. In such a zero-sum game, as the former gained influence within the discipline, the latter was seen as having lost it. This view tends to ignore the host of empirical and theoretical work inspired by political-economy carried out in many areas of geography – such as welfare change (Peck and Theodore, 2001), state restructuring (Brenner, 1999, Macleod and Goodwin, 1999), nature and environment (Castree and Braun, 1998; Harvey, 1996), scale (Brenner, 2001; Swyngedouw, 1997) and regional development (Jones and Macleod, 1999; Lovering, 1999) – let alone the fact that variants of political economy have continued to inspire some of the most vibrant work within economic geography (e.g. Herod, 1998; Peck, 1996; Storper, 1997). Indeed, political economy could be argued to be a victim of its own success, with researchers across many fields of geography now routinely using the approach without necessarily drawing undue attention to this fact. But the declining influence of political economy is a view that has gained considerable credence, so much so that Martin and Sunley (2001) have recently concluded that 'recovering a sense of political economy is one of the most urgent tasks confronting economic geographers' (p155). However, just as the cultural turn was not restricted to geography, so recovering a sense of political economy is a bigger project that encompasses disciplines across the social sciences. In many ways, however, it is a project already well underway. The next section looks at the recent development of this 'new' political economy, to see how this might help in recovering the future for a political economy perspective for geography.

Towards a new political economy

The development of a new political economy has been variously underway across several branches of the social sciences over the past few years. As such it is not straightforward, and indeed the very notion of a new political economy carries at least three different meanings. Hay and Marsh (1999) distinguish between these three approaches according to the manner in which they assess both the novelty of the contemporary social, political and economic processes under study and the adequacy of the theories and methods drawn on to study them. They are summarised in the table below.

The first meaning of 'new' thus refers to new approaches to old problems, implying that:

> 'there has been no qualitative shift in the nature of political and economic processes in recent years, but that a cumulative process of critique, counter-critique and attrition has, over the years, served to discredit many of the assumptions upon which classical... political economy was premised' (Hay and Marsh, 1999, p15)

Table 4.1 What's new about the new political economy?

	Qualitatively new environment?	Obsolescence of old PE in a changed environment?	Limitations and distortions of the old PE?	Purpose of new PE
NPE 1	No or not necessarily	No	Yes – invalid assumptions	To present improved analysis
NPE 2	Yes – 'new times'	No (though some modification required)	No, or these are acceptable	To adapt old PE to illuminate 'new times'
NPE 3	Yes – 'new times'	Yes – 'new times' require a new PE	Not necessarily (old PE was adequate to a different task)	To develop a new PE for 'new times'

Source: Adapted from Hay and Marsh (1999, 15)[1].
Note
[1] Although their original table concerns 'international political economy', the same distinctions can be drawn with reference to political economy. Indeed, in many instances in their article, the term international appears in parenthesis.

As a result, what is needed is an analytical and methodological break with the old political economy, based around 'a new, more interdisciplinary, analysis of political and economic processes' (Hay and Marsh, 1999, pp15–16). A second variant of new political economy implies that there is a qualitative shift in the nature of contemporary capitalism, but nevertheless maintains that we do not require a new approach to political economy in order to study it. The challenge is rather to 'redeploy the existing (and appropriately modified) techniques of … political economy to explain … the "new times" we now inhabit' (Hay and Marsh, 1999, p17). A third meaning of the term 'new' shares this identification of new forms of economic and political life, but also maintains that we require a new political economy in order to analyse these. As the initial editorial of the journal *New Political Economy* put it:

> 'a new stage in the development of the world economic and political system has commenced, a new kind of world order, which is characterised both by unprecedented unity and unprecedented fragmentation. Understanding this new world order will require new modes of analysis and new theories, and a readiness to tear down intellectual barriers and bring together many approaches, methods and disciplines which for too long have been apart' (Gamble *et al*, 1996, p5)

It is important for the argument presented here that both approaches which identify limitations to the old political economy include a call to dismantle academic partitions and pursue more work across disciplinary boundaries.

In terms of what these approaches to 'new political economy' might mean for geography, I want to have my cake and eat it – and then have another piece – by suggesting that we take on board elements of all three variants. The first reminds us that there are some fundamental continuities within the make up of contemporary capitalism – not everything, in other words, is new about the 'new times' we are living through. The economic organisation of our society is still based on the circulation and expansion of capital. This expansion in turn depends on economic surpluses generated by wage labour. And this implies continued antagonistic relationships between those who are seeking to generate a surplus and those who are seeking to maximise their wages. As Neil Smith (1998) has recently argued:

> 'broadly similar conditions of wage labour and exploitation that provoked Marx's brilliant critique persist, sustaining capitalism to the present day. Indeed they are dramatically more pervasive. The very societies that led the capitalist cataclysm of 1997 were still thoroughly feudal when Marx and Engels penned the Manifesto; it was still five years before Commodore Perry would sail into Tokyo Bay to insist on trading rights. The unabashed victory of capitalism at the end of the twentieth century – prosperity, poverty, crises and all – makes Marx's analysis more, not less, relevant for the twenty first' (p163).

Indeed, David Harvey has recently argued that in many ways, when viewed globally, capitalist labour relations are far more exploitative than they have been in the past. The point is that many of the most severe forms of labour exploitation have been spatially displaced from the west, and thus removed from our 'field of vision'.

From the second possible meaning of new political economy we can take the idea that despite these continuities we are also witnessing some widespread discontinuities with previous forms of economic and social organisation. For instance, the rise of a knowledge-driven economy, the development of new commodity forms, the global spread of capitalism into areas such as eastern Europe and China, the increasing interconnection of financial markets, the extent of environmental change and degradation, new forms of terrorism and warfare, and the growth of neo-liberal governing projects all require analysis. The third variant of new political economy reminds us that we do need new intellectual currents in order to understand these very real changes in economics, society, politics and culture. As we noted before, some of these are already underway, including the emergence of political ecology to examine changing nature – society relationships; the growth of discourse theory to analyse the discursive constitution of a range of economic, social and political entities; the development of queer theory to inform our understanding of the instability of identity and meaning; and the rise of critical geopolitics to reflect shifts in international relations in a post-cold war era (see Jessop and Sum, 2001, pp91–2).

Thus, although we are faced with the emergence of new themes and problems to study, these concerns must be properly placed within a set of continuing and pervasive economic and social relations – and these continuities and discontinuities can only be analysed in the context of some major intellectual shifts across the social sciences. I would therefore maintain that those seeking to recover a sense of political economy within geography are best placed do so by incorporating different aspects of all three variants of the 'new political economy'. By using elements of these three, we can identify a series of key themes that should provide the foundation for a renewed engagement between geography and political economy.

The first of these is the need to overcome the separation of economy and politics that has been prevalent for much of the disciplinary phase of political economy. In other words, we need to reunite the twin aspects of the term itself in order to overcome the academic and linguistic construction of politics and economics as two separate fields of enquiry. Such a move would enable us to analyse the 'political economy' in ways that do not assume an *a priori* separation between its constituent elements. The challenge for a renewed political economy is to capture the complex interplay between economy and politics, and to offer an analysis which is capable of discerning 'the articulation of market forces and state intervention in reproducing and regularising capitalism' (Jessop and Sum, 2001, p96). By emphasising this articulation we open up a space to study the ways in which the economy is politically constituted and narrated – indeed, it allows us to appreciate the constant struggles over the definition of the boundary between state and market, between public and private and between the realms of the individual as citizen and as consumer. In turn, we are able to examine how these struggles are pursued through the discursive and material strategies of political and economic institutions, and how their outcomes are central to both 'economic restructuring and the transformation of the state and state intervention' (*ibid.*). Hence, the huge debates currently taking place to define the 'legitimate' extent of state support across a range of economic and welfare programmes in both Europe and North America. How much subsidy should be given to a declining agricultural sector? Should an increasingly expensive higher education system be paid for by its participants via fees or funded from general taxation? Should new hospitals be funded privately or publicly? How do we pay for the pensions of an ever-aging population? Should single parents qualify for unemployment benefit or be forced to work? The answers to these questions will help to define economic performance across western societies in the immediate future, but they are all essentially political questions. As such, a full understanding of this performance is inseparable from an analysis of the political projects and institutional supports that shape economic development. But of course, the nature and extent of these political projects will be partly determined by economic and financial conditions – both nationally and internationally. The key is not to separate the political from the economic but to appreciate the constant articulation between both elements within a single 'political economy', working with the notions of the integral state and the integral economy (see Jessop, 1997).

The second theme we can identify is one that recognises the cultural and social embeddedness of the economy, in addition to its political construction. The notion here is that economic activity is 'set within social relations and cultural contexts that make a difference to those economic processes' (Sayer, 2001, p697). These relations and contexts are both material and discursive. As such, they cover the institutional networks that help to construct the links between different economic activites, as well as the relations of trust and dependency which grow up between different members of these networks. They also refer to the construction and constitution of economic subjects, subjectivities, identities and modes of calculation. As Jessop and Sum (2001) point out, this has always been an area of analysis in which both pre-disciplinary and disciplinary approaches to political economy found considerable difficulty – due to their emphasis respectively on notions of class and rationality. In contrast, recent academic theories have shed light on the ways in which new subjects and social forces are formed, and how these are refigured through a host of practices and discources which, in turn, coalesce to 'generate a new "common sense" that gets selected and repeated' (p98).

Thrift (2001) has noted how these 'common senses' are partly constituted within the discursive apparatus of capitalism itself, via the 'cultural circuit' of business schools, management consultants, management gurus and the media. It is perhaps when these combine with and reinforce dominant political discourses – about the sanctity of the market, 'freedom of choice', flexibility, the efficiency of deregulation and so on – that they are most potent. Of course, there are counter discourses which can be mobilised in opposition to these hegemonic 'common sense' constructions – witness the recent development of the anti-globalisation movement through mass protests against the meetings of the World Bank, the International Monetary Fund, the World Economic Forum and the World Trade Organisation in Seattle, Genoa, London and Prague. A renewed emphasis on the cultural and social constitution of the economy and the state (and of the border between the two), and on the active formation of different political communities and political subjects would allow political economy to reveal 'the multiple sites/levels in which class-relevant projects such as neoliberalism are assembled and contested in material-discursive space' (Jessop and Sum, 2001, p98).

Third, Thrift (2001) points to the need to examine the increasing role of the consumer, now expected to 'make more and more extravagent investments in the act of consumption itself' (p378). Previously, political economy (especially within geography) had tended to concentrate on the production end of the circuit of capital (Lee, 1999), paying far less attention to the elements of exchange and consumption. Now, however, through new technologies such as the Internet and video games, commodities are becoming more interactive, can be jointly developed by producer and consumer, and can be purchased as streams of digital content. As Thrift puts it, 'the self-evident world of things has become something more complex' (ibid.). In response, political economy will have to be more willing to examine the act of consumption as well as production. It will be difficult to analyse the latter without an understanding of the former.

A fourth theme that emerges in recent literature on the new political economy concerns the environment, and is underpinned by new approaches to political ecology (see Watts, 2003; and also the chapters in this volume by Fitzsimmons and Watts). Key themes here are actually developed from a critique of some of the assumptions built into former phases of political economy, concerning the desirability of economic growth and modernisation. Instead, the new political economy stresses the political, social and physical limits to economic development, and also highlights the formation and mobilisation of new environmental political movements. It makes a conscious effort to question some of our taken-for-granted categories, such as 'nature' and 'society', stressing instead the hybridity involved in contemporary environmental transformation (Whatmore, 2002). Watts (2003) highlights how some of the most vibrant work within this new area is emerging in the 'border zones', where the concerns of political ecology are meeting those from work on reflexive modernisation, ecological modernisation, environmental security and environmental rights. Here again we have a pointer to post-disciplinary approaches, moving beyond the confines of traditional disciplinary boundaries to engage in a complex mixing of ideas and approaches – drawn from geography, politics, sociology, philosophy, international relations and anthropology. This approach would also allow us to analyse the politics that shape global environmental agendas – an understanding, for instance, of the US government's refusal to ratify the Kyoto agreement cannot be couched in environmental terms alone, but must be linked to the particular political economy of the USA and the strength of the 'petro-dollar' constituency within the American new right.

Last, but not least, the new political economy points to the critical role played by new spatial forms in helping to constitute the parameters of contemporary capitalism (Thrift, 2001), and to the ways in which these very parameters have particular spatial and temporal horizons of action (Jessop and Sum, 2001). This takes on several guises. First, the geography of production itself continues to be reorganised – both nationally and internationally. In some cases this is leading to increased concentration, partly linked to the emergence of those 'networks of trust' identified above, but changing spatial dynamics are also expressed through increased subcontracting and new logistical networks which allow movements and communications within a firm. Second, and linked to this, new spaces within which production takes place are emerging – the so-called 'Big Sheds' which help to produce a new decentralised landscape. Third, Thrift (2001) points to the new 'spaces of consumption that now criss-cross the landscape … to produce the hard sell in new more seductive ways' (p379). Finally, different political projects and economic formations – such as neoliberalism or Keynesian social democracy – are institutionalised through specific spatio-temporal practices. Critically, what this all adds up to is a political economy that recognises 'the pivotal role of space and time as not merely metrics but resources' (Thrift, 2001, p377).

Concluding comments: spatiality and the new political economy

In pointing out this pivotal role of space, Thrift is beginning to delineate the outlines of an engagement between geography and renewed political economy. My contention is that such an engagement can only be fully drawn by embracing a post-disciplinary perspective – as Thrift (2001) puts it, 'in order to understand contemporary capitalism we need to mobilise many heritages, many viewpoints…' (p379). Central to all these viewpoints, however, needs to be an appreciation of space as a resource and not merely as a metric. Considerable ground has, of course, already been made in this regard by David Harvey (1982), who most fully articulated the role of space within capitalism in his brilliant work *The Limits to Capital*. In this, Harvey set out to 'construct a framework for theorizing about the historical geography of the capitalist mode of production' (pxvii). Notions of space and uneven development figured large within this framework – after all, Harvey set out to 'hammer home' the point that 'the production of spatial configurations is necessarily an active constitutive moment in the dynamics of accumulation' (p440). He did this through several interrelated theoretical manoeuvres which together established how capitalism is constantly beset by contradictory tendencies towards economic integration and differentiation, towards agglomeration and dispersion. Each moment in these tendencies establishes a particular spatial configuration – of, for instance, offices, factories, houses, shopping centres, roads and railways – which aids capital accumulation at one point in time, only to become a barrier to it at another. The upshot is that created social and physical environments – that is, geographies – are continually developed, changed and abandoned.

Even allowing for the incredible richness and complexity of the ideas developed by Harvey (1982) in *Limits to Capital* and subsequent work (1985a, b), he remained located largely within a political economy perspective that was based on economic production and accumulation. Issues to do with consumption, with the distribution of any surplus that was produced, and with the division between the private and public spheres were paid less attention – although the role of the state and the intricacies of socialisation and social reproduction are flagged up as critical areas for future work in the 'Afterword' to the *Limits to Capital*. What Harvey did do, however, was establish the ways in which capitalism as an economic and social system uses space, geographical differentiation and uneven development as a key resource in its ongoing transformation.

The task now is to build this recognition into the new political economy – not from a perspective where geography is set alongside economics, politics and sociology (which would be inter-disciplinary at best), but from a genuinely post-disciplinary position where space and spatial practices are implicated in every aspect of our analyses of contemporary capitalism. As Roger Lee (2002) puts it:

> 'in practice the world is too complex for disciplines which wish to reduce its complexity. The grounds for post-disciplinary conversations are, clearly, less to do with making one discipline's obsessions and norms compatible with another. Rather, they derive from the realization that the day-to-day practices undertaken by people going about their daily lives incorporate multiple influences that cannot be dismissed or downgraded merely because they do not fit within prevailing disciplinary norms of analysis or understanding. On the contrary, it is precisely these misfits that should, perhaps, be the focus of our attention.' (p344).

As an example of such influences we need look no further than the current attempts by various governments in Europe and North America to restructure their economies and societies through the pursuit of various neoliberal projects which are at once political, social, cultural and economic. Unpacking and analysing the contours of these projects cannot be done in isolation – with politics, for instance, taking responsibility for the political components, and economics working on the economic aspects. Instead, we need to draw on an understanding that recognises how the economic, the political, the cultural and the social components of neoliberalism are jointly established and developed. And we also need an analysis that recognises the territorial re-scaling and geographical reshaping which lies at the heart of these projects. As an example of such work we can turn to the recent edited collection by Brenner and Theodore (2002a), which contains 11 essays on different aspects of contemporary urban and regional restructuring. Under the title of *Spaces of Neoliberalism*, the collection explores the intersection between neoliberalism and urban development. It does this through analysing the political and economic logics of state intervention in the contemporary city, and examining the social and spatial outcomes of neoliberal urban policies. From the outset, the collection connects the political with the economic, uniting the twin elements of political economy, and does so within an analysis that stresses the 'polycentric and multiscalar character of neoliberalism as a geopolitical and geoeconomic project' (Brenner and Theodore, 2002b, p3). The collection also recognises the ways in which neoliberalism has been intensified through mechanisms of international and interlocal policy transfer – created and lubricated by a cultural circuit involving 'technocratic elites, think-tanks, opinion formers [and] consultants' (Peck and Tickell, 2002, p51).

We can see various elements of the 'new political economy' present in such an analysis. All are underpinned by a recognition 'not only that neoliberalism affects cities, but also that cities have become key institutional arenas in and through which neoliberalism is itself evolving' (Brenner and Theodore, 2002c, pix). In short, the geographies of various neoliberal projects – where and over what scale they are implemented – are critical to their development and evolution. This point is recognised by all the contributors to the volume – yet not all are geographers. The book includes chapters by those from departments of sociology, urban planning, economics and environmental science. Here we have a sense of a post-disciplinary project – the analyses of neoliberalism – being undertaken with a comon purpose that transcends disiplinary boundaries, and which has at its core an appreciation of issues of space, scale and uneven development. Such analyses would be at the heart of my vision for the future of geography – a future where, paradoxically, the transcendence of disciplinary boundaries should result in a greater appreciation of the constitutive role of space as a resource and not merely a metric.

Bibliography

Barnes, T (2000) 'Political Economy' in Johnston, R, Gregory, D, Pratt, G and Watts, M (eds) *The Dictionary of Human Geography*, Oxford: Blackwell.

Brenner, N (1999) 'Globalisation as reterritorialisation: The rescaling of urban governance in the European Union' in *Urban Studies*, 36, 431–451.

Brenner, N (2001) 'The limits to scale? Methodological reflections on scalar structuration', *Progress in Human Geography*, 25, 4, 591–614.

Brenner, N and Theodore, N (eds) (2002a) *Spaces of Neoliberalism,* Oxford: Blackwell.

Brenner, N and Theodore, N (2002b) 'Cities and the geographies of "actually existing neoliberalism"' in Brenner, N and Theodore, N (eds) (2002a) *Spaces of Neoliberalism*, Oxford: Blackwell.

Brenner, N and Theodore, N (2002c) 'Preface: From the "new localism" to the spaces of neoliberalism' in Brenner N and Theodore N (eds) (2002a) *Spaces of Neoliberalism*, Oxford: Blackwell.

Castree, N (1999) 'Envisioning capitalism: geography and the renewal of marxian political economy', *Transactions of the Institute of British Geographers*, 24, 137–158.

Castree, N and Braun, B (1998) 'The construction of nature and the nature of construction: analytical and political tools for building survivable futures' in Braun, B and Castree, N (eds) *Remaking Reality: Nature at the Millennium*, London: Routledge.

Chorley, R and Haggett, P (eds) (1967) *Models in Geography*, London: Methuen.

Crang, P (1997) 'Cultural turns and the (re)constitution of economic geography' in Lee, R and Wills, J (eds) *Geographies of Economies*, London: Arnold.

Crang, P (2000) 'Cultural turn' in Johnston, R, Gregory, D, Pratt, G and Watts, M (eds) *The Dictionary of Human Geography*, Oxford: Blackwell.

Demeritt, D (1996) 'Social theory and the reconstruction of science and geography', *Transactions of the Institute of British Geographers*, 21, 484–503.

Demeritt, D (1998) 'Science, social constructivism and nature' in Braun, B and Castree, N (eds) (1998) *Remaking Reality: Nature at the Millenium*, London: Routledge.

Deutsche, R (1991) 'Boy's town', *Environment and Planning D: Society and Space*, 9, 5–30.

Gamble, A, Payne, A, Hoogvelt, A, Dietrich, M and Kenny, M (1996) 'Editorial: New Political Economy', *New Political Economy*, 1, 1, 5–11.

Gibson-Graham, J K (1996) *The End of Capitalism (as we knew it)*, Oxford: Blackwell.

Gibson-Graham, J K (1997) 'Re-placing class in economic geographies' in Lee, R and Wills, J (eds) *Geographies of Economies*, London: Arnold.

Gough, I (1979) *The Political Economy of the Welfare State*, London: Macmillan.

Gregory, D (1989) 'Areal differentiation and post-modern human geography' in Gregory, D and Walford, R (eds) *Horizons in Human Geography*, London: Macmillan.

Harvey, D (1973) *Social Justice and the City*, London: Arnold.

Harvey, D (1982) *The Limits to Capital*, Oxford: Blackwell.

Harvey, D (1985a) *The Urbanization of Capital*, Oxford: Blackwell.

Harvey, D (1985b) 'The geopolitics of capitalism' in Gregory, D and Urry, J (eds) *Social Relations and Spatial Structures*, London: Macmillan.

Harvey, D (1996) *Justice, Nature and the Geography of Difference*, Oxford: Blackwell.

Hay, C and Marsh, D (1999) 'Introduction: Towards a new (international) political economy', *New Political Economy*, 4, 1, 5–22.

Herod, A (1998) *Organizing the Landscape: Geographical Perspectives on Trade Unionism*, Minneapolis: University of Minnesota Press.

Jessop, B (1997) 'A neo-Gramscian approach to the regulation of urban regimes' in Lavia, M (ed) *Reconstructing Urban Regime Theory*, Thousand Oaks: Sage.

Jessop, B and Sum, N (2001) 'Pre-disciplinary and post-disciplinary perspectives', *New Political Economy*, 6, 1, 89–101.

Jones, M and MacLeod, G (1999) 'Towards a regional renaissance? Reconfiguring and rescal-ing England's economic governance', *Transactions of the Institute of British Geographers*, 24, 295–314.

Lee, R (1999) 'Production' in Cloke, P, Goodwin, M and Crang, P (eds), *Introducing Human Geographies*, London: Arnold.

Lee, R (2002) ' "Nice maps, shame about the theory?" Thinking geographically about the eco-nomic', *Progress in Human Geography*, 26, 3, 333–355.

Lovering, J (1999) 'Theory led by policy: the inadequacies of the "new regionalism" (illustrated from the case of Wales)', *International Journal of Urban and Regional Research*, 23, 379–395.

MacLeod, G and Goodwin, M (1999) 'Reconstructing an urban and regional political economy: on the state, politics, scale and explanation', *Political Geography*, 18, 697–730.

Martin, R and Sunley, P (2001) 'Rethinking the "Economic" in Economic Geography: broadening our vision or losing our focus?', *Antipode*, 33, 148–161.

Massey, D (1989) 'Foreword' in Peet, R and Thrift, N (eds) *New Models in Geography*, London: Unwin Hyman.

Massey, D (1991) 'Flexible sexism', *Environment and Planning D: Society and Space*, 9, 31–53.

Morris, M (1992) 'The man in the mirror: David Harvey's "condition" of postmodernity', *Theory, Culture and Society*, 9, 253–279.

Peck, J (1996) *Work-Place*, New York: Guilford Press.

Peck, J and Tickell, A (2002) 'Neoliberalizing space' in Brenner N and Theodore N (eds) (2002a) *Spaces of Neoliberalism*, Oxford: Blackwell.

Peck, J and Theodore, N (2001) 'Exporting workfare/importing welfare-to-work: exploring the pol-itics of Third Way policy transfer', *Political Geography*, 20, 427–460.

Peet, R and Thrift, N (eds) (1989) *New Models in Geography*, London: Unwin Hyman.

Sayer, A (1994) 'Cultural studies and "the economy, stupid" ', *Environment and Planning D: Society and Space*, 12, 635–637.

Sayer, A (1995) *Radical Political Economy: A Critique*, Oxford: Blackwell.

Sayer, A (1997) 'The dialectic of culture and economy' in Lee, R and Wills, J (eds) *Geographies of Economies*, London: Arnold.

Sayer, A (2001) 'For a critical cultural political economy', *Antipode*, 33, 687–708.

Smith, D (1984) 'Recollections of a random variable' in Billinge, M, Gregory, D and Martin, R (eds) *Recollections of a Revolution*, London: Macmillan.

Smith, N (1998) 'El Nino capitalism', *Progress in Human Geography*, 22, 159–163.

Storper, M (1997) *The Regional World: Territorial Development in a Global Economy*, New York: Guilford Press.

Swyngedouw, E (1997) 'Excluding the other: the contested production of a new "Gestalt of scale" and the politics of marginalisation' in Lee, R and Wills, J (eds) *Geographies of Economies*, London: Arnold.

Thrift, N (2001) 'Chasing capitalism', *New Political Economy*, 6, 3, 375–380.

Watts, M (2003) 'Political ecology' in Sheppard, E and Barnes, T (eds) *A Companion to Economic Geography*, Oxford: Blackwell.

Whatmore, S (2002) *Hybrid Geographies: Natures, Cultures, Spaces*, London: Sage.

5
Summoning life*

Nigel Thrift

> 'Fine vapours escape from whatever is doing the
> living.
> The night is cold and delicate and full of angels
> Pounding down the living. The factories are all lit
> up,
> The chime goes unheard
> We are together at last, though far apart.'
> (Ashbery, 1967)

Introduction

I have struggled with writing this paper for a considerable amount of time now. I have made all kinds of false starts and laid all kinds of false trails. And still it isn't perfect. Why such frustration? Because – well, for me at least – the stakes are high. They are high because I have already outlined what I call non-representational theory many times and I think it is fair to say that, by and large, these efforts have fallen on stony ground. In part, I am sure, this is a result of my own lack of persuasive skills. But it is also, I am sure, because so few people in human geography, or more generally, have a background in the kind of process-based writings that I call on. The stakes are high as well because what I am attempting to do with non-representational theory is to overturn much of the spirit and purpose of the social sciences and humanities. I consider many of the protocols of the current social sciences and humanities to be not just mistaken, but, what's worse, oppressive. Then the stakes are high because non-representational theory is an attempt to change the role of academics by questioning what counts as expertise and who has that expertise. I want to provide more space for all the everyday skills that get us by – but that is a direct threat to the current intellectual division of labour with its dogmatic image of what counts as thought.

This paper is therefore in the nature of a manifesto. But not, I hope, a hectoring one. As I shall argue, there are good reasons to be modest.

So what does the manifesto consist of? To begin with, I will briefly set out some of the chief antecedents of non-representational theory. What I want to point to here is that

*This paper was completed in 2001.

none of these approaches can be easily pigeonholed and that each of them poses a challenge to the dominant theoretical model which still attempts to set up a stable picture of what the world is like, judges its worth, and then derives programmes of renovation. In contrast, these approaches want to work with that excessive reserve of virtuality[1] which we might call 'uncommon sense'. Then, next, I will – again briefly – describe some of the main tenets of non-representational theory and how they make a difference. My purpose here is not to provide a reprise of my previous (and anyway easily available) attempts at description (e.g. Thrift, 1996, 1997, 1999, 2000; Amin and Thrift, 2002). Rather, it is to point to why these tenets have been derived – in order to produce questions that can express other possibilities of thought. Non-representational theory is, if you like, a machine for multiplying questions, and thereby *inventing new relations between thought and life*. In the penultimate part of the paper I will then be able to concentrate on why non-representational theory constitutes *a kind of politics*, so allowing me, in the final part of the paper, to briefly outline a few cases of the politics of disclosure that are possible. My point in the latter parts of the paper is to destabilise the know-and-tell politics that still bedevils so much thought in the social sciences – produce picture of the world, think up political programme, find allies, put into practice, produce transcendence – for something that is much less certain but may ultimately be more productive. Many readers will be frustrated by this move. They will want to know and then be able to tell. Tough. I am searching for something different, something that takes 'democracy' seriously by ridding the social sciences and humanities of their patrician habit of making everything prior and so open to judgement.

In all of this, care needs to be taken. This is a modest manifesto because, as I hope is already becoming clear, I do not want to become a part of the kind of the boy's game that thinks up an imagined community that one has to 'represent' and then indulges in the kind of macho stance that simply speaks its name and never engages. My inclination is to be affective. My inclination is to emphasise affirmative and therefore collective expression. My inclination is to change the ethos of engagement. My inclination, in other words, is to find other styles of proceeding that can make the world more porous and so open to more questions. Cornelia Parker (2001) puts it rather well:

> 'I'm trying to find uncharted territory in the most visited spot or idea, trying to find space where things are the most crowded. It's like going to the eye of the storm. In the shadow of these movements or icons, there must be the most unstable things in our society, the things that we can't map.' (px)

Communicating at an unknown rate

> 'We are so inveterately wedded to the conceptual decomposition of life that I know that this will seem to you like putting muddiest confusion in place of clearest thought, and relapsing into a molluscoid state of mind. Yet I ask you whether the absolute superiority of our higher thought is so very clear, if all that it can find is impossibility in tasks which sense experience so easily performs.' (James, 1909/1996, p256)

> 'what is, traditionally called 'eternal' in a work is not its meaning – for this is necessarily contingent and historically bound – but rather everything else in it that overspills the meaning, an internal dynamism that engages the perpetual coming-to-be of the world with its own ceaseless, creative (because always oriented to an outside) coming to be.' (Kwinter, 2001, p215)

I admit that at times I can get frustrated with geography. Much of it seems to follow the logic of the corpse, interested in the broken, the static, the already passed.[2] Over the last 20 years or so, I have therefore tried to develop an approach which can act as a means of providing something livelier. I call this approach 'non-representational theory'.

It was not, perhaps, the best chosen of phrases to describe what I am trying to achieve. To begin with, the 'non-representational' element prompts questions like, 'So, are you saying you are not interested in "representation"?'; or 'Are you saying that there are no representations?', or 'Are you saying that you can do without representations?'. Then, the 'theory' element prompts longings I cannot satisfy. People want – want so much – a body of theory that acts out rules and conventions, orders and corrections, that they can sign up to and then legislate the world from: this is bad, this is good, this is passé, this is exciting and so on. I cannot meet those expectations since it is precisely this mechanical notion of theory that I want to junk, in favour of a notion of theory as a modest supplement to practice, helping people to create new ways of living-thinking through which they can explore and add to the world – rather than offering ready-made solutions. For me, theory is a useful toolkit, a means of amplification, but never a panacea. And, finally, the phrase suggests a fixed body of thought. It is certainly true that the phrase can be deployed to point to projects that have important things in common, but these important things all boil down to attempts to rewrite the world so as to allow space for new things to thrive; to value openness, to create new degrees of freedom. But too often, Euro-American thought has resulted in a close-down mode, rather like one of those reading groups – so familiar to us all – that only manage to say negative things.

It is fair to say that Euro-American cultures are naturally perspectivist, that is they try to make the whole world the singular object of the viewer's vision. This popular Cartesianism (see Taylor, 1991), which is reproduced in so much academic writing in either a direct or attenuated form is at the root of so many of the patrician habits of the social sciences and humanities. Such a mode of thought, which has perhaps been the single most important impediment to cross-cultural translation, has its roots in the Judaeo-Christian tradition with its insistence on a monotheism instead of a multiplicity which is based, above all, in a conception of the world as based on a principle of scarcity rather than a principle of plenitude; as Schwarz (2001, px) puts it 'like the divine favour denied Cain, there is not enough blessing to go around' (see also Santner, 2001 and Stark, 2001). Non-representational theory thinks differently. It is not that there is more than one solution. It is that there are many solutions. It is possible to create a lot of 'differents', a manyness. To follow William James, we live in a multi-verse, not a universe, in which intersection, transfer, emergence and paradox are central to life.[3]

How can we throw off such deep-seated monological habits of thought? By turning, I would argue, to non-representational 'theory'. But beware. In the midst of life, nothing can be fixed. So non-representational theory is, in a certain sense, a purposely immature body of work, immature in that it attempts to throw off some of the weight of 'adult' expectations, by privileging renewal and challenging limits. And it is a political programme, not in the sense of formulating a set of demands that have to be met, but in the sense of giving a chance to encounters and interactions that are partially invisible in the dominant regime and are excluded from the definition of what counts as knowledge. It is what remains after the work of redemption (Santner, 2001).

This does not mean, however, simply trying to recover encounters and interactions, as though they were exotica. Such a move both reproduces a colonial imaginary, and is likely – in a world where commercial cultures have become machines for vacuuming up difference – to produce just another marketing opportunity (Hutnyk, 2001). Rather, it is to search for modes of disclosure of, intervention in, and extension of what we are capable of that are *co-produced*. That is not an easy task. It requires the re-imagination of practices of 'good' encounter and interaction which we can often only just sense. It requires practices and ethics of listening, talking, metaphorising and contemplating which can produce a feeling of being in a situation together. This is Vico's 'sensory topic', a feeling of being in some situation together, brought up to date as what Riikonen and Smith (1997, p42) call a *'providential diagnostics'*:

> 'Vico made it clear that the very character of our practical social activity is not finalisable. It always contains possibilities for continuous development and further shaping (Shotter, 1993). This doctrine of "providence" or of "natural provision" is interesting in a world like ours which generally idealises finalised knowledges. If Vico's ideas are sound, there is no final knowledge in the social sphere.
>
> The word "providence", often used in religious contexts, refers to the finding of an abundance or a source of richness. Providential topics or objects do not empty themselves. Like children's toys or lover's eyes, they can be continuous sources of possibilities. It is important to observe that providence in Vico's sense is both unavoidable and conditional. The potentialities can be utilised only if they are seen.'

So what are the antecedents of this new kind of moral imagination? What are the lights that illuminate the path towards a non-representational theory? Of course, non-representational theory has many sources and a long and complicated genealogy which can claim all kinds of ancestors: Spinoza's process-centred logic of connection, Nietzsche's non-theistic gratitude for being, Whitehead's account of an emergent concrescence, Wittgenstein's proto-phasics, Bahktin's notions of utterances and addressivity, Tarde's extraordinary micro-sociology, Lefebvre's transfiguration of everyday life, Serres' reworking of Lucretian tendencies and so on. What each of these accounts hold dear, in a more or less developed form, is all the things that non-representational theory holds dear: a kind of energetics, an interest in moments of indeterminacy, undecideability and ambivalence, the abandonment of subject-predicate forms of thought, an orientation to thought as inclusive of affect, and, in general, a sense of the 'tone' of any situation, the play of singularity which *might* (and only might) produce new virtualisations. In other words, this is a conception of a world in which the event is primary, in which:

> 'Morphological description is replaced by description of dynamic process. Also Spinoza's modes now become the sheer actualities, so that, though analysis of them increases our understanding, it does not lead us to the discovery of any higher grade of reality. The coherence, which the system needs to preserve, is the discovery that the process, or concrescence, of any one actual entity involves the other actual entities among its components. In this way the obvious solidarity of the world receives its explanation.' (Whitehead, 1978, p7)

It would be impossible in this short space to number all the ways in which non-representational theory calls up echoes of past process-based thinking. For now, I will instead point to five current bodies of work that are currently 'live' which might be interpreted as avatars. The first of these is the new vitalism that has arisen from Deleuze's appropriation and reworking of Bergson (e.g. Deleuze, 1988; Ansell-Pearson, 1997, 1999). This kind of work depicts a world of resonances which have the property of generalised affectivity. It stresses temporary articulations of creating/inventing which can then form subsequent articulations in which these temporary articulations are stabilised, often as something quite different. The new vitalism is not the heroic manipulation of genetic codes, or software programs. Rather, it is a recognition of the complementary roles of different elements in the elaboration of new (and perhaps more vivid) forms. Life itself is a process of production of the new. Thus:

> 'At no level is the world static. Creation, the always and ever new, is an ongoing process of contraction, folding in what comes along on the outside, exercising only partial control over what is contacted; thus, the stability of each articulation is only relative in the sense that it is never complete or final.' (Olkowski, 1999, p104)

But beware. Though it may sound grand this is very rarely 'Life' with a capital L. Rather, most of the time, it is 'life in all its sticky and slack human/nonhuman, inorganic/incorporeal, phenomenal/epiphenomenal, and banal/intense everydayness' (Seigworth, 2000, p246).

The second is work on non-cognitive dimensions of embodiment, work which again has a long pedigree through Mauss, Wittgenstein, Merleau-Ponty, Bourdieu, Varela and so on. Human life is largely lived in a non-cognitive world, yet the implications of this statement are only now being thought through. In the quite recent past, the push of the world was too often replaced by models of analytic contemplation which could not capture the practical logics of the body or the restless nature of the body's contact with the world, a contact which is not proximate but intertwined and continually coming to sense (Warnier, 2001). Such a motile notion of embodiment is in direct contradiction to analytic models of contemplation which:

> 'cannot conceive of spontaneity and creativity without the intervention of a creative intention, or finality without a conscious aiming at ends, regularity without observance of rules, signification in the absence of signifying intention' (Bourdieu, 2000, p137).

The third is work on the object world. Too often, 'things are unfairly accused of being just "things"' (Latour, 2000a, p117). But objects are brought into the world as more than mute props to which humans react – or alternatively as overpowering assemblages sucking the life out of humanity. Instead, they are given their own modes of existence and modes of thought. Objects, in other words, are not just seen as arbitrary manipulable entities but as having their own phenomenality. Perhaps the best recent attempt to revive the object world has been actor-network theory, Latour's (1999) attempt to transform 'the solid from what was a substance, a territory, a province of reality' into a circulation (p6). For Latour, objects are part of 'due process'. They 'are much too real to be representations and much too disputed, uncertain, collective, variegated, divisive to play the role of stable obdurate, boring primary qualities finishing the universe once and for all' (Latour, 2000a, p119).

The fourth is psychoanalysis. Here, we can see the dropping of much Freudian baggage. This is not just because more general diagnoses of the social imaginary (which, after all, towards the end of his life, Freud was only too happy to indulge in) have come into favour (Castoriadis, 1997; McNay, 1999; Campbell, 2000). There are a number of other impulses towards change. One is considerable scepticism concerning psychoanalytic accounts of infancy, based especially upon a non-representational account of the infant which argues that senses of self exist prior to self-awareness and language (including sense of agency, of physical cohesion, of continuity in time, of having intentions in mind and so on – Stern, 1998). Another is a much greater sense, oddly enough, of the importance of language, but a language of little words in day-to-day use (Billig, 1999; Parker, 1999). And then, in part following on from these developments, a much greater suspicion of the privileged role of the analyst, leading on to the idea that therapy consists of a mutual construction of reality which has rich consequences; not just that the analyst can no longer bring along a pre-formed conceptual map, but also that there are many possible solutions (see Elkaim, 1990). The result has been an exciting period of experimentation with new therapeutic set-ups (see Elkaim, 1997; McNamee and Gergen, 1999; Campbell and Kear, 2001).

The final stimulus is performance, as the acting out of these and other approaches as part of an archive of genres in art, theatre, fashion, dance and music arising most obviously since the 1960s which have tried to open out the world. This vast archive constitutes a theoretical–practical working out of the 'tension of the present tense' (Phelan, 1997) by providing a history of continuous better-sorry-than-safe experiment, which attempts to imagine the unimaginable, reflect on and augment the passions (for example, through a Humean emphasis on 'returns upon the soul' which are copied and repeated) and rework what counts as the political.[4]

Performance might be described as 'intelligence-as-act' (Melrose, 1994). In particular, it requires an emphasis on procedures of somatic action which can achieve a kind of transcendence as a constant critique of signification. But this somatic action,

> 'does not assume the status of a "word", in recent occidental tradition, as it would need
> to do if we were to speak of body language ... And it cannot be said to be either

> hard-edged or a meaningful unit "in itself", nor within a system of so-circumscribed options. What is practised here is not a single lexical choice within an established and easily read symbolic order: first, because there is no such thing as a "single gesture on stage" since each apparent option interacts in the end space with all others and with what preceeds and follows; second, because a known and easily read, culturally coded option is inadequate to what others might call theatre's "poetics", to its "rhetoric" which, in occidental tradition, requires difference as much as it requires conformity. Nor does it seem that we can claim to recognise a minimally coded (and thus meaning-filled) somatic option that might be "made strange" (as in the convention of Russian Formalism) by a stylistic supplement. Instead, it seems that we need to recognise that injection of energy which is peculiar to performance contexts, which connects the everyday to performance … the shift from everyday's minimal wastage of energy to performance's maximal wastage.' (Melrose, 1994, p82)

These five stimuli may sometimes have different projects in heart and mind, but in their disclosing of the world they share a number of features in common, which are best described as a experimental, demonstrative, relational, ethological and dynamic. So, to begin with, the world is incomplete and inconsistent and must be approached through a spirit of affirmative experimentation. It cannot be made to resolve itself (as in dialectics). Second, the world is demonstrative. It is ruled by the imperative of performance: a desire to show and tell (Read, 2000). Third, the world is built out of various 'polyphonic' forms of relations.[5]

> 'I suggest that one think less in terms of systems composed of individuals in interaction and more in terms of inter-relationships of assemblage. An assemblage can be made up of elements which are genetic, neurophysiological, linked to infancy, to the family, to the mass media, and so forth. The concept of assemblage draws on the assemblages created by certain surrealist painters and sculptors. The simplest example is the famous bull's head created by Picasso in 1942: in this assemblage, a bicycle handlebar placed on a saddle evokes a bull's head. On the basis of separate-elements – heterogeneous elements placed in relationship to one another – an assemblage breathes life into the elements that compose it and induces a novel perception of reality.' (Elkaim, 1997, pxvi)

In other words, the assemblage is a means of constructing narrative in such a way that it cannot be subsumed by a simple model of causality. Rather, it is a structure:

> 'capable of registering at once (and without antinomy), contingency and necessity; that is to say the assemblage is a structure which is able to articulate the slide into oblivion of one mode of thought together with the rise to dominance of another without having to explain it is terms of either successive or negation, but can instead stage it as co-adaptation' (Buchanan, 2000, p118).

Fourth, it follows from this conception that the best means of understanding the world is as a set of constantly-becoming ethologies. Behaviour is not localised in 'individuals' but is understood as a relational structure that constitutes what might be termed an 'extended organism' (Turner, 2000), a 'small' world within which becomings take place in terms of affects and capacities for affecting and being affected.[6] Thus:

> 'the environment is an intrinsic feature of the becoming of the movement of the organism. In this rethinking of the becoming of life, Heidegger's thinking comes close to Deleuze's emphasis on ethology, although Deleuze's analysis takes place on a much more molecular and machinic level which renders the notion of the organism hugely problematic both philosophically and politically' (Ansell-Pearson, 1997, p117).

So, fifth, we must think of the work of the world as a set of dynamic intensities that *produce* different spatial and temporal, intelligibilities – territories of becoming that produce new potentials (May and Thrift, 2001).[7] Why? Because:

> 'if I string together all [the] disciplines that are defined by their creative activity it is because there is a limit that is common to them – a common limit in this whole series of invention, invention of function, the sort of block of movement, invention of concepts, and so on. Common to all these disciplines is 'space–time' (espace–temps). If all these disciplines communicate together, it is at the level of that which never disengages for itself, but that which is engaged in all creative disciplines, to know the constitution of space–time' (Deleuze, 2001, p101).

Of course, how these spatialities and temporalities are disclosed differs from author to author – the refrains of Deleuze and Guattari, the intricately practised space–times of Lefebvre, the circulations of Latour – but they all share the same broad goals and technologies. And they all share the commitment to valuing a practical poetics of everyday life, not just as some idle remnant left to speak only after other 'larger' forces have had their say, but as a viable sphere of politics in its own right, the fount of a constant and ongoing virtuality which exceeds, always exceeds.[8] Everyday life is the rough ground where potentials are worked out, a practical *practice* of composition which, for those of a scholastic disposition, is too easily framed as 'banal'.

> 'The poetic … you intend to speak about as *experience*, another word for voyage, here the aleatory rambling of a trek; the strophe that turns but never leads back to this course, or back home at last, is never reduced to poetry-written, spoken, even sung.' (Derrida, 1991, p225)

So, a certain consistent inconsistency, a commitment to the sway of 'affective and relational virtuality' (Foucault, 1989, p77), an ethological notion of space and territory, a preference for the 'everyday'. This will seem to many to be a recipe for wholesale inconsistency and an irresponsible legitimation of all competing claims. But that is not so, for each of these stimuli is also underpinned by a commitment to rigour, the rigour of experimental encounters that can result in happy recognitions and affective contagions, that can exceed their situation – the rigour of addition, the rigour of risk, the rigour of providing materials with the opportunities to show interest. The more mediations the better (Stengers, 1997; Latour, 2001).

In what follows I will now outline some of the main tenets of non-representational theory. Loosely speaking, non-representational theory can be understood as a pragmatics of 'human' transformation (the question, of course, being 'What is human?' or 'How can we become human?'), which works by the unfolding of concrete multiplicities. Therefore, it is concerned, above all, with the dynamics of situations: 'time is not something to be endured, it is activated, orientated, the object of qualitative change' (Guattari, 1996, p18[9]). And this means that 'the analytic problematic shifts from a backward-looking interpretation of the symptoms of pre-existing latent material to the forward-looking, pragmatic application of singularities, towards the construction of new universes of reference for subjectification' (Genosko, 2000, p150).

Abiding signatures

'For many contemporary thinkers, for numerous artists and writers, representation is inevitable and the composition of a kind of thinking and a series of practices that constitute the ruin of representation is nonsense. However, from the point of view of an ontology of change and becoming, fluid series and system series, creative practices and what might be called transformational practices (including psychologies) are real. Only as an ontology of becoming is the 'spiritual' element, the creation of what has no conditions, the production of the new out of a deepening passive synthesis, found to occur in the domain of living beings and their practices.' (Olkowski, 1999, p211)

'Consciousness is neither the pre-requisite to nor the same thing as the capacity to think and reason.' (LeDoux, 1996, p302)

We can add up the five bodies of work outlined above in all kinds of ways. But they feed into non-representational theory in their emphasis on *how and what it is to 'think'*. Why this emphasis? To begin with, non-representational theory is concerned to avoid what Bourdieu (2000, p21) so aptly calls the scholastic disposition, a sense of distance arising out of 'the emergence of universes which, like the scholastic worlds, offer positions in which one can feel entitled to perceive the world as a representation, a spectacle, to survey it from above and from afar and organise it as a whole designed for knowledge alone'. So, non-representational theory tries to recognise and work with all those kinds of thinking that do not fit the scholastic model, that *live inexpertly*. Then, non-representational theory is concerned to characterise many elements of the world as a part of thinking, thus diversifying what is thought of as thought and enabling *alliances to be made with what was previously regarded as anomalous* (Baker, 2000). And, more generally again, we can therefore seen non-representational theory as an attempt to fight against the terrorised imagination that characterises modern societies by stressing the *primacy of poetic invention*: that primacy of poetic invention is a crucial political move.

Hence, non-representational theory's project. The varieties of stability we call 'representation', howsoever understood (for an excellent review, see Prendergast, 2000), can only cover so much of the world[10]. Much of what is intelligible is left off to one side as either irrational detritus or a sublime other. So what kind of thinking is non-representational theory attempting to amplify?

Well, most thinking is still done in the now. Despite the increasing prominence of technologies that programme the past and future, still the world has to be lived as a clamour of competing priorities which cannot be postponed and must be acted out. And very often these performances involve the animation of powers of invention – of talk, of gesture, of the operation of pen or keyboard or more – that can sometimes be remarkable and may even furnish new principles and resources for thinking. Not less, more.

So let me say it clearly: only the smallest part of thinking is explicitly cognitive. Where, then, does all the other thinking lie? It lies in body, understood not as a fixed residence for 'mind' but as 'a dynamic trajectory by which we learn to register and become sensitive to what the world is made of' (Latour, 2000, p1). It lies in the full range of micro-kinetic nerve languages that call us into being, not just vision (which is so often assumed to be the touchstone of knowledge) but all the senses (including senses of bodily movement like proprioception). It lies in the swell of affective contagion which has its own reasons and logic which we are only just beginning to consider. It lies in the specific circumstances of spaces and times which are able to be sensed and worked with but are often only partially articulated, what Ingold (2000) calls the 'resonance to environment' – the somewheres words can't take you.

All manner of such non-cognitive thinking has been posited. There is the snapping-into-action of the body that lies prior to cognition – the so-called 'half-second delay' (see Thrift, 2000a). There is the notion of affect as a somatic register of bodily rules and processes that are constitutive of the states themselves, a classically Jamesian notion now revived in disciplines as different as sociology (Katz, 1999), psychology (Damasio, 1999) and philosophy (Redding, 1999) and realised to be crucial to the work of modern social orderings. And, there is the deep energetic swell of the unconscious, the bodily *and* technical (see Clough, 2000), the imaginary, which has been conceived of by more than one author as an 'aesthetic intelligence' (Campbell, 2001).

Then, finally, thinking must be seen as an ethology. In a line of thought that stretches back to Bateson and before, there is an ambient ecology of mind; the whole environment acts as a 'processual subjectivity' (Guattari, 1996) – as 'wideware' in Clark's (2000) felicitous phrase – which, through constant interaction, thinks existence. How this 'processual subjectivity' is thought varies, from the moving planes of affective intensity so beloved of Deleuze and Guattari, in which lifelines sweep exuberantly towards assimilation, go beyond meaning, to the more mundane attempts to link history and environment to be found in bodies of work like actor-network theory (see Ingold, 2000).

Notice three things that arise from this brief discussion. First, none of this is meant to suggest that cognition is not important. Rather, it is to problematise what cognitive thought might consist of, to radically extend what thinking might be by extending intelligibility out into the world, and to look more carefully at what the connections between the cognitive and the non-cognitive might be (Clark, 2001). For example, how might we understand the connection between talk and emotion? As a recursive loop of expression and content? (Brown, 2001) As selection for certain kinds of affect? As 'sensual resources that operate as a foreground for our conduct only when they remain outside the foreground of our self-awareness'? (Katz, 1999, p7) Second, the sheer materiality of thinking is constantly stressed. Thought is a kind of performative material intervention, a set of locutionary and illocutionary sites that conjure up different qualities of intensity and experimentation. Third, as is heralded by the mentions of sites and senses, thinking is a set of geographies of the sensible, a set of spaces of various kinds of sensation which resist enclosure in representation because they cannot be codified. They are not symbolic or iconic, but rather diagnostic of possibilities other than the predictive or explanatory.

This latter point deserves expansion. For, to finish matters off, there is space. Non-representational theory takes the world to be a kaleidoscopic mix of space–times, constantly being built up and torn down. These space–times normally co-exist, folding into one another, existing in the interstices between each other, creating all manner of bizarre and unexpected combinations (Massey, 1997). Some space–times are more durable. Their reach is able to be extended by intermediaries, metrics and associated knowledges so that they ultimate instable fashion, and are able to be constantly represented. Other space–times flicker into and out of existence. Still others are simply wormholes within or between larger space–times that are able to form escape routes or new points of exception/inception.

Whilst it is probably the case that the bulk of space–times created by humanity have been based upon the body and its phenomenological correlates like up/down and exten-sion/protension, the growth of various technologies means that, increasingly, what counts as the body's space is redefined by interaction with longer, looser assemblages of instru-ments and the 'phylums' to which they belong.[11] Then space–times are constantly shot through by bearers of unconscious thought, technical substrates of unconscious meaning like the machine, the text and writing which both constitute and haunt so many contem-porary space–times (Clough, 2000). And, finally, this means that in some space–times the body may only be a faint memory. Other things are going on.

What I hope is clear is that space–times almost never consist of a patchwork of con-tiguous territories but rather a set of energetic activations, lines of flight that may or may not be elaborated, ethologies that may or may not be able to establish a lasting refrain. These space–times constantly interfere with one another and these interferences can themselves be formative: there is what Genosko (2000) calls the possibility of an 'amorous transport between territories'. Questioning provides a different problem. Such a view means that we are able to say that space–times perform 'us' as much as we per-form 'them', not least because so many of these space–times are fields of affect which, by their very nature, are im-, pre- or post-personal. They perform the 'individual'.[12]

So, in contrast to so many stories of rationalisation, homogenisation and general impoverishment of the constitution of space–time, it is just as possible to argue that modern societies are characterised by an unparalleled density and richness of space–times that have thickened the past, present and future in ways which provide unparalleled opportunities to boost virtuality and promote heterogenesis. Whatever the case, non-representational theory's job is to run interference on the extant fabric of space–time so as to produce even more 'human kinds' by extracting qualities and converting them into 'markers', new expressive elements that 'stake out, or rather advertise or announce the territory' (Brown, 2001, p187). Performing differently in order to think more differently.

A politics of imaginative generosity

> 'We're strict functionalists: what we are interested in is how something works, functions – finding the machine. But the signifier's still stuck in the question 'what does it mean?' – indeed it's this very question in a blocked form. But for us, the unconscious doesn't *mean* anything, nor does language. … The only question is how anything works, with its intensities, flows, processes, partial objects – none of which *mean* anything.' (Guattari, in Deleuze, 1995, p22)

> 'Grammar is a poor cartographer.' (Phelan, 1997, p87)

And so we came to the nub of the chapter. This kind of approach is often thought of as somehow apolitical. But in fact it is quite the contrary. For what non-representational theory is primarily concerned with is forging new political spaces. It is *not* a political pro-gramme but it *is* a politics, a politics of the creation of the open dimension of being. I want to make this claim in four ways.

First, non-representational theory is an attempt to short-circuit the current role of the intellectual – in human geography and elsewhere – as an under-labourer (or perhaps jester) of the growing class of 'bourgeois bohemians' (Brooks, 2000). This powerful class of highly-educated, culturally-aware business people:

> 'has merged the counter-cultural forces of the 1960s with the enterprising ethos of the 1980s and has thereby legitimised capitalism among the very people who were its most ardent critics, and … has legitimised counter-cultural poses among the business elites' (Brooks, 2000, p139).

It therefore values cultural literacy. Indeed, in modern management thinking the cultiva-tion of such cultural skills is considered a positive advantage, at work and at play (insofar as the two can be separated). This is, then, a class of men and women that (to use a phrase which in retrospect has a rather threatening tone) wants it all, and intellectuals are there to do their bit by informing them what that cultural all is – by providing sexy interpretations, creative cues and general ambience. Non-representational theory is, in part, an attempt to reposition the intellectual outside of this seductive space of cultural celebrity by moving her into different territories of expression that can in turn produce new contents.

Second, non-representational theory is an attempt to open up new spaces of the political by providing new forms of political practice which contain within them that special quality of generosity towards the world. As Agamben (1999) has pointed out, there is a widespread assumption in much recent writing on politics that current 'political' practices *are* the space of the political. This is precisely the assumption that non-representational theory seeks to overturn, chiefly by pursuing a politics of the world-disclosing performance of relations, that is, showing things up that are significant and worthy of notice by responding to new events in ways that sense and hold on to anomaly (Spinosa, Flores and Dreyfus, 1997). This skilful acting into situations is a political art in its own right, one which we all have but which is too often dulled by, for example, the mass media who would prefer to do our thinking for us. Thus, non-representational theory is primarily concerned with offering new means of expression and new modes of agency, especially those to do with expanding the space of virtuality of the body and technology. This openness to the space of virtuality means that we can continue to form the people-to-come rather than be drawn back into the *a priori* segmentations into which society tries to sort us.

A key part of this politics is the opening up of new spaces and times which are caught up in the everyday dynamics of momentum and impetus. These open space–times often constitute modern-day prophecies which have the power to perplex because they do not fit standardised anticipations. As Bennett (2001) argues, enchantment still has its places in the world (see also Thrift, 1997) and there is a battery of spatial and temporal practices that can amplify its powers. Further, such everyday moments of encounter can be cultivated to build an ethics of generosity by stimulating affective energy and by refining the perceptual toolkits necessary to build moral stances.

So, third, non-representational theory is concerned with forging a new kind of ethics, one which is concerned, above all, with changing our stance to the world by working on the faculty of judgement as it is actually exercised – in the immediate present. This is not, therefore, an ethics based upon universal moral rules able to be pulled out and applied to any situation, not only because so many moral systems are simply command and control by another name, but also because the ethical field is 'too fast and coarse to be available to clean representation or articulation without remainders' (Connolly, 2000, p313). Instead, it pursues an ethic of cultivation that 'understands obligation, recognition, responsibility and justice to be secondary effects of a generous sensibility ...' (p313). What we have here, then, is an Aristotelian ethical coping based upon pre-theoretical everyday convictions, indeed, very often upon mental processes that cannot be brought to consciousness at all. This is, then, an ethos of awareness, working experimentally upon virtualities that exceed the realm of conscious control. It is the cultivation of 'expertise' as judgement able to be fully attuned to each event rather than the application of set rules, since truly ethical behaviour does not arise from mere habit or from obedience to patterns of rules. 'Truly expert people act from extended inclinations, and from precepts, and thus transcend the limitations inherent in a repertoire of purely habitual responses' (Varela, 1999, p31). As Varela (1999) puts it:

> 'We have to ask ourselves: why should one conflate ethical behaviour with judgement? Most people answer this question by repeating the received (Western) opinion on this matter, not by describing what they do in everyday life. This is crucial. Consider a normal day in the street. You are walking down the sidewalk thinking about what you need to say in an upcoming meeting and you hear the noise of an accident. You immediately see if you can help. You are in your office. The conversation is lively and a topic comes up that embarrasses your secretary. You immediately perceive that embarrassment and turn the conversation away from the topic with a humorous remark. Actions such as these do not spring from judgement and reasoning, but from an immediate coping with what is

confronting us. We can only say we do such things because *the situations brought forth the actions from us*. And yet these are true ethical actions; in fact, in our daily, normal life they represent the most common kind of ethical behaviour.' (p5, my emphasis)

In turn, this kind of 'reasoning', which prompts Tully's (1989, p172) contention that it is 'not necessary to regard' a way of life '[as] free and natural only if it is founded on some form or other of critical reflection', has been and is being forged into practices of learning which can amplify judgement (see also Mouffe, 2001). Recently, a whole host of writers has tried to outline the acquisition of practical skills that can produce virtuous ways of life, from latter-day Heideggerians like Spinosa, Dreyfus and Flores (1999) through to proto-Nietzcheans like Deleuze and Foucault. Similarly, numerous other body-workers, from performers to therapists, have attempted something similar (see Thrift, 2000a). But perhaps the most obvious contemporary example of such practices is to be found in the 'crazy wisdom' of Buddhism (as symbolised by Varela's books with the Dalai Lama). Buddhism is concerned with cultivating intelligent attention and extension through a gradual progression of spontaneity and rational calculation which ultimately allows the acquisition of expertise which is able to bypass deliberateness altogether, so that it is possible to act from dispositions at the very moment of action (see, for example, Watson, Batchelor and Claxton, 1999).

The progressive and pragmatic actualisation of virtue found in the ability to make an appropriate response to a situation requires a cultivation of judgement (understood in a neo-Aristotelian way) which involves both subjects and environments (insofar as this distinction makes any sense since actor and action become one). This requires the involvement of technologies of the 'empty self' which recognise this kind of ethical stance and encourage appropriate *flourishing*. In other words, what is needed is a pragmatics of human transformation. In particular, this must mean valuing to a greater extent the kind of behaviour we currently group under categories like 'intuition' and 'improvisation'. And there are signs that just such a performative valuation is now taking place in such practical arenas as education (e.g. Claxton, 1997, 1999; Atkinson and Claxton, 2000), and business (Flores, 2000) each of them intent on performing each moment with understanding, by cultivating sensitivity to context. (At the same time these arenas are also being used to question certain managerial orthodoxies such as the vogue for audit with it's cramped and diminished stance to the world).

There is one other reason for wanting to formulate such a politics – perhaps the most important – and that is the changing character of Euro-American society. Things are, in short, becoming more performative. Increasingly, modern western societies are dominated by a new signifying organising principle that is changing who and what we are (Guattari, 1996). The old ways of doing things based on systems of discipline are being replaced by a cluster of changes which have variously been described as the triumph of Foucault's pastoral mode (Rose, 1999), the rise of therapeutic politics (Nolan, 1998)[13], the advent of a society of constant modulation (Deleuze, 1995), or even the wholesale ascendancy of the performance principle (McKenzie, 2001). Howsoever this change is described, and to what exact degree it has taken root, there seems little doubt that what we are looking at here is a new way of doing domination, based in inhuman forces that are redefining what we understand the political subject to be. The expectation that people will practise the world in this new way can be seen as constituting a new desiring machine.

> 'The desire produced by performative power is not moulded by distinct disciplinary mechanisms. It is not a repressive desire; it is instead 'excessive', intermittently modulated and pushing across the thresholds of various limits by overlapping and sometimes competing systems. Further, diversity is not simply integrated, for integration is itself becoming diversified. Similarly, deviation is not simply normalised, for norms operate and transform themselves through their own transgression and derivation.' (McKenzie, 2001, p18).

In other words, the performative principle is multiplying and dividing, making its way into the most unexpected places. And as it does so, so new kinds of person are being created, which we are only just beginning to sense; not least because many of the new stances and anticipations have already begun to be hardwired into our bodily repertoires as they become prior to representation (Thrift, 2000a). It follows that many recent social theoretical excursions often seem to be simply statements about what is going on in practice, or even manifestos for a performative new age.

And what has seized most fervently on these new developments? Why, quite clearly, capitalism. And this is no surprise for what distinguishes modern capitalism is that, like science, it is an experimental system that, like science, constantly reconfigures itself, radically uncertain in its certainty (Thrift, 2001). Capitalism is making a play to make a play out of business, investing in a whole series of projects that can renovate the bodies of workers and managers so that their creative juices will flow, thereby making them into ever more valuable – because expressive – commodities (Thrift, 2000b). The modern state, too, has its interests in providing new forms of personhood. So, for example, education is becoming more and more performative (at least in part because of the dictates of global business). Children must act out knowledge if they are to learn. Similarly, the state's workers must perform for consumers in a direct analogue of what is going on in the private sector.

This is, then, a remarkable change in how bio-power is produced and welded. It aims to produce expressive rather than docile bodies, active yet passive bodies that have been taught to act in to the moment, thereby producing added value for business and the state. It is a nomadic system which is able to be constantly reworked in order to produce new variations that can be rapidly exploited and then cast aside. It attempts to make bodies in ways that capitalise on their virtuality, rather than attempt to block it off (as in systems of discipline). This is power as a mobile entity, leading everywhere and nowhere, able to constantly produce the new and then take advantage of it. This is the gay science made afresh.

In the face of this extraordinary change, too much of the social sciences and humanities remain mute or, what's worse, turn to the past certainties of systems of discipline – and the politics of another age. Yet, as this change takes root (or rather, doesn't) we surely need another kind of politics. In the face of perform – or else, we must perform – or acquiesce. And such a politics is being invented. Using some of the very same tools as capitalist business and the state, plus a mixed bag of other practices invented on the street or in performance a new political book of spells is being found. A kind of dream machine. It is scattered – but not therefore incoherent. It is nomadic – but not therefore inconsequential. It is heterogeneous – but not therefore insignificant. And if we are not to be smothered by a pervasive and insidious regimen – the more pervasive and insidious because it relies so much on harnessing our own powers of invention to produce a new 'post-personal' distribution of intensities – we must become a part of the search for new feats of matter, not so much as a consolation as a means of fuelling our outrage. After all, it is ourselves who are being purloined. Can we form a new uncommon sense? Can we produce new sequences of strange and charmed? Can we form new maps of together?

Cry out

▋ 'I create neither for an audience nor for myself. I create for solutions.' (Ligeti, 2001, p90)

▌ 'Politics is the sphere of pure means, that is, of the absolute and complete gesturality of human beings.' (Agamben, 2000, p60)

So, what, then, am I working towards? What Deleuze has called an 'ontological pragmatics'. Not so much an ideological programme as a stance to the world that can practise 'extra-being' (Rajchman, 2000) rather than simple existence. Something more. More than anything, this means the ability to produce practices that can display a generosity towards the world, an 'insistent craving that zest for existence be refreshed by the ever-present, unfading importance of our immediate actions, which perish and yet live for evermore' (Whitehead, 1978, p351), a care for life.

Necessarily, this is not a prescriptive programme. It is not about drafting futures for people to conform to. It is irredeemably plural. It cannot be said how we will get there or, indeed, what there will be. Instead, as Deleuze once wrote, it involves one value above all: 'that intense and trusting open-endedness, that belief in what we may yet become, and in the peculiar time and logic of its effectuation in ourselves and in our relations with one another' (Rajchman, 2000, p142). And it cleaves to one technique above all: the constant defamiliarisation of received determinations of the human and the real, through the medium of affirmative events: 'the poem is lonely. It is lonely and *en route*' (Celan, cited in Clark, 1997, p279).

At this point, people get edgy. What can all this stuff be *used* for? Insofar as they want to fall back on the usual politics of definitions, I cannot help. But if it is possible to suspend these definitions for a little while, then I think it is possible to outline another kind of politics, the politics of a generous sensibility that values above all the creation of 'joyful encounters' which can boost the powers of all concerned. This kind of 'belonging-by-assemblage' (Lee and Stenner, 1999) is not a be-all and end-all, it may perhaps provide only a modest supplement, but I would argue that it is *what makes life worth living*. It is the kind of politics that is about producing situations in which new 'orders' can speak and, even if in the most limited of ways, produce points of emergence. It is the kind of politics that wants to boost 'the ability to become a little more artistic in relations with others and parts of ourselves' (Connolly, 2000, p310). At least three kinds of politics are involved, each of them of affective, experimental, plural.

Politics 1   The politics of readiness

So much politics ends *before* it starts, with people and communities lacking the confidence to act counter to a situation in which their role is assumed to be given, with the result that their potential capabilities are never addressed. But now all kinds of performative technologies (including various body therapies and stage crafts) can work – and sometimes work well – to short-circuit this kind of ceded power by producing dispositions that are open to the moment, able to take hold of accidents and slips, able to draw on skills that can conjure up other wheres.

Politics 2   The politics of witnessing

The present time provides enormous opportunities to develop a politics of new modes of witnessing the world (Felman and Laub, 1991) which can redefine what constitutes witnessing. As one instance all kinds of technologies of vitality are being produced that promise to produce new apprehensions, new artful revelations. Take, for example, the case of so-called haptic computing and the possibilities it presents through its ability to conjure up 'impossible objects', or take the example of the new kinds of architectures that are being made possible by new materials and emerging technologies, with their ability to conjure up new space–times.

Politics 3   The politics of intercession

Lest this all sounds too personal we must remember Deleuze's desire to carry life to a state of a non-personal power. Such post-human thinking depends upon cultivating all these attempts to redefine the moral technology of Judaeo-Christian discourse by redefining the limits of what we understand the political subject to be – in ways which I have tried to indicate. 'Bless the cup that wants to overflow', as Nietzsche (1969, p39) put it. Strengthen potential. Multiply the position from which it is possible to gather up the multiplicities of lived experience. Inter-seed. Massumi (2000), perhaps the key spokesperson for a new kind of affective politics, puts this rather well when he writes of the need for a political ecology of knowledge practices which acts as a kind of destratified and non-reducible cultural ecology.[14]

> 'The object of *political ecology* is the coming-together or the belonging-together of processually unique and divergent forms of life. Its 'object' is a political ecology collectively engaged in symbiosis … [and] to side with symbiosis *as such*. [This] is a political ecology affectively engaged in symbiosis tending. This is what was meant earlier by acting as an 'arbiter'. But the word arbitration is not quite right. To retain its singular mode of self-activity, political ecology would have to refuse to wield decision-making power, or to act as a moral judge. It would find a quasi-casual role for itself, as one modulating instance among others, but different by virtue of its 'masochism' – its taking the *risk* of neither defending its own interests nor claiming to represent anyone else's in general or in particular. Deleuze uses the word 'intercessor' for this distributed but affectively engaged political risk-taking role.

> A political knowledge-practice that takes an inclusive, non-judgemental approach to tending belonging-together in an intense effectively engaged way is an ethics – as opposed to a morality. Political ecology is an amoral collective ethics. Ethics is a tending of coming-together, a *caring for* belonging as such. (p216)

Perhaps, through these new agencies, so often forged out of obscure and devalued energies, we can produce space–times in which processual potentials can be coaxed into existence, space–times in which all the things our world wants to cheapen – grace, hope, joy, respect, dignity and, yes, fun – can have nesting places. In other words, we need to be *more* political.

Notes

1. I am using virtuality here and throughout the paper in the commonly accepted manner, as to be distinguished from possibility. Lévy (1998, pp24–25) puts it particularly clearly:

   > The possible is already fully constituted but it exists in a state of limbo. It can be realised without any change occurring either in its determination or nature. It is a phantom reality, something latent. The possible is exactly like the real, the only thing missing being existence. The realisation of a possible is not an act of creation in the fullest sense of the word, for creation implies the innovative production of an idea or form. The difference between the possible and thus real is the purely logical.
   >
   > The virtual should, properly speaking, be compared not to the real but to the actual. Unlike the passive, which is static and already constituted, the virtual is a kind of problematic complex, the knot of tendencies or forces that accompanies a situation, object or entity in question and which involves a process of resolution: actualisation. This problematic complex belongs to the entity in question and even constitutes one of its primary dimensions. The seed's problem, for example, is the growth of the tree. The seed *is* the problem, even if it is also something more than that. This does not signify that the seed knows exactly what the shape of the tree will be, which will one day burst into bloom and spread its leaves above it. Based on its internal limitations, the seed will have to invent the tree, co-produce it together with the circumstances it encounters.
   >
   > Actualisation thus appears as a solution to a problem, a problem not primarily contained in its formulation. It is the creation, the invention of a form on the basis of a dynamic conjunction of forces and finalities. Actualisation involves more than simply assessing reading to a possible or selecting from many a range of predetermined choices. It implies the production of new qualities, a transformation of ideas, a true becoming that feeds the virtual in turn.'

2. For example, I am distressed by much teaching in geography which seems to me to be so devoted to turning the world into texts that it never considers other means of expression. Surely, what we need are full-on courses full of spatial experiment – from various kinds of bodywork to performance to buildings to installations. I am particularly in favour of the principle adopted by, for example, courses at MIT Media Lab – that all students should have to make something (for example, a piece of software), whatever that might be. They must not be allowed to just write, for human geography is a discipline concerned with spatial expression and this necessarily means not only the cursive.

3. Like Guattari (1996), I take this to be a political statement. Its assertion itself opens up the world.

4. This archive is obviously vast, and not susceptible to review here. I would point to just a few examples which have a particular resonance. In theatre, work that attempts to take theatre out of theatre into wider performance arenas, which has thereby had to deal with the ecology of theatre (e.g. Kershaw, 2000; Chaudhuri, 1997; Marrancom, 1996; Read 1993); and various forms of street theatre (e.g. Cohen-Cruz, 1997); in dance, that large amount of work reviewed in Thrift (2000a); in performance art, the work on, for example, site-specific art, such as that reviewed in Kaye (2000) and Pearson and Shanks (2001), in architecture the work of 'performative architects' like Holl, Lynn and Woods, in activist protest, the work reviewed in McKay (1998), and Kershaw (2000), in poetry, the work of Celan.... and so on. As histories of performances like that by Carlson (1998) have made clear, much of this work has its genesis in the 1960s and is perhaps another illustrative story to set beside that so ably told by Watts (2001). My only criticism of Watts' wonderful piece is that it does not pick up on what I think will prove to be the longer-lasting legacy of this period, the kinds of reworking of the political itself that are only just struggling into the light, to which I am in part trying to point.

5. It is absolutely crucial to remember the original meaning of relation, being-to-another, with its obvious resonances for this paper. See the important book by Gasché (1999).

6. Von Uexküll's work is of prime importance here for the original imaginative stimulus it gave to this strand of thinking, work which is only now coming to fruition.

7. See, for example, Deleuze's application of C S Peirce's work.

8. Hence, nonrepresentational theory's close affinity to all forms of micro-sociology, and especially the natural history of ethnomethodology and various forms of practice theory (Schatzki, Knorr-Cetina and von Savigny, 2001).

9. And it is therefore concerned with what Bourdieu calls the time of forthcoming.

10. And, even here, it needs to be made clear that nonrepresentational theory questions the existence of any stable representations. Insofar as sign is a useful concept, then it has to be reworked as, for example, Deleuze did on several occasions.

11. Here the work of Leroi-Gourhan (1983) is crucial in the work of Deleuze, Derrida and many other authors. So what better definition of an ethology of being than this? Technical operations, as Leroi-Gourhan recognises, are understood not against a static background but in a world which is itself in motion, whose manifold constituents undergo their own particular cycles. Thus every operation, itself a movement, unfolds within what he calls a 'network of movements'. And it is through their participation in such a network that 'active individuals have their being' (p282). The network as a whole does not beat to a single rhythm but to the concurrent rhythms intrinsic to the life activities of the several beings, both human and animal, caught up in it. Thus, every link of the network is, in effect, an interlocking of rhythms, or what might better be described as a specific resonance .... In the attunement of the individual's motor responses to these multiple external rhythms, says Leroi-Gourhan, lies the work of perception (Ingold, 1999, p26).

12. Similarly, the discipline needs to become more involved in the kinds of dialogical work outlined in this essay. Scholarship must come in many forms, not all of which

are lone. But to do this, human geography would need to get away from the habit of closing down the new, which it currently so successfully pursues – while claiming all the time that it is doing the opposite! Techniques: block the new as 'odd', or 'frivolous'; trivialise the new as 'not political'; contain the new by insisting that it can be incorporated in another body of knowledge; diminish the new by insisting that there is an already constituted collective which is the key. A good recent example of these procedures in action is the reaction to actor-network theory which has been subject to all these deadening strategies (plus some fairly hilarious misunderstandings, such as that actor-network theory needs a theory of scale, needs to be made more dialectical, is concerned with the co-construction of nature and culture and so on).

13. But see also Shusterman's (2000) wonderful account of the emotional resonances of country music as an important counter to seeing this emotion as necessarily false.

14. In a sense, Massumi is echoing Guattari's (1996, p91) earlier work, which argued for a 'virtual ecology' which would 'not simply attempt to preserve the endangered species of cultural life but equally … engender conditions for the creation and development of unprecedented formations of subjectivity that have never been seen and never felt'.

Bibliography

Agamben, G (1999) *Potentialities*, Stanford: Stanford University Press.

Agamben, G (2000) *Means Without End. Notes on Politics*, Minneapolis: University of Minnesota Press.

Amin, A, Thrift, N J (2002) *Cities: Retheorising Urban Theory*, Cambridge: Polity Press.

Ansell-Pearson, K (1997) *Viroid Life*, London: Routledge.

Ansell-Pearson, K (1999) *Germinal Life*, London: Routledge.

Ashbery, J (1967) 'The Ecclesiast' in *River and Mountains*, New York: Holt, Rinehart and Winston.

Atkinson, T and Claxten, G (eds) (1999) *The Intuitive Practitioner. On The Value of Not Always Knowing What One is Doing*, Milton Keynes: Open University Press.

Bateson, G (1973) *Steps to an Ecology of Mind*, London: Paladin.

Bennet, J (2001) *The Enchantment of Modern Life. Attachments, Crossings and Ethics*, Princeton: Princeton University Press.

Billig, M (1999) *Freudian Repression: Conversation Creating the Unconscious*, Cambridge: Cambridge University Press.

Bourdieu, P (2000) *Pascalian Meditations*, Cambridge: Polity Press.

Brooks, D (2000) *Bobos in Paradise*, New York: Simon and Schuster.

Brown, S D (2001) 'Psychology and the art of living', *Theory and Psychology*, 11, 171–192.

Buchanan, I (2000) *Deleuzism: A Metacommentary*, Durham, NC: Duke University Press.

Campbell, J (2000) *Arguing with the Phallus, Feminist, Queer and Postcolonial Theory*, London: Zed Books.

Campbell, P and Kear, A (eds) (2001) *Psychoanalysis and Performance*, London: Routledge.

Carlson, M (1998) *Performance*, New York: Routledge.

Castoriadis, C (1997) *World in Fragments. Writings on Politics, Society, Psychoanalysis and the Imagination*, Stanford: Stanford University Press.

Chaudhuri, M (1997) *Staging Place. The Geography of Modern Drama*, Ann Arbor: University of Michigan Press.

Clark, A (2001) *Mindware*, Oxford: Oxford University Press.

Clark, T (1997) *The Theory of Inspiration*, Manchester: Manchester University Press.

Claxton, G (1997) *Hare Brain, Tortoise Mind*, London: Fourth Estate.

Claxton, G (1999) *Wise Up. The Challenge of Lifelong Learning*, London: Bloomsbury.

Clough, P T (2000) *Autoaffection. Unconscious Thought in the Age of Teletechnology*, Minneapolis: University of Minnesota Press.

Connoly, W (2000) *Why I Am Not A Secularist*, Minneapolis: University of Minnesota Press.

Damasio, A (1999) *The Feeling of What Happens*, London: Allen Lane.

Deleuze, G (1995) *Negotiations*, New York: Columbia University Press.

Deleuze, G (1994) *Difference and Repetition*, New York: Columbia University Press.

Deleuze, G (1998) *Bergonism*, New York: Zone Books.

Deleuze, G (2001) 'What is the creative act?' in Lotringer, and Cohen, S (eds) *French Theory in America*, New York: Routledge.

Derrida, J (1991) ' "Eating Well", or the calculation of the subject: an interview with Jacques Derrida' in Cadava, E, Conner, P and Nancy, J L (eds) *Who Comes After the Subject?* New York: Routledge.

Elkaim, M (1990) *If You Love Me, Don't Love Me. Undoing Reciprocal Double Binds and Other Methods of Change in Couple and Family Therapy*, Northvale: NJ, Aronson.

Felman, S and Laub, D (1991) *Testimony. Crises of Witnessing in Literature, Psychoanalysis and History*, New York: Routledge.

Flores, F (2000) 'Heidegger, thinking and the translation of business practice' in Wrathal, M and Malpas, J (eds) *Heidegger, Coping and Cognitive Science: Essays in Honor of Hubert L Dreyfus*, Volume 2, 271–292. Cambridge, Mass: MIT Press.

Foucault, M. (1989) *The Archaeology of Knowledge*, Harmondsworth: Penguin.

Gasché, R (1999) *Of Minimal Things. Studies on the Nature of Relation*, Stanford: Stanford University Press.

Genosko, G (2000) 'The life and work of Felix Guattari' in Guattari, F *The Three Ecologies*, London: Athlone.

Guattari, F (2000) *The Three Ecologies*, London: Athlone.

Guattari, F (1996) *Chaosmosis*, Sydney: Feral.

Hutnyk, J (2001) *Critique of Exotica*, London: Pluto Press.

Ingold, T (1999) 'Tools for the hand, language for the face; an appreciation of Leroi-Gourham's *Gesture and Speech*', *Studies of the History and Philosophy of Biological and Biochemical Sciences*, 30, 411–453.

Ingold, T (2000) *The Perception of the Environment*, London: Routledge.

James, W (1909/1996) *A Pluralistic Universe*, Lincoln: University of Nebraska Press.

Katz, J (1999) *How Emotions Work*, Chicago: University of Chicago Press.

Kaye, N (2000) *Site-Specific Art*, London: Routledge.

Kershaw, B (2000) 'The theatrical biosphere and ecologies of performance' 122–131.

Kwinter, (2001) *Architectures of Time Towards a Theory of the Event in Modernist Culture*, Cambridge, Mass: MIT Press.

Latour, B (1999) 'After ANT' in Hassard, J and Law, J (eds) *Actor Networks and After*, Oxford: Blackwell.

Latour, B (2000a) 'Body, cyborg and the politics of commotion' http://www.ensmp.fr/PagePerso/SCI/Bruno-Latour. html/artpap/p-80cyborgs.html

Latour, B (2000b) 'When things strike back: a possible contribution of science studies to the social sciences', *British Journal of Sociology*, 51, 107–124.

Latour, B (2001) 'Good and bad science: the Stengers – Deprest falsification principle' in Akrich, M and Berg M (eds) *Bodies on Trial*, Durham, NC: Durham University Press.

Le Doux, J. (1998) *The Emotional Brain*, London: Weidenfeld & Nicolson.

Lee, N and Stenner, P (1999) 'Perpetuum mobile: substance, force and the sociology of translation' in Law, J, Hssard, J (eds) *Actor Network Theory and After*, Oxford: Blackwell.

Leroi-Gourhan, A (1993) *Gesture and Speech*, Cambridge, Mass: MIT Press.

Lévy, P (1998) *Becoming Virtual*, London: Pleunum Press.

Ligeti, G (2001) 'Fighting Shy', *The Economist*, July 28 2001, 88–90.

Massey, D (1997) in Golding, S (ed) *Eight Technologies of Otherness*, London: Routledge.

Massumi, B (2000) 'Too-blue: colour patch for an expanded empiricism', *Cultural Studies*, 14, 177–226.

May, J and Thrift, N J (eds) (2001) *TimeSpace*, London: Routledge.

McKay, G (1998) *Senseless Acts of Beauty*, London: Verso.

McKenzie, J (2001) *Perform – or Else*, New York: Routledge.

McNamee, S and Gergen, K (1999) *Relational Responsibility: Resources for Sustainable Dialogue*, Thousand Oaks, CA: Sage.

McNay, L (1999) *Gender and Agency*, Cambridge: Polity Press.

Melrose, S (1994) *A Semiotics of the Dramatic Text*, London: Macmillan.

Mouffe, C (2001) *The Democratic Paradox*, London: Verso.

Nietzsche, F (1969) *Thus Spoke Zarathustra*, Harmondsworth: Penguin.

Nolan, J L (1998) *The Therapeutic State*, Albany: New York Press.

Olkowski, D (1999) *Gilles Deleuze and the Ruin of Representation*, Berkeley: University of California Press.

Parker, C (2001) 'Anarchy and Ecstasy', *The Economist*, June 9 2001, p133.

Parker, I (ed) (1999) *Deconstructing Psychotherapy*, London: Sage.

Patton, P (2000) *Deleuze and the Political*, London: Routledge.

Pearson, M and Shanks, M (2001) *Theatre/Archaeology*, London: Routledge.

Phelan, P (1997) *Mourning Sex*, London: Routledge.

Prendergast, C (2000) *The Triangle of Representation*, New York: Columbia University Press.

Rajchman, J (1999) *Constructions*, Cambridge, Mass: MIT Press.

Rajchman, J (2000) *The Deleuze Connections*, Cambridge, Mass: MIT Press.

Read, A (1995) *Theatre and Everyday Life*, London: Routledge.

Read, A (2000) 'Acknowledging the imperative of performance in the infancy of theatre', *Performance Research*, 5, 61–69.

Redding, J (1999) *The Logic of Affect*, Ithaca: Cornell University Press.

Riikonen, E and Smith, G M (1997) *Re-Imagining Therapy. Living Conversations and Related Knowing*, London: Sage.

Rose, N (1999) *Powers of Freedom*, Cambridge: Cambridge University Press.

Santner, E L (2001) *On the Psychotheology of Everyday Life. Reflections on Freud and Rozen*, Chicago: University of Chicago Press.

Schatzki, T, Knorr Cetina, K and von Savigny, E (eds) (2001) *The Practice Turn in Contemporary Theory*, London: Routledge.

Schwarz, R M (2001) *The Curse of Cain. The Violent Legacy of Monotheism*, Chicago: University of Chicago Press.

Seigworth, G (2000) 'Banality for cultural studies', *Cultural Studies*, 14, 227–268.

Shotter, J (1993) *Cultural Politics of Everyday Life*, Milton Keynes: Open University Press.

Shusterman, R (2000) *Performing Live. Aesthetic Alternatives for the Performing of Art*, Ithaca: Cornell University Press.

Spinks, L (2001) 'Thinking the post-human: literature, affect and the politics of style', *Textual Practice*, 15, 23–46.

Spinosa, C, Flores, F and Dreyfus, H (1997) *Disclosing New Worlds*, Cambridge, Mass: MIT Press.

Stark, R (2001) *One True God*, Princeton, Princeton University Press.

Stengers, I (1997) *The Invention of Modern Science*, Minneapolis: University of Minnesota Press.

Stern, (1998) *The Interpersonal World of the Infant*, London: Karnac.

Suderberg, E (ed) (2000) *Space, Site, Intermediation. Situating Installation Art*, Minneapolis: University of Minnesota Press.

Taylor, C (1991) *Sources of Self*, Cambridge: Cambridge University Press.

Thrift, N J (2000) 'Steps to an ecology of place' in Allen, J, Massey, D (eds) *Human Geography Today*, Cambridge: Polity Press.

Thrift, N J (1996) *Spatial Formations*, London: Sage.

Thrift, N J (1997) 'Cities without modernity, cities with magic', *Scottish Geographical Magazine*, 113, 138–149.

Thrift, N J (1999) 'The still point: resistance, embodiment and dance' in Pile, S, Keith, M (eds) *Geographies of Resistance*, London: Routledge.

Thrift, N J (2000a) 'Afterwords', *Environment and Planning D. Society and Space*, 18, 213–255.

Thrift, N J (2000b) 'Still life in nearly present time: the object of nature', *Body and Society*, 6, 34–57.

Thrift, N J (2001) 'Performing Cultures in the New Economy', *Annals of the Association of American Geographers*, 90, 674–692.

Tully, J (1989) 'Wittgenstein and political philosophy: understanding practices of critical reflection', *Political Theory*, 17, 172–204.

Turner, J S (2000) *The Extended Organism. The Physiology of Animal – Built Structures*, Cambridge, Mass: Harvard University Press.

Varela, F (1999) *Ethical Know-How: Action, Wisdom and Cognition*, Stanford: Stanford University Press.

Warnier, J P (2001) 'A praxeological approach to subjectivation in the material world', *Journal of Material Culture*, 6, 5–24.

Watson, G, Batchelor, S and Claxton, G (eds) (1999) *The Psychology of Awakening*, London: Weiser Books.

Watts, M (2001) '1968 and all that …', *Progress in Human Geography*, 25, 157–188.

Whitehead, A N (1978) *Process and Reality*, New York: Free Press.

6

Postcolonial geographies: spatial narratives of inequality and interconnection

Catherine Nash

Introduction

In her book *Edge of Empire: Postcolonialism and the City*, Jane Jacobs (1996) poses one of the most significant questions for contemporary human geography: 'Can the spatial discipline of geography move from its positioning of colonial complicity towards producing postcolonial spatial narratives?' (p163). Here she points both to the intimate relationships between geography as a formal academic discipline and European imperialism that have been explored in recent work on the historiography of geography (Barnett, 1998; Bell, Butlin and Heffernan, 1995; Godlewska and Smith, 1994; McEwan, 1998), and looks to the future direction of human geography informed by postcolonial perspectives. This chapter is written with Jacobs' question in mind. My response is that yes, geography can move towards producing postcolonial spatial narratives, but not in any simple, easy or uncomplicated way. Postcolonial perspectives are important for human geography and geography is important to questions of postcolonialism, but bringing them together is necessarily challenging as well as productive for both. Postcolonialism, as I will argue, destabilises some of the certainties of geography. At the same time, geography differentiates global perspectives on colonialism and directs attention to the materiality of colonial and postcolonial processes, something that has been relatively neglected in comparison to the analysis of colonial and postcolonial writing and visual representations. While the term postcolonial is sometimes used to mark a time period after the end of colonial rule, or to describe the social, cultural and political characteristics of societies shaped by colonialism, postcolonialism describes a complex and debated set of analytical and theoretical perspectives, variously informed by feminist, Marxist, post-structural and sometimes psychoanalytic theories, which critically explore the histories and geographies of colonial practices, discourses, impacts and legacies. Despite the different theoretical tools and focus of interest within this growing interdisciplinary field, its core concerns are the centrality of colonialism to the patterns of global power from the early modern period to the present, and the construction of the identity of the 'coloniser' as well as the 'colonised' through often racialised ideas of difference. Postcolonialism is both historical and contemporary in its focus, interrogating the historical geographies of colonisation as well as challenging their continued effects in the present. A critical engagement with colonialism and its continued legacies is central to postcolonialism.

The impacts of Western imperialism and colonialism have been profound. They include loss of land, livelihoods and lives and the disruption of pre-colonial cultural and social systems. Colonialism involved material processes, knowledges and modes of representation. As Stephen Greenblatt (1988) has written of early modern European encounters with the New World, the 'possession of weapons and the will to use them on defenceless people are cultural matters that are intimately bound up with discourse: with the stories that a culture tells itself, its conceptions of personal boundary and liability, its whole collective system of rules' (p64). Colonialism was not just political or economic, but also a cultural process that required legitimation through discourses of difference and superiority, and in which the experiences and identities of colonised people were shaped through damaging forms of cultural as well as political domination (Fanon, 1952, 1967; Nandy, 1983). The histories and identities of colonial powers were also deeply shaped by colonialism. For both former colonies and former colonial powers, the legacies of colonialism live on: in new patterns of ethnicity, racialised inequalities and identity politics shaped by migration from former colonies to former colonial powers; in relationships between indigenous people, descendants of white European settlers and more recent migrants in white settler colonies; in the civil wars and ethnic separatist movements in states brought into being in their modern form through colonialism; in new forms of domination that follow and extend old imperial lines of unequal interconnection. Postcolonialism explores the complex and effective relationships between issues of *power, inequality* and *exploitation* and themes of *identity, knowledge* and *representation*. These themes are, of course, central to the huge body of work which interrogates the structures, spaces and ideologies of modernity. What makes postcolonialism distinctive is its attention to colonisation alongside class, gender, nationhood and other axes of identity and oppression.

This critical focus on colonialism has been enormously influential. Recent glossaries, introductory texts and readers indicate the current level of interest in postcolonialism. They also evidence the range of themes in postcolonial criticism: the nation-state, ethnicity, representation and resistance, the relationship between postcolonialism and feminism or postmodernism, and key terms in postcolonial theory such as ambivalence, hybridity, mimicry, miscegenation or the subaltern (Ashcroft, Griffiths and Tiffin, 1989, 1995, 1998; Williams and Chrisman, 1997; Gandy, 1998; Loomba, 1998; Moore-Gilbert, 1997). Postcolonial critics have posed awkward and unavoidable questions about Western world views, Western traditions of knowledge production and the ways in which colonialism was implicated in the development of disciplines, from those like history, literature and art history which constructed notions of European superiority and cultural achievement, to those involved in the 'discovery', naming, classification and representation of colonialised lands and people – cartography, biology, botany, anthropology and geography.

Postcolonialism has prompted a critical reflection on the roles these disciplines played in producing colonial knowledge and colonial discourses, and has made questions of colonialism central to their contemporary concerns. But this is not just an academic exercise. Postcolonial perspectives are also deployed by a whole range of political activists and cultural practitioners who actively work to criticise colonialism and challenge the problems and patterns of inequality that have followed in its wake and continue with new forms of domination by powerful states and global capitalism.

It is frequently argued that postcolonialism was inaugurated in the field of literary criticism, most famously with Edward Said's account of the 'Western' imagination of the 'East' in *Orientalism* (1978), and developed through the work of Gayatri Spivak (1987) and Homi Bhabha (1994). In one sense postcolonialism has been dominated by literary studies, but if postcolonialism is understood more widely as a critical exploration of colonialism, its origins and locations are more diffuse and include writers and intellectuals like Frantz Fanon, C L R James and W E B DuBois, whose writing predates these key figures (King, 1999). Despite the impact of postcolonialism on a wide range of disciplines, much postcolonial work remains focused on cultural representations. Yet, as I want to show in this chapter, geographical attention to spatial difference and the simultaneously symbolic and material shaping of places and social relations, can contribute significantly to postcolonial studies. As Jane Jacobs (1996) notes, while ideas of difference are central to postcolonial theory, its theoretical abstractions do not always adequately connect to the specific, concrete and local conditions of everyday life. The development of postcolonial theory has been closely linked to literary criticism, and much postcolonial work continues to explore questions of culture and representation in a wide range of media and cultural forms including film, travel writing, art, photography, museums and exhibitions. This focus on colonial discourses and postcolonial strategies in cultural products has been one avenue for postcolonial geography too (Blunt, 1994; Blunt and Rose, 1994; McEwan, 1994; Phillips, 1997; Ryan, 1997). Yet, human geographers' attention to the relationships between the symbolic and material in the production of space, at least potentially counters the textualist tendencies of some postcolonial work. In one sense, geography can ground postcolonialism though its focus on the material forms as well as symbolic dimensions of place, space, nature and landscape. Attention to colonial architecture, urban form, spatial context and the built environment has until recently been largely neglected in postcolonialism (King, 1995). As Anthony King has argued, this overlooks the spatial conditions of all social relations. 'Moreover, such spatial and built form arrangements are not simply symbolic signifiers of power and control, they also materially affect life chances of those who live within them' (King, 1999, p108). Human geographers can challenge postcolonial generalisations by exploring the specific character of different postcolonial locations; by focusing on the different scales of imperial and colonial processes and their geographies; by paying attention to the ways in which colonialism and its legacies have shaped economic, political, social and cultural geographies differently in different places; and by tracing the interconnections between different postcolonial locations.

Yet, at the same time, postcolonialism erodes the grounding of popular and academic geography in neat maps of identity and difference: the mosaic of nation-states 'naturally' organising social, economic, cultural and political relationships; the West and non-West; the local and global; the centre and periphery. Postcolonialism both directs attention to the history of geography and its role in European imperialism and colonialism, and provides fresh theoretical perspectives. The discipline's imperial history haunts contemporary human geography in ways that are both challenging and productive. This awareness of the politics of knowledge, prompted by the historiography of geography and empire, disturbs grand claims and grand theory. Postcolonialism challenges the authority of western geographical knowledge, the privileging of western traditions of representation, and the primitivism and exoticism of western geographical claims to know, theorise and represent the rest of the world. It directs geographers' attention to questions of discourse, provides new ways of understanding the relationships between place and identity, and focuses attention on the colonial dimensions of capitalism, development and environmental change. As geographical engagements with postcolonialism have shown, human geography can be enriched by the work of postcolonial theorists and, in turn, geography can make for better postcolonial work.

This chapter presents an argument for the necessary but necessarily difficult task of moving towards postcolonial human geographies. Though most postcolonial work in human geography has been on the history of the discipline and the cultural analysis of colonial texts, other avenues are opened up by bringing together the concerns and insights of geography and postcolonialism; postcolonial development, economic, urban and environmental geographies are just a few possible areas of intersection. Yet this is not a call for simply attaching the prefix 'postcolonial' to disciplinary or sub-disciplinary titles, but rather proposes a critical and constructive engagement with both postcolonial perspectives in human geography and with the complex geographies of postcolonialism. Crucially, adopting the term postcolonial to describe or recast contemporary human geography is misjudged, reductive and politically inadequate if it simply means re-inscribing oversimplified distinctions between the coloniser and colonised, between the imposed/foreign and native/indigenous, or between colonial geographies of bounded cultural differences and postcolonial geographies of cultural fluidity. My focus is especially, but not only, on geographies of culture and identity, but I also want to give some indication of the mutually informing relationships possible between postcolonialism and other disciplinary concerns, such as environmental, economic and development geographies. My focus here is also explicitly spatial. It is on the geographical imaginations of colonial discourse, the different geographies of colonialism's culture, the different geographies of postcolonial theory and on the situated politics of theories of place and belonging. The first section of this chapter outlines the broad cultural frameworks and imaginative geographies through which European societies have understood and figured the rest of the world. The second provides a commentary on the general arguments of the first by considering the need to attend to the specific and different histories and geographies of colonialism and postcolonialism. Finally, I turn to the theme of place, culture and belonging to illustrate the possibilities and problems of a postcolonial human geography.

Colonial geographical imaginations

Colonialism was both a practical and ideological project. It involved early modern European expansion and exploration of formerly 'unknown' parts of the world, the making of the world market through the expansion of world trade, capital investment in colonial enterprises, the development of export-orientated production in the colonies for markets and industries elsewhere, and transfer of profit back to the 'centre'. Colonialism included the creation of imperial spheres of influence, military conquest and political control. It has involved the transformation of environments, the displacement of colonised peoples and settlement of European migrants in colonised lands. For colonised people it meant the imposition of new systems of rule and culture, and the disruption and destruction of lives, ways of life and livelihoods. The practical work of colonisation was entwined with cultural practices and discourses used to legitimate colonial projects and strengthen colonial authority, and with ideas of cultural difference. One of the most important themes within postcolonial theory has been the way European colonial countries made sense of the world increasingly dominated by European imperialism and colonial control. European expansion was accompanied by efforts to sort out, order and exploit colonised people and knowledge; to make the world profitable and to make all its variety and difference make sense. This attention to the ways in which colonised people and places were understood and represented in a wide range of European disciplines – biology, geography, history, anthropology – and media – literature, painting, photography, travel writing, scientific texts – involves more than the identification of overt racism and colonial stereotyping, though this has been a necessary critique. Work on the production of knowledge and representation has involved exploring the wider ways in which colonial domination and colonial identities were profoundly linked to the production of knowledge about the colonial world (Richards, 1993).

From the early modern period onwards European encounters with non-European societies fuelled political and philosophical debates about human nature and difference. This preoccupation with difference effectively produced the category 'race'. Arguments about the superficiality or immutable nature of physical differences were entwined with debates about culture. Rationalists argued that despite ostensible cultural differences all human minds were capable of reason and thus reform. Though apparently non-hierarchical, this understanding of difference justified a 'civilising mission' to raise other cultures and societies to European standards of 'reason'. In reaction to this Enlightenment rationalism, romantics argued for the natural, organic and permanent separation of cultures. Again, though potentially pluralist, its focus on comparison and difference opened the way for the hierarchical ranking of societies on scales of more or less civilised. Europe's location on these hierarchies is predictable. Though apparently contradictory, these different models of cultural difference were deployed strategically according to context and colonial intention. Thus, flexible but resilient colonial binaries of 'self' and 'other' were mapped onto geographical imaginations of the 'centre' and 'periphery' as well as West and East. Distance from the European colonial centre was constructed as distance in time; colonised people and places were figured as less civilised, and in need of the 'civilising' work of colonialism. Africa, for example, the focus of imperial interest in the late nineteenth century, was constructed as the 'Dark Continent', feminised and racialised as unknown and darkly threatening, virgin and desirable, and in need of the light of European civilisation (Brantlinger, 1985).

Colonialism was accompanied by efforts to fix the identity of the coloniser and colonised through ideas of absolute difference that worked to create an ideology of European super- iority and non-European inferiority. One key starting point in the work of uncovering, analysing and deconstructing these colonial discourses, has been Edward Said's (1978) enor- mously influential account of the construction of the 'East' or 'Orient' in nineteenth- and early twentieth-century English, French and Northern American scholarship and literature. Orientalism, Said argued, divides the world into two halves distinguished by their essential difference. This colonial imaginative geography constructed the character of the 'West' and 'East' in ways that justified English and French colonial ambitions. Figuring the East as splendid but despotic, exotic but irrational, mysterious but weak and passive, dark and depraved, enabled the West to be constructed in contrast as democratic, rational, active, strong, enlightened, civilised. Building on this work, other postcolonial theorists have pro- vided accounts that explore the gendered and differentiated nature of Orientalism in a wide range of cultural forms (Lewis, 1996; Lowe, 1991). Orientalism is one extremely powerful and persistent version of the binary structure of imperial ideology, which as Abdul JanMohammed (1995 [1985]) describes, polarises the cultures and identities of the coloniser and colonised into irreconcilable Manichean categories of good and evil. Despite the limited and often contradictory efforts by colonialist writers to imaginatively identify with the colonised, generally '[t]roubled by the nagging contradiction between the theoretical justification of exploitation and the barbarity of its actual practice' colonial discourse 'attempts to mask the contradiction by obsessively portraying the supposed inferiority and barbarity of the racial Other, thereby insisting on the profound moral difference between self and other' (p23). As Frantz Fanon (1952, 1967) argued, colonialism made both 'coloniser' and 'colonised' through this hierarchy of immutable racial and cultural distinctions.

Colonial binaries are familiar, persistent and often perpetuated in academic as well as popular representations. The repertoire of contrasts between modern/traditional, core/ periphery, First World/Third World, developed/underdeveloped, advanced/backward, figure routinely in Western representations of the rest of the world. Bringing together the insights of colonial discourse theory and the study of development is one challenging but innovative direction for human geography (Simon, 1998). Postcolonialism challenges representations which continue to used colonial frameworks to describe or 'invent' the 'Third World' (Schech and Haggis, 2000). Western development theories of the 1950s and 1960s, which equated development with modernisation and Westernisation, both drew on Enlightenment ideals of modernity and progress, and on colonial discourses of the 'civilising mission'. Improvement in material conditions of life required 'Third World' states becoming more Western, maturing out of a childlike state of inefficiency, corruption, incompetence and irresponsibility, with the paternal guidance of the West. Taken for granted universal ideals or apparently disinterested objectives – 'democracy', 'modernisation', 'progress' and 'development' – can be shown to be discursive tools that justify the neoliberal march of free market capitalism. Yet, rather than herald the end of development studies, Susanne Schech and Jane Haggis (2000) argue that postcolonial perspectives on culture and representation offer constructive directions for development studies and development intervention. In turn, the concern with addressing the problems of uneven development created by colonialism – displacement, disease, war, repression, poverty and environmental degradation – within development studies, counters some forms of postcolonialism which make colonisation seem a bloodless affair of texts and theories far removed from contemporary patterns of inequality. Postcolonialism, similarly, points to the limits of work on North–South relations in geopolitics or the field of international relations, which fails to take seriously the ways in which constructions of 'North' and 'South' draw on colonial traditions of representation, legitimate policies on foreign aid, human rights and military intervention and promote the hegemony, security and economic benefit of powerful Northern states (Doxy, 1996).

Challenging colonial discourses requires understanding their construction and the productive relationships between knowledge and power. Recent work on colonial cartography, photography and other forms of representation and colonial practices of collection and display illustrates the connections between knowledge and the power to materially transform places and structure often violently unequal social relations. European exploration and appropriation set a world of things in motion: ships, documents, objects, people. From the eighteenth century especially, botanical and zoological specimens were collected, compared, measured and classified according to newly devised systems of ordering which attempted to sort out all the world according to European taxonomies and forms of knowledge (Withers, 1995). These natural histories, represented in encyclopaedia and displayed in zoos and botanical gardens, were claims to global authority. They were also tied to more utilitarian concerns and reflected the colonial construction of nature as a resource for development (Willems-Braun, 1997). Plants like rubber, coffee and tea especially were transported, studied in economic botany and planted for profit as colonial ecologies were shaped by plantation agriculture and, in settler colonies, new pastoral systems (Griffiths and Robin, 1997; Grove, 1995). Maps, lists, paintings, diagrams, written descriptions and objects brought back to Europe figured colonial people for European audiences. Colonised people were also subject to Western scientific efforts to classify and categorise. In the late nineteenth century, racist hierarchies of racial difference which drew on Darwinian evolutionary thinking were formulated and supported by the newly devised sciences of phrenology and craniology that linked head size and shape to levels of intelligence. Deeply pernicious and often sexualised notions of 'native savagery' were constructed through scientific as well as cultural representations of the bodies of colonised people, as their bodies were depicted in texts and images as well as put on display for Europeans (Gilman, 1986).

Colonial collecting also extended to the material cultures of colonised people, which were classified and exhibited according to European frameworks of knowledge. From the mid-nineteenth century, European museums, colonial exhibitions and world fairs were powerful sites for the production and circulation of colonial discourses of European development and civility, the benevolence of European imperialism and the savagery, exoticism and chaotic disorder of colonised people and cultures (Breckenridge, 1989; Coombes, 1994; Greenhalgh, 1988). Museums distinguished between the 'art' of Western Europe and the material culture of colonised people (Clifford, 1988). Though early twentieth-century artists in France looked to non-Western material culture as a source of creative inspiration, their celebration of the 'primitive' and rejection of the 'modern' reinforced the colonial model of Western 'civilisation' and non-Western 'savagery' (Foster, 1985; Hiller, 1991; Perry, 1993; Pollock, 1992). Non-Western artefacts were placed alongside European archaeological exhibits to illustrate an evolutionary process through which non-European cultures, supposedly, had yet to pass. The 'native' villages and 'native' people put on display in the world fairs of the early twentieth century commodified colonial relationships for the entertainment and education of European audiences. Shared enjoyment of the safe spectacle of difference and the condensed global colonial geographies that could be travelled from colonial palaces to dominion pavilions, encouraged, it was hoped, a shared investment in imperialism that would neutralise socialist, suffragist, or nationalist threats to the social order at home. These exhibitionary practices were also part of the European colonial tendency to imagine the whole world as an exhibition to be viewed, investigated, experienced and enjoyed by Europeans (Mitchell, 1989; see also Gregory, 1994, pp15–69; Gregory, 1995).

However, this was not just a matter of visual pleasure and possession. In colonial discourses and colonial representations, cultural appropriations were always inextricably linked to processes of material dispossession. In visual and written accounts of the land in colonial contexts, the absence as well as presence of figures in the landscape register a range of cultural and political as well as personal claims to space. Within European colonial discourses new lands were classically portrayed as empty, virginal, Edenic and awaiting development. Indigenous people were often simply ignored or reduced to elements of the natural fauna. When native people were represented in landscape paintings they were depicted as if in an idyllic pre-contact pattern of life that did not register the effects of European intrusion, as objects for scientific curiosity, as a wild undifferentiated nomadic horde, as last survivors of a naturally vanishing people, or as emblematic icons that marked the landscape as distinctly non-European, and so supported the cultural work of white settler nation building. In Australia, for example, these romantic and sublime, but distinctly non-European landscape paintings were used in efforts to create an imaginative national landscape and collective identity, but 'Aboriginal people are never presented as co-viewers of the landscape, but they are features within it, and elements in its wildness' (Thomas, 1999, p82). In this and in other colonial contexts, the apparent failure of indigenous people to cultivate and improve the land was used to sanction colonial settlement.

Said argued that the colonial categories of 'us' and 'them' were remarkably historically constant. Yet, as other postcolonial theorists have shown, all this work of trying to fix the identities of the coloniser and colonised reveals the unstable, vulnerable and fractured nature of colonial discourse. Faced with the complexities of colonial encounters and the flows of cultural and other forms of identification between European colonists and colonised people, the work of fixing the absolute distinction between the coloniser and colonised was never quite done. The 'centre' itself was not a homogenous realm and internal differences of ethnicity, class and gender had to be worked over to forge the image of the colonial self. Men and women were assigned gendered colonial identities that were in turn differentiated by class. Shared investment in Empire, it was hoped, would override ethnic difference within the British state. Social differences and different degrees of support for the imperial project at home and amongst the colonial agents abroad troubled the neatness and stability of the colonial binary. Recent attention to the activities and ambiguous subjectivities of Western women in colonial contexts has been an important challenge to the undifferentiated model of the white male coloniser (Burton, 1992; Chaudhuri and Strobel, 1992; Ware, 1992). Ideas of gender have been central to the making of metropolitan identities, to colonial discourses and to the differentiated experience of empire (Hall, 1992). At the same time, postcolonial critics have challenged the colonial assumptions and authority of white Western feminism (Mohanty, 1988; Radcliffe, 1994). The focus on overlapping identities and inequalities between and within categories of class, gender, race and sexuality is central to the development of postcolonialism.

The rigid ideologies of colonial discourse did not travel out from the 'centre' unchanged, but were threatened, challenged, negotiated, made and remade in the encounters between those brought together through colonialism. Anthropologists like Nicholas Thomas (1994) have traced the complexity of colonial encounters. In white settler contexts, for example, the representation of land and people could reveal more ambivalent relationships to colonial settlement and dispossession:

> 'Some denied an indigenous presence which others acknowledged, but those who acknowledged that presence did so in different ways. Some framed it nostalgically and sentimentally; some romanticized the colonial endeavour; others acknowledged its imperfections and struggled with the question of dispossession.' (Thomas, 1999, p33)

The stability of the coloniser/colonised model has also been criticised from a more conceptual direction in the work of Homi Bhabha (1994). Colonial discourse, he argues, was marked by ambivalence. Orientalism, primivitism and exoticism were all characterised by often sexualised and racialised desire for the difference of the 'other' and insistence on the dangerous savagery of the 'inferior' colonial subject. Since the definition of the colonial 'self' depended on the colonised 'other', this 'self' could never be realised as autonomous, independent and completely self-fashioned. Furthermore, colonialism was fed by a desire to reform the colonised – effectively to make colonised people more like the colonisers – yet at the same time depended upon ideas of absolute difference. In particular, the ability of colonised elites to 'mimic' Western culture unsettled these essentialist boundaries of difference. Racist anxieties about 'miscegenation' were the more virulent and overt expressions of these anxieties about the stability of the coloniser identity.

The neatness of the 'coloniser–colonised' model has thus given way to a more complex sense of the internal diversity of the colonial and colonised country. Hierarchies of gender and class, and the diversity of ethnicities in both contexts, challenge images of social and cultural homogeneity in the colonised and colonising country. Colonialism has emerged in recent postcolonial work as differentiated socially as well as temporally and spatially, contested in the 'centre' and resisted in the 'periphery', more ambivalent and less certain. Yet colonial discourses were effective precisely because they were enormously flexible and adaptable. The tensions and ambiguities of colonial representations speak of a less monolithic but no less problematic colonial project characterised by unequal exchange and partial understanding. Again, postcolonial geography needs to retain a critical perspective on the material and cultural costs of colonialism while at the same time producing more complex accounts of colonial encounters. It needs to examine colonial discourses critically without denying agency to colonised people or overlooking practices of resistance and appropriation (Yeoh, 2000).

To this point, thus, I have argued that postcolonialism rightly attunes human geographers to the implication of geographical knowledge in colonial discourses and representational practices. I have highlighted especially the dualistic imaginative geographies of colonialism, at the same time pointing to their production through more complex spaces of colonial encounter and transaction. Yet writing this through, I have been aware of the limits of generalising at this level. As we have seen, postcolonial perspectives increasingly have deconstructed the crude model of the coloniser and colonised through the focus on gender, class and the 'antagonistic intimacy' (Thomas, 1999, p10) of colonial encounters. Nonetheless, I want to suggest, the 'colonial' and 'postcolonial' need to be further refined, qualified and differentiated by geography. The postcolonial human geography I envisage is one in which geography is seen to matter.

Colonial and postcolonial geographies

I now propose to shift from a broad account of colonial imaginative geographies to a focus on the specific and differentiated geographies of colonialism and postcolonialism. This move reflects the double task of *both* theorising the broad structures of colonialism *and* attending to the specific nature, impact and legacies of colonisation in different times and places. Postcolonial criticism has generated a productive and critical engagement with established traditions across a wide range of subjects and areas. Yet postcolonialism has also been criticised for its use as a generalising term, which collapses the differences between different colonial experiences and for implying a temporal break that elides continued neo-colonial processes and internal oppressions (McClintock, 1992; Parry, 1987; Mishra and Hodge, 1991).

One of the strongest criticisms of the term has centred on the way the prefix 'post' in postcolonial seems to simply imply a time after colonialism. Critics of postcolonialism argue that it prematurely celebrates the end of colonialism and overlooks the ways in which its legacies still shape contemporary societies, in neo-colonial forms of political and economic domination through which the West continues to exploit much of the world. Though most former colonies have gained political independence, economic and cultural inequalities persist long after national liberation. Concentrating on the moment of independence from formal political control by a European power, fails to account for the much longer history of informal colonisation, continued colonial domination and the long histories of anti-colonial resistance that precede and follow national liberation. The moment of political independence is a crucial part of the decolonising process, but it does not mark the end of colonialism. Neither did the period of formal overseas control mark its beginnings. Though the late nineteenth century and early twentieth century, as a period in which large parts of Africa and Asia came under formal European colonial domination, was a crucially formative era, it was also a stage in a much longer process of European expansionism. As Stuart Hall (1996) has written, colonisation:

> 'references something more than direct rule over certain areas of the world by imperial powers. It signifies the whole process of expansion, exploration, conquest, colonisation and imperial hegemonisation which constituted the "outer face", the constitutive outside, of European and then Western capitalist modernity after 1492.' (p249)

Postcolonial is most appropriate not as a name for the period after the end of formal colonisation, but as a term which refers to a complex process of disengagement from the colonial power that often preceded and continues long after independence. This disengagement can also be from imperial domination in places where direct colonisation did not accompany colonial exploitation. Rather than simply celebrate the achievement of formal independence, postcolonial critics argue for a longer and more critical perspective that charts the different extended histories and extensive geographies of colonialism and postcolonialism.

Thus, this sense of longer and more complex histories should be matched by attention to the differentiated geographies of colonialism and postcolonialism. Much of the debate about postcolonialism has been generated by the tension between the political appeal of a grand narrative of colonial domination, resistance and national liberation and the need to pay attention to the diversity and specificity of colonial and postcolonial economic, political and cultural formations. The development of postcolonial thinking has been driven by the desire to both address critically colonialism and its global impacts and to understand its highly localised patterns and forms.

The experience of European colonisation has been very different in different places, since colonialism was both global in its reach and marked by very different geographies and temporalities. Former colonies may all be called postcolonial, but they are not postcolonial in the same way. They differ significantly in the nature and timing of their colonisation, from those based on trade, settler colonisation or on the exploitation of resources and native labour, and in their forms of government. The territories of the British empire were variously ruled by consuls, governors, British officials, commercial companies, or existed as relatively autonomous dominions. If 'postcolonial' refers very broadly to the process of political, cultural and economic decolonisation, it must also refer to the highly differentiated, uneven processes of colonisation and decolonisation. Ex-colonised countries have different relationships to the European metropolitan core, different ethnic and class structures, different histories of decolonisation, and different post-independence political, cultural and economic geographies. As Stuart Hall (1996) writes:

> 'Australia and Canada, on the one hand, Nigeria, India and Jamaica on the other, are certainly not "postcolonial" *in the same way*. But this does not mean that they are not "postcolonial" *in any way*. In terms of their relation to the imperial centre, [...] they were plainly all "colonial", and are usefully designated now as "postcolonial", though the manner, timing and conditions of their colonisation and independence varied greatly. So, for that matter, was the US, whose current "culture wars", conducted throughout with reference to some mythicised Eurocentric conception of high civilisation, are literally unintelligible outside the framework of America's colonial past.' (pp245–6)

Postcolonial theory is itself shaped by these different geographies. The specific emphasis and direction of postcolonial theory in different places reflects the different timing and nature of colonialism and anticolonial resistance, specific patterns of privilege and social division, continued relationships to former colonial powers and new forms of neo-colonial domination, and different transnational networks that link as well as bypass the 'centre'. Postcolonialism thus includes, for example, the engagement with histories of colonialism in the present in Britain, double critiques of colonialism and the post-independence nation in Ireland, uncovering the lives of those who have been marginalised both in the postcolonial nation and under colonialism in 'subaltern studies' in India (Guha and Spivak, 1988), and questions of indigenous peoples' political, economic and cultural rights in countries like New Zealand, Canada and Australia. These different postcolonial critical agendas in different postcolonial locations, work against postcolonialism becoming a kind of monolithic or universal theory that can be applied without modification world wide. Ruth Frankenberg and Lata Mani (1993) have argued that:

> 'the concept must be carefully specified, used to describe moments, social formations, subject positions and practices which arise out of an unfolding axis of colonization/decolonization, interwoven with the unfolding of other axes, in *uneven, unequal* relations with one another'. [They] 'argue against the idea that there is such a thing as "the postcolonial" in any simple sense. This does not mean, however, that we are against theorizing the term, nor that it is without utility. Rather, as we have said, we would argue that the notion of the "postcolonial" is best understood in the context of a rigorous politics of location, of a rigorous conjuncturalism.' (p237)

This focus on the politics of location or what I describe as different postcolonial locations (Nash, 1999), works against postcolonialism becoming a set of impressive theoretical tools that are never challenged by the particular, complex, messy material of social relations in different places. Rather than conceptualise the postcolonial as a bounded set of attributes or characteristics that is used as a yard stick to measure the degree of postcoloniality exhibited in different places, the postcolonial can be understood as a diverse range of responses to different colonialisms that have been differently experienced, encountered and dealt with in different times and places. The term 'postcolonial locations' gestures towards the need to explore the ways in which detailed empirical research about specific settings shaped by histories of colonialism and contemporary global interconnections, and theoretical debates about postcolonialism may be challenged by and interpreted in relation to one another. Thinking geographically about colonialism counters the globalising risks of postcolonial theory by considering: the distinctive and different forms of colonialism enacted and experienced; the different situations into and through which these forms were enacted; and the consequent different inflections of these forms in different local settings.

This more complex sense of the postcolonial allows for a critical return to the colonial 'metropole' though postcolonial eyes. Though some have argued against describing former colonial powers or white settler countries as postcolonial (Williams and Chrisman, 1994), rather than restrict the term to non-Western colonised societies, it is, I would argue, more useful to allow the term to encompass, without occluding, very different colonial trajectories and legacies. Instead of locating the postcolonial only in the non-white non-European world, in ways which replicate the move to somehow locate the tainted histories of colonialism in racialised peripheries, postcolonialism works a more effective critique by exploring the postcolonial character of white settler colonies and metropolitan colonising countries. Again, this does not negate the continued hierarchies of power or privilege *within* settler colonies nor *between* former colonial powers and former colonies, but it opens up the complexities of these different postcolonial contexts. Rather than use it as an evaluative term that can only be awarded places that are somehow unambiguously anti-colonial, the term postcolonial is better deployed to highlight the diversity of colonial legacies for both 'centre' and 'periphery' and the complexity of their interconnections.

Indeed, one of the most useful aspects of postcolonial theory is its attention to the way colonialism has been integral to the shaping of imperial metropolitan societies, and not just something that happened to other places. As Catherine Hall (1996) has argued:

> 'In Britain the traces of those imperial histories appear everywhere – in the naming of streets, the sugar in tea, the coffee and cocoa that are drunk, the mango chutney that is served, the memorials in cemeteries, the public monuments in parks and squares. Such traces are frequently left unexplored, or are refracted through a golden glow of better days, days when Britons led the world.' (p67)

In one sense at least, images of the colonial past linger on in Western cinema, advertising, fashion and tourism. This is an imperial past remembered as outside rather than within the 'centre'. Presented as an innocent retrospective of a lost world of privilege, elegance, decorum, order, luxury and opportunity, this 'imperial nostalgia', as Renato Rosaldo (1989) has described it, is characterised also by mourning for those cultures, peoples and environments changed or destroyed by colonialism, or regretfully but inevitably lost in the march of 'progress' to 'civilisation' and 'development'. Salvage ethnography, for example, attempted to record the cultures being affected by the intrusion of the 'modern', including the ethnographers themselves. Rosaldo argues that the apparently natural, harmless, innocence of the nostalgic mode, typified in extravagant film and television period costume dramas of white colonial society, disguises histories of domination with evocative but superficial elegies for an imperial past and romantic recollections of cultures before colonisation. But the alternative to 'imperial nostalgia' should not be the guilty relegation of British imperial history to a best-forgotten and distant past. Catherine Hall (1996), for example, calls for a different way of remembering that can provide ways of imagining different forms of belonging in Britain today. This 'memory work' of empire means remembering empires differently though a 'recognition of inter-connection and inter-dependence, albeit structured through power, rather than a notion of hierarchy with the "centre" firmly in place and the "peripheries" marginalised' (*ibid.*, p67). By tracing the interwoven chain of connections between England, the Caribbean and other colonial contexts in the nineteenth century she shows how debates about class-based and gendered versions of citizenship and identity in Britain were inseparable from debates about empire (Hall, 1992, 1993, 1994). Formative periods in the making of Englishness and the British nation-state, she argues, cannot be understood outside a colonial framework. White English class and gender identities were constituted through colonial relationships and interconnections, some far flung, some very immediate. This attention to the political, economic and cultural networks, which linked people variously positioned in an imperial world in intimate but unequal ways, challenges the model of an ethnically pure nation and myths of racial or cultural homogeneity with a critical sense of diversity and interconnection.

I should emphasise that this postcolonial work of critically exploring the ways in which the cultures, economies and identities of former European colonial powers were made though their imperial enterprises is not incompatible with the important, and also postcolonial critique of Eurocentric models of culture, history, civilisation, progress and development. Postcolonialism always entails multiple strategies: here of de-centring or 'provincialising Europe' (Chakrabarty, 1992) by relocating Western narratives of progress in their wider colonial histories *and* rethinking the 'centre' by resituating it in its complex web of colonial interconnections. Postcolonialism interrupts the smooth historiography of modern European capitalism developing in the 'centre' and spreading to its 'peripheries' by making global colonial interconnections central rather than subordinate to a story of European development (Hall, C. 1996). Though postcolonialism is founded on the critique of *European* colonialism, postcolonialism therefore also entails the critique of eurocentricism. In eurocentric models of modernity, progress and development all other histories are irrelevant or subordinated (Shohat and Stam, 1994). All world-changing developments diffuse outwards from the 'centre' (Blaut, 1993). Postcolonial geographies have to mediate a tension between, on the one hand, paying attention to the problematic impact of European colonisation and, on the other, challenging the eurocentrism endemic in Western culture. Postcolonial arguments about the inseparability of economic, social, cultural and political change in Europe from the complex encounters and mutual flows of culture, capital, objects and people between Europe and the colonised world, decentres Europe, while retaining the critical focus on European colonisation. This is, of course, not an easy task.

As well as providing alternatives to notions of pure colonial centres, ideas of interconnection also problematise models of pure pre-colonial cultures radically transformed by colonialism. But how can the focus on interconnection rather than colonial encounters between isolated and independent cultures and societies make for an effectively critical postcolonial geography? Is it possible both to reject models of autonomous and pure cultures and still critically examine the social changes and cultural transformations effected by colonialism and neo-colonialism? An alternative to the model of the pure, unchanging, previously isolated culture radically disrupted by colonialism, is a critical perspective that sees 'societies' as always already interconnected. Here, the nature, scale and degree of interconnection and the pace of cultural change are the focus, not simply cultural corruption. Colonialism can then be understood as a significantly hierarchical, unequal and asymmetrical form of interconnection with often sudden, dramatic and destructive impacts. As Gupta and Ferguson (1992) argue:

> 'instead of assuming the autonomy of the primeval community, we need to examine how it was formed as a community out of the interconnected space that always already existed. Colonialism, then, represents the displacement of one form of interconnection by another. This is not to deny that colonialism, or an expanding capitalism, does indeed have profoundly dislocating effects on existing societies' (p8).

Colonialism disrupts already 'creolized' rather than pure cultures – 'intrinsically of mixed origin, rather than historically pure and homogenous.' (p8)

Though colonial discourses insisted on the cultural difference between the 'coloniser' and 'colonised', much recent postcolonial work has focused on the complexity and contradictions of colonial encounters. Mary Louise Pratt (1992) has re-conceptualised the space of colonial encounter as the 'contact zone' – the space in which people previously separate historically and geographically come into contact with one another in relations of dominance and subordination. Rather than rely on ideas of cultural corruption she figures this contact zone as a space of 'transculturation' in which colonial models of subordinated people were, in part, shaped by colonised people, who in turn reworked, selectively reinvented, and reappropriated the cultural materials of the colonial metropole. There is more space in this model for the active agency of colonised peoples even in contexts of colonial domination. The idea of transculturation also allows for a more dynamic version of culture, one that challenges the image of pre-colonial cultures as timeless, pure and unchanging. For sure, narratives of the dramatic destruction of indigenous cultures, and their tales of previously isolated societies devastated by colonial contact, are potent critiques of colonialism. Nativist desire to go back to a pre-colonial culture is a significant moment in the disengagement from colonial cultural domination. The cultural projects of anti-colonial nationalism have frequently sought to recreate the nation in the image of a pure pre-colonial culture, strong and unsullied by colonial contact. Yet these narratives of national purity bring with them exclusive models of culture and ethnicity and social conservatism fuelled by anxieties about the threat of cultural corruption. For women charged with maintaining the ethnic purity of the nation and for minority ethnic groups, anti-colonial nationalism can create new forms of domination (Chatterjee, 1993). Though the commemoration of pre-colonial culture and condemnation of colonial corruption reflect the violent and destructive histories of colonialism, they figure the pre-colonial culture as pure, homogenous, static and isolated in ways which reproduce the colonial image of the pre-modern, timeless, unchanging periphery. The narrative of the obliteration of indigenous culture by colonisation also figures Western culture as all-powerful. No resistance is registered, echoing earlier colonialist accounts of 'fatal impact' in which indigenous people are figured as the tragic victims of colonialism, inevitably vanishing in the encounter between 'savagery and civilisation', rather than as agents who 'often effectively, resisted, accommodated or domesticated' colonial intrusions (Thomas, 1999, pp43, 65).

These sorts of arguments have wider resonances. For example, the tendency for critics of the effects of (colonial) Western cultural influence to represent other cultures as weak and easily eroded, and their populations as passive consumers of Western culture, is paralleled in contemporary debates about cultural globalisation. The argument that local 'authentic' cultures are being swamped by mass media, new communication technologies and global multinational companies leading to the Westernisation or, more specifically, the Americanisation of the world is problematic. It seems to imply that cultural flows are all one way, that local cultures somehow exist in unchanging isolation until the arrival of new Western media, and fails to recognise the complex ways in people receive, interpret and selectively appropriate new cultural influences. Local cultures, it is argued, are made through, rather than destroyed by, consumption of the global (Miller, 1992). The development of new terms to describe the complex outcomes of these cultural exchanges and flows – such as *hybrid, creole, border* and *syncretic* cultures – reflects this complexity and rejects colonial discourses of cultural purity and colonial anxieties about cultural or racial mixing, pathologised as miscegenation (Hannerz, 1996; Young, 1995). These efforts are also paralleled in recent approaches to environmental history and ecology. Criticisms of the environmental impacts of colonialism and the dispossession of indigenous people have sometimes reproduced the romantic and primitivist image of native people living in isolated harmony with nature in a golden age before colonialism. The complexity of social relations, social stratification and relationships to the environment are reduced to the classically colonialist model of the 'noble savage'. Historical geographies of long-term pre-colonial human intervention challenge Western fantasies of native harmony with nature that figure contemporary indigenous people as emblems of a pre-colonial past, at the same time as they trace the dramatic environmental impact of western capitalism and colonialism (Head, 1999).

So far in this chapter, I have argued for three ways in which human geography might pursue its engagement with postcolonialism. First, through a critical focus on the imaginative geographies of colonial discourse and the colonial character of geographical knowledge. Second, through an attention to different postcolonial locations and trajectories, including the colonising as well as the colonised. And third, through a conceptualising of these locations in terms of spatial narratives of interconnection rather than separation and obliteration. In the final section of this chapter, I want to push this argument one step further, turning directly to recent postcolonial perspectives on identity and location. In so doing, I caution against an overly simplistic adoption of the spatial narratives of interconnection that I have been advocating – for example, through invoking 'routes' rather than 'roots' – and instead emphasise the need for postcolonial human geographies to offer more nuanced accounts of the relations between place and identity. I want to illustrate this further way in which geography and postcolonialism can challenge and inform each other though a specific example. My focus is on genealogy – tracing ancestry and making family trees – and in particular the interest in Irish roots amongst descendants of Irish migrants in settler colonial contexts. As I have discussed in more detail elsewhere (Nash, 2002), genealogy is all about ideas of cultural identity, attachments to places, senses of belonging, ideas of 'race', ethnicity, nationhood and other models of collective identity. Tracing Irish roots links locations where questions of belonging, authenticity and ethnicity are shaped in different ways by the broad processes and specific patterns of European settlement, colonisation and nationalism, the displacement of colonised people and population movements of the twentieth century. My interests are in locating popular genealogy in specific postcolonial contexts and tracing the flows of imagination and desire that are enacted when people travel in search of roots, and in considering what this may say about wider theories of place, politics and identity.

Postcolonial roots

In one sense my interest in roots runs counter to postcolonial interests in flows and movement, but it also an engagement with them. Postcolonial theorists have challenged colonial models of a world neatly ordered into discrete cultural units and the hierarchies of 'race' and 'civilisation' into which they have been fitted, the idea of natural 'races' and notions of racial purity, and the primitivism of models of culture that can only imagine cultural encounters in terms of corruption and erosion. This critique of collective rootedness and cultural purity has also been directed to the nation-state conceived as a political unit composed of racially or ethnically homogenous people. In response to racism, ethnic fundamentalism and global experiences of cultural dislocation, much recent work in postcolonialism has questioned the traditional idealisation of unified national culture, pure identities, fixed residence and secure roots. As I have already argued, ideas of cultural flow, hybridity, movement, interconnection and creolisation have provided important challenges to colonial models of bounded cultures, purity and neat maps of 'racial' homelands. Liisa Malkki (1992) has used the term 'sedentarist metaphysics' to describe the idea of a racially 'rooted' community, with its homogenising and exclusive language of pure and primordial cultures and races assigned to politically differentiated spaces, that pathologises internal difference and external 'others'. The search for alternative models of culture and identity – through tracing transnational geographies of movement, dispersal and spatial interconnections that override the boundaries of the nation-state – has been a very significant theme within postcolonialism. Most famous is Paul Gilroy's (1997) conceptualisation of diasporic consciousness as a sub-national and transnational, non-territorial collective identity formed out the experience of displacement. Diaspora, he argues, disrupts the fundamental power of territory to determine identity by breaking the simple sequence of explanatory links between place, location and consciousness. Diasporic identities challenge the codes of modern citizenship because they are based on multiple identifications and multiple belongings always in motion between the place of residence and other places.

This is important and necessary work. Yet, with it has come a tendency to value unquestioningly geographies of fluidity as progressive and effectively postcolonial, and to see claims to rootedness, belonging and attachments to place as perpetuating regressive colonial geographies of bounded places and pure cultures. Gilroy's concept of the diaspora does not mean abandoning ideas of origins, but instead involves rethinking the relationship between cultural origin and contemporary cultural location. Nevertheless, the critical rejection of ideas of rootedness is often evoked when authors point to the contrast between 'routes' and 'roots'. Rather more complicated and challenging critical perspectives are required to understand and evaluate what is at stake when ideas of roots circulate. Following my argument about postcolonial locations, I want to explore the implications of ideas of ancestry, ethnicity and descent in different contexts, as well as the interconnected geographies that emerge when ideas of rootedness are set in motion. This is not an attempt simply to recover notions of roots, but to trace critically the ways in which political implications of genealogical identities shift as the idea of roots travels between different places. Nor is it to argue that ideas of roots should somehow replace mobility as the core concept for describing and understanding contemporary global society, but it is a criticism of the reduction of the complexity of the world to satisfying but superficial oppositions – the very binary structures of thinking, in this case 'roots' and 'routes' that have been deconstructed in postcolonialism.

Genealogy has been rightly criticised for the way it has been used to claim power and privilege and define the ethnic origins of the nation-state. National histories in Europe and the 'new world' often valorise specific genealogies. Joined to a language of race and nationality genealogy can be a handy tool for any group seeking grounds for subtle or violent forms of racial or ethnic discrimination. The claim to belong to and have legitimate rights of ownership and authority over a place through genealogical roots – the bonds of 'blood', 'race', ancestry and territory – is a familiar and powerful cultural discourse. However, though this discourse of roots can very easily become an exclusive and exclusionary ideology, claims to be native and rooted have significantly different implications in different places. The absolute rejection of rootedness sits awkwardly alongside the political claims of indigenous people, for example. In European settler societies, the language of being genealogically rooted can be deployed by indigenous groups to challenge their cultural and economic subordination, in face of benevolent but depoliticised discourses of multiculturalism (Jacobs, 1996). Through its focus on the prior existence of 'first peoples', indigenousness may productively unsettle the narrative of heroic nation building (Gelder and Jacobs, 1998) – the creation of a civilised and productive land out of wilderness – yet it also excludes more recent arrivals such as refugees and asylum seekers. Yet, complicating the situation still further, in the United States as well as Australia, the language of ethnic identity and indigenousness that has come out of anti-racist and indigenous land rights campaigns has been taken up by significant numbers of the white majority population. For those positioned between the 'First Nations' and the recent migrants of the late twentieth and early twenty-first centuries, genealogy can be an appealing tool for navigating through tangled questions of culture and belonging, and the current popularity of looking for white European roots elsewhere is in part at least a response to the potency of the idea of being indigenous. But this longing is not always matched by a recognition of the political claims of ethnic minorities or indigenous people. In settler colonial contexts in which ideas of home, roots, belonging, authenticity and the indigenous are so loaded by the histories of colonisation, imperialism, slavery and the dispossession of native people as well as more recent migrations and First Nation political claims, genealogical versions of ethnicity are inextricably bound up with the shaping of postcolonial identities.

Tracking the flows of genealogical desire between Ireland and other places reveals the contradictory and spatially differentiated cultural politics of genealogy and the different geographies of postcolonial identity politics. In the study tours and archives where amateur genealogists in Ireland and overseas visitors in search of ancestry meet and share stories, research support and resources, the practice of research involves encountering all the complexity of shared, different and cross-cutting identities and identifications. For genealogical tourists the motivation for doing genealogy is always both personal and connected to wider social issues. Genealogical tourism has been encouraged in Ireland to both generate revenue and to promote the recognition of cultural diversity in Ireland through the idea of the Irish diaspora. As this well-intentioned promotion of plural versions of Irishness through the idea of the Irish diaspora travels, it intersects with local cultural politics. In the United States, for example, interest in Irish ancestry (both Catholic post-Famine and earlier Ulster-Scots) amongst white Americans has been prompted both by the language of multiculturalism and by anxieties about new migrant flows from Central and South America. In Australia, the turn to specifically Irish roots registers both a postcolonial rejection of the English imperial connection, the negotiation of an Asian cultural and economic location and the powerfully unsettling effects of the language of Aboriginal indigenousness.

Yet even those who begin with romantic images of Irishness and who defensively want to assert a white European identity, can find that ideas of ethnic purity are fundamentally undermined in the process of doing genealogy. The certainties of blood become less secure faced with social and cultural difference in Ireland. American visitors to the Public Record Office of Northern Ireland sometimes visibly proclaiming their Irishness with shamrocks and slogans on sweatshirts and wind-cheaters, sit next to local researchers busy tracing different genealogical identities and ethnicities as Irish, Northern Irish, Ulster-Scots and/or British in Northern Ireland. Meetings with distant relatives in Ireland are often occasions for managing differences, as cousins from abroad perform versions of Irishness – having learnt to play or enjoy Irish folk music, speak Irish or do Irish dancing, for example – that do not always match the interests or attitudes of their relations in Ireland. Being in Ireland can challenge the meaning of genealogical descent. Yet at the same time, the work of amateur genealogists often points to absences in the traditional narratives of the Irish nation, as they trace ancestors whose lives and experiences have been edited out of the traditional heroic and respectable accounts of Irish history – Irish men who fought in the British army, or unmarried mothers who emigrated to avoid shame and social censure. In Ireland, genealogy can work to challenge the legacy of anti-colonial nationalism and its discourses of ethnic and cultural purity, revealing diversity, uncovering interconnection, charting complexity, as well as reveal the costs of colonial domination. Genealogy can feed as well as unfix a range of perspectives on politics, culture and identity, but it is significant that family history and genealogy are being used in Northern Ireland to encourage more inclusive senses of belonging and awareness of cultural diversity rather than division. In the recently touring exhibition, *Local Identities*, a family tree was used to illustrate the complex interconnections rather than the isolation of the 'two communities' in Northern Ireland. There is, therefore, nothing stable or predictable about the relationship between genealogy, diaspora and nationhood. Genealogy can serve to anchor and protect exclusive national cultures. It can be used to rework the nation as hybrid and heterogeneous. It can uncover pre-national cultural interconnections, between Scotland and the north of Ireland, for example, as well as enact contemporary transnational collective identities.

Though often prompted by a sense of uneasy location between the claims of the indigenous and the 'invasion' of new migrants, the genealogical work of white settlers can problematise notions of racial purity by revealing the thoroughly hybrid nature of the family tree. While many continue to skip back in time to focus on an Irish ancestor and use this as the basis of romantic identification with Ireland, many others, encouraged by the rules of proper genealogy, find that their own family trees figure the antagonistic intimacy of European settlers and indigenous people in settler societies – resistance to as well as insistence on racialised boundaries, hierarchies of ethnicity amongst migrant groups and discourses of miscegenation. Doing genealogy can map flows and contaminations rather than confirm pure identities and fixed locations. For descendants of European settlers, genealogy can lead to a more politicised and historicised sense of location, that acknowledges the impacts of European settlement and refuses the choice between sense of belonging in the place of residence and attachment to other places. The political implications of ideas of being native, settled or indigenous, and ideas of cultural hybridity, authenticity or plurality are different in different places.

Conclusion: postcolonial locations

Returning to the question posed at the beginning of this chapter, 'Can the spatial discipline of geography move from its positioning of colonial complicity towards producing postcolonial spatial narratives?' (Jacobs, 1996, p163), at least some broad points can be made in response. Despite the different positions and perspectives within what is broadly called postcolonialism, the work of colonial discourse theorists and postcolonial critics provide an agenda for human geography, schematically summarised here: for addressing the complexity of colonial relations as well as their broad structures; for critically considering cultures of domination, resistance and hybridity; and for exploring the ethnic, classed and gendered differences of privilege and power within the colonising, colonised and, importantly, post-independence state. Postcolonialism maintains a critical perspective on colonial relations of power, while at the same time challenging the binary categories of homogenous colonising and colonised groups. It also challenges hierarchies of power in the de-colonised nation-state. A human geography informed by postcolonialism retains a critical awareness of its disciplinary history of colonial complicity, and deploys its consequent sensitivity to the politics of knowledge and the danger of grand narratives to locate postcolonial theories, dismantling their globalising implications by attending to the specificities of different postcolonial contexts. The implications, nature and usefulness of postcolonial theories also have their own geography and are shaped by the specific historical experiences of colonisation, imperialism, settlement and political independence in different places. We need to differentiate the geographies of colonialism and postcolonialism, to pay attention to the specific configurations of contact, conquest, and influence, pre-colonial social structures and ethnicities, different trajectories of independence and different social patterns and politics between indigenous populations, settlers and more recent migrants. Postcolonial geography attends to the differentiated nature of colonialism and to the hierarchical relationships and complex interconnections between places affected by the long history of European colonialism. Postcolonial geographies critically explore the power-laden discourses and practices of both colonialism and nationalism and the interconnections, interdependencies and power relations between people, structured though class and gender as well as ethnicity. As I have argued elsewhere (Nash, 1999), the imperative of the present, with its globalising as well as separatist impulses, is to enlist history and geography to rethink creatively and critically, rather than simply deconstruct ideas of identity and belonging. Postcolonial geographies of the sort I have outlined here are a significant contribution to that project.

Bibliography

Ashcroft, B, Griffiths, G and Tiffin, H (eds) (1989) *The Empire Writes Back. Theory and Practice in Postcolonial Literatures*, London: Routledge.

Ashcroft, B, Griffiths, G and Tiffin, H (eds) (1995) *The Postcolonial Studies Reader*, London: Routledge.

Ashcroft, B, Griffiths, G and Tiffin, H (eds) (1998) *Key Concepts in Postcolonial Studies*, London: Routledge.

Barnett, C (1998) 'Impure and worldly geography: the Africanist discourse of the Royal Geographical Society', *Transactions of the Institute of British Geographers*, 23, 2, 239–252.

Bell, M, Butlin, R A and Heffernan, M J (eds) (1995) *Geography and Imperialism, 1870–1920*, Manchester: Manchester University Press.

Bhabha, H (1994) *The Location of Culture*, Routledge: London.

Blaut, J M (1993) *The Colonizer's Model of the World: Geographical Diffusionism and Eurocentric History*, New York: Guilford Press.

Blunt, A (1994) *Travel, Gender and Imperialism: Mary Kingsley and West Africa*, New York and London: Guilford Press.

Blunt, A and Rose, G (eds) (1994) *Writing Women and Space: Colonial and Post-Colonial Geographies*, New York: Guilford Press.

Brantlinger, P (1985) 'Victorians and Africans: The Genealogy of the Myth of the Dark Continent', *Critical Enquiry*, 12, 166–203.

Brealey, K G (1995) 'Mapping them "out": Euro-Canadian cartography and the appropriation of the Nuxalk and Ts'ilhqot'in First Nations' territories, 1793–1916', *Canadian Geographer*, 39, 140–156.

Breckenridge, C A (1989) 'The Aesthetics and Politics of Colonial Collecting: India at World Fairs', *Comparative Studies in Society and History*, 31, 195–216.

Burton, A (1992) *Burdens of History: British Feminists, Indian Women and Imperial Culture*, Chapel Hill, NC: University of North Carolina Press.

Burton, A (1998) *At the Heart of Empire; Indians and the Colonial Encounter in late Victorian Britain*, Berkeley, CA: University of California Press.

Chakrabarty, D (1992) 'Postcoloniality and the Artifice of History: Who Speaks for "Indian" Pasts?', *Representations*, 32, 1–24.

Chatterjee, P (1993) *The Nation and its Fragments: Colonial and Postcolonial Histories*, Princeton, NJ: Princeton University Press.

Chaudhuri, N and Strobel, M (eds) (1992) *Western Women and Imperialism: Complicity and Resistance*, Bloomington, IN: Indiana University Press.

Clifford, J (1988) 'On collecting art and culture' in *The Predicament of Culture: Twentieth-century Ethnography, Literature, and Art*, Cambridge, Mass: Harvard University Press.

Coombes, A (1994) *Reinventing Africa*, London: Yale University Press.

Doxy, L R (1996) *Imperial Encounters: The Politics of Representation in North-South Encounters*, Minneapolis: University of Minnesota Press.

Fanon, F (1952) *Black Skin: White Masks*, London: Pluto Press.

Fanon, F (1967) *The Wretched of the Earth*, Harmondsworth: Penguin.

Foster, H (1985) 'The "Primitive" Unconscious of Modern Art, or White Skin Black Masks' in *Recodings; Art, Spectacle, Cultural Politics*, 181–208.

Frankenburg, R and Mani, L (1993) 'Crosscurrents, Crosstalk: Race, "Postcoloniality" and the Politics of Location', *Cultural Studies*, 7, 2, 292–310.

Gandy, L (1998) *Postcolonial Theory: a Critical Introduction*, Edinburgh: Edinburgh University Press.

Gelder, K and Jacobs, J M (1998) *Uncanny Australia: Sacredness and Identity in a Postcolonial Nation*, Melbourne: University of Melbourne Press.

Gilman, S (1986) 'Black Bodies, White Bodies: towards and Iconography of Female Sexuality in late Nineteenth-century Art, Medicine and Literature', in Donald, J and Rattansi, A (eds) *'Race', Culture and Difference*, London: Sage.

Gilroy, P (1997) 'Diaspora and the detours of identity' in Woodward, K (ed.) *Identity and Difference*, London: Sage in association with the Open University.

Godlewska, A and Smith, N (eds) (1994) *Geography and Empire*, Oxford: Blackwell.

Greenhalgh, P (1988) *The Expositions Universelles, Great Exhibitions and World's Fairs, 1851–1938*, Manchester: Manchester University Press.

Gregory, D (1994) *Geographical Imaginations*, Oxford: Blackwell.

Gregory, D (1995) 'Imaginative Geographies', *Progress in Human Geography*, 19, 4, 447–485.

Greenblatt, S (1988) *Marvelous Possessions: The Wonder of the New World*, Oxford: Clarendon Press.

Griffiths, T and Robin, L (eds) (1997) *Ecology and Empire: Environmental History of Settler Societies*, Edinburgh: Keele University Press.

Grove, R H (1995) *Green Imperialism: Colonial Expansion, Tropical Island Edens and the Origins of Environmentalism*, Cambridge: Cambridge University Press.

Guha, R and Spivak, G C (eds) (1988) *Selected Subaltern Studies*, New York: Oxford University Press.

Gupta, A and Ferguson, J (1992) 'Beyond "Culture": Space, Identity and the Politics of Difference', *Cultural Anthropology*, 7, 1, 6–23.

Hall, C (1992) 'Missionary Stories: gender and ethnicity in England in the 1830s and 1840s', in Hall, C, *White, Male and Middle-Class: Explorations in Feminism and History*, Cambridge: Polity Press.

Hall, C (1993) ' "From Greenland's Icy Mountains … to Afric's Golden Sand": Ethnicity, Race and Nation in Mid-Nineteenth Century England', *Gender and History*, 5, 212–230.

Hall, C (1994) 'Rethinking Imperial Histories: The Reform Act of 1867', *New Left Review*, 208, 3–29.

Hall, C (1996) 'Histories, empires and the postcolonial moment', in Chambers, I and Curti, L (eds) *The PostColonial Question: Common Skies, Divided Horizons*, London: Routledge.

Hall, S (1996) 'When was the "postcolonial"? Thinking at the Limit' in Chambers, I and Curti, L (eds) *The Postcolonial Question: Common Skies Divided Horizons*, Routledge: London.

Hannerz, U (1996) *Transnational Connections: Culture, People, Places*, Routledge: London.

Head, L (1999) *Second Nature: the History and Implications of Australia as Aboriginal Landscape*, Syracuse: Syracuse University Press.

Hiller, S (ed.) (1991) *The Myth of Primitivism; Perspectives on Art*, London: Routledge.

Jacobs, J M (1996) *Edge of Empire: Postcolonialism and the City*, London: Routledge.

JanMohammed, A R (1995) 'The Economy of Manichean Allegory' in Ashcroft, B, Griffiths, G and Tiffin, H (eds) *The Postcolonial Studies Reader*, London: Routledge (originally published in 1985).

King, A D (1995) 'Writing Colonial Space: A Review Essay', *Comparative Studies in Society and History*, 37, 541–554.

King, A D (1999) '(Post)colonial Geographies: Material and Symbolic', *Historical Geography*, 27, 99–118.

Lewis, R (1996) *Gendering Orientalism: Race, Femininity and Representation*, London: Routledge.

Loomba, A (1998) *Colonialism/Postcolonialism*, London: Routledge.

Lowe, L (1991) *Critical Terrains: French and British Orientalisms*, Ithaca, NY: Cornell University Press.

Malkki, L (1992) 'National Geographic: The Rooting of Peoples and the Territorialisation of National Identity Among Scholars and Refugees', *Cultural Anthropology*, 7, 1, 24–44.

McClintock, A (1992) 'The Angel of Progress: Pitfalls of the Term "Postcolonialism" ', *Social Text*, 31/32, 84–98.

McEwan, C (1994) 'Encounters With West African Women: Textual Representations of Difference by White Women Abroad', in Blunt, A and Rose, G (eds) *Writing Women and Space: Colonial and Postcolonial Geographies*, New York: Guilford Press.

McEwan, C (1998) 'Cutting power lines in the palace? Countering paternity and eurocentrism in the "geographical tradition" ', *Transactions of the Institute of British Geographers*, 23, 3, 371–384.

Miller, D (1992) 'The Young and the Restless in Trinidad: A Case of the Local and the Global in Mass Consumption' in Silverstone, R and Hirsch, E (eds) *Consuming Technology*, London: Routlege.

Mishra, V and Hodge, B (1991) 'What is Post(-)colonialism?', *Textual Practice*, 5, 3, 399–414.

Mitchell, T (1989) 'The World as Exhibition', *Comparative Studies in Society and History*, 31, 217–236.

Mohanty, C (1988) 'Under Western Eyes: Feminist Scholarship and Colonial Discourses', *Feminist Review*, 30, 61–88.

Moore-Gilbert, B (1997) *Postcolonial Theory: Contexts, Practices, Politics*, London: Verso.

Nandy, A (1983) *The Intimate Enemy: Loss and Recovery of Self under Colonialism*, New Delhi: Oxford University Press.

Nash, C (1999) 'Irish placenames: postcolonial locations', *Transactions of the Institute of British Geographers*, NS 24, 4, 457–480.

Nash, C (2002) 'Genealogical identities', *Environment and Planning D: Society and Space*, 20, 1, 27–52.

Parry, B (1987) 'Problems in Current Theories of Colonial Discourse', *Oxford Literary Review*, 9, 27–58.

Perry, G (1993) 'Primitivism and the "modern" ', in Harrison, C, Francina, F and Perry, G, *Primitivism, Cubism and Abstraction; The Early Twentieth Century*, New Haven and London: Yale and Open University Press.

Phillips, R (1997) *Mapping Men and Empire: A Geography of Adventure*, London: Routledge.

Pollock, G (1992) *Avant-Garde Gambits 1888–1893, Gender and the Colour of Art History*, London: Thames and Hudson.

Pratt, M L (1992) *Imperial Eyes: Travel Writing and Transculturation*, London: Routledge.

Radcliffe, S (1994) '(Re)presenting post-colonial women: authority, difference and feminisms', *Area*, 26, 1, 25–32.

Richards, T (1993) *The Imperial Archive: Knowledge and the Fantasy of Empire*, London: Verso.

Rosaldo, R (1989) 'Imperialist Nostalgia', *Representations*, 26, 107–122.

Ryan, J (1997) *Picturing Empire: Photography and the Visualization of the British Empire*, London: Reaktion.

Said, E (1978) *Orientalism: Western Conceptions of the Orient*, London: Penguin (1991).

Schech, S and Haggis, J (2000) *Culture and Development: A Critical Introduction*, Oxford: Blackwell.

Shohat, E and Stam, R (1994) *Unthinking Eurocentricism: Multi-culturalism and the Media*, London: Routledge.

Simon, D (1998) 'Rethinking (post)modernism, postcolonialism, and posttraditionalism: South-North perspectives', *Environment and Planning D: Society and Space*, 16, 219–245.

Spivak, G C (1987) *In Other Worlds: Essays in Cultural Politics*, New York and London: Methuen.

Thomas, N (1994) *Colonialism's Culture: Anthropology, Travel and Government*, Cambridge: Polity Press.

Thomas, N (1999) *Possessions: Indigenous Art/Colonial Culture*, London: Thames and Hudson.

Ware, V (1992) *Beyond the Pale: White Women, Racism and History*, London: Verso.

Willems-Braun, B (1997) 'Buried Epistemologies: The Politics of Nature in (Post)colonial British Colombia', *Annals of the Association of American Geographers*, 87(1): 3–31.

Williams, P and Chrisman, L (eds) (1994) *Colonial Discourse and Postcolonial Theory: A Reader*, New York: Columbia University Press.

Withers, C W J (1995) 'Geography, Natural History and the Eighteenth-Century Enlightenment: Putting the World in Place', *History Workshop Journal*, 39, 137–164.

Yeoh, B S A (2000) 'Historical Geographies of the Colonised World' in Graham, B and Nash, C (eds) *Modern Historical Geographies*, Harlow: Prentice Hall.

Young, R (1995) *Colonial Desire: Hybridity in Theory, Culture and Race*, London: Routledge.

7

Feminist geographies: spatialising feminist politics

Geraldine Pratt

Introduction

In recent years I have given an annual lecture on feminist geography to the introduct-ory human geography graduate seminar. The story that I tell is this: in the 1970s feminist geographers began a critique of the sexism and masculinism, both institutional and intel-lectual, of the discipline. Monk and Hanson (1982) described the varied ways that geogra-phers ignored the everyday lives of women, from their choice of research topics to their analyses of empirical evidence. Other feminists envisioned rebuilding the city to better accommodate women (MacKenzie, 1989). The objectives of feminist geographers were clear: to make space for women, in the concrete, everyday practices of the university and beyond, and in the knowledges that we produce about these worlds. By the 1990s, the organising objectives were more diffuse. It became less clear how or even whether women could or should be united across differences of sexuality, race and class. Bell and Valentine (1995), for example, recommended that feminist geography and geographies of sexuality be 'divorced', or at least temporarily separated to assess whether they could co-inhabit the same intellectual space. My lecture, nevertheless, ends with the assertion that feminist geography can accommodate all of these differences because it is now about the geographical production of difference, not just gender difference, but a range of other marginalising differences as well (e.g. sexuality and race).

I want to pause over this expansionary portrayal of contemporary feminist geography by considering an event that happened on December 6, 2000 in Toronto, Canada. The day is an emotionally charged one for Canadian feminists; it marks the anniversary of the deaths of 14 female engineering students at Montreal's Ecole Polytechnique in 1989. Before Marc Lepine killed them, witnesses say that he yelled, 'I am here to fight against feminism, that is why I am here ... You're all a bunch of feminists. I hate feminists'. In 1991, the Canadian Parliament declared December 6 a national day of remembrance and action on violence against women. Nine years later, on the same day, Charles Rackoff, 'an award winning' computer science professor at the University of Toronto responded to an email notifying recipients of commemorative events for the day:

> 'It is obvious that the point of this is not to remember anyone. The point is to use the deaths of these people as an excuse to promote the feminist/extreme left-wing agenda. It is no different, and no more justified, than when organizations such as the Klu-Klux-Klan [sic] use the murder of a white person by a black person as an excuse to promote their agenda. (Even the KKK, as far as I know, has never suggested that all Black people should wear white ribbons [as many observers do on December 6] to apologize for the collective sins of their race).' (Freeze, 2000, A8)

This event is fascinating to read against my simplified and optimistic chronology of feminist geography. Professor Rackoff deploys a complicated rhetoric of difference. He links feminist and *extreme* left-wing class politics. This drastically constricts the membership of the group that feminism can represent. If you are a feminist you are also an extreme left-winger. Rackoff extends his argument that feminists are imposing their narrow interests by then summoning up a lively debate that emerged within feminism in the 1980s, namely, that feminism represented white women's interests over those of non-white women. He does this by judging feminist political strategy to be even worse than that of the Ku Klux Klan (and, in a novel twist, equates the plight of men with that of African Americans). Rackoff was interpreted as engaging only in 'a free exchange of ideas', and a university spokeswoman predicted that the university would take no action: 'the university takes a fairly broad view on issues of controversy' (Freeze, 2000, A8).

Rackoff's remarks offer a sobering vision of where the decentering of feminist objectives, from gender equity to a more open field of difference, might go. Rather than expanding the potential to build alliances, among women and between women and other marginalised groups, a focus on difference, rather than on gender difference more specifically, can be deployed to exploit ambiguities of what feminism is and who it represents, and to marginalise feminism as a political and intellectual force.

I want to turn now to pursue this hesitation about what feminist politics might be within a field of difference. I do this by paying close attention to the ways in which differences among women came to the attention of feminist geographers and, in particular, to the destabilising influence of Judith Butler's anti-essentialist theorising. I argue that Butler's responses to her many critics implicitly foreground the importance of context and geography for feminist politics. I attempt to make this geographical argument much more explicit. My vision of feminist geography is that it is more than a subdiscipline within geography. It has a much larger task within feminism of building alliances across women and other marginalised groups through analyses that are both sensitive to difference and committed to universal norms. Geographical analyses are essential to feminist attempts to navigate the difficult line between recognising difference and universalist commitments to equality.

A set of suspicions about gender as a category

Through the 1980s it became less obvious that women share a common set of interests. Professor Rackoff's portrayal of feminism as aligned with particular leftist politics and racialised interests echoes one strand of this questioning. At the simplest level it became apparent that feminists, including many feminist geographers, who tended to be white and heterosexual, had taken their own social locations for granted and then overgeneralised the experiences of heterosexual white women. To cite an example in which I am implicated, a number of feminist geographers demonstrated that in the United States married women with young children tend to find paid employment very close to home (within about ten minutes). This narrows their field of opportunities, and exacerbates the tendency for women to work in low-paid, dead-end jobs (Hanson and Pratt, 1995). But when feminist geographers absorbed the criticisms made by non-white feminist theorists and thought to consider the experiences of differently racialised women, they found that many African American women with dependents have very long commutes to paid employment (McLafferty and Preston, 1992, 1997). Feminist geographers' descriptive narratives of the world thus had been racialised in unacknowledged ways and they simply did not describe the lives or relevant geographies of many non-white women. Alternatively, different geographies, other than spatial constraint, may haunt the work lives of lesbian women. In one of the first articles to address sexuality and space, Valentine (1993) chronicled the discomfort and/or veiled existence lived by many British lesbian women in heterosexual workplaces.

The recognition of differences among women has tugged in two directions, neither of which leaves feminism, as a political and intellectual movement, on firm footings. One has been to insist, as I have just done, on the specificity and incommensurability of different women's identities and experiences (identity politics). The other (anti-essentialism) is a criticism of identity politics insofar as it asks whether any categorisation, including that of women or lesbian, is exclusionary. The latter argument is that identity is formed through a logic of exclusion: one defines oneself through what one is not. This involves a dualistic mode of thought and a radical simplification of the plurality of experience. I want to elaborate this argument through the writing of Judith Butler because, as much as any feminist theorist, Butler has shaken the ontological foundations of feminism.

Butler destabilises the assumption that gender is a social construction built on the foundations of biological difference: sex. She cites (1990), for example, the small but not insignificant number of babies born with indeterminate sex characteristics, and the societal impossibility of leaving them in a space between the binaries of male and female. The compulsory norms of heterosexuality – heteronormativity – dictate two sexes. In a move that reverses the standard feminist account of the relations between gender and sex, Butler argues that gender norms dictate two sexes and not vice versa. This is different from a typical social constructivist position insofar as she is arguing that biological sex itself is produced and it is not just gender that is socially constructed. Gender, including the category woman, thus loses its interiorised, biological foundation. Butler reconceptualises gender as performative. We come to understand our identity as girl/woman or boy/man because we repeatedly perform it: 'There is no gender identity behind the expression of gender; that identity is performatively constituted by the very "expressions" that are said to be its results' (Butler, 1990, p25). These performances are not arbitrarily chosen. They are compelled and sanctioned by heteronormativity. Butler retells the story of Herculine Barbin to make this point abundantly clear. Herculine was a nineteenth-century hermaphrodite, famously discussed by Foucault (1980), whose sexual ambiguity was discovered and disallowed by the medical profession, the church and the state. S/he was forced to assume an unambiguously male body and identity, and her/his life ended in bitterness and suicide.

Butler's rendering of gender performance opens a number of interesting political possibilities. By arguing that discourses of heteronormativity literally bring binarised sex and our understandings of our physical bodies into being, she is saying that what we take for granted as material and immutable (e.g. two sexes) is produced, and can be produced differently.

Nevertheless, a familiar reaction to Butler's theory is that it restricts opportunities for women to organise politically because it removes the ontological, biological foundation for the category, woman, and offers a restricted notion of agency. In an extended critique of the effects of Butler's (and other feminists') use of poststructuralist theory, Benhabib (1995) worries that it leads to the loss of an emancipatory, utopic vision. Benhabib imagines utopia in a broad sense as a 'longing for the "wholly other"…, for that which is not yet' (p36). 'I want to ask,' writes Benhabib, 'how in fact the very project of female emancipation would even be thinkable without … a regulative principle of agency, autonomy, and selfhood' (p21). There are two aspects of Butler's theorising that are troubling to Benhabib and many other feminists. First, it is often argued that Butler's theory of performativity robs the feminist subject of agency (Allen, 1998; Nelson, 1999; Webster, 2000). Benhabib asks: 'If we are no more than the sum total of the gendered expressions we perform, is there ever any chance to stop the performance for a while, to pull the curtain down, and let it rise only if one can have a say in the production of the play itself?' (1995, p21). Within Butler's theoretical framing, the answer would have to be: no. She sees the autonomous, rational subject, who has the capacity to stand off-stage and refuse the script, as a product of liberal ideology, a construction that disavows dependency and the social relations through which we are produced. A second and related concern is that, having destabilised the ontological foundations of identity, including the identity of woman, the basis for political solidarity is unclear and uncertain. According to Butler's theory, any collective solidarity must be seen as a political accomplishment and it is an achievement that is inherently linked to processes of exclusion. Achieving solidarity around the category, woman, necessarily involves suppressing differences among women. Butler recognises the necessity for such solidarity, but argues that making a political choice to do so is different from assuming unity *from the start*. Nevertheless, critics are concerned that Butler's emphasis on the ways that processes of exclusion and inclusion are intertwined leaves under-theorised the basis for solidarity and the effects of collective empowerment (Allen, 1998; Weir, 1996; Webster, 2000). I briefly present responses to these two concerns about agency and the basis for political solidarity to open up a more geographical reading of an anti-essentialist feminist politics.

Possibilities for feminist agency

From Butler's perspective, we become subjects through the performances demanded by discursive regimes. We act within these discursive conventions and are constituted by and through those very acts; this is the productive power of discourse. Performativity is a 'regularized and constrained repetition of a norm' (Butler, 1993, p95).[1] Although this may seem to restrict our capacity for agency, as Webster (2000) observes: 'While Benhabib claims that Butler *loses* an account of agency, Butler considers herself to *gain* one' (original emphasis, p2). Let me explain.

There are four ways to understand agency within Butler's account of the subject. First, although Butler develops her ideas from Foucault's theory of power and discourse, she turns to psychoanalysis to develop a richer theory of the subject than Foucault provides. In Butler's (2000b) assessment, Foucault's theory of the subject neither theorises agency or the 'instabilities of identificatory practices' (p151). She takes from psychoanalysis the understanding that the unconscious sets limits on what we can perform: 'What is exteriorized or performed can only be understood by reference to what is barred from performance, what cannot or will not be performed' (1997, pp144–5). While this is hardly a model of conscious agency – quite the opposite – it provides one way of understanding slippage across performances and a rationale for subverting the tyranny of gender roles. Butler, for example, speculates that in order to achieve *a* gender we must reject some of our sexual attachments. For an infant, this would include desire for a parent of the same sex. The loss of these implicitly homosexual attachments (e.g. a girl for her mother) can be neither avowed nor grieved: homosexuality 'produces a domain of unliveable passion and ungrievable loss' (1997, p135). Because we cannot openly grief this loss, homosexual desire continues to 'panic gender' (p136); hence the incessant, insistent performance of a gender ideal that can never be stabilised or finally achieved. This dynamic model of 'panicked' heterosexuality is not a model of static repetitions of fixed gender roles.

Second, discourses are polyvalent and can have effects that are not intended by their users. A much-cited example of this comes from Foucault (1978), who notes that discourses of sexuality (which he dates from the eighteenth century) created the stigmatised, marginalising identity of homosexual. Before this time, homosexual acts occurred but did not define a person's identity. The identity of homosexual, however, has been taken up in radicalised ways to decriminalise homosexuality. In other words, a stigmatising identity that disciplined and criminalised can be redeployed in liberating ways.

Third, although we have no capacity to stand outside discursive conventions, we do have the 'possibility of reworking the very conventions by which we are enabled' (Butler, 1995, p136). There are possibilities of subverting norms through each performance.

Fourth, and most important to the argument that I wish to develop, we force social change because of the politics of exclusion and the promise of inclusion inherent in the formation of social collectivities. Identity categories such as 'woman' or 'working class' can draw us together – politicise – but are never fully descriptive of those who are gathered under their name. As Webster (2000) notes, 'the political signifier (such as 'woman') is politically effective precisely because of its power to produce and constitute its political field and its simultaneous failure to ever fully describe and represent that which it names' (p14). The inevitable failure to describe fully, to be fully inclusive, keeps the category open and under contestation and rearticulation; this is the promise and practice of democratic politics. From this perspective, the rise of identity politics in the 1980s and the discovery that feminism was exclusionary was an important moment of democratisation that led feminism to be resignified as a category and political movement, and to be reconfigured in new ways with queer and other minority struggles. Most importantly, the capacity for agency is not a static property of human beings secured through theoretical debate; it is a capacity contingent upon and bound up with historical conditions. For Butler (1995), the pressing question is specific and concrete rather than metaphysical: her question is, 'what are the conditions under which agency becomes possible' (p136)?

Contingent universality

If the possibilities for agency within poststructuralist feminist theory (such as Butler's) has been a subject of debate, a second criticism is that its anti-essentialism robs feminism of its uniting principles. Allen (1998) criticises Butler for obscuring the 'not-so-contingent foundations' to her theory; if there is no normative foundation to Butler's theory, she asks, 'why should we resignify norms? Why expose them as unnatural? Why denaturalize sex?' (p466). Allen's view is that feminism cannot persist without unifying norms, and that Butler should 'admit' that normative concepts are already 'lurking within her text' and 'spend some time and energy defending' them (p466).

Butler's position on universal norms is now less covert than when Allen made this suggestion in 1998; for several years she has engaged in public dialogue with Ernesto Laclau on new ways of conceiving universality (Butler, 2000b). They chart a course between the particularity of identity politics and transcendental universal norms by conceiving the particular and universal as intertwined and articulated through democratic politics. By particularity, they refer to the primacy given to cultural difference, which can lead to cultural relativism whereby norms are seen as group specific. By universal, they are referring to norms that apply across groups, places and possibly times. Within feminism, a particularly contentious site for debate about cultural relativism is the issue of female cliteradectomy. Is this a cultural practice that ought to be respected, or one that feminists should condemn as an expression of patriarchal values?

Laclau's (1996) argument against the particularism of identity politics, which he develops in relation to separatist multiculturalism, is two pronged, and worth repeating here. First, identity-based groups are never totally separate because they assert their difference through norms and principles that transcend their difference, often through the language of rights. In other words, they rely on shared universal norms to assert their particularity. Second, he argues that particularism is self-defeating for members of non-dominant groups because they cannot assert a differential identity without distinguishing themselves from a context, thereby reinscribing their marginality within a dominant community. At the same time, both Butler and Laclau resist the 'return of the universal' in its ideal, transcendental form by arguing that what is understood as universal is achieved through an ongoing and conflictual process of mediation across social groups through which common social objectives and political strategies are articulated (Zerilli, 1998). There is no fixed meaning of universality and competing notions of universality must be translated and articulated to achieve common understandings. Different struggles at different times embody this universal function. Lara (1998) argues, for example, that feminist and US black civil rights movements have been particularly successful in shifting public opinion over the last century and expanding the 'public sphere' insofar as they have held the particularity of their experiences in tension with norms of universality – for example, universal principles of freedom and human rights. But because the universal emerges within the political field and out of political struggle, it always carries the trace of particularity, and the struggle to expand who has access to that which is guaranteed by universal norms is never finished. The paradoxical relation between the universal and particular is the precondition of democratic politics. Universality is never fully achieved, nor is it 'a preexisting something (essence or form) to which individuals accede but, rather, the fragile, shifting, and always incomplete achievement of political action; it is not the container of a presence but the placeholder of an absence, not the substantive content but an empty place' (Zerilli, 1998, p15).

The implications of this model of universality for feminism are two fold. First, it qualifies and makes understandable my claim that feminist geography is now about the geographical production of a range of marginalising differences, including but extending beyond gender difference. I am claiming that a chain of equivalence has been forged across struggles through overlapping critiques of the particularity of hegemonic versions of the universal. The shared critique is that historically the universal has veiled particularistic interests (i.e. white, male, heterosexual, Western) (Rose, 1993). There are shared commitments to universal norms of justice and equality that involve expanding 'the human' beyond current particularistic readings.

Second, it changes our understanding of feminist universal claims; they can be thought of as part of a political process of generating intersubjective agreement rather than applications of pregiven rules or identities. This reinterpretation of feminism also changes the substance and process of feminist politics. To return to the Montreal massacre, Chun (1999) details the conflicts that emerged among Canadian women after the murders at the Ecole Polytechnique. In particular she describes the anger that some younger, post-feminist women engineering students, who survived the massacre, felt toward older feminists who absorbed their distinctive experiences as yet another instance of generalised male violence. Some of these younger women refused to be cast as victims of the shootings and generalised male violence. And yet, Lepine cited his hatred of feminists as a rationale for his act, and a suicide note found in his apartment indicated his intent to kill several high-profile older feminists. Chun advocates a model of listening that would admit the particularity of the experiences of the women who survived the event while acknowledging the chain of citations that link this event to the feminist movement and other instances of male violence. She is advocating a performative notion of feminist identification whereby the particularity of experiences is acknowledged and respected, even as a chain of identifications is produced. 'Such a contract of listening', she argues, 'would allow for history' (p140).

And what about geography? A number of geographers have noted Butler's silence on the matter of space and geography. In Thrift's and Dewsbury's (2000) assessment: 'Butler makes little room for space. Period.' (p414). Nelson's (1999) position is that Butler's attenuated reading of agency actively prevents geographical analyses: 'The kinds of questions many geographers ask cannot be adequately addressed by a strictly performative understanding of identity, an approach that assumes an already abstracted, time and placeless subject' (p351). It is true that Laclau and Butler engage geography most explicitly as spatial metaphor.[2] In staging their discussion of space through metaphor, they repeat a familiar tendency in social and cultural theory (Smith and Katz, 1993; Harvey, 2000). Nonetheless, Butler's and Laclau's efforts to retheorise universality do highlight the need to assess both agency and universal norms within concrete circumstances. In arguing thus, they direct us to a fuller geographical project, because a concrete analysis is not only historically specific; it is geographically specific. Agency is not only a characteristic of the subject, it is contingent on time and place. The meanings of universal norms that bind feminists, norms such as justice and equality, are negotiated and translated by different groups in the same and different places.

How might feminist geographers take up this challenge of understanding the contingency of agency and the paradox of the interdependency of particularity and universality, both of which place geography at the centre of feminist theories and practice? How might we engage the challenge of 'taking Butler elsewhere' (Gregson and Rose, 2000)? We can do this by understanding first how geographies are often the medium for naturalising differences among women, and then how they can be used to link struggles across differently positioned women. At stake is the question of how to build a feminist movement that cannot take its identity for granted.

Geographies that naturalise differences among women

The differences that divide feminist and other struggles are not just group/identity based; these identities and groups are produced in and through space. Particularity is located (Pratt and Hanson, 1994), and, as Harvey (2000) notes, it is precisely the banality of this observation – the extent to which we take geographical difference for granted – that makes geography such an important social force. Differences are produced through space, and both knowledge and strategic use of these differences are critical for generating intersubjective agreement across women in the absence of a pregiven identity or *a priori* universal norms.

Rather than building alliances through an understanding of the bounded nature of social life, many feminists have been attracted by metaphors of nomadism or mobility as a way of building alliances among women. Fragmented, multiple, unstable identities seem to allow movement or points of partial contact across difference (Ferguson, 1993). I have argued elsewhere (Pratt, 1999) that this focus on mobility needs to be complemented by a careful consideration of the geographical production of difference (for critiques of metaphors of mobility, see also Kaplan, 1987; Wolff, 1993).

Another compelling image is that of the new *mestiza*, a cultural subject who builds political unity in the borderlands between and not contained within particular nations (Anzaldua, 1987). But working at the same border as Anzaldua, the border between Mexico and the United States, Wright (1998) hesitates over this image of the new *mestiza* (see also Mitchell (1997) for a critique of the 'hype of hybridity'). Wright argues that we must understand how discourses of geographical difference persist in the material-isation of political subjects living at the border.

I want to pursue Wright's argument because she provides a convincing demonstration of how the articulations of identities and difference (in this case class, gender and nation-ality) are performed through space. Drawing on an ethnography of a *maquiladora* (an export-processing factory) in Ciudad Juarez, she shows how national and gender div-isions rigidly regulate class relations within the firm. The sequestering of *mexicanas* within poverty-level, minimum wage jobs was rationalised by American managers in terms of their national attributes (self-evident through bodily adornment and comportment), and close surveillance was demanded by their dangerous propensity to go out of control: 'all women employees at [the firm] had to stake her position as non-*mexicana* or risk being interpreted as another instance of her dangerous corporeal configuration' (Wright 1998, p120). So it was that when a Mexican woman was promoted into administration – for the first time in the company's history – she literally shed her Mexican body by buying new clothes across the border in the United States: 'her dress suits changed to darker hues; her hems grew longer and her heels shorter' (p123). She moved herself and her family to El Paso: in fact residence on the other side of the border, in the United States, was an explicit requirement of the job. In a context where geographic difference nat-uralised and legitimised extreme levels of gendered class exploitation: 'the failure to recognize the politics of geographic difference in the *maquiladoras* is disastrous for a *mexicana* who aspires to improve her own material standing' (p124).

It is also disastrous for a feminist movement that seeks to articulate across this geog-raphy. We have to understand the many, insidious ways that banal geographic difference is written onto and into women's bodies so as to naturalise social differences. Exemplifying Butler's point that 'there is no reference to a body that is not, at the same time, a further production of that body' Wright (1999a, p1608) argues that the produc-tion of *mexicana* bodies as low-quality, untrainable labour – as the personification of waste – not only locks them into poverty but makes understandable several kinds of era-sure. It provides a way of understanding the public reactions to the murders of almost 200 women in Ciudad Juarez in the mid to late 1990s, insofar as a common narrative that was used to explain the murders called upon the women as exemplars of cultural and moral decline (Wright, 1999b). It makes understandable the sequestered invisibility of *mexicanas* within the factory and American male managers' obsessive control of their bodies. Following the logic that the trace of low-value labour remains in the products that she produces, Wright argues that 'the trick [for managers] is to guarantee that she disappears from the things that she makes' (1999a, p1604) by ensuring that American customers remain unaware that Mexican women have built parts of the products they buy. The consolidation of a particular geographical imaginary of differences (Mexican/ American) within Mexican women's bodies radiates from the disciplined factory body, to the dumping of hundreds of murdered bodies in the desert, to the internal structuring of the firm. We find our common understandings as feminists by unraveling these productions of difference. As Wright (1998, p116) notes, theories of performativity carve 'out a political space between discourse and matter, in which ... political action can include efforts to disturb the codes for constructing subjects from the materials identified to be located in their bodies.'

Social differences are produced at and through a variety of geographical scales, within and not just across national borders. Tang (2000) analyses, for example, how the difference between the narratives constructed about Southeast Asian immigrants, as opposed to African Americans, including those constructed by social scientists, discourage analyses of common problems and experiences. Despite high rates of poverty and welfare dependency (Tang cites a rate of about 80% among California's Southeast Asian population) the experiences of Southeast Asian immigrants are persistently interpreted through geographies of immigration (even for second and third generation immigrants), rurality and tight-knit familial networks. Similar experiences of high fertility rates and long-term unemployment are interpreted differently for Asian and African Americans; in the case of the former they are interpreted as aberrant and temporary, in the case of the latter, as evidence of the chronic black underclass. These imaginative geographies – of mobile immigrants as opposed to ghettoised underclass – concretise social differences and take the focus away from common experiences as working or jobless poor surviving the collapse of the welfare state.

If the banality of geography naturalises differences at a variety of scales, Harvey argues that it also creates the conditions for the 'double positions' taken in the name of universal norms. An example would be supporting sexual harassment legislation in a country such as the United States or Canada, and accepting the rights of US or Canadian firms to operate outside of these norms in other contexts (e.g. *maquiladoras*). Often these doubled positions emerge because there are competing universalisms at stake (women's equality versus economic liberalism) but, as Harvey (2000) notes, the contradictions of competing universalisms can be eased or the uneven application of universal principles go undetected if these contradictions or inconsistencies happen in different places: 'Failure to specify or investigate ... geographic conditions makes such double positions entirely feasible all in the name of universal ethics' (p546).

Butler (2000a) argues that the 'claim to universality always takes place in a given syntax, through a certain set of cultural conventions in a recognizable venue' (p35), and thus always carries the trace of geographical and cultural particularity. Historically, some notions of universality have worked through sexist and racist conceptions of 'civilised men' which exclude significant portions of the population. But universality is decided in an open-ended political struggle through which those who have been excluded can lay claim to universal rights. Such claimants produce a 'performative contradiction' (Butler, 2000a, p38) whereby they expose the particularity of universality even as they insist on access to universal rights. The effectiveness of such claims depends, in part, on a political discourse that sustains certain questions: 'What, then, is a right? What ought universality to be? How do we understand what it is to be a 'human'? The point is … not to answer these questions, but to permit them an opening' (Butler, 2000a, p41). Banal geographies that naturalise social difference and uneven access to universal rights tend to foreclose these questions; feminist geography keeps them alive by denaturalising the geographical processes that are part of the production of social differences among women.

Feminists strategise geographically

Geography does more than produce difference and ease doubled positions *vis à vis* universal norms. I want to outline, through concrete examples, different ways that feminists are working geographically to extend the meaning of who counts as human within the practice of universal norms.

One obvious but important point is that mapping contradictions in space can be an effective way of visualising exclusion and building alliances across excluded groups. In the documentary film, *Sa-I-Gu: From Korean Women's Perspectives* by Christine Choy, Elaine Kim and Dai Sil Kim-Gibson, several Korean American women speak of their experiences during and after the Los Angeles riots/uprisings on April 29, 1992. The film narrative is structured so that at the beginning of the film they speak of their profound losses that resulted from the event: the death of a son for one, and the loss of businesses for others. They direct their considerable anger and blame toward African Americans, including African American children in their neighbourhood who frequented their stores. In a discussion with the three co-producers that follows the film, we are told that the film has been criticised for allowing these Korean women the opportunity to air their (racist) views. This criticism ignores the fact that, as the film progresses, the Korean women begin to express anger toward white Americans for their responsibility for the uprising. 'At first I didn't notice,' says one woman, 'but I slowly realized … the rioters were very poor … The riots happened because of the gap between the rich and poor. The police could have stopped the riots. The media promoted the Black/Korean conflict' to veil the conflict between whites and blacks. These women begin to speak about the uneven access to police services in Los Angeles: 'All night we were asking: "Where is police? Where is police? Where is police?"' A young Korean man tells of calling the police and being told that the police would not come to Koreatown. 'Do you know where the police troops were?' he asks, 'They were in Japantown. They were guarding Beverly Hills'. The perception that Los Angeles police chose to sacrifice their lives and livelihoods in order to protect those of other, more privileged groups raised fundamental questions about the universality of norms of equality in the United States. It is a moment that concretised the particularity of access to services, to justice, to equality, and caused a reassessment of political opponents and allies. These Korean women shopkeepers began to see equivalencies between their situations and those of African and Latino Americans which previously they had not 'noticed'. It was the visible, audible, tactile, olfactory mapping of inequality – of noticing which areas of the city lay in smouldering rubble after the uprising, and which remained unscathed – that led them to this realisation.

Seeing inequality written starkly into the landscape can provide concrete evidence of the limits of universality. It is for this reason that a project such as *The State of Women in the World Atlas* (Seager, 1997) is an important one in feminist geography, as are recent feminist engagements with GIS (Kwan, 2002). The discipline of geography's technologies of visualisation have a long masculinist, imperialising history (Harley, 1992; Smith and Godlewska,1994), but they are technologies that can be deployed to different ends.

One of the points of interest of the film, *Sa-I-Gu*, is that it maintains the tension between a political alliance with others who are excluded from full citizenship rights in the United States and the particularity of Korean-Americans' experiences. Their experience is not mapped simply onto the experiences of others. The title, *Sa-I-Gu*, means 4.29 or April 29. It follows 'after the manner of naming other events in Korean history ... [as in] 4.19 (Sa-il-ku), or April 19, 1960, when the first student movement in the world to overthrow a government began in South Korea. The ironic similarity between 4.19 and 4.29 does not escape most Korean Americans' (Kim, 1993). Lowe (1996) argues that this allusion to Korean nationalism through the naming of the film is 'not a direct transference of Korean nationalism but a discontinuous rearticulation of it that includes the crucial consideration of the racialization of Korean immigrants in the United States as workers of color' (p423). These subtle mappings of continuities and discontinuities, which involve a partial folding of one geography into another, are acts of translation and articulation that respect the particularities of history and geography.

The metaphor of the fold evokes Rose's (1993) discussion of paradoxical space: the location of being in two locations, both inside and outside, simultaneously. Rose uses the concept to theorise the subjectivity of women and other marginalised groups that are never fully insiders in the spaces that they inhabit. It is not a comfortable space but it can be a productive one if we take seriously Lara's (1998) claim that the success of the women's and civil rights movements in the United States in extending the meaning of universality depended on strategic negotiations of particularity and universality, on the paradoxes of being the same and different, on being both insiders and outsiders. Rose locates particular subjects in paradoxical spatial locations, but we might rethink paradoxical space as a feminist tool. A concrete example of the political potential of paradoxical space is provided in Lowe's (2000) description of the empirical research that she and Laura Pulido have done with Mexican *maquiladora* workers on sexual harassment in the workplace. With the knowledge that no Latin American country has a national law that defines sexual harassment as a human rights violation, the data from the workers' survey may be used in a struggle to test whether international law will extend relevant US Civil Rights legislation to subjects working in US plants outside of the United States. It is the ambiguity of the US firms' position: both inside and outside the US, that opens this opportunity for feminist organising to extend 'universal' rights for women from one context to the other. Another fascinating example of this use of paradoxical space involves the recent conviction of a French citizen for sexually violating an 11-year-old girl in Thailand while on holiday as a sex tourist. A 1998 law authorises French courts to try 'sexual aggression committed abroad' even when the deed is not considered a crime in the country in which it is committed. As Llosa (2001) notes, if this principle could be extended to other countries from which sex tourists originate, this could have a significant impact on the sexual exploitation of children in developing countries.

Gibson, Law and McKay (2001) provide another example of feminist organising that works with geographical difference to extend universal rights, in this case for Filipina contract workers. They oppose two identities given to Filipina overseas contract workers: the identity of 'heroine' that circulates within a nationalist discourse in recognition of the significance of domestic workers' remittances as a major source of foreign currency for the Philippines' economy; and the identity of 'victim' of capitalist development popularised by many non-governmental organisations (NGOs) working with contract migrants and leftist critics of the Philippine state. They argue that geographical mobility, interpreted through a non-essentialist reading of class processes, places overseas migrant workers in a multitude of class positions that they can use strategically to reposition themselves and, potentially, the Philippines' economy. They are particularly interested in the 'Reintegration Program' of the Asian Migrant Centre in Hong Kong, through which savings from work as domestic workers (which Gibson *et al.* classify as a slave class position) in one context are being pooled to invest in collectively-owned cooperatives (a communal class process) in the Philippines. Unlike the stereotype of victim, '[t]his NGO's politics are based on a vision of the subject as full of potentiality rather than lack' and make strategic use of geographical uneven development as a means of overcoming it. The women's activities have the intent and effect of extending economic rights in both locations, within the particularity of their class positions in each. As women acquire new skills and economic relations as entrepreneurial businesswomen, they develop resources to fight for their rights as workers in Hong Kong. Their understanding of their work experiences in Hong Kong are then used to build social values beyond profit maximising into their business ventures in the Philippines.

Geographical translations

The contested politics of committed feminist organising of Filipina overseas contract workers – the question of whether to cast Filipina contract workers as victims or mobile class subjects – brings into relief the difficult, negotiated process of building feminist alliances. The process of translation across cultural groups always carries the colonising potential of one group imposing their (e.g. first world feminist) version of universality on another. Drawing on Spivak, Butler (2000a) urges an anti-colonial mode of translation that marks the non-convergence of discourses and the ruptures that defy translation and exposes 'the limits of what the dominant language can handle' (p37; see also Pratt, 2000; Rose, 1997).

For feminist geographers this would mean that we consider the limits of our geographical readings as we enter conversations with other groups in other locations (of identification and place). Wendy Brown (2000) argues that subjects of gender, class, nationality, race and sexuality are created through 'different histories, different mechanisms and sites of power, different discursive formations, different regulatory schemes' (p235). We can add: different geographies. These different forms of subjection do not operate independently of each other, but their particularity is important and makes understandable the different meanings given to the same geography. Brown (2000), for example, cites privacy as a geographical category that works differently for those in differently marked identities. For many feminists privacy is a suspect category that depoliticises 'many of the constituent activities and injuries of women – reproduction, domestic assault, incest, unremunerated household labor, and compulsory emotional and sexual service to men' (p236).[3] But if we take seriously Brown's argument that powers that produce socially subordinate subjects occur in radically different modalities that 'touch different surfaces and depths, form different bodies and psyches' (p236), then we can expect that claims to privacy rights will operate within a different context for women who are not middle class, heterosexual and white. We can understand the strong defence of home and privacy that has been made by African American women in these terms (e.g. hooks, 1990, Williams, 1991). The defence of privacy from the perspective of gay men again operates differently, in relation to a different modality of power. Consider David Bell's (1995) argument about the need to protect the intimacy of gay men from the intrusion of the state. Feminists who attempt to build consensus about universals across differences will need to work with such ruptures in translation. These ruptures are important moments because they show us the limits of our thinking. The different positions on privacy indicate some dimensions of privacy that white, heterosexual, middle-class feminists have taken for granted.

We might think more fully, not only about the limits of our knowledge of geography, but the limits of our knowledges across geography. Appadurai (2000) has noted the disjunction between the knowledge of globalisation and the globalisation of knowledge, the latter sadly trailing the former. In his opinion, this is because Western intellectuals have failed to appreciate the extent to which what we understand as research is culturally determined and narrowly prescriptive. He argues that there are other traditions of doing research and making knowledge claims in other parts of the world, and invites a conversation about what counts as knowledge, about plural communities of judgement and accountability, and how we might translate across them. These are concerns that feminist geographers have begun to address in creative ways. One example is the pairing of Okoko's (1999) analysis of gendered responses to widespread environmental degradation in the rural communities of Ibeno, Nigeria with commentaries by three Anglo/American feminists. This begins a conversation in print across an significant North/South divide. Both Robson (1999) and Ramirez (2000) reflect on the difficulty faced by women of the south in publishing in international journals because of the lack of material resources and access to journals. They also note a certain blindness on the part of northern feminists to the theoretical analyses of southern feminists, and a tendency to envision the latter as atheoretical empiricists. This repeats a colonising posture that casts southern women as informants and northern women as the intellectually superior theorists. We will need to continue to explore creative ways of building a postcolonial feminism through a critical reappraisal of our writing and publishing practices.

Conclusion

I want to return to the expansionary portrayal of feminist geography with which I began: a feminist geography that is about the production of difference, all differences; and my parallel worries that post-structuralist critiques of foundational categories and principles open feminism to the narrowing and destabilising set of manoeuvers deployed by Professor Rackoff. My present perspective is that both my and Professor Rackoff's portrayals of feminism repeat the same mistake, the mistake of compressing histories and geographies: in the first, feminism colonises other differences; in the latter, the fullness of the careful alliances that must be developed within feminism are ignored and feminism is collapsed and restricted to a narrow set of other identifications. I have drawn upon Butler's theorising about the contingency of agency and the paradoxical relation between universal norms and particularity to find a place between these two extremes, a place that foregrounds geography.

Feminist politics is alert to the suspicion that women are not fully included in the universalisms of our day. A feminist geography not only details the geographies that lull us into submission by naturalising differences; it is a persuasive resource for building alliances among women and with other marginalised groups. It is a resource that is a persistent reminder of the particularity that inhabits universal claims, that urges careful and necessarily incomplete translations, and insists on the difference that difference can make.

Acknowledgements

I thank Trevor Barnes, Phil Crang and Juanita Sundberg for reading a first draft of this paper and their help in clarifying my argument.

Notes

1. Butler draws upon Derrida's reformulation of the performative to avoid an implication of the autonomous liberal subject that may be drawn from J L Austin's account of performative language: this is, the subject has the power to call phenomena into being through his or her utterances. In Derrida's reformulation, the performative

utterance is a derivative citation rather than a founding act, and the speaker is neither the 'origin or owner of what is said' (Butler, 1993, p227). When a religious or state official, for example, brings the social relation of marriage into being through the performative speech act: 'I pronounce you man and wife', this is because it calls upon a history of convention, and a chain of previous citations.

2. They disagree about the appropriate spatial metaphor to describe universality (empty space as opposed to non place). Butler (2000a) rejects the metaphor of empty space on the grounds that it implies that universality is exterior to politics; Laclau disagrees.

3. Oddly forgetful of this point, Brown herself (1995) has elaborated an extended critique of Patricia Williams' defence of individual privacy rights, which was articulated from Williams' perspective as an African American woman.

Bibliography

Allen, A (1998) 'Power Trouble: Performativity as Critical Theory', *Constellations*, 5, 456–471.

Anzaldua, G (1987) *Borderlands/La Frontera: The New Mestiza*, San Francisco: Spinsters/Aunt Lute Press.

Appadurai, A (2000) 'Grassroots Globalization and the Research Imagination', *Public Culture*, 12(1), 1–19.

Bell, D and Valentine, G (eds) (1995) *Mapping Desire*, London and New York: Routledge.

Bell, D (1995) 'Perverse Dynamics, Sexual Citizenship and the Transformation of Intimacy' in Bell, D and Valentine, G (eds) *Mapping Desire*, London and New York: Routledge.

Benhabib, S (1995) 'Feminism and Postmodernism: An Uneasy Alliance' in Benhabib, S, Butler, J, Cornell, D and Fraser, N (eds) *Feminist Contentions: A Philosopical Exchange*, New York: Routledge.

Brown, W (1995) *States of Injury*, Princeton: Princeton University Press.

Brown, W (2000) 'Suffering Rights as Paradoxes', *Constellations*, 7, 230–254.

Butler, J (1990) *Gender Trouble: Feminism and the Subversion of Identity*, New York: Routledge.

Butler, J (1993) *Bodies That Matter: On the Discursive Limits of 'Sex'*, New York: Routledge.

Butler, J (1995) 'For a Careful Reading', in Benhabib, S, Butler, J, Cornell, D, and Fraser, N (eds) *Feminist Contentions: A Philosophical Exchange*, New York: Routledge.

Butler, J (1997) *The Psychic Life of Power: Theories of Subjection*, Stanford: Stanford University Press.

Butler, J (2000a) 'Restaging the Universal: Hegemony and the Limits of Formalism' in *Contingency, Hegemony, Universality: Contemporary Dialogues on the Left*, Butler, J, Laclau, E and Zizek, S, London and New York: Verso.

Butler, J (2000b) 'Competing Universalities' in *Contingency, Hegemony, Universality: Contemporary Dialogues on the Left*, Butler, J, Laclau, E and Zizek, S, London and New York: Verso.

Choy, C, Kim, E and Kim-Gibson, D S (producers) *1993 Sa-I-Gu: From Korean Women's Perspectives*. Distributed by National Asian American Telecommunications Association, 346 Ninth Street, San Francisco, CA 94103.

Chun, W H K (1999) 'Unbearable Witness: Toward a Politics of Listening', *Differences: A Journal of Feminist Cultural Studies*, 11,112–149.

Ferguson, K (1993) *The Man Question: Visions of Subjectivity in Feminist Theory*, Berkeley: University of California Press.

Foucault, M (1978) *The History of Sexuality, Volume One*, tr. R. Hurley, New York: Vintage.

Foucault, M (ed.) (1980) *Herculine Barbin, Being the Recently Discovered Memoirs of a Nineteenth-Century Hermaphodite*, tr. R. McDongall, New York: Colophon.

Freeze, C (2000) 'Klan' furor mars massacre vigils', *The Globe and Mail*, December 7 2000, A1, A8.

Gibson, K, Law, L and McKay, D (2001) 'Beyond Heroes and Victims: Filipina Contract Migrants, Economic Activism and Class Transformations', *International Feminist Journal of Politics*, 3, 365–86.

Gregson, N and Rose, G (2000) 'Taking Butler Elsewhere: performativities, spatialities and subjectivities', *Environment and Planning D: Society and Space*, 18(4), 433–452.

Hanson, S and Pratt, G (1995) *Gender, Work and Space*, London and New York: Routledge.

Harley, J B (1992) 'Deconstructing the map' in Barnes, T J and Duncan, J S (eds) *Writing Worlds: Discourses, Text and Metaphor*, London: Routledge.

Harvey, D (2000) 'Cosmopolitanism and the Banality of Geographical Evils', *Public Culture*, 12, 529–564.

hooks, B (1990) *Yearning: Race, Gender, and Cultural Politics*, Toronto: Between the Lines.

Kaplan, C (1987) 'Deterritorializations: the rewriting of home and exile in Western feminist discourse', *Cultural Critique*, 6, 187–198.

Kim, E (1993) 'Home is Where the Han Is' in Gooding-Williams, R (ed.) *Reading Rodney King, Reading Urban Uprisings*, New York: Routledge.

Kwan, M-P (2002) 'Introduction: feminist geography and GIS', *Gender, Place and Culture*, 3, 261–262.

Laclau, E (1996) *Emancipation(s)*, London: Verso.

Lara, M P (1998) *Moral Textures: Feminist Narratives in the Public Sphere*, Cambridge: Polity Press.

Llosa, M V (2001) 'Crossing the Moral Boundary', *The New York Times*, January 7, WK 17.

Lowe, L (1996) 'Imagining Los Angeles in the Production of Multiculturalism' in Gordon, A and Newfield, C (eds) *Mapping MultiCulturalism*, Minneapolis: University of Minnesota Press.

Lowe, L (2000) 'Toward a Critical Modernity', *Anglistica*, 4, 69–90.

Mackenzie, S (1989) 'Women in the City' in Peet, R and Thrift, N (eds) *New Models in Geography, Vol. 2*. London: Unwin Hyman.

McLafferty, S and Preston, V (1992) 'Spatial Mismatch and Labor Market Segmentation for African-American and Latina Women', *Economic Geography*, 68, 406–431.

McLafferty, S and Preston, V (1997) 'Gender, Race, and the Determinants of Commuting: New York in 1990', *Urban Geography*, 18, 192–212.

Mitchell, K (1997) 'Different diasporas and the hype of hybridity', *Environment and Planning D: Society and Space*, 15, 533–553.

Monk, J and Hanson, S (1982) 'On not excluding half the human in geography', *Professional Geographer*, 34, 11–23.

Nelson, L (1999) 'Bodies (and Spaces) do Matter: the limits of performativity', *Gender, Place and Culture*, 6(4), 331–353.

Okoko, E (1999) 'Women and Environmental Change in the Niger Delta, Nigeria: evidence from Ibeno', *Gender, Place and Culture*, 6(4), 373–378.

Pratt, G and Hanson, S (1994) 'Geography and the construction of difference', *Gender, Place and Culture*, 1, 5–29.

Pratt, G (1999) 'Geographies of Identity and Difference: Marking Boundaries' in Massey, D, Allen, J and Sarre, P (eds) *Human Geography Today*, Cambridge: Polity Press.

Pratt, G (2000) 'Research Performances', *Environment and Planning D: Society and Space*, 18(5), 639–651.

Ramirez, B (2000) 'The politics of constructing an international group of critical geographers and a common space of action', *Environment and Planning D: Society and Space*, 18(5), 537–543.

Robson, E (1999) 'Problematising Oil and Gender in Nigeria', *Gender, Place and Culture*, 6(4), 379–390.

Rose, G (1993) *Feminism and Geography: The Limits of Geographical Knowledge*, Minneapolis: University of Minnesota Press.

Rose, G (1997) 'Situating knowledges: postcoloniality, reflexivities and other tactics', *Progress in Human Geography*, 21, 305–320.

Seager, J (1997) *The State of the Women in the World Atlas*. New rev. second edition, London: Penguin.

Smith, N and Katz, C (1993) 'Grounding metaphor: towards a spatialized politics', in Keith, M and Pile, S (eds) *Place and the Politics of Culture*, London: Routledge.

Smith, N and Godlewska, A (1994) (eds) *Geography and Empire*, Cambridge, MA. and Oxford: Blackwell.

Tang, E (2000) 'Collateral Damage: Southeast Asian Poverty in the United States', *Social Text*, 18, 55–79.

Thrift, N and Dewsbury, J-D (2000) 'Dead geographies – and how to make them live', *Environment and Planning D: Society and Space*, 18 (4), 411–432.

Valentine, G (1993) '(Hetero)sexing space: lesbian perceptions and experiences of everyday spaces', *Environment and Planning D: Society and Space*, 11, 395–413.

Webster, F (2000) 'The Politics of Sex and Gender: Benhabib and Butler Debate Subjectivity', *Hypatia*, 15, 1–22.

Weir, A (1996) *Sacrificial Logics: Feminist Theory and the Critique of Identity*, New York: Routledge.

Williams, Patricia J (1991) *The Alchemy of Race and Rights*, Cambridge, Mass.: Harvard University Press.

Wolff, J (1993) 'On the road again: metaphors of travel in cultural criticism', *Cultural Studies*, 7, 224–239.

Wright, M (1998) 'Maquiladora Mestizas and a Feminist Border Politics: Revisiting Anzaldua', *Hypatia*, 13, 114–131.

Wright, M W (1999a) 'The politics of relocation: gender, nationality, and value in a Mexican macquiladora', *Environment and Planning A* 31, 1601–1617.

Wright, M W (1999b) 'The Dialectics of Still Life: Murder, Women and Maquiladoras', *Public Culture*, 11, 453–474.

Zerilli, L M G (1998) 'This Universalism Which is Not One', *Diacritics*, 28, 3–20.

8

Poststructuralist geographies: the essential selection

Marcus A Doel

'We gotta get back into the goddam world somehow. If we don't, we'll regret it. Maybe not today—'

'What? We'll forget it?'

'No, I said—'

'What?'

'Never mind.'[1]

Poststructuralist geography: passwords and driftworks

'What strikes me as odd is not that everything is falling apart, but that so much continues to be there. It takes a long time for a world to vanish, much longer than you would think.'[2]

1. Contrary to popular opinion, **we have no *special* (some would say 'unnatural') interest in language**. We are not besotted with texts, writing, signs, images and such like. We do not believe that since reality is only accessible to us through language, then reality *itself* must be lost to us in language; that all we have are *signs* of things, rather than the things themselves; that having been emancipated from their bondage to an élite band of actually existing real-world referents (such as people, places, events and objects), signs will at last be free to float in the void, enjoying untroubled and lazy halcyon days. We are not locked into the so-called 'prison-house of language'. Still less do we think that since reality is constructed out of language it is dematerialised and desubstantialised. There is no danger of the world falling into desuetude. We do not take the view that everything is made out of language: that everything is 'discourse,' for example. So, when Jacques Derrida declares that 'there is nothing outside the text' [*il n'y a pas de hors-texte*], do not imagine that he subscribes to any of the above.[3] 'There is', 'nothing', 'outside', 'the text' are not especially concerned with language: they have much more to do with bringing the spacing and timing of events to the fore, logistical considerations that are ordinarily allowed to slip into the background of the taken-for-granted. 'There is nothing outside the text' means 'there is

nothing outside context'. No text without context. No event without spatialisation and temporalisation. And just to show how far we are from cultivating either a 'theology of the Text'[4] or promulgating 'a new "idealism" … of the text,'[5] suffice to say that 'we can call "context" the entire "real-history-of-the-world,'' if you like.'[6]

2. Language, sign-systems, representations and discourses interest us neither more nor less than anything else. If they appear to do so, then it is only because they happen to provide opportune materials for some of our most well-publicised experiments. So, let us be crystal clear on the following point: **our equalitarianism knows no bounds**. We are willing to embrace everything. Nothing is privileged. Nothing is held in reserve.

> 'What I call "text" implies all the structures called "real", "economic", "historical", socio-institutional, in short: all possible referents. … That does not mean that all referents are suspended, denied, or enclosed in a book, as people have claimed, or have been naive enough to believe and to have accused me of believing. But it does mean that every referent, all reality has the structure of a differential trace, and that one cannot refer to this "real" except in an interpretive experience. The latter neither yields meaning nor assumes it except in a movement of differential referring. That's all.'[7]

3. If reality is structured as a language, as a text, and as a context, then it is in the sense of a **differential trace**: signs refer to other signs; flows refer to other flows; materials refer to other materials; encounters refer to other encounters; events refer to other events; forces refer to other forces; and so on. And note that we do not say that reality is structured 'like' a language, text or context: this is no mere metaphor, analogy or pedagogic and heuristic device. Whatever there is takes place as a differential trace. Hence our resolve to decline all forms of pointillism – 'I don't like points'[8] – so that we may 'never miss a twist or a fold'.[9] For we will only unlock the power of poststructuralist geography to the extent that we embrace nothing but relations and co-relations, their folding and unfolding.[10] 'The model for the sciences of matter is the "origami", as the Japanese philosopher might say, or the art of folding.'[11] Consequently, poststructuralist geography is a kind of spatial science, one that is maddened and radicalised by the diabolical twists and turns of so-many differential relations.[12] 'One does indeed find folds everywhere.'[13]

4. Obviously, the differential trace is **manifold** – it can be folded in many ways – and given its heterogeneous materials and varied complexion it is certainly not 'of a piece'. And since we are speaking of differential traces and *nothing but* differential traces, they are necessarily without a last resort: there is no transcendental signifier; no final instance; no settling of accounts; no definitive judgements; no ultimate way of being. Hereinafter, everything will have been **relative**: that is to say, everything will have been related and co-related to other differential relations which can themselves be ramified and pullulated to infinity and beyond. We will never be finished with the work of contextualising and recontextualising. We are reminded of one of Gilles Deleuze's throwaway lines: 'Speaking always as geographers …'.[14] For example, the novelist Georges Perec takes an instant in the everyday life of an apartment block at 11 Rue Simon-Crubelier in the Monceau district of Paris: the twenty-third of June

nineteen seventy-five, a moment before eight o'clock in the evening. In 99 chapters he attempts to lay out all of the differential traces that make up *this* instant:

> 'CHAPTER ONE
>
> *On the Stairs, 1*
>
> Yes, it could begin this way, right here, just like that, in a rather slow and ponderous way, in this neutral place that belongs to all and to none, where people pass by almost without seeing each other, where the life of the building regularly and distantly resounds. What happens behind the flats' heavy doors can most often be perceived only through those fragmented echoes, those splinters, remnants, shadows, those first moves or incidents or accidents that happen in what are called "common areas", soft little sounds damped by the red woollen carpet, embryos of communal life which never go further than the landing. The inhabitants of a single building live a few inches from each other, they are separated by a mere partition wall, they share the same spaces repeated along each corridor, they perform the same movements at the same time, turning on a tap, flushing the water closet, switching on a light, laying the table, a few dozen simultaneous existences repeated from storey to storey, from building to building, from street to street.'[15]

Not withstanding his recourse to a structural formula that would remain constant across the various cases, Perec's task of exposition proves interminable: 'I owe myself infinitely to each and every singularity'.[16] *On the one hand*, despite the constriction of place, the traces of the event spill out to embroil innumerable other spaces both within and without 11 Rue Simon-Crubelier:

> 'He would paint himself painting, and already you would be able to see the ladles and the knives, the serving spoons and door handles, the books and newspapers, the rugs, jugs, firedogs, umbrella stands, dishstands, radios, bedside lamps, telephones, mirrors, toothbrushes, washing lines, playing cards, cigarette stubs in ashtrays, family photographs in insect-repellent frames, flowers in vases, radiator shelves, potato mashers, floor protectors, bunches of keys in saucers of small change, sorbet makers, catboxes, racks of mineral water, cradles, kettles, alarm clocks, Pigeon lamps, and universal spanners. And …'[17]

On the other hand, despite the constriction of time, the traces of the event spill out into innumerable other times:

> 'CHAPTER NINETY-FOUR
>
> *On the Stairs, 12*
>
> *Draft Inventory of some of the things*
> *found on the stairs over the years*
> *(second and final instalment)*
>
> 25 A set of "Fact Sheets" on dairy farming in the Poitou-Charentes region
> a macintosh bearing the brand name 'Caliban' made in London by Hemmings & Condell,
>
> six varnished cork glass-mats portraying the sights of Paris: the Elysée palace, Parliament House, the Senate Building, Notre-Dame, the Law Courts, and the Invalides,

> a necklace made from the spine of an alosa,
>
> a photograph taken by a second-rate professional of a naked baby lying prone on a sky-blue tasselled nylon cushion,
>
> a rectangular piece of card, about the size of a visiting card, printed on one side: *Have you ever seen the Devil with a nightcap on?* and on the other side: *No! I've never seen the Devil with a nightcap on!*
>
> a programme for the *Caméra* cinema, 70 Rue de l'Assomption, Paris 16, for the month of February 1960:
>
> 3–9: *The Criminal Life of Archibaldo de la Cruz,*
>
> BY LUIS BUÑUEL
>
> 10–16: JACQUES DEMY FESTIVAL ….'[18]

5. When one attends to the *fabric* or *structure* of differential relations, the task stretches out before us like an infinitely receding horizon. 'How joyous the notion that, try as we may, we cannot do other than fail and fail absolutely and that the task will remain always before us, like a meaning for our lives.'[19] Establishing the context of any event – that is to say, of any portion of 'the entire real-history-of-the-world' – becomes unsaturable, unlimitable and uncontrollable since 'the total milieu … is constantly being reinscribed and thrown back into play.'[20] At each and every turn, a labyrinth of time complicates a labyrinth of space.[21] Such is Jorges Luis Borges' and Franz Kafka's duplicity. *On the one hand*: 'all my surroundings seem filled with agitation'. *And on the other hand*: 'But all remained unchanged'.[22] This duplicity lets us glimpse the secret passwords of poststructuralist geography: 'and', 'but'. They enable us to follow the cracking open of the event.

6. Everything **takes place** (and note the vacillation of this phrase between what is in place and what is swept out of place; between what is off-set and what is set off; between what takes *place* and what *takes* place) by way – relay, delay – of a disjoined and disadjusted context that remains perpetually open to being worked over by other differential relations. To the extent that we affirm the ineluctability of these iterable and innumerable forces of destabilisation and differentiation, we will henceforth practise an unstable and undecidable form of structuralism. Poststructuralism boils down to this: '*One cannot assume a position* on the twisted, shock-ridden, electrified labyrinthine band. One's got to get this into one's head'.[23]

7. But what about poststructuralism's position *vis-à-vis* structuralism? Let's start with the obvious: poststructuralism comes *after* structuralism. Once we are done with structuralism, poststructuralism is what responds to the call: 'And *then* …?'[24] So, we may take up poststructuralism once we have finished with structuralism: once we have completed, exhausted or abandoned structuralism. On this basis, poststructuralism will offer something else: something different. Consequently, do not expect poststructuralism to have anything whatsoever to do with structuralism. Having broken with structuralism – having renounced all connection – we might just as well call poststructuralism 'anything-whatsoever'. Postmodernism, perhaps. Or postindustrialism. Or humanism gone berserk. Or deconstruction, schizoanalysis, idealism, etc. With the slate wiped clean, we would be able to begin all over again: right here, right now. By a strange twist of fate such a poststructuralism would usher in Year Zero at the dawn

(yawn?) of a new millennium. We would then be ideally placed for the task of envisaging and manifestoing for a new kind of geography rising Phoenix-like from the ashes of by-gone ways of doing geography. 'If we don't, we'll regret it. Maybe not today –'

8. 'What? We'll forget it?' Surely not! For when one is done with structuralism, the call 'And then… ?' must be taken as a plea for continuation, as if structuralism had been unexpectedly interrupted or broken off; as if, having been seduced by and interpolated into the structuralist universe, the dénouement and comeuppance had been snatched from us. Poststructuralism would then be the *continuation* of structuralism *after the fact*. Like Donald Barthelme's postindustrial reworking of the everyday banality of thirty-something *Snow White*[25] or Robert Coover's old-man *Pinocchio in Venice*,[26] we will encounter the characters, situations, and stakes of structuralism elsewhere. In phenomenology, perhaps. Or empiricism. Or humanism gone berserk. Or deconstruction, schizoanalysis, idealism, etc. Such a poststructuralism – a structuralism postponed, relayed or despatched – would respond to the call 'And *then*…?' by sifting through what is ostensibly not structuralist in order to recover what will have become of structuralism: to snatch the dénouement and comeuppance *back from* such things as structuration theory, critical realism, actor-network theory, etc. Always in hot pursuit, the poststructuralist would be doggedly after structuralism, even when its prey runs to ground. 'If we don't, we'll regret it. Maybe not today –'.

9. 'What? We'll forget it?' 'And *then* …?' Or else, not the mere *continuation* of structuralism after the fact, but the continuation of structuralism *by other means*: an othering of structuralism; structuralism becoming estranged from itself. Like the frustrated reader of Italo Calvino's novel *If on a Winter's Night a Traveller*, one will encounter a continual mutation and differentiation without origin or end.[27]

10. Let's return to the obvious: poststructuralism comes *after* structuralism. 'And *then*…?' Poststructuralism as: Indifference? Forgetting? Continuation? Othering? Anything-whatsoever? From the off, then, we might expect five visions and five manifestos (at least). But this is only to take account of poststructuralism's relation to structuralism. In addition (assuming that it is a matter of addition, rather than, say, of multiplication or differentiation), one must take account of poststructuralism's other relations (which are innumerable). Putting all of this to one side, let's simply agree that poststructuralism comes *after* structuralism, but this 'after' will have to resonate in several disparate registers and be read on a surrealist clock lent to us by Salvador Dalí (a clock with warped face, melted hands and dislocated numbers). Despite picking up on the obvious thing, the *timing* of poststructuralism turns out to be problematic.[28] This should be understood in the Althusserian sense: poststructuralism *poses problems* for timing.[29] So, perhaps we would be better to pick up not on the *timing* of poststructuralism, but on the *spacing* of poststructuralism. Poststructuralism comes after structuralism – and goes after structuralism. It comes from behind. It takes structuralism from behind.[30] It is off-set at a distance and set off in motion. 'And *then*…?' Poststructuralism as: Laggard? Decrepit? Youthful? Suspenseful? Twisted? 'Never mind.'[31]

11. Contrary to popular opinion, we do not wish to elude the gravitational pull of the world in order to float freely amongst signs and images. Rather, we affirm the falling back of signs and images into the play of the world. We remain – as always – resolutely

materialist. So, we are struck by the *force* of signs, by the *intensity* of images, and by the *affects* of language. 'The evil demon of language resides in its capacity to become object, where one expects a subject and meaning.'[32] 'Writing is a flow among others; it enjoys no special privilege and enters into relations of current and counter-current, of backwash with other flows – the flows of shit, sperm, speech, action, eroticism, money, politics, etc.'[33] So, we no longer recognise anything other than material and immaterial **forces**, the differential relations between forces, and their incessant shuffling. Whatever there may be, it always *strikes* someone or other as an articulation of force.

12. As fanatical materialists, **we are struck by everything** – nothing will be set aside from the play of force; nothing will be spirited away onto a higher plane or exorcised into a nether-world. One does not have to be a magician, market-maker or medium to know that onto-theology and diabolism act in our world. It is true that we take up signs, words, images, quantities, figures, maps, photographs, money, hypertext, gardening advice, lipstick traces, the exquisite corpse and so on and so forth – but we take them up as force: as strikes and counter-strikes; as blows and counter-blows. 'Representation no longer exists; there's only action.'[34]

13. Being struck by everything, **we hold nothing in reserve**. Of course, this does not prevent values and judgements from raining down on us: what is said to be true, proper, necessary, just, good, beautiful, tasteful, apt, timely, essential, etc. We are reminded of Raoul Vaneigem's taunting of consumer society:

> 'Today the promises of the old society of production are raining down on our heads in an avalanche of consumer goods – the instruments of comfort, all equally revolutionary according to the publicity handouts – that nobody is likely to call manna from heaven. You can hardly believe in the magical power of *gadgets*.'[35]

So too with values and judgements. Though they reign over us, they are not manna from heaven. They are fragments of practice – one or two snatched from an infinite array – that are thrown up into the sky before falling back in order to constrain and regulate other fragments of practice. Take your hand: it is capable of an infinite number of practices – to shake other hands, to stroke Formica worktops, to underscore a gesture, to be cold, to hold a cigarette, to cut and be cut, to labour … Hence the folly – or the despotism – of trying to make one or two of these practices its essential property. For example: 'Stop! Look! A hand *is* made for working'. We are struck by everything, but only as 'passwords' for 'driftworks,' never as 'order-words' that must be obeyed. We may even subscribe to an essential selection – on condition that it has built-in obsolescence.

> 'The essential thing is not to become inured. For habits are deadly. Even if it is for the hundredth time, you must encounter each thing as if you have never known it before. No matter how many times, it must always be the first time. This is next to impossible, I realize, but it is an absolute rule.'[36]

14. In *The Communist Manifesto* of 1848, Karl Marx and Frederick Engels thought that they knew what a hand was good for: 'WORKING MEN OF ALL COUNTRIES, UNITE!' 'THE PROLETARIANS HAVE NOTHING TO LOSE BUT THEIR CHAINS.'[37] And we

understand the tactical reasons for such a call to arms. So long as hands are put to work in the interests of capital accumulation, these hands will remain estranged and alienated from themselves. However, this condition of estrangement and alienation is far from being *the whole game*. The labouring hand is indeed one element in play – amongst others. But in seeking to loosen the grip of exploitation and alienation, Marx and Engels risked collapsing the infinite potential of what hands are capable of doing to a single imperative: 'Labour!' In doing so, they forgot what *other* stakes were in play. This emaciation of the virtual is especially dangerous given that the labouring-hand is the source of value; that in being set to work – or in setting itself to work – it makes value, use-value and exchange-value possible. Hence Jean Baudrillard's realisation that far from challenging and opposing the logic of capitalism, Marxism is not only its accomplice and alibi, it is also its most devoted fanatic: 'Hands of the world unite. Work! Labour! Be useful!' Hence our preference for a *desiring*-revolution.[38] We are neither seduced by the *mirror* of production[39] nor tremble with shame before the accusation of having created 'a waste of space'[40] filled with nothing but 'theoretical glitter'[41] in which all of our critical energy is squandered[42] (a style of working and living that would no doubt be ideal for geographers who act like ballroom dancers, disco dancers or glam-rockers, but dreadful for those of us who prefer the spaced-out 'zombie dance'[43] of Goths, punks, psycho-billies and ravers: even more so than it pains those who prefer to jerk about in suits and ties as if they were at the wedding or sale of the century). So, we have absolutely 'nothing to admit'[44] – least of all to those who dress up politics and morality as fashion advice: 'You can't go out like *THAT!*'; 'Do we look apolitical and amoral in *THIS*?' Instead, we prefer to follow the lead of Marcel Duchamp and fabricate 'celibate machines', paying 'homage to their pointlessness'.[45] But do not think that this is an easy trick to pull off:

> 'I have tried to think several times of an apartment in which there would be a useless room, absolutely and intentionally useless. It wouldn't be a junkroom, it wouldn't be an extra bedroom, or a corridor, or a cubby-hole, or a corner. It would be a functionless space. It would serve for nothing, relate to nothing. For all my efforts, I found it impossible to follow this idea through to the end. … A space without a function. Not "without any precise function" but precisely without any function; not pluri-functional (everyone knows how to do that), but a-functional.'[46]

An infernal machine is being assembled: 'the racing of a discursive machinery….'[47] For while we are not wholly averse to being *put to use* and *minimising the expenditure of energy*, we will only tolerate these things as passwords and not as order-words; as phases of play and not as the essence of the game.[48] There is no overarching rule for the game – least of all usefulness, efficacy and efficiency. 'Now, my question is this. What happens when a thing no longer performs its function?'[49] We are reminded of Bartleby, the grey-eyed scrivener,[50] whose disinclination to have work verified – and thereby *valorised*[51] – destabilises the established libidinal economy of the legal chambers in which he works to the point of collapse:

> 'being much hurried to complete a small affair I had in hand, I abruptly called to Bartleby. In my haste and natural expectancy of instant compliance, I sat with my head bent over the original on my desk, and my right hand sideways, and somewhat

> nervously extended with the copy, so that, immediately upon emerging from his retreat, Bartleby might snatch it and proceeded to business without the least delay.
>
> In this very attitude did I sit when I called to him, rapidly stating what it was I wanted him to do – namely, to examine a small paper with me. Imagine my surprise, nay, my consternation, when, without moving from his privacy, Bartleby, in a singularly mild, firm voice, replied, "I would prefer not to." '[52]

From the moment that the lawyer commands Bartleby to engage in verification, valorisation and judgement, all entreaties for him 'to be a little reasonable'[53] will be taken up with the same indefinite and dysfunctional reply: 'I would prefer not to.' 'You *will* not?' asks the lawyer. 'I *prefer* not', replies Bartleby.[54] The advance withdrawal of Bartleby's formula 'hollows out an ever expanding zone of indiscernibility or indetermination between some nonpreferred activities and a preferable activity. All particularity, all reference is abolished. The formula annihilates 'copying'. The only thing that remains is suspense. Bartleby 'can survive only by whirling in a suspense that keeps everyone at a distance'; whence 'the vertiginous impression, each time, that everything is starting over again from zero'.[55] Indeed, the more immobile and passive he becomes, the more he sets the world of social production in motion and agitation: 'Nothing so aggravates an earnest person as a passive resistance.'[56] '"*Prefer not*, eh?" gritted Nippers – "I'd *prefer* him, if I were you, sir," addressing me – "I'd *prefer* him; I'd give him preferences, the stubborn mule! What is it, sir, pray, that he *prefers* not to do now?" Bartleby moved not a limb.'[57] Bartleby has suspended all action – and yet everything remains on edge, teetering on the brink of delirium:

> 'Somehow, of late, I had got into the way of involuntarily using the word 'prefer' upon all sorts of not exactly suitable occasions. And I trembled to think that my contact with the scrivener had already and seriously affected me in a mental way. … The next day I noticed that Bartleby did nothing but stand at his window in his dead-wall reverie.'[58]

By *neither* accepting *nor* refusing, Bartleby frustrates a 'logic of expectation' by responding with the 'superior irrationalism' of a 'logic of preference.' Even though he seems to be ensconced in his hermitage and shut off from the world around him, Bartleby remains engaged in *collective* action and *social* production (or rather, anti-production).

> 'As days passed on, I became considerably reconciled to Bartleby. His steadiness, his freedom from all dissipation, his incessant industry (except when he chose to throw himself into a standing revery behind his screen), his great stillness, his unalterableness of demeanor under all circumstances, made him a valuable acquisition. One prime thing was this – he was always there – first in the morning, continually through the day, and the last at night.'[59]

But he participates without copying or belonging: he remains indifferently and indefinitely detached. He has become a suspended transformer. One might say that Bartleby has found a way of working without labouring: 'nature does not labour: … it *creates*'.[60]

15. In addition to the reduction of hands and bodies to labour-power – the source of value – we must also caution against their transformation into a **force of**

consumption, especially when it masquerades as a desiring-revolution: the so-called 'right' to satisfy need, and the 'freedom' to want, desire, and enjoy. Mass production *demands* mass consumption. Consumption is imperative: Eat! Drink! Use! Enjoy! Buy! – *Anything whatsoever*. So, rather than being a freedom, a right or a liberty, consumption has become one's civic duty and a collective responsibility.[61] As citizens of consumer societies we are duty-bound to consume. We are *obliged* to have needs, wants and desires.[62] When all is said and done, we *must* make use. Consequently, 'use' and 'utility' are not natural categories, but moral ones. We are reminded of one of Sophie Calle's double games, in which she asked the novelist Paul Auster to invent a fictive character for her to resemble in 'real life' for a period of up to one year. In response, Auster wrote her a *Gotham Handbook: Personal Instructions for S.C. On How to Improve Life in New York City (Because she asked…)*, which required her: (1) to smile when the situation didn't call for it; (2) to flatter strangers with small-talk; (3) to give sandwiches and packs of cigarettes to beggars and homeless people; and (4) to cultivate a piece of New York since nearly everything is falling apart. In taking up the latter she chose a double phone booth (the one on the right).

> 'I cover the telephone company's NYNEX logo, the name of which is displayed across the top of the booth, with a sign that reads 'HAVE A NICE DAY', the American expression which punctuates every conversation and which I hate the most after 'Enjoy!' (But I couldn't bring myself to use that. Imagine, putting pleasure in the imperative like that!).'

But 'The worst is yet to come. Tomorrow, Wednesday, September 21, I must get down to business and start smiling.'[63] So, holding nothing in reserve – least of all the injunction to 'work and be useful!' and still less the demand to 'smile and enjoy!'[64] – and all the time being struck by everything, we wish only to return to *the whole game*: 'REVOLU-TIONARY GAMESTERS OF ALL COUNTRIES, UNITE! YOU HAVE NOTHING TO LOSE BUT YOUR DIE.'[65] For when all is said and done, it is Life – and not just labour-power – that is at stake. But **life is nothing personal**. It is collective, manifold and impersonal. It takes place betwixt and between, according to the fortuitous articulation of differential relations of force and by way of the cracking open of events: chaosmosis.[66] 'Like everyone else, I have problems with the words *performance, performer*. … I propose to replace *performer* by *transformer*.'[67] The hand that is articulated with a keyboard is not the same hand that is articulated with a chilled beer-glass.

> 'The hardness of which we speak is this: Pushed, seduced into factories, into mines, the ex-peasants are placed before an unacceptable challenge, for instance, to work with a 20,000-Hz noise in their ears. They accept it. How? By transforming their bodies: for example, the noise gets neutralized in their auditory spectrum. The metamorphosis of bodies and minds happens in excitement, violence, a kind of madness … when there is no common measure between what you're coming from (the old body) and where you're going. Always incommensurability, here in the projection of the human figure, starting from a familiar space, on to another space, an unknown one. To accept that is to extend your power.'[68]

In any event: and, but, metamorphosis.

16. We encounter anything whatsoever, are struck by its composition of forces, and experiment with how it might be taken up. Crucially, 'you do not know beforehand what good or bad you are capable of; you do not know beforehand what a body or a mind can do, in a given encounter, a given arrangement, a given combination'.[69] You do not know how forces will strike out and (s)play out. Even the simplest tasks and most obvious operations pose problems: What to do with an egg?[70] Or my personal favourite: What to do with a *set* of calendars?[71] Every day life poses problems – most obviously for infants and the recently disabled: How to eat? How to drink? How to walk? How to speak? How to dance? How to sleep?[72] Life is creative and experimental: germinal life; viroid life; the artifice of life.[73] We are all artists of everyday life; 'we are all handymen: each with his little machines' – 'all the time, flows and interruptions. ... And rest assured that it works ... Something is produced: the effects of a machine, not mere metaphors.'[74] We all experiment with the materials of everyday life.

> 'The Bauhaus was an answer to the question: What 'education' do artists need in order to take their place in the machine age? Our practical conclusion is the following: we are abandoning all efforts at pedagogical action and moving toward experimental activity.'[75]

Take any apparently stabilised state of affairs, such as an event, a place or a body.

17. **And then?**

> 'Open the so-called body and spread out all its surfaces: not only the skin with each of its folds, wrinkles, scars, with its great velvety planes, and contiguous to that, the scalp and its mane of hair, the tender pubic fur, nipples, nails, hard transparent skin under the heel, the light frills of the eyelids, set with lashes – but open and spread, expose the labia major, so also the labia minora with their blue network bathed in mucus, dilate the diaphragm of the anal sphincter, longitudinally cut and flatten out the black conduit of the rectum, then the colon, then the caecum, now a ribbon with its surface, all striated and polluted with shit; as though your dress-maker's scissors were opening the leg of an old pair of trousers, go on, expose the small intestines' alleged interior, the jejunum, the ileum, the duodenum, or else, at the other end, undo the mouth at its corners, pull out the tongue at its most distant roots and split it, spread out the bats' wings of the palate and its damp basements, open the trachea and make it the skeleton of a boat under construction; armed with scalpels and tweezers, dismantle and lay out the bundles and bodies of the encephalon; and then the whole network of veins and arteries, intact, on an immense mattress, and then the lymphatic network, and the fine bony pieces of the wrist, the ankle, take them apart and put them end to end with all the layers of nerve tissue which surround the aqueous humours and the cavernous body of the penis, and extract the great muscles, the great dorsal nets, spread them out like smooth sleeping dolphins.'[76]

So far so good, but we still have a long way to go before we embrace everything and hold nothing in reserve, before we have exhausted the laying out of a body's spatial formation and being-in-formation in all of its manifold relations.

> 'And this is not all, far from it: connected onto these lips a second mouth is necessary, a third, a great number of other mouths, vulvas, nipples. And adjoining the skin of the fingertips, scraped by the nails, perhaps there should be huge silken beaches of skin, taken from the inside of the thighs, the base of the neck, or from the strings of a guitar. And against the palm, all latticed with nerves, and creased like a yellow leaf, set potter's

> clays, or even hard wooden handles encrusted with jewels, or a steering wheel, or a drifter's sail, are perhaps required. Don't forget to add….'[77]

18. **And *then?*** Cast adrift amidst these disparate materials we will take them up and make an event, a place or a body out of them. We will lend them a certain consistency, and we will make something function on the basis of this materialist delirium. Whatever it turns out to be, it will be an assemblage of heterogeneous pieces and differential relations. 'What a mistake to have ever said *the* id. Everywhere *it* is machines – real ones, not figurative ones: machines driving other machines, machines being driven by other machines, with all the necessary couplings and connections.'[78] Henceforth, the forces of conjunction (*and*) and the indefinite (*a*) perpetually sweep away the counter-forces of injunction (*is*) and the definite (*the*): 'it's along this line of flight that things come to pass, becomings evolve, revolutions take place. … An AND, AND, AND which each time marks a new threshold, a new direction of the broken line, a new course for the border.'[79] Pick it up…

19. 'There is no general recipe. We are finished with all globalising concepts. Even concepts are haecceities and events'.[80] We affirm the incalculable power of virtual multiplicities and the manifold articulation of force within seemingly secure, sedimented and stabilised material artefacts and states of affairs. Along with deconstruction, schizoanalysis and rhizomatics, we affirm the 'destabilization on the move in, if one could speak thus, "the things themselves"', such that the 'de' of destabilization and 'deconstruction signifies not the demolition of what is constructing itself, but rather what remains to be thought beyond the constructivist or destructivist scheme.'[81] Accordingly, in any situation whatsoever we are attuned to both what **remains** in the wake of stabilisation and what is **remaindered** by the forces of stabilisation. Hence our fondness for margins, residuals, error terms, leftovers, outliers, outcasts, deviants, vagrants, misfits, the repressed, the excommunicated, the subhuman and the non-human, and so on and so forth. And yet, the forces of stabilisation can only proceed on the basis of what is remaindered. They can only proceed by remaindering:

> 'even when the capitalist machine is humming in the apparent general boredom and when everybody seems to do their job without moaning, all these libidinal instantiations, these little *dispositifs* [apparatuses] of the retention and flow of the influxes of desire are *never unequivocal*'.[82]

Despite the worst of intentions, what remains participates without belonging: 'stabilization is relative even if it is sometimes so great as to seem immutable and permanent. It is the momentary result of a whole history of relations of force.'[83] Stability 'is by definition what is destabilizable.'[84]

20. How will we take up a body? Following Spinoza, Deleuze suggests that we will not take it up as a form or a function, and still less as an individual object or subject, but as a set of relations (relations of speed and slowness, acceleration and deceleration, movement and rest, proximity and distance) and as a differential power to affect and to be affected. A body is an articulated being (jointed – and by the same token – disjointed): a spatial formation; an actor-network; a matrix. There is no position (no identity, no stability) that is not worked over by ex-position (differentiation and metamorphosis).[85] One becomes amongst others: that's all.

21. So, if we are to engage in envisioning and manifestoing we cannot emphasise strongly enough that geography will not be given to us: neither as a gift of nature nor as a virtual ready-made. Geography will not have been a found object – like a long-lost treasure or heirloom that one could polish and put on permanent display. Whatever it is, it will have to be assembled more or less from scratch and lent a transient consistency in contexts that are still to come and according to passwords and driftworks that are barely discernible.

22. Where to find the materials for an up-and-coming body of human geography? Where to find the stirrings of a geographical delirium? Where to pick up the risks, the game and the stakes? Human geographers can become excited by almost anything. A random enumeration: maps, drawings, data, conversation, car-boot sales, advertisements, allotments, the World Bank, motorway service stations, photographs, magic mushrooms, sewers, exotic fruit, toys, Africa, poems, merchant bankers, children, daytime television, domestic violence, cemeteries, language, stainless steel, asylum seekers, canals, popular organ music, kazoo bands.... But it is not just human geographers who can become excited by almost anything: maps, drawings, data, conversation, car-boot sales, advertisements, allotments, the World Bank, motorway service stations, photographs, magic mushrooms, sewers, exotic fruit, toys, Africa, poems, merchant bankers, children, daytime television, domestic violence, cemeteries, language, stainless steel, asylum seekers, canals, popular organ music, kazoo bands.... Enamoured by these pleasing prospects I consult the latest version of *The Dictionary of Human Geography*[86] to see which 'P's (why not?) interest human geographers, and find in the volume's 'comprehensive' index five pages of 'P's spread out before me, each with three columns of densely packed entries. Excluding subheadings, authors and cross-references, the listing for 'Pr' alone is as follows:

> practice; pragmatism; pre-industrial cities; pre-industrial societies; prediction; preference system (trade); prehistory; prejudice; prescriptivism; presence (metaphysics of); preservation; pressure groups; prices; pricing; pricing policies; Primary Metropolitan Statistical Areas; primary productivity; primary products (trade in); primate cities; primitive accumulation; primitive communism; principal components analysis; prison; prisoner's dilemma; privacy; private interest developments; private property; private sphere; private-security policing; privatization; probabilism; probability; probability: maps, matrix, theory; problem-solving; problematic concept; processes; producer cooperatives; producer services; product life cycles; production; production complexes; production of: knowledge, nature, scale, space; productive forces; productivity; profane space; professional ethics; professionalization; profit cycle; profits; progress; projections; proletarianization; property; property classes; property rights; prostitution; protest movements; Protestants; and protoindustrialization.

23. Having glanced at the 'Po's and the 'Ps's, and scanned forlornly row after row of books and journals that are strewn out across the walls of my office, an office that is only a stone's throw from the hundreds of thousands of items that huddle together in the University Library, and a mouse-click away from innumerable electronic journals and discussion lists, not to mention the materials of everyday life that are spread out across the face of the Earth, I begin to wonder whether it might be better to strike-out any hope of envisioning and manifestoing a future for human geography. Surely, only a despot or recklesshead would attempt to cut a dash through such a disparate range of

materials that can be extended infinitely. Don't forget to add: pranks; praxis; prayer; precept; precinct; predacity; prefabrication; prefecture; pregnancy; presentation; pretence; pretext .... As fanatical materialists we will not fall back on so-many values, beliefs, demands and expectations that we have held in reserve. We will not try to impose a certain combination of materials on you (say: 'production', 'property' and 'protest movements'), nor a certain combination of interests (say: 'practice', 'pragmatism' and 'probability'). Instead, we will take up Georges Perec's advice: 'Force yourself to see more flatly.'[87] Hereinafter, **privileges are anathema to us**. This is why we are contemptuous of the privileging of words, images and simulations no less than we are contemptuous of the privileging of so-called reality, nature and normalcy. We want it all: the whole caboodle. What a wonderful list of would-be materials: a, aa, aac, aak, aakin, aal, aald, Aalenian, aam, aan, aandblom, aane, aar, aard-vark, aard-wolf, aare, Aaron, Aaronic, Aaronical, Aaron's-beard, Aaron's rod, aas, aasvogel, aat, ab, aba, abac, abaca, abacinate, abacination... Smile and enjoy!

24. Rather than announce with a blare of trumpets the order-words that we wish you would submit to (say: 'orientation', 'distance' and 'relative position'[88] or 'justice', 'nature' and 'difference'[89]), we applaud Kenneth Goldsmith's painstaking collection and systematisation of some potential materials. Between February 7, 1993 and October 20, 1996, Goldsmith amassed 606 pages of words, sound-bites and phrases that were circulating in America – in books, advertisements and conversation; and on television, radio and film – arranged according to their syllable count, alphabetic nature and sound structure: from 1 to 7,228 syllables.[90] Page one opens with: 'A, a, aar, aas, aer, agh, ah, air, är, are, arh, arre, arrgh', while page 606 closes with a single 7,228-syllable 'phrase': the complete text of D. H. Lawrence's *The Rocking Horse Winner*. The work – a list poem – is refreshingly advertised as a 'carefully crafted ... typographic rant of total gibberish', a 'useless collection of perishable information.'[91] Such is Life, the Essential Selection: a 'perfectly astonishing miscellaneity'.[92] So, we would rather sink without trace into the gibberish of everyday life than attempt to impose privileges.[93]

25. Given the plethora of materials and the gibberish of everyday life, how can we compose a body, a machine, a desiring-machine, an event, an 'it happens' out of all this – and so much more beside?

> 'We live today in the age of partial objects, bricks that have been shattered to bits, and leftovers. We no longer believe in the myth of the existence of fragments that, like pieces of an antique statue, are merely waiting for the last one to be turned up, so that they may all be glued back together to create a unity that is precisely the same as the original unity. We no longer believe in a primordial totality that once existed, or in a final totality that awaits us at some future date. ... We believe only in totalities that are peripheral. And if we discover such a totality alongside various separate parts, it is a whole *of* these particular parts but does not totalize them; it is a unity *of* all of these particular parts but does not unify them; rather, it is added to them as a new part fabricated separately.'[94]

Our vision and manifesto for geography amounts to this: pick it up ... Not as an order-word, but as a password: an 'and', a 'but', a force of differentiation and metamorphosis. This distinction can best be grasped by counter-posing

> 'two ways of reading a book: either we consider it a box which refers us to an inside, and in that case we look for the signified; if we are still more perverse or corrupted, we search for the signifier. And then we consider the following book as a box contained in the first one or containing it in turn. And we can comment, and interpret, and ask for explanations, we can write about the book and so on endlessly. Or the other way: we consider a book as a small a-signifying machine; the only problem is "Does it work and how does it work? How does it work for you?" If it doesn't function, if nothing happens, take another book. This way of reading is based on intensities: something happens or doesn't happen. There is nothing to explain, nothing to understand, nothing to interpret. It can be compared to an electrical connection.'[95]

As a password, pick it up and experiment with how it takes place and goes off, neither of which is set in advance.

26. > 'It is the twenty-third of June nineteen seventy-five, and it is eight o'clock in the evening. Seated at his jigsaw puzzle, Bartlebooth has just died. On the tablecloth, somewhere in the crepuscular sky of the four hundred and thirty-ninth puzzle, the black hole of the sole piece not yet filled in has the almost perfect shape of an X. But the ironical thing, which could have been foreseen long ago, is that the piece the dead man holds between his fingers is shaped like a W.'[96]

27. Turning to page X,[97] I happen upon a section of *The Dictionary of Human Geography* entitled 'How to Use This Dictionary'. It has three sentences. The first sentence refers readers to 'keywords' (we will treat them as passwords that *unlock*, rather than as order-words that *clamp down*), the second to 'cross-references and other entries' (we will treat them as passageways for *driftworks*, rather than as bindings for *constriction*), and the third and final sentence suggests that 'Readers may trace other connections through the comprehensive index at the back of the book' (we assume that we are invited to inhabit the fabric of the text, activate the schizoid switchboard and create a *Life*).

28. **Passwords, driftworks, switchboard**: *The Dictionary of Human Geography* promises 'a hinge-logic, a hinge-style'.[98] The problems it poses for us are those of burrowing into a context that is forever turning and returning; and of finding a way to inhabit it without succumbing to despair, despotism or paranoia. These problems are the ones addressed by Kafka in *The Trial, The Castle,* and *The Burrow*.[99]

> 'How can we enter into Kafka's work? This work is a rhizome, a burrow… . Yet it might seem that the burrow in the story of that name has only one entrance… . But this is a trap arranged by the animal and by Kafka himself; the whole description of the burrow functions to trick the enemy. We will enter, then, by any point whatsoever; none matters more than another, and no entrance is more privileged even if it seems an impasse, a tight passage, a siphon.'[100]

Eschewing privileges we will pick up on anything whatsoever: this or that; here or there; big or little; pivotal or trivial.

29. Even though we give ourselves over to encounters, encounters that force us to pose problems with respect to the infinite potential of the materials to hand, this does not prevent the misers from attempting to **force a constriction**: to insist on the conservation of energy, the minimisation of effort and the optimisation of expenditure and

return; or else to narrow things down to their 'proper' limits, 'essential' uses and 'rational' kernel, for example. Passwords are invariably crushed by order-words: 'A hand is really fit for…'; 'A place is really good for…'[101] and so on and so forth. Such are the reserves (and conceits) of common sense, accepted codes and habitual expectations. Needless to say, the repressed returns:

> 'At times the schizophrenic loses his patience and demands to be left alone. Other times he goes along with the whole game and even invents a few tricks of his own, introducing his own reference points in the model put before him and undermining it from within. … He deliberately *scrambles all the codes*, by quickly shifting from one to another, according to the questions asked of him, never giving the same explanation from one day to the next, never invoking the same genealogy, never recording the same event in the same way.'[102]

Obviously, children are the most adept at 'desimplifying' the constrictions that are forced upon us and set into place: they know how to lead things astray. They are masters of the surrealist, situationist and psychogeographical arts of diversion, deflection, deterritorialisation, seduction, metamorphosis and shape-shifting.

> 'The bed became a trapper's cabin, or a lifeboat on the raging ocean, or a baobab tree threatened by fire, a tent erected in the desert, or a propitious crevice that my enemies passed within inches of, unavailingly. I travelled a great deal at the bottom of my bed.'[103]

Such are the 'voyages in place,' 'motionless trips' and 'molecular revolutions' that we love so much: becoming-other; becoming-animal;[104] becoming-imperceptible….[105] Being cast adrift is not subordination to randomness but *complete insubordination* to constriction and habit.[106]

> 'One shouldn't complicate things for the pleasure of complicating, but one should also never simplify or pretend to be sure of such simplicity where there is none. If things were simple, word would have gotten around … Those who wish to simplify at all costs … are in my eyes dangerous dogmatists and tedious obscurantists. No less dangerous (for instance, in politics) are those who wish to purify at all costs.'[107]

30. Between our spendthrift materialism that holds nothing in reserve and the miserly onto-theology that would strike us down by restricting our action there is a **slippage of practice**. This slippage casts a **shadow** over practice – echoes of Gothic Marxism[108] – far worse than any elevation of privileges. It is force turned against itself. In every case our response will be the same: to return the great pretender whence it came. For we are 'in love with a sun which casts no shadows'.[109] When Henri Lefebvre draws out a distinction between the '*lived space*' of bodies (a spatial formation that is a direct and immediate extension of the social body; a production of space that enhances the body's capacity for collective action; a sensuous space that is fitting, appropriate, and fully embodied) and the '*abstract space*' of cold calculation (a space wrenched from the body and given over to number, money, geometry, capital, Logos, Phallus, Power, etc.) – such that the latter falls upon, crushes and overcodes the former – he insists that they are nevertheless composed of the same substance, the same force: each is born of spatial practice and sustained through spatial practice.[110] So, abstract space is simply lived space that has 'slipped' from the immediate and proper grasp of the body, only

then to turn back on the body with a vengeance: *abstract space is to lived space as capital is to labour* (hence the alienation, reification, vampirism and fetishism of space whenever it is estranged from bodily practice; hence also the complicity of spatial practice in its own estrangement). What appears abstract and alien – or more frequently natural and inalienable – is returned whence it came: to socio-spatial practice. Where we depart from Lefebvre – and Marx before him – is over the lingering onto-theology in the guise of a moralising humanism. They both take for granted the 'proper' form, nature and organic composition of the social body: not cold, calculating and quantified but passionate, creative and qualified; not abstract, disembodied and preconceived, but concrete, embodied and lived; not fragmented, disjointed and inorganic but whole(some), tightly knit and organic. Georges Bataille, Gilles Deleuze, Félix Guattari and Jean-François Lyotard have all reminded us that coldness *is also an intensity*, that cruelty *is also lived*, that calculation *is also a passion*, that capital *is also desiring-production* and that *there will never have been a whole body*.[111]

31. There are nothing but forces, forces that are set into place. We remain dumbstruck by the structuralist insistence that the differential play of force is a *set* piece, eternally frozen like Damien Hirst's *The Physical Impossibility of Death in the Mind of Someone Living*.[112] Structure is that which holds fast between otherwise seemingly disparate and incommensurate contents. Like the rules of a game, structure is homologous. Structure *is* relation and co-relation: 'the vacuum cleaner goes into the broom closet; exhausted bodies into the bedroom: the two functions are the same, of recuperation and maintenance.'[113]

32. The first structural revolution in geography established **the set pieces of a spatial science**, invariably with an eye towards the transformation of process into pattern, structure into event, and law into case: co-relation, friction of distance, least effort, etc. Eventually, David Harvey, Gunnar Olsson and many others shrugged.[114]

33. The second structural revolution in geography established **the set pieces of a socio-spatial science**: the dialectical tension between the forces and relations of production (capitalism) and reproduction (patriarchal heterosexuality); between structure and agency, subject and object, space and place, power and resistance, etc. No doubt it will not have escaped your attention that these set-piece 'spatial formations' have suffered badly over recent decades: from wears and tears; mixing and matching; incredulity and parody; obsolescence (built-in?) and resurrection. Everywhere we are struck by the same wearisome turns and returns, and by the hysterical and not-so-hysterical 'call to arms': to become relevant, useful, profitable, engaged – or engaging – popular, critical, revolutionary, etc.[115] Having failed to budge an inch, it is almost as if they were trying to find relief from the burdensome force of structure in the materials of everyday life. As if they could lose themselves – or rather, lose the problems posed for themselves – in the fabric of the Real (call it what you will: 'context', 'situation', 'place', 'milieu', 'network', 'map', 'location', 'setting', 'geography', 'geometry', 'universe', 'world', 'landscape', 'stage', 'glocale' – and ramify it if you must: 'contexts', 'situations', 'places', 'milieux', 'networks', 'maps', 'locations', 'settings', 'geographies', 'geometries', 'universes', 'worlds', 'landscapes', 'stages', 'glocales').

34. No matter how much we may feel at home amid the seemingly secure comforts and plush fabric of our preferred set-piece surroundings – '*The desert of the real*'[116] – we will always drift towards the force of a problem that *insists* on being posed: What's the

set up? What's going on? What will have gone on? These are **problems without a solution**; problems that are re-posed precisely to the extent that they are resolved (from the Latin, *re-solvere*: re-release). We must go on. We can't go on. We'll go on.

35. Or the other way: the set-ups are **solutions without a problem**; solutions that demand the creation of a problem that is worthy of them. For example, in 1895, Louis Lumière, the inventor of the *cinématographe* – a combined film camera and projector that could take and re-present 'living photographs' – famously responded to Georges Méliès' expression of interest in the device by calling it 'an invention without a future'. Nevertheless, after a decade of being struck by the aleatory drift of so-many disparate and contingent encounters, 'living photographs' had more or less invented a problem worthy of themselves: *the engineering of space and time*[117] (a problem that is often obscured by a widespread and misplaced fixation on the false problem of *telling stories*, especially as exemplified by the 'narrative cinema' of the Hollywood studio system[118]). However, the problems posed by the force of this resolve remain in place. We must continue to pick them up. So, no matter what the set-up, nothing is ever settled – finally. 'This trench will bring me certainty, you say? I have reached the stage where I no longer wish to have certainty.'[119] As we have noted in passing, even the most minimal and constricted articulation of forces can be ramified to infinity and beyond, just like the pullulation wrought on someone set between the facing off of mirrors. Take Meursault in his prison cell:[120]

> 'The main problem ... was killing time. I ended up not being bored at all as soon as I learnt how to remember things. Sometimes I'd start thinking about my room and, in my imagination, I'd set off from one corner and walk round making a mental note of everything I saw on the way. At first it didn't take very long. But every time I did it, it took a bit longer. Because I'd remember every piece of furniture, and on every piece of furniture, every object and, on every object, every detail, every mark, crack or chip, and then even the colour or the grain of the wood. At the same time, I'd try not to lose track of my inventory, to enumerate everything. So that, by the end of a few weeks, I could spend hours doing nothing but listing the things in my room. And the more I thought about it, the more things I dug out of my memory that I hadn't noticed before or that I'd forgotten about. I realised then that a man who'd only lived a day could easily live for a thousand years in a prison.'[121]

36. Having left nothing in reserve, having been struck by everything and having resolved to pose problems, it is still not enough, however, to be fanatical about one's disparate materials: 'proclaiming 'Long live the multiple' is not yet doing it, one must do the multiple.'[122] In the wake of the structural revolutions, embedment in a set-up of differential forces may entail a fate worse than death: **still lives** – which is to say, **stilled lives**. Having drifted from the frozen poses of structuralism it is all too easy to find oneself in the frozen poses of empiricism. Whence the difference between structuralism and poststructuralism. For the latter, structure is not just *set*, it is set *in motion*. Space *takes* place. Such is the (double) movement and (duplicitous) expenditure – the dis-placement and dis-possession – of a polymorphously perverse libidinal economy. The most powerful password in Kafka's fiction is: 'But' (*aber*).

> 'Of all German authors, Kafka uses the adversative conjunction *aber* by far the most. Indeed, he uses it on the average two or three times more often … The cause of this lies in the remarkable complexity of a soul which cannot simply see and feel in a straight line, a soul which didn't doubt and hesitate out of cowardice and caution, but rather out of clear-sightedness. A soul which at every thought, every perception, every assertion, instantly heard a little devil whispering to him: *aber* … . And then this soul had to write down this devilish *aber* to our greater "confusion inside of clarity"'.[123]

Such is Kafka's paratactic style of disjunctive synthesis and ambivalence. Innumerable series are laid out alongside one another, but their co-ordination lacks integration, hierarchy and subordination, so that we will never know which series should be preferred, which series should be followed, or even which series is commensurable or compossible with any other series.[124] 'They each follow their course without merging; at best they slide over each other like tectonic plates, and occasionally their collision or subduction creates fault lines into which reality rushes. Fate is always at the intersection of these two lines of force.'[125] By way of disjunctive syntheses – 'and', 'but', 'meanwhile' – events crack open and '*everything … returns to the surface*'.[126] For horizontal thinkers, one does indeed find folded surfaces everywhere.[127] This is why we live in a scrumpled and disadjusted universe.[128]

37. As always, we are fated to maintain the disparate: 'and', 'but', 'meanwhile'… . 'Not to maintain together the disparate, but to put ourselves there where the disparate itself *holds together*, without wounding the dis-jointure, the dispersion, or the difference, without effacing the heterogeneity of the other.'[129]

38. Energy can be neither created nor destroyed – only redistributed and transformed into 'new archipelagoes of matter'.[130] We are all transformers caught up in the delirium of desiring-production. Everything is suspended in perpetual circulation. Everything is set in motion. Everything is cast adrift.[131] So, do not confuse reality with fidelty or fealty. And do not expect us to be faithful or trustworthy. There is nothing original or authorized under the sun. Reality is a transformer – that's all. Continuous remix.

39. And *then*…?

40. 'Much later, when he was able to think about the things that happened to him, he would conclude that nothing was real except chance. But that was much later. In the beginning, there was simply the event and its consequences.'[132]

Notes

1. Robert Coover (1989) *A Night at the Movies. Or, You Must Remember This* (Paladin, London) p186.
2. Paul Auster (1989) *In the Country of Last Things* (Faber & Faber, London) pp28–29.
3. Jacques Derrida (1976) *Of Grammatology*, trans. Gayatri Spivak (Johns Hopkins University Press, Baltimore, MD) p158.
4. Jacques Derrida (1981) *Dissemination*, trans. Ben Johnson (Athlone, London) p258.
5. Jacques Derrida (1981) *Positions*, trans. Alan Bass (University of Chicago Press, Chicago, IL) p66.
6. Jacques Derrida (1988) *Limited Inc* (Northwestern University Press, Evanston, IL) p136.

7. Jacques Derrida (1988) *Limited Inc* (Northwestern University Press, Evanston, IL) p148.

8. Gilles Deleuze (1995) *Negotiations, 1972–1990*, trans. Martin Joughin (Columbia University Press, New York, NY) p161.

9. Jacques Derrida (1989) 'Introduction: desistance' in *Typography: Mimesis, Philosophy, Politics*, Philippe Lacoue-Labarthe, ed. Christopher Fynsk (Harvard University Press, Cambridge, MA) p10.

10. Marcus Doel (1999) *Poststructuralist Geographies: The Diabolic Art of Spatial Science* (Edinburgh University Press, Edinburgh); Marcus Doel (2000) 'Un-glunking geography: spatial science after Dr Seuss and Gilles Deleuze' in *Thinking Space*, eds Mike Crang, Nigel Thrift (Routledge, London) pp117–135.

11. Gilles Deleuze (1993) *The Fold: Leibnitz and the Baroque*, trans. Tom Conley (University of Minnesota Press, Minneapolis, MN) p6.

12. Deborah Dixon, John-Paul Jones III (1996) 'For a *supercalifragilisticexpialidocious* scientific geography' *Annals of the Association of American Geographers*, Vol. 86, No. 4, pp767–779; Deborah Dixon, John-Paul Jones III (1998) 'My dinner with Derrida, *or* spatial analysis and poststructuralism do lunch', *Environment and Planning A*, Vol. 30, No. 2, pp247–260; Marcus Doel (2003) 'Gunnar Olsson's transformers: the art and politics of rendering the co-relation of society and space in monochrome and Technicolor', *Antipode*, Vol. 35, No. 1, pp 140–167; Gunnar Olsson (1991) *Lines of Power/Limits of Language* (University of Minnesota Press, Minneapolis, MN).

13. Gilles Deleuze (1995) *Negotiations, 1972–1990*, trans. Martin Joughin (Columbia University Press, New York, NY) p156.

14. Gilles Deleuze (1983) 'Politics' in *On the Line*, Gilles Deleuze, Félix Guattari, trans. John Johnston (Semiotext(e), New York, NY) p83.

15. Georges Perec (1996) *Life A User's Manual*, trans. David Bellos (Harvill, London) p3.

16. Jacques Derrida (1986) 'Remarks on deconstruction and pragmatism' in *Deconstruction and Pragmatism*, ed. Chantal Mouffe (Routledge, London) p86.

17. Georges Perec (1996) *Life A User's Manual*, trans. David Bellos (Harvill, London) p227.

18. Georges Perec (1996) *Life A User's Manual*, trans. David Bellos (Harvill, London) p465.

19. David Barthelme (1991) 'Nothing: a preliminary account' in *Sixty Stories* (Minerva, London) p248.

20. Jacques Derrida (1981) *Dissemination*, trans. Ben Johnson (Athlone, London) p339.

21. Jorges Luis Borges (1985) 'The garden of forking paths' in *Fictions* (John Calder, London) pp79–92.

22. Franz Kafka (1993) 'The burrow' in *Franz Kafka: Collected Stories* (David Campbell, London) p501 and p503, respectively.

23. Jean-François Lyotard (1993) *Libidinal Economy*, trans. Iain Hamilton Grant (Athlone, London) p11.

24. Robert Coover (1989) *A Night at the Movies. Or, You Must Remember This* (Paladin, London) p187.

25. Donald Barthelme (1978) *Snow White* (Atheneum, New York, NY).

26. Robert Coover (1991) *Pinocchio in Venice* (Linden, New York, NY).

27. Italo Calvino (1981) *If on a Winter's Night a Traveller*, trans. William Weaver (Picador, London).

28. Need we recall that many of the key works taken to be of a poststructuralist inclination were composed before those taken to exemplify structuralism?

29. See, for example: Jean Baudrillard (1986) 'The year 2000 will not take place' in *Future*Fall: Excursions into Postmodernity*, eds Elizabeth Grosz, Terry Threadgold, David Kelly, Alan Cholodenko, Edward Colles (Power Institute of Fine Arts, University of Sydney, Sydney) pp18–28; Gilles Deleuze (1991) *Bergsonism*, trans. Hugh Tomlinson, Barbara Habberjam (Zone, New York, NY); Jacques Derrida (1992) *Given Time: 1. Counterfeit Money*, trans. Peggy Kamuf (University of Chicago Press, Chicago, IL); Jean-François Lyotard (1991) *The Inhuman: Reflections on Time*, trans. Geoffrey Bennington, Rachel Bowlby (Polity, Cambridge).

30. Gilles Deleuze (1977) 'I have nothing to admit', *Semiotext(e)*, Vol. 2, No. 3, pp111–116.

31. Should we mention the fact that poststructuralism poses problems for spacing? The space of poststructuralism is anathematic through and through.

32. Jean Baudrillard (1988) *The Ecstasy of Communication*, trans. Bernard Schutze, Caroline Schutze (Semiotext(e), New York, NY) p84.

33. Gilles Deleuze (1977) 'Intellectuals and power' in *Language, Counter-Memory, Practice*, Michel Foucault (eds), trans. Donald Bouchard, Sherry Simon (Cornell University Press, Ithaca, NY) p144.

34. Gilles Deleuze (1977) 'Intellectuals and power' in *Language, Counter-Memory, Practice*, Michel Foucault (eds), trans. Donald Bouchard, Sherry Simon (Cornell University Press, Ithaca, NY) pp206–207.

35. Raoul Vaneigem (1979) *The Revolution of Everyday Life*, trans. John Fullerton, Paul Siekeking (Rising Free Collective, London) URL: http://Library.nothingness.org/articles/SI.

36. Paul Auster (1989) *In the Country of Last Things* (Faber & Faber, London) p7.

37. Karl Marx, Frederick Engels (1986) *Manifesto of the Communist Party*, trans. Samuel Moore (Progress, Moscow) p70.

38. 'Anti-Oedipus' (1977) *Semiotext(e)*, Vol. 2, No. 3.

39. Jean Baudrillard (1975) *The Mirror of Production*, trans. Mark Poster (Telos, St Louis); Jean Baudrillard (1981) *For a Critique of the Political Economy of the Sign*, trans. Charles Levin (Telos, St Louis).

40. Tim Unwin (2000) 'A waste of space? Towards a critique of the social production of space …' *Transactions of the Institute of British Geographers*, Vol. 25, pp11–29.

41. Chris Hamnett (2001) 'The emperor's new theoretical clothes, or geography without origami' in *Market Killing: What the Free Market Does and What Social Scientists Can Do About It*, eds Greg Philo, David Miller (Longman, Harlow) p166.

42. Ron Martin (2001) 'Geography and public policy: the case of the missing agenda', *Progress in Human Geography*, Vol. 25, No. 2, pp189–210; Michael Storper (2001) 'The poverty of radical theory today: from the false promises of Marxism to the mirage of the cultural turn' *International Journal of Urban and Regional Research*, Vol. 25, No. 1, pp155–179.

43. The Cramps (1980) 'Zombie dance' on *Songs the Lord Taught Us* (Illegal Records, London).

44. Gilles Deleuze (1977) 'I have nothing to admit', *Semiotext(e)*, Vol. 2, No. 3, pp110–116.

45. Jean-François Lyotard (1990) *Duchamp's TRANS/formers,* trans. Ian McLeod (Lapis, Venice, CA) p69.

46. Georges Perec (1999) *Species of Spaces and Other Pieces,* revised edition, trans. John Sturrock (Penguin, Harmondsworth) p33.

47. Jean-François Lyotard (1993) *Libidinal Economy,* trans. Iain Hamilton Grant (Athlone, London) p97.

48. Cf. The collection of papers collected under the title 'Radical Geography', ed. Richard Peet (2000) *Environment and Planning A,* Vol. 32, Nos 6 and 7; Noel Castree (2000) 'Commentary: what kind of critical geography for what kind of politics?', *Environment and Planning A,* Vol. 32, No. 12, pp2091–2095; David Harvey (2000) *Spaces of Hope* (Edinburgh University Press, Edinburgh); Michael Pacione (1999) 'Applied geography: in pursuit of useful knowledge', *Applied Geography,* Vol. 19, pp1–12; 'Relevance in human geography' (Special issue), *Scottish Geographical Journal,* Vol. 115, No. 2.

49. Paul Auster (1987) *The New York Trilogy* (Faber & Faber, London) p77. He addresses this question most fully in *The Invention of Solitude* (1989) (Faber & Faber, London) and *In the Country of Last Things* (1989) (Faber & Faber, London).

50. A scrivener may be a professional writer; a scribe or copyist; a clerk, secretary or amanuensis; or a notary. Bartleby is employed solely for the purpose of copying legal documents: 'word by word'.

51. As a comparative method, *verification* ensures that what would otherwise be singular (a copy which may or may not accord with an original) is rendered commensurable, exchangeable and substitutable (a faithful reproduction of the same). Verification is therefore not only authorisation: it is valorisation. Verification underwrites the proper identity of a piece of writing and thereby authorises its issuance as exchange-value. Only after verification may a copy enter into licit circulation (cf. Jacques Derrida, 1992, *Given Time: 1. Counterfeit Money,* trans. Peggy Kamuf, University of Chicago Press, Chicago, IL).

52. Herman Melville (1968) *Bartleby and the Lightning-Rod Man* (Penguin, Harmondsworth) p11.

53. Herman Melville (1968) *Bartleby and the Lightning-Rod Man* (Penguin, Harmondsworth) p25.

54. Herman Melville (1968) *Bartleby and the Lightning-Rod Man* (Penguin, Harmondsworth) p17.

55. Gilles Deleuze (1997) 'Bartleby; or, the formula' in *Essays Critical and Clinical* (University of Minnesota Press, Minneapolis, MN) p71.

56. Herman Melville (1968) *Bartleby and the Lightning-Rod Man* (Penguin, Harmondsworth) p15.

57. Herman Melville (1968) *Bartleby and the Lightning-Rod Man* (Penguin, Harmondsworth) p26.

58. Herman Melville (1968) *Bartleby and the Lightning-Rod Man* (Penguin, Harmondsworth) pp26–27.

59. Herman Melville (1968) *Bartleby and the Lightning-Rod Man* (Penguin, Harmondsworth) pp18–19.

60. Henri Lefebvre (1991) *The Production of Space,* trans. Donald Nicholson-Smith (Blackwell, Oxford) p70.

61. 'Consumption is an active, collective behaviour: it is something enforced, a morality, an institution. It is a whole system of values, with all that expression implies in terms of group integration and social control functions. [T]he current training in systematic, organised consumption is *the equivalent and extension, in the twentieth century, of the great nineteenth-century-long process of the training of rural populations for industrial work*' (Jean Baudrillard, 1998 *The Consumer Society: Myths and Structures*, trans. Chris Turner, Sage, London, p81). Cf. Zygmunt Bauman (1983) 'Industrialism, consumerism and power', *Theory, Culture & Society*, Vol. 1, No. 3, pp32–43; Zygmunt Bauman (1998) *Work, Consumerism and the New Poor* (Open University Press, Buckingham).

62. 'consumerist man regards *enjoyment as an obligation*; he sees himself as *an enjoyment and satisfaction business*. He sees it as his duty to be happy. … Hence the revival of a *universal curiosity* …. You have to try *everything*, for consumerist man is haunted by the fear of "missing" something' (Jean Baudrillard, 1998 *The Consumer Society: Myths and Structures*, trans. Chris Turner, Sage, London, p80).

63. Sophie Calle (1999) *Double Game* (Violette Editions, London) p246.

64. 'Smile!' enjoins the BBC's Breakfast weather-presenter quite out of the blue one dank Friday morning: 'It's National Smile Week!' To which the grimacing news-presenter replies: 'We'll try'. National Smile Week turns out to be an oral health awareness campaign organised each May by the British Dental Health Foundation. URL: http://www.dentalhealth.org.uk/smile/

65. Anonymous (1960) 'Manifesto', *Internationale Situationiste*, No. 4 URL: http://librarynothingness.org/articles/SI

66. Félix Guattari (1992) *Chaosmosis: An Ethico-Aesthetic Paradigm*, trans. P Bains, Julian Pefanis (Power Publications, Sydney).

67. Jean-François Lyotard (1990) *Duchamp's TRANS/formers,* trans. Ian McLeod (Lapis, Venice, CA) p31.

68. Jean-François Lyotard (1990) *Duchamp's Trans/formers,* trans. Ian McLeod (Lapis, Venice, CA) pp18–19.

69. Gilles Deleuze (1988) *Spinoza: Practical Philosophy*, trans. Robert Hurley (City Lights, San Francisco, CA) p125.

70. Cf. Georges Bataille (1982) *The Story of the Eye*, trans. Joachim Neugroschal (Penguin, Harmondsworth).

71. David Clarke, Marcus Doel (2000) 'Cultivating ambivalence: the unhinging of culture and economy' in *Cultural Turns/Geographical Turns: Perspectives on Cultural Geography*, eds Ian Cook, David Crouch, Simon Naylor, James Ryan (Pearson, Harlow) pp214–233.

72. Marcus Doel, David Clarke (1999) 'Dark Panopticon. Or, Attack of the Killer Tomatoes' *Environment and Planning D: Society and Space*, Vol. 17, No. 3, pp427–450; Marcel Mauss (1992) 'Techniques of the body' in *Incorporations: Zone 6*, eds Jonathan Crary, Sanford Kwinter (Zone, New York, NY) pp455–477.

73. Keith Ansell-Pearson (1997) *Viroid Life: Perspectives on Nietzsche and the Transhuman Condition* (Routledge, London); Keith Ansell-Pearson (1999) *Germinal Life: The Difference and Repetition of Deleuze* (Routledge, London).

74. Gilles Deleuze, Félix Guattari (1984) *Anti-Oedipus: Capitalism and Schizophrenia*, trans. Robert Hurley, Mark Seem, Helen Lane (Athlone, London) pp1–2.

75. Asger Jorn (1989) 'Notes on the formation of an Imaginary Bauhaus, 1957' in *An Endless Adventure … An Endless Passion … An Endless Banquet … A Situationist scrapbook*, eds Iwona Blazwick (ICA/Verso, London) p23.

76. Jean-François Lyotard (1993) *Libidinal Economy*, trans. Iain Hamilton Grant (Athlone, London) p1.

77. Jean-François Lyotard (1993) *Libidinal Economy*, trans. Iain Hamilton Grant (Athlone, London) pp1–2.

78. Gilles Deleuze, Félix Guattari (1984) *Anti-Oedipus: Capitalism and Schizophrenia*, trans. Robert Hurley, Mark Seem, Helen Lane (Athlone, London) p1.

79. Gilles Deleuze (1995) *Negotiations, 1972–1990*, trans. Martin Joughin (Columbia University Press, New York, NY) p45.

80. Gilles Deleuze (1983) 'Politics' in *On the Line*, Gilles Deleuze, Félix Guattari, trans. John Johnston (Semiotext(e), New York, NY) p108.

81. Jacques Derrida (1988) *Limited Inc* (Northwestern University Press, Evanston, IL) p147.

82. Jean-François Lyotard (1993) *Libidinal Economy*, trans. Iain Hamilton Grant (Athlone, London) p114.

83. Jacques Derrida (1988) *Limited Inc* (Northwestern University Press, Evanston, IL) p145.

84. Jacques Derrida (1988) *Limited Inc* (Northwestern University Press, Evanston, IL) p151.

85. Marcus Doel (2001) '1a. Qualified quantitative geography', *Environment and Planning D: Society and Space*, Vol. 19, No. 5, pp555–572.

86. Ron Johnston, Derek Gregory, Gerry Pratt, Michael Watts (eds) (2000) *The Dictionary of Human Geography*, fourth edition (Blackwell, Oxford).

87. Georges Perec (1999) *Species of Spaces and Other Pieces*, revised edition, trans. John Sturrock (Penguin, Harmondsworth) p51.

88. John Nystuen (1963) 'Identification of some fundamental spatial concepts', *Papers of the Michigan Academy of Science, Arts and Letters*, Vol. 48, pp373–384.

89. David Harvey (1996) *Justice, Nature and the Geography of Difference* (Blackwell, Oxford).

90. Kenneth Goldsmith (1997) *No. 111.2.7.93–10.20.93* (The Figures, Great Barrington, MA).

91. URL: http://wings.buffalo.edu/epc/authors/goldsmith/111/info.html

92. Georges Perec (1999) *Species of Spaces and Other Pieces*, revised edition, trans. John Sturrock (Penguin, Harmondsworth) p196. Cf. Paul Auster (1989) *The Invention of Solitude* (Faber & Faber, London).

93. Cf. Gaston Bachelard (2000) 'Rhythmanalysis' in *The Dialectic of Duration*, trans. Mary McAllester Jones (Clinamen, Manchester) pp136–155; Michel de Certeau (1984) *The Practice of Everyday Life*, trans. Steven Rendall (University of California, Berkeley, CA); Henri Lefebvre (1995) 'Part V: Elements of rhythmanalysis' in *Writings on Cities*, trans. Eleonore Kofman, Elizabeth Lebas (Blackwell, Oxford) pp219–240.

94. Gilles Deleuze, Félix Guattari (1984) *Anti-Oedipus: Capitalism and Schizophrenia*, trans. Robert Hurley, Mark Seem, Helen Lane (Athlone, London) p42.

95. Gilles Deleuze (1977) 'I have nothing to admit', *Semiotext(e)*, Vol. 2, No. 3, p114.

96. Georges Perec (1996) *Life A User's Manual*, trans. David Bellos (Harvill, London) p497.

97. Cf. David Clarke, Marcus Doel (1994) 'The perfection of geography as an aesthetic of disappearance: Baudrillard's America', *Ecumene*, Vol. 1, No. 2, pp317–321.

98. Jean-François Lyotard (1990) *Duchamp's Trans/formers*, trans. Ian McLeod (Lapis, Venice, CA) p123.

99. Franz Kafka (1992) *Kafka: The Complete Novels* (Minerva, London); Franz Kafka (1993) 'The burrow' in *Franz Kafka: Collected Stories* (David Campbell, London) pp467–503.

100. Gilles Deleuze, Félix Guattari (1986) *Kafka: Toward a Minor Literature*, trans. Dana Polan (University of Minnesota Press, Minneapolis, MN) p3.

101. Cf. Robert Mugerauer (1994) *Interpretations on Behalf of Place: Environmental Displacements and Alternative Responses* (SUNY, New York, NY); Edward Relph (1976) *Place and Placelessness* (Pion, London).

102. Gilles Deleuze, Félix Guattari (1984) *Anti-Oedipus: Capitalism and Schizophrenia*, trans. Robert Hurley, Mark Seem, Helen Lane (Athlone, London) pp14–15.

103. Georges Perec (1999) *Species of Spaces and Other Pieces*, revised edition, trans. John Sturrock (Penguin, Harmondsworth) p17.

104. 'Any cat-owner will tell you that cats inhabit houses much better than people do. Even in the most dreadfully square spaces, they know how to find favourable corners' (Georges Perec, 1999, *Species of Spaces and Other Pieces*, revised edition, trans. John Sturrock, Penguin, Harmondsworth, p24).

105. Gilles Deleuze, Félix Guattari (1988) *A Thousand Plateaus: Capitalism and Schizophrenia*, trans. Brian Massumi (Athlone, London); Félix Guattari (1996) *Soft Subversions*, trans. David Sweet, Chet Wiener (Semiotext(e), New York, NY).

106. Brian Massumi (1992) *A User's Guide to Capitalism and Schizophrenia: Deviations from Deleuze and Guattari* (MIT, Cambridge, MA).

107. Jacques Derrida (1988) *Limited Inc* (Northwestern University Press, Evanston, IL) p119.

108. Jacques Derrida (1994) *Specters of Marx: The State of the Debt, the Work of Mourning, and the New International*, trans. Peggy Kamuf (Routledge, London); Michael Löwy (1996) 'Walter Benjamin and surrealism: the story of a revolutionary spell', *Radical Philosophy*, No. 80, pp17–23; Michael Löwy (1998) 'Consumed by night's fire: the dark romanticism of Guy Debord', *Radical Philosophy*, No. 87, pp31–34.

109. Albert Camus (1983) *The Outsider*, trans. Joseph Laredo (Penguin, Harmondsworth) p119.

110. Henri Lefebvre (1991) *The Production of Space*, trans. Donald Nicholson-Smith (Blackwell, Oxford).

111. Gilles Deleuze, Félix Guattari (1984) *Anti-Oedipus: Capitalism and Schizophrenia*, trans. Robert Hurley, Mark Seem, Helen Lane (Athlone, London); Jean-François Lyotard (1993) *Libidinal Economy*, trans. Iain Hamilton Grant (Athlone, London); Jean-François Lyotard (1998) *The Assassination of Experience by Painting – Monory*, trans. Rachel Bowlby (Black Dog, London).

112. Damien Hirst (1991) *The Physical Impossibility of Death in the Mind of Someone Living*. Dead tiger-shark suspended in a 7 ft × 17 ft × 7 ft glass-and-steel tank filled with formaldehyde (Saatchi Collection, London).

113. Georges Perec (1999) *Species of Spaces and Other Pieces*, revised edition, trans. John Sturrock (Penguin, Harmondsworth) p31.

114. David Harvey (1973) *Social Justice and the City* (Arnold, London); Gunnar Olsson (1975) *Birds in Egg* (University of Michigan, Ann Arbor).

115. Cf. Doreen Massey (2000) 'Editorial: practising political relevance', *Transactions of the Institute of British Geographers*, Vol. 25, pp131–133; Ron Martin (1999) 'Editorial: the "new economic geography": challenge or irrelevance?', *Transactions of the Institute of British Geographers*, Vol. 24, pp387–391; Jamie Peck (1999) 'Editorial: grey geography?', *Transactions of the Institute of British Geographers*, Vol. 24, pp131–135 (and the 'Exchange' of views that ensued in *Transactions of the Institute of British Geographers*, Vol. 25, pp243–258); Susan Smith (2001) 'Editorial: emotional geographies', *Transactions of the Institute of British Geographers*, Vol. 26, pp7–10.

116. Jean Baudrillard (1983) *Simulations* (Semiotext(e), New York, NY) p2.

117. Marcus Doel, David Clarke (2002) 'An invention without a future, a solution without a problem: motor pirates, time machines, and drunkenness on the screen' in *Lost in Space: Geographies of Science Fiction*, eds Rob Kitchin, James Kneale (Continuum, London) pp136–155.

118. Marcus Doel (1999) 'Occult Hollywood: unfolding the Americanization of world cinema' in *The American Century: Consensus and Coercion in the Projection of American Power*, eds David Slater, Peter Taylor (Blackwell, Oxford) pp243–260.

119. Franz Kafka (1993) 'The burrow' in *Franz Kafka: Collected Stories* (David Campbell, London) p502.

120. Meursault is the stranger who killed an Arab in Albert Camus' (1958) *The Outsider*, trans. Joseph Laredo (1985 edition, Penguin, Harmondsworth). Contrary to what one might expect, the killing was not something for which Meursault was responsible, even though he calmly pulled the trigger of the gun. There was nothing personal about it. The killing was wholly impersonal, without motive, and bereft of reason – and so it is not unreasonable for Meursault to be without 'regret'. When pressed on the matter of regret at his trial, Meursault suggests that his only regret is that it happened, which is more of an 'annoyance' than a regret. Meursault is the stranger who happened to kill an Arab – that's all. As with Bartleby, Meursault frustrates a 'logic of expectation' – the expectation that one can pin responsibility, a motive, an explanation, and a regret on someone – with a 'logic of preference': it could have been otherwise, but what would it matter? Little wonder, then, that in the 'Afterword' to *The Outsider*, Camus should suggest that Meursault 'is condemned because he doesn't play the game' (p118). For Meursault, the killing happened – that's all. 'There is nothing to explain, nothing to understand, nothing to interpret' (Gilles Deleuze, 1977, 'I have nothing to admit', *Semiotext(e)*, Vol. 2, No. 3, p114). Cf. Jean Baudrillard (1996) *The Perfect Crime*, trans. Chris Turner (Verso, London).

121. Albert Camus (1958/1983) *The Outsider*, trans. Joseph Laredo (Penguin, Harmondsworth) p77. The same time-wasting technique is employed by Marco Stanley Fogg as he waits for an old and frail blind man to die: 'By the end, I had pushed myself to such lengths of precision that it took me hours to work my way around the room. I advanced by fractions of an inch, refusing to let anything escape me, not even the dust motes hovering in the air. I mined the limits of that space until it became inexhaustible, a plenitude of worlds within worlds' (Paul Auster, 1992, *Moon Palace*, Faber & Faber, London, p219). Cf. Marco Polo's geo-historical reading

of the ebony and ivory squares that compose the seemingly 'empty structure' of the Great Khan's imperial chessboard, as recounted in Italo Calvino's (1974) *Invisible Cities*, trans. William Weaver (Secker & Warburg, London) pp131–132: '*The quantity of things that could be read in a little piece of smooth and empty wood overwhelmed Kublai …*'

122. Gilles Deleuze, Claire Parnet (1987) *Dialogues*, trans. Hugh Tomlinson, Barbara Habberjam (Athlone, London) p16.

123. Herman Uytersprott, quoted in Zygmunt Bauman (1991) 'Kafka, or the difficulty of naming' in *Modernity and Ambivalence* (Polity, Cambridge) p179.

124. Gilles Deleuze (1990) *The Logic of Sense*, trans. Mark Lester with Charles Stivale, ed. Constantin Boundas (Columbia University Press, New York, NY).

125. Jean Baudrillard (1996) *The Perfect Crime*, trans. Chris Turner (Verso, London) p97.

126. Gilles Deleuze (1990) *The Logic of Sense*, trans. Mark Lester with Charles Stivale, ed. Constantin Boundas (Columbia University Press, New York, NY) p7.

127. A brief account of 'radically horizontal thought' – with particular reference to Gilles Deleuze's Nietzschean play of differential repetition – is provided by John Lechte (1994) *Fifty Contemporary Thinkers: From Structuralism to Postmodernity* (Routledge, London) pp101–105; Yve-Alain Bois, Rosalind Krauss (1997) *Formless: A User's Guide* (Zone, New York, NY).

128. Marcus Doel (1996) 'A hundred thousand lines of flight: a machinic introduction to the nomad thought and scrumpled geography of Gilles Deleuze and Félix Guattari', *Environment and Planning D: Society and Space*, Vol. 14, pp421–439. Cf. Yves-Alain Bois, Rosalind Krauss (1997) *Formless: A User's Guide* (Zone, New York, NY).

129. Jacques Derrida (1994) *Specters of Marx: The State of the Debt, the Work of Mourning, and the New International*, trans. Peggy Kamuf (Routledge, London) p29.

130. Paul Auster (1989) *In the Country of Last Things* (Faber & Faber, London) pp36.

131. See for example: Primo Levi (2000) 'Carbon' in *The Periodic Table*, trans. Raymond Rosenthal (Penguin, Harmondsworth) pp188–195; Victor Pelevin (1996) 'The life and adventures of shed Number XII' in *The Blue Lantern and Other Stories*, trans. Andrew Bromfield (New Directions, New York) pp138–149; Thomas Pynchon (1975) *V* (Picador, London).

132. Paul Auster (1987) *The New York Trilogy* (Faber & Faber, London) p3.

9

Computing geographical futures

John Pickles

Introduction

> 'I believe we need a "Digital Earth". A multi-resolution, three-dimensional representation
> of the planet, into which we can embed vast quantities of geo-referenced data.'
> (Vice President Gore, January 31, 1998 http://www.digitalearth.gov/)

> 'The virtual class has driven to global power along the digital superhighway. Representing
> perfectly the expansionary interests of the recombinant commodity-form, the virtual
> class has seized the imagination of contemporary culture by conceiving a techno-utopian
> high-speed cybernetic grid for traveling across the electronic frontier…. As the CEOs
> and the specialist consultants of the virtual class triumphantly proclaim: "Adapt or you're
> toast."… Always working on the basis of the illusion of enhanced interactivity, the digital
> superhighway is a big real estate venture in cybernetic form….' (Kroker and Weinstein,
> 1994, p7)

The transformations wrought by digital computers are giving rise to a variety of new 'cyber-
geographies' and new geographical imaginaries. From the utopian pragmatism of Vice
President Gore to the techno-pessimism of Kroker and Weinstein's analysis of the age of
the cybernetic grid as the age of dead information and 'roadkill' on the digital super-
highway, all agree that digitality and cybernetic systems of data collection, storage, analysis,
representation and communication are transforming society and space alike. As Crang,
Crang and May (1999) have pointed out:

> 'Whether framed through the more generalized notion of cyberspace, or the more
> specific phenomena of the internet, the World Wide Web, virtual reality, hypertext and
> genres of science fiction such as cyberpunk, it is hard to miss the proliferating debates
> over the social and geographical significance of new technologies of computer mediated
> communication.' (p1)

This chapter began as an invitation to write on the future geographies of these emerging
systems and practices, and I began by focusing on the changes wrought by contemporary
debates about Geographical Information Systems (GIS), particularly those resulting from
GIS-society initiatives in the United States. In practice, however, the issues involved in GIS-
society debates are increasingly merging with broader science-technology-society debates.
In turn, these debates, particularly surrounding the generalisation of cyberspaces in

everyday life, are also being affected by the interaction and merging of diverse imaging technologies.[1] As a result, the chapter has mutated into a series of reflections on the role of digital information and imaging systems in constructing new worlds, and secondly on the limits of computational representations.

As my title suggests, I am interested in the ways in which future geographies are being produced by computational information and imaging technologies. But, I am also interested in the ways that issues of non-equivalence and non-representability resist such productions and provide opportunities for new ways of using such technologies. I illustrate some aspects of these emerging cyber-geographies, discuss some of the ways in which digitality is transforming a variety of concrete and scholarly worlds, and provide a critique of the some of the triumphalist readings of cyberspace and the new worlds they seem to promise. In particular, the chapter aims to broaden the emerging discussion of 'the world in the wires' (with its attendant fixations on cyberspaces, virtual reality (VR) and gaming simulations) to a consideration of 'the wires in the world'. The chapter then turns to the implications of spatial data and imaging technologies, critical geography and democratic practice.

Global visions

'I will take as my point of departure a single feature, one that immediately defines our object of study. Scientific knowledge is a kind of discourse. And it is fair to say that for the last forty years the "leading" sciences and technologies have had to do with language: phonology and theories of linguistics, problems of communication and cybernetics, modern theories of algebra and informatics, computers and their languages, problems of translation and the search for areas of compatibility among computer languages, problems of information storage and data banks, telematics and the perfection of intelligent terminals…' Lyotard (1984, pp3–4)

'Growing bigger than ever. Redefining the social landscape. Building the first truly global economy. And the story is just beginning. What is it all about? Information communication technology (ICT), of course.' WITSA (2000, p2)

To say that the computer has changed the world is now little more than a trite commonplace. Computerisation has transformed many aspects of life, from the home to the most global of production, commercial or civil interchange. In recent years, digitality has begun to extend the scope and range of its influences across wider arenas of life and is rapidly producing new digital and digitised landscapes. From telecommunications in the home, roboticised production lines in the workplace, databases of the therapeutic and security agencies of the state, media based political campaigns, sophisticated self-guided missile systems, to 3-D imaging systems of the internal organs of the human body, cybernetic systems and cyborgs have been incorporated into social life. Consumers for these new products and practices have been painstakingly produced. New metaphors have been deployed to promote further adoption. Desert Storm and the Gulf War, in particular, showcased the new imaginary of digital reach, as Iraq's giant canon (symbol of old centralised warfare?) was pitted against mobile units carving their way through desert landscapes triangulating their positions using Global Positioning Systems (GPS) and smart bombers slipping massive bombs into the turrets and chimneys of 'military targets'. This showcasing of the power of new digital technologies became a full-blown public celebration of the new era of hyper-reality (and media and military hyperbole) in the daily broadcasts of NATO briefings of pin-point bombing in the Third Balkan War (see Ali, 2000).[2]

Beyond a political economy and geopolitics of technical change, a political technology of the social body and a corresponding regime of morality is also emerging, in which our understanding of the 'subject' itself is being reconfigured (see Hillis, 1999; Uebel, 1999). Felix Guattari (1991) has called this 'the fabrication of new *assemblages* of enunciation, individual and collective' (p8) in which actors and scales of action are no longer only governments and nation states, but complex assemblages that go well beyond the military industrial complex of the 1950s and 1960s.

In 1995, in *Ground Truth*, I argued that geographers should think in similar ways about Geographical Information Systems (GIS), and that they needed to begin to embed discussions about technology and its uses in wider disciplinary and social contexts. The book argued that geographers needed a social history of the origins and development of GIS, an account of its contemporary public and private uses and a discussion about its effects in transforming Geography and geographies.[3] The book asked geographers to consider, what might be the implications of the merger of spatial data handling and imaging systems with a host of other spatially referenced databases? What would happen as GIS began to merge with other technologies that included the internet and the World Wide Web? And, what opportunities might these provide for new disciplinary and social uses of geographical information technologies?[4]

Although some readers interpreted *Ground Truth* as 'a declaration of war' against GIS and 'a call to arms' for GIS practitioners, at the heart of the book was an attempt to focus attention on two aspects of digital spatial information systems. The first was to multiply situate the discussion of geographical information and imaging technologies within conceptual and interpretative frameworks in ways that might change how the everyday practice of GIS was understood. The second aspect on which we focused was the ways in which developments in GIS could be seen as part of a series of generic and global social and technological transformations. These included the ways in which geographic and digital information technologies more broadly had also become a part of the practices of war, peace and diplomacy, the ways in which they had become integral to corporate economic strategy, and the ways in which the building of large geo-referenced digital databases were beginning to pose serious threats to personal privacy, security and safety (and how these concerns were then deployed to surveil and regulate space).

In this sense, *Ground Truth* sought to broaden the scope of the nascent debate about GIS, science and society, and offer conceptual frames for dealing with what Giddens had earlier called the acknowledged and unacknowledged preconditions and intended and unintended consequences of action. In so doing, the authors sought to open up conversations in geography about the ways in which technology was already and always a thoroughly socio-geographical practice, how 'it' is shot-through with political and geopolitical imperatives, and how 'it' is institutionally embedded. But, it was also about how the representations 'it' produces and circulates are always dialectical, open, contingent and contestable. The collected essays sought to do this by providing a range of interpretative moments for understanding the new worlds being constructed. Optimistically, many saw in the new digital information and imaging systems what Michael Joyce (1999) has called 'a gesture of the parenthetical, the dialectic, the thematic, the rhythmic, the fugal, the isobaric, the metonymic, the list, the link, the litany, as well as any and all other – whether en-dashed or no – appositional stitchery [that] constitute the space of hypertextuality.'(p236) But they also warned about the ways in which new visual regimes and particular epistemologies were being emplaced. In the next section, I turn attention to five examples of large-scale cyber-engineering projects, at the heart of which are important new conceptions of space, bodies and subjects.

Emerging cyber-geographies: space, bodies and subjects

'The human capacity to visualize the globe, to place ourselves beyond our world and look in on it, is historically very recent and culturally quite specific. It is part of our inheritance from the European Renaissance, now diffused among all peoples. Global thinking is a capacity of enormous significance if for no other reason than that we all assume for ourselves the position that most peoples have historically reserved for God. No longer confined by the local worlds of our direct experience, the conception of the globe allows us to make *geography*, first to predict and then to discover new spaces, new worlds, new peoples. It is important to remember that geography is always imagined before it is seen and mapped.' Cosgrove (1989, p13)

In 1994/5, I was primarily concerned with the modernist and empiricist epistemologies that seemed to lie at the heart of the triumphalist claims made for GIS by its strongest adherents (Openshaw 1991, 1992). I was also concerned to draw attention to the scope and scale of the social engineering project that geographical information and imaging technologies represented. At the time, however, I was largely unaware of some of the more innovative engineering projects that are building new computational spaces and new geographies, and that will almost certainly change the ways in which we think about geographical information and imaging. It is to these that I now turn. The first is the Digital Earth Initiative, the second is medical imaging technologies, the third deals with a NASA project on the Vegetation Cover Lidar, and the fourth deals with virtual reality and full immersion computing environments.

The Digital Earth Initiative (DEI) is a coordinated effort on the part of federal government and non-government agencies to construct 'a virtual representation of our planet that enables a person to explore and interact with the vast amounts of natural and cultural information gathered about the Earth' (http://www.digitalearth.gov/main.html). The initiative was introduced in 1998 by then Vice President Gore as a means of mobilising government and non-governmental agencies to work together to integrate systems for collecting, retrieving, and representing geo-referenced data. DEI is specifically charged with addressing technical and organisational difficulties with managing and making available high quality georeferenced data through programs on computational science, mass storage, satellite imagery, broadband networks, interoperability and metadata.

> 'Imagine, for example, a young child going to a Digital Earth exhibit at a local museum. After donning a head-mounted display, she sees the Earth as it appears from space. Using a data glove, she zooms in, using higher and higher levels of resolution, to see continents, then regions, countries, cities, and finally individual houses, trees, and other natural and man-made objects. Having found an area of the planet she is interested in exploring, she takes the equivalent of a 'magic carpet ride' through a 3-D visualization of the terrain. Of course, terrain is only one of the numerous kinds of data with which she can interact. Using the system's voice recognition capabilities, she is able to request information on land cover, distribution of plan and animal species, real-time weather, roads, political boundaries, and population. She can also visualize the environmental information that she and other students all over the world have collected as part of the GLOBE project. This information can be seamlessly fused with the digital map or terrain data. She can get more information on many of the objects she sees by using her data glove to click on a hyperlink. To prepare her family's vacation to Yellowstone National Park, for example, she plans the perfect hike to the geysers, bison, and bighorn sheep that she has just read about. In fact, she can follow the trail visually from start to finish before she ever leaves the museum in her hometown.
>
> She is not limited to moving through space, but can also travel through time. After taking a virtual field-trip to Paris to visit the Louvre, she moves back in time to learn about French history, perusing digitized maps overlaid on the surface of the Digital Earth, newsreel footage, oral history, newspapers and other primary sources. She sends some of this information to her personal e-mail address to study later. The time-line, which stretches off in the distance, can be set for days, years, centuries, or even geological epochs, for those occasions when she wants to learn more about dinosaurs.' (Gore: http://www.digitalearth.gov/VP19980131.html)[5]

There is much that could be said about this initiative, and several of us have already debated the implications of the initiative (see Goodchild, 2000; Pickles, 2000; Rhind, 2000). The boldness, scope and level of investment in the initiative are certainly astounding, and the integration of data institutions and practices it promises offers stunning possibilities for expanding geographical research questions.

In many ways, DEI is a global engineering project based on computer scientist David Gelernter's *Mirror Worlds*. In *Mirror Worlds*, Gelernter (1992, p1)

> 'describes an event that will happen someday soon. You will look into a computer screen and see reality. Some part of your world – the town you live in, the company you work for, your school system, the city hospital – will hang there in sharp color image, abstract but recognizable, moving subtly in a thousand places.'

The mirror world of virtual reality and spatial images is a 'true-to-life mirror image trapped inside a computer – where you can see and grasp it whole' (p3). These images 'engulf some chunk of reality' (p6) and the mirror world 'reflects the real one' (p6). 'Fundamentally these programs are intended to help you comprehend the powerful, supertechno-glossy, dangerously complicated and basically indifferent man-made environments that enmesh you, and that control you to the extent that you don't control them' (p6).

How is this to happen? How will the 'place' of mirror world permit one to enter, stroll around and retrieve archival and live-medium information?

> 'The picture you see on your display represents a real physical layout. In a City Mirror World, you see a city map of some kind. Lots of information is superimposed on the map, using words, numbers, colors, dials – the resulting display is dense with data; you are tracking thousands of different values simultaneously. You can see traffic density on the streets, delays at the airport, the physical condition of the bridges, the status of markets, the condition of the city's finances, the current agenda at city hall and the board of education, crime conditions in the park, air quality, average bulk cauliflower prices and a huge list of others.
>
> This high-level view would represent – if you could achieve it at all – the ultimate and only goal of the *hardware* city model. In the software version, it's merely a starting point. You can dive deeper and explore. Pilot your mouse over to some interesting point and turn the *altitude* knob. Now you are inside a school, courthouse, hospital or City Hall. You see a picture like the one at the top level, but here it's all focussed on this *one* sub-world, so you can find out what's really going on down here. Meet and chat (electronically) with the local inhabitants, or other Mirror World browsers. You'd like to be informed whenever the zoning board turns its attention to Piffel Street? Whenever the school board finalizes a budget? Leave a software agent behind.' (Gelernter, 1992, pp16–17)

Like the Digital Earth Initiative, Gelernter's world is one of all information about a particular place available and mapped immediately, limited only by the speed of moving the mouse and dropping the agents. The new digital world is a mirror world – a world of hyper-textual information, geo-coded to a virtual globe, and devised to provide 'all information about one place'.

A similar kind of imaging technology has also emerged in recent years in medicine. Medical imaging systems are producing new representations that render the human body as transparent and its forms in depth.[6] These transparency models have already changed the way in which medicine operates, enabling a host of relatively non-invasive procedures to be developed in treating patients who previously would have required invasive surgery and long and difficult rehabilitation. These imaging technologies are, however, also producing new visual regimes and epistemologies that are no longer bound by an ontology of surfaces and bodies. In their places, doctors and geographers are beginning to deal with chimera, ghosts and holographs, or with monsters whose reality exceeds the 'real'.

This chimeric world of vision that penetrates solid objects, or what I have called elsewhere an ontology 'investing objects in depth' (Pickles, 2004) has captured the imagination of scientists dealing with both environmental and social problems. How do we carry out sophisticated and important analysis and make informed policy judgements about, for example, global warming without detailed knowledge about the process of forest growth and biomass exchanges? To know that, we need to know in detail the vertical structure of forest biomass. But how do we know about such vertical layers since, in most forests of the world we cannot see them either from the top because of canopy cover or from the bottom other than by guesswork. This is the goal of the Vegetation Canopy Lidar (VCL) project run out of the University of Maryland under NASA's Earth System Science Pathfinder (ESSP) program (http://www.geog.umd.edu/vcl/). The principal goal of VCL is the characterisation of the three-dimensional structure of the earth, in particular the mapping of the vertical and horizontal structure of the earth's vegetation cover and land surface topography.[7] The project will use:

> '5 diode-pumped, Q-switched Nd:YAG lasers, generating 15 mJ, 10 ns-wide Gaussian shaped pulses at a wavelength of 1064 nm. The lasers operate at frequencies of 10 Hz (over oceans) and 242 Hz (over land). Lasers are in a circular configuration which from a 400 km-high orbit will span an 8 km-wide area. Laser footprints are 25 m wide. They are near contiguous in the along track direction, and spaced 2 km apart across track … Global Positioning System (GPS) and Satellite Laser Ranging (SLR) techniques provide the spacecraft orbit to 15 cm (1 sigma) accuracy.' (http://www.geog.umd.edu/vcl/)

Here, the forest is being rendered visible in depth and, as a result, new spaces of information are being constructed and opened. Perhaps the boldest of these 'spaces of revealment' are the pictures of the 'real' earth or the 'earth as it really is', cleaned of clouds and dust to reveal a thoroughly de-natured earth, an image that is fast becoming iconic in earth science circles, particularly on the World Wide Web. But, the denaturing is the production of a new second nature – a transparent holographic earth, and it is this holographic imaginary seems to be at work in so many current efforts to model and reproduce the natural and social environment in digital informational terms. It is in holography, virtual reality (VR) machines and full immersion environments that this impulse reaches its zenith, both in terms of the technical advances being made and in the commercial and military interest in them. Full immersion environments and VR simulations push these ontologies of transparency to their full extension and, like the examples we have discussed, invest their subjects in depth. Gone are ontologies of non-penetrable surfaces and objects. Now all objects are bundles of information that can be imaged in as many ways as they can be imagined: the boundary layer of clouds is wiped 'clean' from 'cloud-free globes' (http://www.earth-images.com/haz.htm), the surface boundary of the earth is rendered plastic and transparent, the forest canopy is rendered in depth and the privacy of the home is rendered as resource for polling and sales.

There is much that could be made of the power and value of such holographic and immersive technologies, but for my present purposes I want to link our current fascinations with those of a different era, through a brief reading of Walter Benjamin's *Passagen-Werk* and his discussion of four representational technologies – part of a previous representational transition – taken from nineteenth-century Paris (Benjamin, 1999).[8]

Benjamin's *Passagen-Werk* project was carried out in Paris up to and during the early years of the Second World War. The explicit goal of the project was an investigation of the cultural and economic transformations at work in nineteenth-century Paris at a time of major capitalist restructuring, a time very much akin to our own end-of-century period of restructuring and change.

In turning to Paris it is significant for our purposes to note that what was new at the time was not the urban brilliance and luxury of the city, but secular public access to them (Susan Buck-Morss, 1989). Paris was, in this sense, a 'looking-glass city' and a Mirror City that dazzled the crowds, reflecting images of new consumer goods and consumers, but 'keeping the class relations of production virtually invisible on the looking glass's other side.' This spectacle of Paris Benjamin called '"phantasmagoria" – a magic lantern show of optical illusions, rapidly changing size and blending into one another' (Buck-Morss, 1989, p81). 'In this system everything desirable came to be transformed into fetishised images of commodities-on-display...'

Benjamin sought to unmask this fetishised Mirror World of end-of-century Paris by describing what he called the 'ur-forms of the phantasmagoria of progress'. Four such ur-forms are of direct interest to our present discussion: the panorama, the arcade, the world exhibition and the plate-glass shop window. Each represents elements of the informational transition that was occurring in the late nineteenth century as Western capitalist economies internationalised and new global imperial geographies were built. The panorama was a new technology of visual representation organised and moved around different cities to present spectacles of one form or another to eager middle-class consumers. The panoramas provided sweeping views that rolled by the viewer at varying speeds, giving the impression of movement through the world at accelerated speed (Buck-Morss, 1989, p82). Panoramas were a common feature of the new commercial arcades springing up throughout the city ('the original temple of commodity capitalism'); and it was in the arcades that the flow of images and the flow of commodities came together (Figure 9.1). The arcades were the precursors of the department store and, in more contemporary form, the panorama and the arcade conjoined as precursors for the digital world of the internet and on-line shopping. But it was not just shopping that was so commodified. Information itself was being rendered into a fetishised commodity, and its high point was the emergence of the great world exhibitions, the first being in London in 1851 – a Mirror World of a different kind; a Crystal Palace (Figure 9.2). It was in these great international exhibitions and

Figure 9.1   *Panorama*

OPENING OF THE GREAT EXHIBITION, HYDE PARK.

(After the Picture by Eugène Lamé.)

Figure 9.2 *Crystal palace exhibition*

fairs that the 'pleasure industry' has its origin, and it is they that:

> 'refined and multiplied the varieties of reactive behaviour of the masses. It thereby prepares the masses for adapting to advertisements. The connection between the advertising industry and world exhibitions is thus well-founded.' Buck-Morss (1989, p85)

The exhibitions and arcades incorporated another technology that became fundamental to a modernist sensibility: the large plate-glass window. This leant to sellers the ability to display goods for view, but prevented consumers from touching. Pleasure was now to be derived from the visual spectacle alone. The representation of far away places and possible ways of life came, in itself, to be a source of pleasure, as was the broadening experience and promise of movement, global reach and speed. Exhibitions and arcades were, then, for Benjamin the source of a broader phantasmagorical politics: 'a promise of social progress for the masses without revolution' (Buck-Morss, 1989, p86). 'Each successive exhibition was called upon to give visible "proof" of historical progress toward the realization of these utopian goals, by being more monumental, more spectacular than the last' (p87), and each show-cased the technologies that enabled the movement of goods around the globe. Speed, information and access came to symbolise progress.

I think Benjamin's *fin de siècle* modernity provides a useful corrective to the triumphalism of our own contemporary techno-hype. But, unlike Kroker and Weinstein with whose technophobia we began this chapter, Benjamin struggled constantly to read social and technical change in terms of dialectical images.

Global reach and combined and uneven development

> 'The gold rush is on. The hypermedia are happening. Whatever you call it, here come interactive graphics, text, video, all somehow user-chosen. But how will they tie together? If producers knew where all this was going, the rush would rival the advent of the Talkies. Meanwhile, each manufacturer says its gizmo will be the centerpiece of the hypermedia gold rush.' Nelson (1992, p157)

> 'A depiction is never just an illustration. It is the material representation, the apparently stabilised product of a process of work. And it is the site for the construction and depiction of social differences. To understand a visualisation is thus to inquire into its provenance and into the social work that it does. It is to note its principles of exclusion and inclusion, to detect the roles that it makes available, to understand the way in which they are distributed, and to decode the hierarchies and differences that it naturalizes. And it is also to analyze the ways in which authorship is constructed or concealed and the sense of audience is realised.' (Fyfe and Law, 1988, p1)

What kind of objects and identities are being produced in the digital transition? What forms of territorialisation are at work in the Digital Earth project? I have already suggested that Vice President Gore's vision is both about a digital informational world *and* it is about retraining and recomposition of the US labour force and the restructuring of the US economic and geopolitical position in the world. It is, in a Gramscian sense, a new Americanism – a thorough-going post-Fordism, with important implications for the ways in which notions of social progress are being written, global relations understood and an American (and global) future is being mapped. This emerging geography of the 'digital transition' is, of course, difficult to describe, in part because it is changing so quickly. Last year's cautions about the 'over-reaching' claims of boosters are over-matched by the growth, diffusion and accessibility of this year's products. Writing any geography of the transition is fraught with danger and likely to be overly conservative in its judgments. But there are some things we can say.

First, underpinning contemporary claims for the democratising potentials of informatics is a strong liberal notion of the public sphere in which people (usually 'men') of good faith join in debate about their collective futures predicated on notions of individual autonomy, private property and effective state power. The promise and possibility of informed open discussion is mobilised through claims to providing more information and more access to information; providing tools for sustaining and enlarging opportunities for 'voice' and 'access' in an arena of reasoned, open, un-coerced discourse. In this digital public sphere, technology provides new possibilities for access to information, subject formation and the flourishing of civil society, albeit against an increasingly transparent backcloth of monopoly control and differential access and benefit.

Second, like all highways, the information highway requires capital investment, points of access, navigation skills and spatial and cultural proximity for effective use. Like the automobile highway, the information highway fosters new rounds of creative destruction and differentiates among users and between users and non-users. As Roszak (1986, p28) so presciently argued in the case of the United States:

> 'It is thanks to the financial leverage provided by this firm commitment to the warfare state that the corporate community has been able to engineer the wrenching break with America's industrial past we now find ourselves in. In large part, the advent of the information economy means that our major corporations are rapidly retiring two generations of old capital or moving it abroad. As they do so, with the rich support of military contracts, they are liberating themselves from the nation's most highly unionized labor so that investment may be transferred into more profitable fields. High tech is not only glamorous; it pays off handsomely, especially if those who are collecting the profits are excused from paying the social costs that result from running down old industrial centers and disempowering their work force…'

The result has been a massive reinvestment in the computerisation of every aspect of economic, political and social life, and a major contributor to the growth of the US economy in the 1990s. North America is by far the largest regional market for Information Communication Technology (ICT), spending $796 billion in 1999 alone, resulting in growing differentials between it and all other regions (Table 9.1). The top ten national information economies account for 80% of the global ICT market, whereas the bottom 10 represent a collective share of less than one percent (WITSA, 2000, p7).

The serious nature of the digital divide has prompted response at the highest levels of the US government. But, the same solutions are often pursued with recommendations

Table 9.1 Information Technology spending by country as % of world spending

	1992	1993	1994	1995	1996	1997
US	35.2	36.5	36.6	35.1	35.1	35.8
Japan	16.4	17.1	17.3	17.6	17.5	17.6
Germany	8.3	8.0	7.6	7.9	7.3	6.6
United Kingdom	5.9	5.3	5.3	5.4	5.4	5.7
France	6.0	5.7	5.4	5.7	5.4	5.1
Italy	3.5	2.9	3.0	2.9	2.9	2.8
Canada	3.0	2.9	2.8	2.6	2.6	2.6
Brazil	1.0	1.2	1.0	1.2	1.5	1.9
Australia	1.7	1.7	1.8	1.7	1.8	1.9
China (PRC)	0.6	0.7	0.8	1.3	1.5	1.6
Korea	1.2	1.2	1.3	1.5	1.8	1.5
Netherlands	1.7	1.6	1.6	1.7	1.6	1.5

Source: WITSA: Digital Planet: The Global Information Economy Report, formerly posted at http://www.aiia.com.au/international/WITSstudy.html

for further rounds of investment in the same technologies that produced the divide in order to diffuse access and use across wider areas and social groups:[9]

> 'a national initiative is required to close the gap between the information haves and have-nots. Thus, we were very encouraged by your [President Clinton] December Executive memorandum, Narrowing the "Digital Divide": Creating Opportunities for All Americans in the Information Age, directing various cabinet agencies to develop strategies and strengthen programs to make information infrastructure accessible to the information "have-nots" … .
>   … information technology tools and applications can provide opportunities that transcend barriers of race, gender, disability, age, income, and location'.
> President's Information Technology Advisory Committee (2000, cover letter and p1)

Third, as market ideology and monopoly capital extend their sway through an economy of 'information' more aspects of individual life become objects of counting, measuring and analysis. Modern technological society even sets up human beings and nature as objects of manipulation in such ways that '[o]ur whole human existence everywhere sees itself challenged – now playfully and now urgently, now breathlessly and now ponderously – to devote itself to the planning and calculating of everything' (Heidegger, 1969, pp34–35).[10] Not only do contemporary data technologies treat all data and information within a universal calculus and binary logic, and imaging technologies reach without break across socially and historically differentiated territories, but the tools themselves permit types of surveillant intervention that restructure everyday life itself (Pickles, 1991; Lyon, 1994; Curry, 1995; Goss, 1995; Graham, 1999). Thus, if the modernising impulse of electronic technology is interpreted by some as liberatory – as creating new opportunities for civil society to forge 'communities' of correspondence such as the emergence of computerised e-mail networks and bulletin boards – others are more sanguine about the rationalising effects of such modernising technologies. New systems of knowledge engineering raise many questions about freedom, civil society and democratic practice.[11]

For some the future of geo-referenced information technologies must be understood in terms of past rounds of investment in territorial mapping. As Hall (1992) and Chrisman (1997a, b) have each demonstrated so nicely, the last great state-led project of mapping – the topographic surveys of the nation states – itself produced a highly uneven geography with terrible consequences for some. Arguing that the origins and early history of GIS has been curiously ignored, John Cloud's accounts of what he calls its 'clandestine history' traces the development of present geographic science technologies during the Second World War and the Cold War, and argues that these histories are 'complexly entangled with global geopolitics and the most secret technologies and programs in modern history' (Cloud, 2000).[12] These projects, amongst others, are beginning to document the ways geographers have too easily forgotten their own histories and the ways in which practices and technologies have been shaped by very real social considerations, many beyond the control or knowledge of the researchers involved.[13] These unacknowledged foundations have prefigured the choices already made in the construction and development of both technologies and their related practices, and they continue to 'act' through the complex ways in which research and development is funded and underwritten.[14]

The convergence of information and imaging systems provides rich new opportunities for the geographical imagination. One particularly interesting example is Martin Dodge's *An Atlas of Cyberspaces*, which maps the 'new electronic territories of the Internet, the World Wide Web and other emerging Cyberspaces' (http://www.cybergeography.org/atlas/atlas.html).

> 'These maps of cyberspaces – cybermaps – help us visualise and comprehend the new digital landscapes beyond our computer screen, in the wires of the global communications networks and vast online information resources. The cybermaps, like maps of the real world, help us navigate the new information landscapes, as well being objects of aesthetic interest. They have been created by "cyber-explorers" of many different disciplines, and from all corners of the world.'

The atlas is rich and varied, and the maps illustrate well the geographically uneven nature of access, connectivity and interaction in this new 'world in the wires' (Figure 9.3). Not surprisingly, older patterns of geographical and social investment and disinvestments are often reproduced in the new cyber-geographies, and the resulting 'digital divides' are as startling as many of the other economic and demographic divides that characterise the modern world.

Disintegration in the process of creation: possibilities for a democratising economy of the sign

> 'They are just letters of the alphabet on a page; you can scroll up such a poem like a map. The syntax has come apart. The letters are scattered and assembled again in a rough-and-ready way. There is no language anymore … it has to be invented all over

Figure 9.3 *Source: An Atlas of Cyberspaces. http://www.cybergeography.org/atlas/atlas.html.*
Copyright © Stephen G. Eick. Used with permission.

again. Disintegration right in the innermost process of creation.' Hugo Ball (1915)
referring to the work of Futurist Marinetti, quoted in Melzer (1976, p29)

'Communities are to be distinguished, not by their falsity/genuineness, but by the style in
which they are imagined.' Anderson (1983: p6)

In this final section I want to turn to the Dadaist impulses reflected in Hugo Ball's
response to Marinetti's work and ask, with Benedict Anderson, what communities are possible and how we might imagine new forms of community and the deployment of information technologies appropriate to them, while holding on to a healthy skepticism about the
origins, embeddedness and uses of digital information systems. That is, what are the possibilities of opening digital spatial data technologies to new social practices? In what ways are
new metaphors, technical capacities and social practices emerging around a reworking of
our understanding of cybernets and cyber-geographies? Specifically, to where might we
turn to begin to think further about new axes of thought and practice for dealing with
information technologies?

Three largely discrete areas of work seem to me to offer some promise for extending
both the technical capacities and creating new forms of digital information and visualisation systems, and for allowing new relationships and new balances between technology
and societal users. The first is technical and derives from the convergence of digital information technologies (see Pickles (1999) for a parallel argument dealing with technical
convergence and the future role of GIS). As Toulouse (1997, p3) illustrates, in discussing
HTML, information systems are increasingly converging and becoming inter-operable:

'Hyper Text Markup Language freed network computing from the confines of academia
by generating an alternative to the ugly esoteric "know-the-code" command-line interfaces

of UNIX and DOS. In conjunction with the rapid development of desktop CPUs by Intel and Motorola, HTML browsers like Netscape's Navigator have made it possible for ordinary middle-class computer owners who obtain an Internet connection to point-and-click to display Web pages and to bounce from website to website around the globe. Sites now feature sound and the Web is beginning to revolutionise the distribution of images as it exerts its technological prowess over the magazine, in terms of speed of distribution, and the television set, in terms of picture quality.'

These convergences are producing many more user-friendly interfaces.

As we have seen, powerful information technologies are changing all aspects of social life, directly in OECD countries and less directly or only indirectly in poor countries of the South. But, for the moment, we have only poor languages and inadequate architectures for fostering interactivity at the point of the production, analysis and representation of digital data. At all points, complex expert systems and sophisticated technical expertise are required to mediate person and machine to enable the new forms of social interaction, communities of dialogue and interactive settings that are being produced.

Certainly, it is true that even within existing architectures access is hard to deny, networks are quite difficult to control, information is readily accessible and used by individuals and groups with limited budgets and expertise, and the ability to use the technology in depth permits civic and environmental groups to pursue worthy goals. Moreover, as Harvey and Chrisman (1998) have insisted, there are cultural geographies to all technological adoptions, even to the extent that the 'same software' run on the 'same hardware' following the 'same rules' can result in different forms, depending the tacit cultures and norms of practice. Vattimo has been even more emphatic about this reading of informatics: even within the constraints of digital data and expert knowledge systems that underpin so much geographical information technology,

'generalized communication explodes like a multiplicity of "local" rationalities – ethnic, sexual, religious, cultural or aesthetic minorities – that finally speak up for themselves. They are no longer repressed and cowed into silence by the idea of a single true form of humanity that must be realized irrespective of particularity and individual finitude, transience and contingency' (Vattimo, 1992, p9).

In the place of a national media, networks of remote correspondents are emerging dropping in and out of on-going 'conversations' and information exchanges, surfer-citizens gliding through hyperspace and cyber-gates, cruising the virtual night for contact and data, empowered by the 'unregulated' flow and 'open access' to new worlds of information, new communities of solidarity, and new spaces for action. For Vattimo at least there is something at the very heart of computerised information technologies that keeps open the possibility of new uses and new users. In taking apart worlds of meaning and smashing them into little pieces of data: ones and zeros, bits and bytes, digital information systems enable reassemblages into new meaning systems with new representational forms; digital Dadaism for democracy!

The second area of work is social and falls under the general rubric of participatory GIS, in which struggles for more democratic control over the development and use of GIS technologies are producing new discursive practices within GIS and geography itself, as well as reconfigurations of the processes and practices of GIS development. More sensitive to public needs and access, participatory GIS nonetheless contains within it rich political and social strains of thinking and is itself a highly contested terrain of social struggle over technology and social practice.

While few in geography have been as triumphalist as Vattimo about the possibilities for new social uses of geographical information technologies (although see Oppenshaw, 1991), there have been several efforts to engage with the possibilities of building more accessible and interactive geographical information systems, what has come to be called GIS2.[15] One such undertaking is the Public Participation GIS Project (PPGIS).[16] Growing out of an NCGIA initiative on GIS and Society, PPGIS quickly captured the imagination of geographers interested in issues of access and control over information and technology. There were also exciting new technical issues about the types of data that were represented, the forms of representation appropriate to different categories of users and the possibilities for building new information systems. These would need to have more open architectures, be amenable to different types of user needs and would stress the conflicts, errors and ambiguities of particular data and representational choices. As the ability to integrate geographical data of a wide range of types has increased, so have the kinds of user and needs broadened. In this regard, two issues seem crucial to me.

How do we build architectures that address the issue of interactivity, not only in terms of integrating and accessing various forms of geographical information (including spatial data, imagery, sound, video for places and areas), but also in ways that enable individuals and groups to 'build' their own geographical repositories and databanks? The issue is both technically and organisationally challenging, involving as it does the need for complex new architectures and ethnographic practices for information gathering in settings in which community groups are directly controlling the agenda. The issue is challenging because it requires a rethinking of the relationship between science and society, between the representation of information and the representation of citizens. This leads to the third new area of work.

In *We Have Never Been Modern*, Bruno Latour asked what it means to ask whether the project of modernity was, or could ever be, fulfilled. Through a discussion of the debate between Boyle and Hobbes in the mid-seventeenth century, Latour showed how a modern notion of representation came into being at the same time that a binary distinction between science and politics emerged to frame the way we understand the modern world. The Boyle–Hobbes debate stands, in this discussion, for an originary moment from which sprang two notions of representation, underpinned by a single anxiety about the necessity of moulding and controlling the masses. One notion of representation involves the political representation of the views of citizen in an emerging democracy – representative democracy. In this notion of representation, a modern notion of 'society' is born as that structure of social relations that *must be* represented and regulated politically; a Leviathan that will require maps of its territory and information about its citizens and places. A second notion of representation involves natural objects and through such representations 'nature' as we now know it was produced. The 'constitution' of modernity is therefore the structure of science and politics that keeps society and nature distinct and subject to regimes of representation by experts: political leaders on the one hand and scientific scholars on the other.

Latour's point is that even our most basic categories of 'society' and 'nature' have been produced historically as what he calls a governing 'constitution' of the modern world. However, as the title of the book indicates, We Have Never Been Modern, Latour believes that the constitution and binary geometry of modernity have never been, and can never be, the structure of practice of everyday life of actual citizens. Instead, the constitution that separates society and nature, politics and science, representer and represented has given birth to unrepresented/unrepresentable monsters and hybrids.

I take two primary lessons from Latour's argument. The first is that issues of democratic representation cannot be severed from issues of scientific representation. The two notions of representation mark the structure of the constitution of modernity and in this historical sense they are mutually constitutive. As a result, efforts to 'open' the technology to 'the people' are not only about the process of increasing access and levels of participation. Democratising technology must also involve an interrogation (and deconstruction) of the positionality and politics of expert systems and scientific knowledge production. That is, democracy is about politics and epistemology.

The second lesson is that the modern constitution has never been and can never be achieved 'in practice'. Scientific representation has always been a form of political representation, both in its silence about its political commitments (e.g. 'positivism') and in the ways in which its political roles have always been contested. As a result, the modern constitution of representation has produced new assemblages, hybrids and monsters that indeed 'represent' the inability of politics or science to hold separate the two economies of representation. But, these assemblages, hybrids and monsters are, and have always been, the possibility of something different; the 'spaces of hope' (Harvey, 2000) that refuse totalisation.

As Eric Sheppard has asked, are the futures of geographical information technologies and computational geographies to lie in building bigger and better mousetraps – a larger Leviathan such as the Digital Earth? Or do digitality and IT offer possibilities for contesting further the very constitution of representational science and politics? In this sense, democratisation rests not on 'representation' per se, but on the deepening of the Enlightenment imperative of keeping open the possibility that that which we take for the 'real' could always be otherwise. Is there, for example, in digital systems already emerging a hybrid iconographic, non-representational, cartography? (see Pickles (2004) for further elaboration of this point.) For Landow and Delany (1992), digital information systems, and specifically hypertext, are already producing new ways of theorising information and representation. The apparently infinite malleability and reproducibility of spatial information in digital systems allows, even forces, us to rethink the relations among objects and practices that have been set in concrete for hundreds of years under the regime of print capitalism (Anderson, 1991). Textuality, narrative, margins, inter-textuality and the roles and functions of readers and writers are all reconfigured in the digital text. The digital transformations of geo-mapping in Roland Barthes' terms point to the possibility of the production of writerly (rather than readerly) texts, which do not dominate the reader and insist on particular readings, but engage the reader as an 'author' and insist upon the openness and inter-textuality of the text – that is, its openness to other texts and readings. That is, digitality opens up again the question of the participation of the masses and provides new opportunities for interactivity lost to an earlier nineteenth century information revolution. This is the direction that Stengers (2000, p118) has been pushing us in her calls for a 'guerrilla' epistemology:

> 'the problem of the contemporary sciences is not, for me, one of scientific rationality but of a very particular form of mobilization: it is a matter of succeeding in aligning interests, in disciplining them without destroying them. The goal is not an army of sol-diers all marching in step in the same direction; there has to be an initiative, a sense of opportunity that belongs rather to the guerrilla.'

But, in this sense, Stengers does not go far enough, still caught in a vanguardist logic of expert systems in which 'the guerrilla has to imagine himself [sic] as belonging to a discip-lined army, and relate the sense and possibility of his local initiatives to the commands of staff headquarters'.

Gillian Rose (1993) has struck even further at the heart of modernist 'Cartographic anx-ieties' in suggesting that the conception of the mirror and the Imperial Eye, so prevalent in the history of modern cartography, is also thoroughly masculinist. In its place, she suggests, we need to think in terms a different epistemology of mapping, one in which the mirror has been broken into a thousand pieces, each shard still reflecting, but without coherence, without the possibility of the universal view, without the possibility of control. Is this a future that is possible or even desirable in the 'digital transition/transformation'? Is this a future way of thinking about mapping practice? Is this a new cartography?

Like Walter Benjamin, Allucquere Rosanne Stone (1995) also seems to have grown tired of trying to think of these issues in terms of utopian or dystopian perspectives, and – like Benjamin – she asks in *The War of Desire and Technology at the Close of the Mechanical Age*, what is happening in the deployment of emergent digital technologies, what kinds of 'counter-images' are available to us, and what new forms of identity are being produced?

> '*The War of Desire and Technology* is about science fiction, in the sense that it is about the emergent technologies, shifting boundaries between the living and the nonliving, optional embodiments … in other words, about the everyday world as cyborg habitat. But it is only partly about cyberspace. It is also about social systems that arise in the phantasmatic spaces enabled and constituted through communication technologies…. I am interested in prosthetic communication for what it shows of the 'real' world that might otherwise go unnoticed. And I am interested because of the potential of cyberspace for emergent behavior, for new social forms that arise in a circumstance in which *body, meet, place*, and even *space* mean something quite different from our accustomed understanding. I want to see how tenacious these new social forms are in the face of adversity, and what we can learn from them about social problems outside the worlds of the nets.'

And this is, surely, one of the challenges for any future critical computational, prosthetic geographies. The phantasmatic spaces are contestable, but they will be contested by the very forces of monopoly power and totalitarian logics that led Walter Benjamin with his manuscript of the Arcades Project into the hills along the French–Spanish border where both he and his particular project of dialectical images met their end.[17]

Acknowledgements

This paper owes a great deal to the extended discussions of the History of GIS group (particularly David Mark, Patrick McHaffie, Ken Hillis and Michael Curry), the GIS and Society group of NCGIA Initiative 19 (particularly Eric Sheppard, David Mark, Michael Curry, Daniel Weiner, Francis Harvey, Nick Chrisman), and the participants of the conferences and workshops of each.

Notes

1. I made this point in *Ground Truth* in 1995, and again in Pickles (1998). The convergence and generalisation of digital information technologies presents geographers with an exciting opportunity to find new ways of talking about and using computational informational and imaging technologies. For an excellent collection of essays that do just this see Crang, Crang and May (1999). On the social aspects of computing see the bibliography by Agre (1998).

2. See Libicki (1994) 'The Mesh and the Net: Speculations on Armed Conflict In an Age of Free Silicon', http://www.ndu.edu/ndu/inss/macnair/mcnair28/m028cont.html. In a related vein see also the Institute for the Advanced Study of Information Warfare (IASIW), http://www.psycom.net/iwar.1.html.

3. See the NCGIA Initiative 19, GIS and Society http://www.geo.wvu.edu/i19/; the History of GIS Project http://www.geog.buffalo.edu/ncgia/gishist/ (David M Mark, Nicholas Chrisman, Andrew U Frank, Patrick H McHaffie, John Pickles, 1997); the Varenius Project http://www.ncgia.ucsb.edu/varenius/ncgia.html; and the projects of the University Consortium for Geographic Information Science http://www.ucgis.org/.

4. Of course, this begs what might be the more important question of what will come to constitute identifiably 'geographical' information technologies as research on complex representational forms and systems, such as solid body imaging, immersive environments and virtual reality technologies, begin to merge with current technologies and practices. See, for example, Baraff (1989, 1994) on computer simulation of non-penetrating rigid bodies, http://www.cs.cmu.edu/~baraff/papers/sig89.pdf and http://www.cs.cmu.edu/~baraff/papers/sig94.pdf, Youngblut *et al* (1996) on virtual environment interface technology, www.hitl.washington.edu/scivw/IDA/, and Cruz-Neira *et al* (1993) on surround-screen projection-based virtual reality, http://www.evl.uic.edu/EVL/RESEARCH/PAPERS/CRUZ/sig93.paper.html.

5. Other sources for Digital Earth include: http://digitalearth.gsfc.nasa.gov/; http://www.digitalearth.gov/; http://www.digitalearth.gov/vision.html; http://www.icase.edu/~tom/DigitalEarth/DEResources.html. See also the Global mapping project at http://www1.gsi-mc.go.jp/iscgm-sec/.

6. See the US Institute of Health's Visible Human Project: http://www.nlm.nih.gov/research/visible/visible_human.html and http://www.nlm.nih.gov/research/visible/visible_gallery.html. http://www.madsci.org/~lynn/VH/planes.html

7. This will be the first systematic mapping of the vertical structure of most forest on the globe.

8. This reading was originally presented at the International Cartographic Association Congress in Ottawa (Pickles, 1998) and has been developed in regard to the Digital Earth Initiative in Pickles (2000). I am grateful to editors of *Cartographic Perspectives* for permission to draw on this text here.

9. See the President's Information Technology Advisory Committee (PITAC) Report, *Information Technology Research: Investing in Our Future* (http://www.ccic.gov/ac/ report/). In April 2000, a United Nations panel urged the world organisation to redirect its aid programs to help poorer countries with less internet access catch up. The panel's chair, former Costa Rican president Jose Maria Figueres-Olsen, said panel members were disturbed by the lack of a UN strategy for helping spread technologies such as the Internet, and suggested the world body allocate more money. 'The United Nations has a series of unconnected, small initiatives, all trying to do their own to' push information technology, Figueres-Olsen said. He added that the world body should make the same commitment to technology that it has to combating HIV/AIDS and fostering gender equality. The panel, assembled by UN Secretary-General Kofi Annan, is comprised of 18 government and business leaders. Source: UN Wire, http://www.unesco.org/webworld/news/000425_un_digidivide. shtml.

10. Telemarketing, junk mailing and the availability of individual information such as credit information on the web, all of it geo-coded, makes the 'individual' and the 'household' ever more available for commercial and political users. These examples seem to me to be precisely the kind of colonising of lifeworlds and the rendering of home life and family increasingly as resource or standing reserve for consumption to which Heidegger was pointing.

11. See, for example, the interesting work on subject formation in regard to the practices and effects of cyber-porn by Michael Uebel (2000), privacy by Michael Curry (1996) and surveillance and individual behavior in the city by Stephen Graham (1999).

12. David Mark has also begun to write a history of the military involvement in the development of TIN (Triangular Independent Networks). 'TIN, or Triangulated Irregular Network, represents a topographic elevation surface by a tesselation of non-overlapping triangles, with elevations at their corners' (Mark, 1997). This work is being carried out under the rubric of the History of GIS Project currently administered by David Mark at the University of Buffalo. See http://www.geog.buffalo.edu/ ncgia/gishist/.

13. This issue recently came home to me again in watching a PBS documentary on 'Military Weapons' in which senior executives of the company that gathers and disseminates SPOT imagery could not contain their delight when describing how SPOT imagery had serviced the needs of the Defense Department in Desert Storm and NATO in Kosovo (Public Broadcasting Service, 2000).

14. See Eric Sheppard's (1995) wonderful essay on the partially determined nature of technological choice. See also Sheppard (1993).

15. The term was suggested by Stan Openshaw at Friday Harbor meeting of the NCGIA Initiative 19 on GIS and Society.
16. Details are available at http://www.ncgia.maine.edu/ppgis/ppgishom.html and http:// www.ncgia.ucsb.edu/varenius/ppgis/ncgia.html.
17. On his journey to Spain to flee the Nazis in France, Benjamin is known to have carried a suitcase. He told a friend this contained the manuscript of a life's major work. It is thought this may have been the only copy of the Arcades Project.

Bibliography

Agre, P (1998) 'Social aspects of computing' http://www.tao.ca/wind/rre/0330.html.

Ali, T (ed.) (2000) *Masters of the University: NATO's Balkan Crusade*, London: Verso.

Anderson, B (1983/1991), *Imagined Communities: Reflections on the Origin and Spread of Nationalism*, London: Verso.

Baraff, D (1989) 'Analytical methods for dynamic simulation of non-penetrating rigid bodies', *Computer Graphics* (Proc. SIGGRAPH), 23, 223–232.

Baraff, D (1994) 'Fast contact force computation for nonpenetrating rigid bodies' *Computer Graphics* (Proc. SIGGRAPH), 28, 23–34

Benjamin, W (1999) *The Arcades Project*, trans. Howard Eiland and Kevin McLaughlin, Cambridge, Mass.: Harvard University Press.

Buck-Morss, S (1989) *The Dialectics of Seeing: Walter Benjamin and the Arcades Project*, Cambridge, MASS.: The MIT Press.

Chrisman, N (1997a) *Exploring Geographic Information Systems*, London: Wiley.

Chrisman, N (1997b) 'GIS as Social Practice: or why standards are doomed to failure', presented at UCGIS Annual Retreat, Bar Harbor Maine, June, http://faculty.washington.edu/chrisman/Present/ BarHarb.html.

Cloud, J G (2000) 'Hidden in Plain Sight: The Clandestine Histories of GIS', UCGIS Summer Assembly 2000, Oregon, http://www.ucgis.org/oregon/entries.html.

Cosgrove, D (1989) 'Looking In On Our World: Images of Global Geography', *The Globe: Representing the World*, York: Allanwood Press, 13–18.

Crang, M, Crang, P and May, J (eds) (1999) *Virtual Geographies: Bodies, Space and Relations*, London: Routledge.

Cruz-Neira, C, Sandin, D J and DeFanti, T A (1993) 'Surround-Screen Projection-Based Virtual Reality: The Design and Implementation of the CAVE', in *Proceedings of SIGGRAPH '93 Computer Graphics Conference*, ACM SIGGRAPH, August, 135–142. http://www.evl.uic.edu/EVL/RESEARCH/PAPERS/CRUZ/sig93.paper.html.

Curry, M (1995) 'On the inevitability of ethical inconsistency in geographical information systems' in John Pickles, (ed.) *Ground Truth: The Social Implications of Geographic Information Systems*, New York: Guilford Press.

Curry, M (1996) 'In plain and open view: Geographic information systems and the problem of privacy', *Proceedings of the Conference on Law and Information Policy for Spatial Databases*, Santa Barbara, CA: National Center for Geographic Information and Analysis. http://www.spatial.maine.edu/tempe/curry.html.

Curry, M (1998) *Digital places: Living with Geographic Information Technologies*, London: Routledge.

Dodge, M (2000) 'An Atlas of Cyberspaces', http://www.cybergeography.org/atlas/atlas.html.

Fyfe, G and Law, J (1988) *Picturing Power: Visual Depiction and Social Relations*, London and New York: Routledge.

Gelernter, D (1992) *Mirror Worlds: Or the Day Software Puts the University in a Shoebox. How it Will Happen and What it Will Mean*, New York: Oxford University Press.

Goodchild, M (2000) 'Cartographic Futures on a Digital Earth', *Cartographic Perspectives*, 36, Spring: 1–9.

Goss, J (1995) 'Marketing the New Marketing: the Strategic Discourse of Geodemographic Information Systems' in *Ground Truth: The Social Implications of Geographical Information Systems*, Pickles, J (ed.), New York: Guilford Press.

Graham, S (1999) 'Geographies of surveillant simulation' in Crang, M, Crang, P and May, J (eds) *Virtual Geographies: Bodies, Space and Relations*, London: Routledge.

Guattari, F (1991) 'Regimes, Pathways, Subjects' in Crary, J and Kwiter, S (eds) *Incorporations*, Zone 6, New York: Urzone.

Hall, S (1992) *Mapping the Next Millenium: How Computer-Driven Cartography is Revolutionizing the Face of Science*, New York: Vintage Books.

Harvey, F and Chrisman, N (1998) 'Boundary objects and the social construction of GIS technology', *Environment and Planning A*, 30(9), 1683–1694.

Harvey, D (2000) *Spaces of Hope*, Berkeley and Los Angeles: University of California Press.

Heidegger, M (1969) *Identity and Difference*, Trans. J Stambaugh, New York: Harper and Row.

Hillis, K (1999) *Digital Sensations: Identity, Embodiment and Space in Virtual Reality*, Minneapolis: University of Minnesota Press.

Joyce, M (1999) 'On boundfulness: the space of hypertext bodies', in Crang, M, Crang, P and May, J (eds) *Virtual Geographies: Bodies, Space and Relations*, London: Routledge.

Kroker, A and Weinstein, M A (1994) *Data Trash: The Theory of the Virtual Class*, New York: St Martin's Press.

Landow, G and Delany, P (1992) *Hypertext: The Convergence of Contemporary Critical Theory and Technology*, Baltimore: The Johns Hopkins University Press.

Liverman, D, Moran, E, Rindfuss, F, Ronald, R and Stern, P C (eds) (1998) *People and Pixels: Linking Remote Sensing and Social Science*, Washington D.C.: National Research Council.

Lyon (1994) *The Electronic Eye: The Rose of Surveillance Society*, Minneapolis: University of Minnesota Press.

Lyotard, J F (1984) *The Postmodern Condition: A Report on Knowledge*, Trans. by G Bennington and B Massumi. Minneapolis: University of Minnesota Press.

Mark, D (1997) 'The History of Geographic Information Systems: Invention and Re-Invention of Triangular Irrelgular Networks (TINs)', Proceedings, GIS/LIS'97. Available at http://www.geog.buffalo.edu/ncgia/gishist/GISLIS97.html.

Mark, D, Chrisman, M N, Frank, A U, McHaffie, P H and Pickles, J (1997) 'The History of GIS Project', http://www.geog.buffalo.edu/ncgia/gishist/bar_harbor.html.

Melzer, A H (1976) *Dada and Surrealist Performance*, Baltimore and London: Paj Books, Johns Hopkins University Press.

Nelson, T H (1992) 'Virtual World Without End: The Story of Xanadu', in Jacobson, L (ed.) *Cyberarts: Exploring Art and Technology*, San Francisco: Miller Freeman.

Openshaw, S (1991) 'Commentary. A view on the GIS crisis in geography, or, using GIS to put Humpty-Dumpty back together again', *Environment and Planning A*, 23: 621–628.

Openshaw, S (1992) 'Commentary: Further thoughts on geography and GIS: a reply', *Environment and Planning A*, 24: 463–6.

Pickles, J (1991) 'Geography, GIS, and the Surveillant Society', *Papers and Proceedings of the Applied Geography Conferences*, Frazier, J W, Epstein, B J, Schoolmaster III, F A and Moon, H E (eds) Vol. 14: 80–91.

Pickles, J (1995) *Ground Truth: The Social Implications of Geographic Information Systems*, New York: Guilford Press.

Pickles, J (1999) 'Arguments, debates and dialogues: the GIS-social theory debate and the concern for alternatives', in Longley, P A, Goodchild, M F, Maguire, D J and Rhind, D W (eds), *Geographical Information Systems: Principles, Techniques, Applications, and Management*, New York: Wiley.

Pickles, J (2003) *A History of Spaces: Cartographic Reason, Mapping, and the Geo-Coded World*, London and New York: Routledge.

Pickles, J (2004) 'Cartography, Digital Transitions, and Questions of History', *Cartographic Perspectives*, 37 (Fall): 4–18.

President's Information Technology Advisory Committee (2000) *Information Technology Research: Investing in our future*, http://www.ccic.gov/ac/report.

Public Broadcasting Service (2000) 'Weapons', *Frontline*, http://www.pbs.org/wgbh/pages/frontline/gulf/weapons/gps.html.

Rhind, D (2000) 'Business, Governments, and Technology: Inter-Linked Causal Factors of Change in Cartography', *Cartographic Perspectives*, 37 (Fall): 19–25.

Rose, G (1993) *Feminism and Geography: The Limits of Geographical Knowledge*, Minneapolis: University of Minnesota Press.

Roszak, T (1986) *The Cult of Information: The Folklore of Computers and the True Art of Thinking*, New York: Pantheon Books.

Sclove, R E (1999) *Democratic Politics of Technology: The Missing Half: Using Democratic Criteria in Participatory Technology Decisions*, Amherst: The Loka Insitute. http://www.Loka.org/idt/intro.htm.

Sheppard, E (1993) 'Automated Geography: What Kind of Geography for What Kind of Society', *The Professional Geographer*, 45(4), 457–460.

Sheppard, E (1995) 'GIS and Society: Towards a Research Agenda', *Cartography and Geographical Information Systems*, 22: 5–16.

Stengers, I (2000) *Power and Invention: Situating Science*, Minneapolis: University of Minnesota Press.

Stone, A R (1995) *The War of Desire and Technology at the Close of the Mechanical Age*, Cambridge, MA: MIT Press.

Toulouse, C (1997) 'Introduction to "The Politics of Cyberspace"', *New Political Science*, 41–42 (Winter) http://www.urbsoc.org/cyberpol/intro.shtml.

Uebel, M (1999) 'Toward a Symptomatology of Cyberporn', *Theory and Event*, 3:4, http://muse.jhu.edu/journals/theory_and_event/v003/3.4uebel.html.

Vattimo, G (1992) *The Transparent Society*, Baltimore: The Johns Hopkins University Press.

Virilio, P (2000) *The Information Bomb*, London: Verso.

WITSA, (2000) 'Digital Planet: The Global Information Economy' http://www.witsa.org/DP2000sum.pdf.

Youngblut, C, Johnson, R E, Nash S H et al. (1996) 'Review of Virtual Environment Interface Technology', *Institute for Defence Analysis Paper*, P–3186. March, www.hitl.washington.edu/ scivw/IDA/.

10
Morality, ethics and social justice

David M Smith

Introduction

At the last Labour Party Conference of the twentieth century, Prime Minister Tony Blair looked forward to a new Britain for the next millennium. He invoked a new moral purpose manifest in the creation of a model nation, based not on privilege, class or background but on the equal worth of all. He illustrated his notion of social injustice by a maternity ward with two babies side by side, delivered by the same doctors and midwives, yet with two quite different lives ahead:

> One returns with his mother to a bed and breakfast that is cold, damp, cramped. A mother who has no job, no family to support her. Sadder still, she has no-one to share the joy and triumph of the new baby, a father nowhere to be seen. That mother loves her child like any other mother. But her life and her baby's life is a long, hard struggle. For this child, individual potential hangs on a thread.
>
> The second child returns to a prosperous home, grandparents desperate to share the caring and a father with a decent income and even larger sense of pride. They're already thinking about schools, friends she can make, new toys they can buy. Expectations are high, opportunities truly limitless. (Tony Blair, 28 September 1999, as reported in *The Mirror*)

Tony Blair recognised that he had been lucky, and wished that all could share this experience.

Neither the infant Blair nor the children in his illustration deserve their good or bad fortune. It originated in a situation over which they had no control, and in which the geographical inheritance is deeply implicated. There is a growing recognition of the spatial inequity or unfairness of life in contemporary Britain, expressed in such notions as a 'postcode lottery' with respect to local variations in health and education services, for example. While the wheel of fortune is supposed to allocate lottery prizes with mechanical impartiality, inequalities in life prospects from family to family and place to place arise within a socio-spatial structure with no guarantee of fair outcomes. And, whereas buying a National Lottery ticket is a matter of individual choice, no one in Britain can avoid the 'lottery of life' and the possibility of exposure to its unfortunate consequences.

As to the wider world, the tenth annual United Nations *Human Development Report* (UNDP, 1999), the last of the old millennium, pointed to serious manifestations of the globalisation of economic relations. The 1990s showed an increasing concentration of income, resources and wealth among people, corporations and countries, arising from the operation of global markets. At the same time, competitive pressure has put a squeeze on public goods, care activities and the environment, to which the poor are especially vulnerable. The lot of the individual world wide is very much a matter of luck, as it is in Britain: of being in the right place (or otherwise) on an increasingly uneven development surface the form of which is largely beyond local control. The United Nations sees market expansion outpacing governance, which must be strengthened if the opportunities and benefits of globalisation are to be more widely shared. Thus, 'a new commitment is needed to the ethics of universalism set out in the Universal Declaration of Human Rights' (UNDP, 1999, p2).

However, the experience of much of today's world is not so much the cosmopolitanism associated with modernity, but more a resurgence of parochialism. This is exemplified by British reaction to the arrival of growing numbers of refugees, displaced by mounting economic, political and environmental crises elsewhere. Such pejorative terms as 'economic migrant' and 'bogus asylum seeker' are deployed, along with faintly disguised ethnic and racial chauvinism, in discourses designed to give moral credibility to a politics of exclusion reminiscent of reactions to an earlier generation of immigrants from the Caribbean and the Indian subcontinent. While academic apostles of postmodernism invoke such notions as fluidity, porous places and an age of post-sovereignty, governments of well-to-do and supposedly liberal states strengthen borders against outsiders (Smith, 2004). The post-socialist era may well have been characterised by increasingly transnational economic relations, accompanying the universalisation of capitalism, but the political response is left largely to individual nation-states. The notion of a 'united nations' significantly moderating the local economic and environmental impacts of globalisation is proving fanciful, in the face of national self-interest and corporate power.

Hence the tension between global forces and local outcomes, which has been such a feature of geographical concern in recent years. While owners of capital are free to move their assets from one part of the globe to another with the instantaneous efficiency of an electronic impulse, the struggles of the victims of disinvestment, restructuring and environmental degradation are more locally confined. And so it is for those who have suffered or survived the 'ethnic cleansing' perpetrated by regimes pandering to rediscovered nationalisms. As to culture, the process of globalisation (or universalisation) of a specifically 'Western', materialist way of life is being resisted by some powerful local forces, including religious fundamentalisms with their own unyielding conceptions of the good. Meanwhile, different 'other' identities based on such criteria as disability and sexuality, as well as ethnicity, are challenging crude universalist notions of human nature, seeking local havens of recognition and security in which to realise the moral ideal of equal worth applauded by Tony Blair.

It will be clear from these introductory remarks that the contemporary world raises deep moral issues, with obvious geographical content. This chapter outlines geography's recent exploration of links with ethics, or moral philosophy. It goes on to consider some of the implications for geographical perspectives on social justice, examining the tension between the particularism encouraged by geographical preoccupation with context and the universalism characteristic of much mainstream moral theory. It advances a conception of social (and environmental) justice which transcends undeserved geographical differences in life chances. Its underlying theme is that, if geographers are to make claims to a role in the creation of a better world, this should be built on as firm a moral foundation as the intrinsically contested pursuit of the right and the good will permit.

Engaging morality and ethics

As an academic discipline with scientific pretensions, geography is sometimes supposed to be value free. However, geographers are far from reticent in suggesting that their inquiries can improve life on Earth. In arenas ranging from facility location to resource conservation, assertions that some arrangements are better than others are frequently made. There is also concern with more general questions of social and environmental justice. Even when value neutrality is most convincingly claimed, as in statistical analysis and numerical modelling, the initial choice of research problem is likely to be based on considerations of social relevance. Professional geography is a normative project.

However, it is rare for geographers to examine the philosophical basis of their value judgements in any depth. Human geographers have become familiar with various other cognate disciplines, most obviously economics, political science and sociology, and with some aspects of the philosophy of science. They contribute to such interdisciplinary fields as cultural studies, development planning and urban and regional analysis, and seek to incorporate space into social theory. They have also become technically sophisticated, for example in the development of geographical information systems. But despite long-standing engagement with matters of social concern, it is only recently that geographers in Britain and elsewhere have begun to explore links with the subject of ethics (Smith, 2003). And moral philosophers remain almost entirely ignorant of the work of geographers. The interface with ethics is one of the final disciplinary frontiers inviting geographical exploration, the outcome of which could be crucial to the wisdom required to address issues on which the very survival of a decent and sustainable form of human life on Earth may depend.

Insofar as conceptions of right or wrong, good or bad, are implicated in any human activity, all geographies are in some sense moral creations. They reflect the various ways in which moral values and ethical understandings guide humankind, in the social practice of making a living. However, the term 'moral geography' has been adopted in recent years as a label for a particular style of geographical investigations with a moral dimension. Some writers prefer the usage of 'moral landscape', 'moral location', 'moral terrain' or 'moral topography' (for reviews, see Smith, 1998a, pp14–18; 2000b, Chapter 3). The most obvious theme of these studies is that of moral differences: spatial variations in moral beliefs, codes and practices. Another is the role of environments in the construction of morality, reflecting the geographer's traditional preoccupation with behavioural responses to both nature and built form. There is also a focus on the power to prescribe who may do what, where and with whom: 'moral geographies operate not only through a dominative power of control and exclusion but also through performative powers of spatial practice' (Matless, 1994, p396). These studies raise, in various guises, the question of the 'right' place for certain kinds of human beings and behaviour.

Studies conducted under the rubric of moral geography and the like have been described as exercises in 'thick' descriptive ethics (Proctor, 1998, p13). Empirical observation fuses with contextual interpretation, to reveal different ways in which the right and the good is understood and acted upon, by real people in actual situations. However, they are only tenuously connected to the field of ethics, and their significance has yet to be acknowledged by moral philosophers. This lack of cross-disciplinary interaction is symptomatic of a failure to bring the theoretical power of philosophy to bear on the interpretation of moral issues in geography. Similarly, there is insufficient attention on the part of moral philosophy to what can be learned from the carefully constructed case study, in bringing context and local specificity to theoretical abstractions. Thus, bridging this disciplinary divide should bring benefits on both sides.

The discovery and cultivation of common ground between geography and ethics goes back barely a decade. A prelude was provided by Yi-Fu Tuan (1986, 1989), whose humanism involved a variety of moral interpretations of culture and landscape. More recently, morality was assigned a central role in the framework for understanding 'homo geographicus' elaborated by Robert Sack (1997). There has also been an edited collection on topics connecting geography with ethics (Proctor and Smith, 1999), a book relating the notion of moral geographies to ethics in a world of difference (Smith, 2000b), and extended reviews of the accumulating literature (Proctor, 1998; Smith, 1998a). The recent exploration of moral issues by geographers is linked to a growing interest in development ethics and environmental ethics, and to a broader normative turn in social theory (Sayer and Storper, 1997).

A central issue at the interface of geography and ethics is the distinction between particular moral beliefs and practices manifest in the specific localities, which traditionally excite geographical curiosity, and more general principles towards which human imagination in the form of moral theory is often drawn. The intellectual spirit of the beginning of the new millennium, influenced as it is by postmodernism, is wary of universal principles associated with the Enlightenment. Yet respect for the local and particular can easily degenerate into a critically impotent form of moral relativism. These issues come to the fore in the discourse of social justice, which has a special capacity to arouse public indignation and political response.

Resurrecting social justice

A major feature of geography's recent moral turn has been the resurrection of interest in social justice (Smith, 2000c). This has generated three books (Smith, 1994; Harvey, 1996; Low and Gleeson, 1998), the last two of which introduce nature into the subject, in recognition of a growing concern with environmental justice and 'green' politics. Other recent developments, reflecting changing understandings of social justice in moral and political philosophy, include criticism of the distributive paradigm with which the established notion of 'territorial' social justice is closely associated, and concern with the domination and oppression of groups of 'others' defined by ethnicity, gender, race, sexuality and so on. Especially important has been a reconnection of justice with broader considerations of the good life, characteristic of some classical accounts (Smith, 1997). Thus, if what is taken to be good varies from place to place, with the cultural, economic and social context, then so will the requirements of justice. This sets up a tension between particularity and generality, which requires sensitive resolution if progress is to be made towards envisioning a better world which is recognised as such both locally and globally.

The importance of this issue is highlighted by the contemporary preoccupation with difference, which has been a special concern of feminist perspectives in geography (Kobayashi, 1997). This requires us to 'establish ways of criticizing universalistic claims without completely surrendering to particularism' (McDowell, 1995, p292). A danger, to which the so-called new cultural geography has been prone, is that exaggerated preoccupation with difference pulls the perspective too close to particularism. This can lead to a failure to adopt a perspective general enough to transcend specific cultures or ways of life, the justice of which may be open to critique. That some insights can be found in moral philosophy helps to make the case for greater geographical attention to this field. The conventional universalist claim, that 'a theory of justice cannot simply be a theory of what justice demands in this particular society but must be a theory about what justice is in any society' (Barry, 1995, p6), has been augmented by recognition that abstract principles 'can guide context-sensitive judgement without lapsing into relativism' (O'Neill, 1992, p53).

The work of Onora O'Neill (1992) may be used to elaborate the point. She distinguishes between idealised and relativised theories of justice, the former stressing the need to abstract from particularities, the latter conceding to them. Her first move is to argue for abstract principles of universal scope, 'that can be adopted in any plurality of potentially interacting beings' (p64). One is the principle of non-injury: 'commitment to universal principles of justice is most effectively expressed through specific institutions that limit risks of injury, so helping to secure and maintain basic capacities and capabilities for action for all' (O'Neill, 1996, pp179, 191). Care and concern for others follows, which implies an ethic of care of the kind promoted in some feminist accounts of justice (e.g. Clement, 1996; Bowden, 1997; see also Smith, 1998b).

After deriving abstract universal principles, the second move takes account of 'the context and particularities of lives and societies' (O'Neill, 1992, p53). Significant differences in actual cases are recognised, but the application of universal principles across them 'need not prescribe or proscribe, recommend or reject rigid uniformity of action or entitlement' (O'Neill, 1996, p77). Principles do abstract from difference, but need not concede to ideal conceptions of persons which reflect traditions or practices in particular societies while denying salient differences. Her defence of universal principles against particularism is at the same time a recognition that they can be applied in particular contexts without accepting relativism:

> '[T]he diversity of situation and pluralism of belief found in different times and places do not undermine principles of justice [which] can be justified quite generally, and can be used to judge the specific constructions of justice which, quite rightly, take different forms at different times and places.' (O'Neill, 1996, pp173–4)

An alternative to this strategy is to begin with the full expression of difference, and to respect it, including different conceptions of social and environmental justice. However, this concedes too much to relativism, for, if all we can say to another person is, 'Your conceptions of justice are true for you, in your cultural context, but mine are true in my context', meaningful debate about justice must cease (Low and Gleeson, 1998, p197). To undertake normative evaluation implies that there is a basis for comparison, and the possibility of some kind of moral truth transcending time and place. This is required to challenge outcomes of the kind of idealism to which O'Neill objects, which may incorporate local gender and racial stereotypes, for example, and support the restricted social roles which some cultures may prescribe.

O'Neill's strategy may be compared with Michael Walzer's version of communitarianism, which gives greater weight to particularity. His connection between justice and the good is expressed in the axiom that we are distributing lives of a certain sort, and what counts as justice in distribution depends on what that 'sort' is (Walzer, 1994, p24). Thus: 'Justice requires the defence of difference – different goods distributed for different reasons among different groups of people' (p33), reflecting the values of particular cultures and societies. His recognition of the significance of the local and particular, in the context of new or resurgent 'tribalisms', suggests that moral minimalism at the universal level leaves room for all the tribes, 'and so for all the particularist versions of justice' (p64). However, the danger is that this room may harbour various forms of domination and oppression. That these can be perpetrated by 'tribes' (communities or nations), as well as under the totalitarian rule to which he takes exception, is a horrific fact of recent experience in various parts of the world, like central Africa and the Balkans.

Milton Fisk (1995) reminds us that there are various kinds of communities, not all of which provide 'a foundation for political morality in general or even justice in particular' (p231). Indeed, some are characterised by hierarchy and patriarchy, and remain conspicuously repressive of difference (Smith, 1999a). He sees the problem of justice as finding a way, beyond the contending schools of liberalism (universality) and communitarianism (particularity), of resolving conflicting claims so as to perpetuate the social bond. It must therefore reach out beyond any particular interest to draw in some potentially conflicting interests. But this will still be done from some standpoint, of an individual, group or nation, so cannot escape into pure universality. 'The problem then arises as to how justice can be sufficiently universal so as to draw different tendencies together if it is never more than justice from a particular standpoint' (Fisk, 1995, p222).

This neatly captures the problem of advancing a specific conception of justice as both theoretically defensible and responsive to the real world of the new millennium. It is with a sketch of such a conception that this chapter proceeds.

Towards context-sensitive universalism in social justice

That the contemporary world is characterised by vast and increasing inequalities in levels of living requires no demonstration here (for evidence, see, for example, UNDP, 1999). And it would take exceptional imagination to construct a theory of justice, or of the good, capable of providing a moral defence of a world in which some persons in some places enjoy almost impregnable economic, political and social security along with living standards embellished by the latest fashion accessories and electronic gadgetry, while others elsewhere endure such cruelty at the hands of an opposing ethnicity or repressive state that the uncertain fate of the refugee seems a preferable alternative. These inequalities in human life chances arise in large part from specific manifestations of what has been elaborated elsewhere as 'the place of good fortune' (Smith, 2000a). This expression incorporates three meanings of place: the role or part played by good fortune in people's lives, position in some social structure and place in its geographical sense.

The effect of fortune was highlighted in the introduction to this chapter. It is central to the liberal egalitarian perspective on social justice initiated by John Rawls (1971). He recognised that differential occupational achievement depends on natural talents or abilities and on social-environmental circumstances, which are morally arbitrary in the sense that no one deserves to benefit from them. Life chances are thus the outcome of three separate lotteries: the natural lottery which distributed genetic endowments, the social lottery which distributes more or less favourable environments and the lottery of pure luck (Barry, 1989, p226). Transcending them implies that there is no moral case for anything except equality in the distribution of requirements for human well-being, like Rawls's primary goods of liberty and opportunity, income and wealth and the bases of self-respect. This 'argument from arbitrariness', or 'luck egalitarianism', has featured prominently in subsequent work on social justice.

The prescription commonly referred to as 'equality of fortune' has stimulated extensive debates in moral and political philosophy. The focus tends to be on individual attributes which are outcomes of misfortune, and which might therefore warrant compensation. For example, persons unlucky in the lottery distributing physical disabilities that constrain life prospects might be compensated in some way. However, problems arise in distinguishing between conditions for which individuals cannot be held responsible and those for which they can. Congenital disability is a clear case of the former, whereas inclination for effort might not be convincingly attributed to the chance of nature, or even nurture. Some ludicrous outcomes arise in attempts to even out all individual circumstances, like compensating people for the misfortune of having expensive tastes that require more money than others to satisfy.

However, the moral quagmire into which the argument from arbitrariness so easily sinks is avoided if the focus is not on personal attributes but on the place of good fortune in its geographical sense. This is readily incorporated into the equality of fortune perspective: 'Part of its appeal comes from the force of the obviously correct claim that no one deserves their genetic endowments or other accidents of birth, such as who their parents were or *where they were born*' (Anderson, 1999, p290; emphasis added). Local resources, including infrastructure, clearly contribute to the environmental effect in its broadest sense. So do the local economic, political and social relations within which persons are embedded. The chance of birth in a particular place on the highly uneven surface of human opportunities carries no greater moral credit than being born to a rich or poor family, able-bodied or otherwise, male or female, black or white. And such initial advantage as arises from the place of good fortune is readily transferred to future generations, similarly devoid of moral justification. As for the possibility of the disadvantaged seeking better opportunities elsewhere, for most people the capacity to change their place, from a poorly endowed to richly resourced location (or state), may be as limited as it is to change their gender or skin pigmentation. Economic migrants are increasingly made unwelcome.

It follows that there is a strong case for the equality of populations identified by place: the traditional focus of territorial social justice. The crucial question is: equality of what? Should it be Rawls' primary goods, resources, opportunities, capabilities, welfare outcomes, or what? This has been debated at length by luck egalitarians (for references, see Anderson, 1999, p293). The question is complicated by the fact that the individual freedom to choose life plans so revered by liberals means that everyone might require a unique set of assets. Added to this is the contemporary respect for difference, which similarly works against some common conception of the good and of what is required to attain it.

Two arguments may be advanced to facilitate an approach to social justice in practice, attempting Fisk's task of drawing different tendencies together. One is to talk in terms not of equality but of *equalisation* (Smith, 1994). This strategy recognises that achieving equality is virtually impossible, by any criteria, but that moves in this direction are both possible and morally justifiable. The process of equalisation might be constrained by the 'difference principle' proposed by John Rawls (1971, p302), which requires social and economic inequalities to be arranged so that they are 'to the greatest benefit of the least advantaged'. Even if the argument from arbitrariness undermines the moral credit for most if not all individual achievement, this principle is a defensible concession to the possibility that some inequalities can work to the advantage of everyone and especially the worst-off. A recent version of luck egalitarianism avoids the problem of compensating everyone for every conceivable misfortune by giving priority to the well-being of those who are badly-off, 'and not substantially responsible for their condition in virtue of their prior conduct' (Arneson, 2000, p340).

The second argument relates to the objects of distribution. What people actually require for life is much the same, whoever and wherever they are, because they are themselves naturally much the same. This may be disputed at the higher levels of living prevailing among the privileged minority of the world's population, with the freedom to indulge in markedly different life styles. But for the vast majority of the world's population, living at little above subsistence level, the striking thing is the similarity of their poverty and of what is required to alleviate it. This is the point of the ethical naturalism, or essentialism, condemned from the privileged situation of a postmodern intellectual élite who seem so preoccupied with difference as to be unable to accept the truth that some things really are essential to a recognisably human form of life.

The natural fact of human similarity leads to the identification of common human needs. All persons share one obvious need: to avoid injury (O'Neill, 1996; see above), or serious harm (Doyal and Gough, 1991). This goes beyond threat to survive in a physical sense, to include impaired participation in the prevailing social milieu. From this follow needs for the physical health to continue living and functioning effectively, and for the personal autonomy or ability to make informed choices in a given context. Actual need satisfiers, in the form of goods and services, may be culturally specific, as opposed to the universality of the needs themselves (Doyal and Gough, 1991). This cut through the dualism of universality and particularity is similar to the capabilities approach adopted by Amartya Sen (1992), in which the notion of poverty is considered absolute or universal in the sense of impairing people's capability to function, but relative with respect to the commodities required to alleviate it. The incorporation of physical hazards relevant to the avoidance of injury or serious harm, like exposure to polluted air, land and water, along with access to such natural resources as clean water and land suitable for farming, housing and so on, broadens the scope to incorporate environmental as well as social justice. And again, what is actually required, by way of both physical resource and environmental conservation, will be relative to the local context.

This focus on human needs and capabilities is sensitive to contemporary currents of anti-essentialism and suspicion of universalism, but without conceding to them. For example, Martha Nussbaum (1992, p205) finds that 'legitimate criticism of essentialism still leaves room for essentialism of a certain kind: for a historically sensitive account of the most basic human needs and human functionings'. These are, surely, universal. She suggests that to give up on all evaluation, and in particular on a normative account of human being and functioning, is to turn things over to a world in which the forces affecting the lives of women, minorities and the poor are rarely benign. Although the capabilities approach advances cross-cultural norms, this universalism 'derives support from a complex understanding of cultures as sites of resistance and internal critique' (Nussbaum, 1998, p770): echoes of popular themes in contemporary geography.

All this suggests a restricted set of criteria required universally to sustain a distinctively human form of life, the interpretation and satisfaction of which will be to some extent culturally and hence locally relative. But it would be surprising if what was required differed very much, at the relevant level of living endured by the world's poor. The satisfaction of these basic needs can then be asserted as a human right, and a criterion for political action.

An emphasis on basic need satisfaction has some radical implications for social justice. Rawls (1971) adopted liberal convention in prioritising liberty over social and economic equality, but there is nothing sacred about this. A reformulation from a Marxian perspective proposes the first priority of meeting basic security and subsistence rights: everyone's physical integrity is to be respected, and everyone is to be guaranteed a minimum level of material well-being (Peffer, 1990). This requires such hallowed tenets of liberalism as private property rights and freedom from imposed conceptions of the good to yield to the basic needs of the worst-off. Care for the vulnerable becomes a supreme virtue.

Given limits to global resources, satisfying everyone's basic needs here and now, never mind provision for future generations, greatly limits the scope for inequality (Sterba, 1998). The wider the spatial reach of (re)distribution, as well as the more generous the conception of need, the more severely egalitarian its consequences. And the more egalitarian the outcomes, the greater the limitations on individual or group indulgences based on conceptions of the good which require disproportionate shares of the Earth's finite resources. Social justice as equalisation clearly has implications for the good, which rule out ways of life unattainable to large majorities of the population.

This kind of conception of social justice has been subject to the criticism that its emphasis on (re)distribution overlooks the processes whereby difference becomes a source of disadvantage through domination and oppression (Young, 1990). Thus, Elizabeth Anderson (1999) advocates 'democratic equality', which aims to abolish socially created oppression, rather than following luck egalitarianism in correcting what is taken to be injustice generated by the natural order: a relational theory against the concern of the equality of fortune perspective with a pattern of distribution. She sees the proper aim of egalitarian justice as 'not to ensure that everyone gets what they morally deserve, but to create a community in which people stand in relations of equality to others' (pp288–9). However, in deriving principles from her theory, Anderson recognises that they 'must identify certain goods to which all citizens must have effective access over the course of their whole lives' (p314). This leads her to embrace Sen's capabilities approach, but with an emphasis on avoiding repression: 'people are entitled to whatever capabilities are necessary to enable them to avoid or escape entanglement in oppressive social relationships' (p316). She identifies three aspects of human functioning: as a human being, as a participant in a system of cooperative production, and as a citizen of a democratic state:

> 'To be capable of functioning as a human being requires effective access to the means of sustaining one's biological existence – food, shelter, clothing, medical care – and access to the basic conditions of human agency – knowledge of one's circumstances and options, the ability to deliberate about means and ends, the psychological conditions of autonomy, including the self-confidence to think and judge for oneself, freedom of thought and movement. To be capable of functioning as an equal participant in a system of cooperative production requires effective access to the means of production, access to the education needed to develop one's talents, freedom of occupational choice, the right to make contracts and enter into cooperative agreements with others, the right to receive fair value for one's labor, and recognition by others of one's productive contributions. To be capable of functioning as a citizen requires rights to political participation, such as freedom of speech and the franchise, and also effective access to the goods and relationships of civil society.' (Anderson, 1999, pp317–18)

This is, in effect, an inventory of universal human needs, and arguably human rights, which gives due emphasis to relational as well as possessional aspects of life.

A conception of social justice can therefore been constructed, beginning with the moral arbitrariness of sources of inequality (especially those associated with place), and then moving from recognition of human sameness to basic needs for human functioning, and to their satisfaction as of right. From the initial identification of inequality, social justice requires a process of equalisation over time, as expeditiously as possible, until the constraint of Rawls' difference principle is reached. And what is to be equalised are the requirements for distinctively human being in society with others, not merely of physical survival.

This general conception reflects some of the particularities of the world in which we now live, with its gross inequalities, residual egalitarian sentiments and abiding faith in grand projects for human betterment (actual experience and postmodern scepticism notwith-standing). Within this world, the perspective advanced is broad and flexible enough to do the initial work required of universal principles: to engage the specific manifestations of inequality in particular societies in a manner which facilitates comparison and further gen-eralisation. In the process, contextual thickening will take place, as understanding of the par-ticular society is built up. The findings can then be related to others: 'past resolutions begin to lay a basis for formulating principles of justice that achieve a higher level of universality than what would be involved if cases were taken in isolation' (Fisk, 1995, p227).

Envisioning social justice: the case of South Africa

South Africa provides an example of what is involved in working between the universal and the particular in pursuit of social justice (following Smith, 1999b; 2000b; see also Smith, 2002). Under apartheid, a singularly immoral geography was created, in association with the social construction of difference in terms of race. People were classified accord-ing to officially defined 'race groups' ('African', 'coloured', 'Indian' and 'white'), which pre-scribed where they could live in segregated residential space. Differences in the quality of housing, infrastructure and social services among 'group areas' added to the discrimination associated with racial designation itself. The immorality of this system arose from the fact that race is an unchosen identity beyond individual control, and from which no moral credit or otherwise should therefore be derived. Geographically, to have been born in the poverty of a black township or informal settlement, rather than in an affluent white neighbourhood, was simply a matter of luck.

Following the abolition of apartheid at the beginning of the 1990s, social justice was initially defined very much in terms of racial redistribution, prioritising the basic needs of the poor, largely black population. This strategy could be regarded as a context-specific version of the universal principle of social justice as equalisation. However, bringing it to bear in the particular circumstances of contemporary South Africa revealed limitations of a narrowly (re)distributive perspective, for it is impossible to redistribute resources in a manner which would equalise living standards up to the level currently enjoyed by the privileged, largely white minority. Such standards of material affluence are unattainable to most of the historically disadvantaged population within the lifetime of present South Africans, given the existing resource constraints and any conceivable scenario of economic growth.

This leads to the question of an alternative conception of justice, based on an alternative, less materialistic conception of the good life. One possibility would be to replace a distributive perspective focused on individual material well-being by a relational perspective prioritising an ethic of care for disadvantaged members of an emergent national community. Precedents can be found in the practice, and philosophy, of pre-modern African society, with its communal property ownership and communitarian ethics. Some see this as a distinctive Afro-centric morality: an alternative to the prioritisation of individual freedom associated with liberalism and of the collectivism exemplified by socialism (Shutte, 1993). The guiding concept of *ubuntu*, or group solidarity, has attracted interest among those seeking an alternative development ethics which values authenticity of indigenous culture. However, a realistic appraisal of a somewhat idealised past recognises that traditional African communal society could be brutally repressive. And a realistic consideration of the present, including the strength of modern individualistic and material values, reveals the difficulty of promoting alternative ethics.

As it is, development aspirations have had to come to terms with the international context of global economic relations, within which post-apartheid South Africa operates. The initial emphasis on basic needs soon gave way to a macroeconomic strategy of reduced state spending, investment incentives, wage restraint, labour market flexibility and privatisation, which strongly resembled the neoliberal policies promoted elsewhere by the International Monetary Fund. The aim is to generate conditions conducive to attracting capital investment, in competition with other countries seeking to do the same. As one South African economist puts it: 'While international capital flows may not yet hold the key to a county's economic life or death, policy makers ignore this power at their peril' (Nattrass, 1996, p39).

The inevitable consequence of this strategy will be the rough justice of the marketplace, characterised by the persistence of inequality but with the inherited racial divides augmented by those of class. A poignant picture of the material reality of life in the 'new' South Africa is provided by a critical sociologist, in terms invoking our central notion of the place of good fortune:

> 'We live in a society where millions of people are condemned to extreme deprivation even before they are born. Regardless of their own qualities, they are condemned to misery and humiliation. A few others are born into utter luxury, and waited on hand and foot for the rest of their lives. Ours is a world where it is natural for some inhabitants to eat R500 [£50] meals while others, literally metres away, cannot afford even a loaf of bread.' (Desai, 1999, p63)

He concludes that one cannot really comprehend the evil of it all, centred on the global worship of money. It is to negate such outcomes that the struggle to identify, assert and implement an alternative conception of social justice must continue.

Envisaging a moral geography

In South Africa as elsewhere, the meaning of social justice is defined and redefined in practice. This involves ongoing dialogue between what might claim to be universal principles and the particular context within which they have to work. At the level of general theory, it is not hard to envision a moral geography in which the first call on society's collective resources is the satisfaction of people's basic needs. From the present levels of (spatial) inequality, a process of convergence would be set in motion, with priority given to the places with worst-off people. The achievement of decent living conditions for all, in the sense of material well-being and social security, would leave little scope for luxury consumption on the part of those more fortunately placed. In any event, caring for others would carry its own moral imperative, and reward.

The crucial question is whether such an aspiration is feasible, in the world as it has come to be. Equality of opportunity for human functioning, in the sense identified by Anderson (1999) above, is clearly impossible under the social relations of capitalism, with markets driven by pre-existing inequalities in resources and capabilities. Uneven development is reproduced at various spatial scales: global, national, regional and local. While the United Nations and the likes of Tony Blair acknowledge surface manifestations of the problem, and its moral significance, a resolution seems beyond their vision, constrained as it is by failure to recognise how deeply embedded the origins of inequality are in the structure of contemporary society, its culture, economy and polity.

Returning to the case of the two babies with which this chapter began, the one born to its lone mother is likely to be inheritor of the outcome of generations of struggle to make a living in the harsh environment of industrial Britain, learning to become labour in poor schools, prone to occupational health hazards, the community finally crushed and family perhaps broken by factory or mine closure, redundancy and long-term unemployment. The other child is likely to be inheritor of the outcome of generations of cumulative privilege manifest in well-remunerated and secure employment, nice homes and neighbourhoods, good schools and health services (possibly private) and the transferable skills required to make the most of the emerging information economy. And all these differences are in one of the richest countries in the world, and innovator of the welfare state. These deeply geographical sources of inequality, exacerbated in countries with less aggregate wealth and weaker commitment to social security, are part of the very fabric of society. It requires more than stronger governance to change them, helpful though that might be in blunting the cutting edge of injustice.

It is in seeking the new institutions and social arrangements required to equalise human life prospects, whoever and wherever people are, that the creation of a moral geography can be envisaged. But it is ultimately a political project, and one of such revolutionary implications that it will be conceivable only if driven by the most powerful moral argument. And, rather than to the postmodern, or even to the post-socialist, it is to a post-capitalist and perhaps post-market morality that the vision must be directed. For as long as free-market fundamentalism prevails, in a world with such undeserved inequality of the means of influencing markets, their outcomes will lack moral justification. The ultimate challenge of the new millennium is, then, to devise an environmentally sustainable system of resource allocation which will put the satisfaction of basic human needs first, for everyone, everywhere, within caring social relations. If such a formidable task is within the intellectual capacity of humankind, then this chapter should have shown that some points of departure may be found in a morally informed geographical imagination.

Acknowledgements

Parts of this chapter draw on sections of earlier publications, identified in the text. The initial research was supported by a Leverhulme Fellowship.

Bibliography

Anderson, E S (1999) 'What is the point of equality?', *Ethics*, 109, 289–337.

Arneson, R J (2000) 'Luck egalitarianism and prioritarianism', *Ethics*, 110, 339–349.

Barry, B (1989) *Theories of Justice (A Treatise on Social Justice, Volume 1)*, London: Harvester-Wheatsheaf.

Barry, B (1995) *Justice as Impartiality (A Treatise on Social Justice, Volume II)*, Oxford: Clarendon Press.

Bowden, P (1997) *Caring: Gender-sensitive Ethics*, London: Routledge.

Clement, C (1996) *Care, Autonomy, and Justice: Feminism and the Ethic of Care*, Oxford: Westview Press.

Desai, A (1999) *South Africa Still Revolting*, Johannesburg: Impact Africa Publishing.

Doyal, L and Gough, I (1991) *A Theory of Human Need*, London: Macmillan.

Fisk, M (1995) 'Justice and universality', in Sterba, J P, Machan, T R, Jagger, A *et al.* (1995) *Morality and Social Justice: Point/Counterpoint*, London: Rowman Littlefield.

Harvey, D (1996) *Justice, Nature and the Geography of Difference*, Oxford: Blackwell Publishers.

Kobayashi, A (1997) 'The paradox of difference and diversity (or, why the threshold keeps moving)' in Jones, J P, Nast, H J and Roberts, S M (eds) *Thresholds in Feminist Geography: Difference, Methodology, Representation*, Oxford: Rowman and Littlefield.

Low, N and Gleeson, B (1998) *Justice, Society and Nature: An Exploration of Political Ecology*, London: Routledge.

McDowell, L (1995) 'Understanding diversity: the problem of/for theory' in Johnston, R J, Taylor, P J and Watts, M J (eds) *Geographies of Global Change: Remapping the World in the Late Twentieth Century*, Oxford: Blackwell Publishers.

Matless, D (1994) 'Moral geographies in Broadlands', *Ecumene*, 1, 27–56.

Natrass, N (1996) 'Gambling on investment: competing economic strategies in South Africa', *Transformation*, 31, 25–42.

Nussbaum, M C (1992) 'Human functioning and social justice: in defence of Aristotelian essentialism', *Political Theory*, 20, 202–246.

Nussbaum, M C (1998) 'Public philosophy and international feminism', *Ethics*, 108, 762–796.

O'Neill, O (1992) 'Justice, gender and international boundaries', in Attfield, R and Wilkins, B (eds) (1992) *International Justice and the Third World*, London: Routledge.

O'Neill, O (1996) *Towards Justice and Virtue: A Constructive Account of Practical Reasoning*, Cambridge: Cambridge University Press.

Peffer, R G (1990) *Marxism, Morality, and Social Justice*, Princeton, N.J.: Princeton University Press.

Proctor, J D (1998) 'Ethics in geography: giving moral form to the geographical imagination', *Area*, 30, 8–18.

Proctor, J D and Smith, D M (eds) (1999) *Geography and Ethics: Journeys in a Moral Terrain*, London: Routledge.

Rawls, J (1971) *A Theory of Justice*, Cambridge, Mass.: Harvard University Press.

Sack, R D (1997) *Homo Geographicus: A Framework for Action, Awareness, and Moral Concern*, Baltimore and London: The Johns Hopkins University Press.

Sayer, A and Storper, M (1997) 'Ethics unbound: for a normative turn in social theory', *Environment and Planning D: Society and Space*, 15, 1–17.

Sen, A (1992) *Inequality Reexamined*, Oxford: Clarendon Press.

Shutte, A (1993) *Philosophy for Africa*, Rondebosch: University of Cape Town Press.

Smith, D M (1994) *Geography and Social Justice*, Oxford: Blackwell Publishers.

Smith, D M (1997) 'Back to the good life: towards an enlarged conception of social justice', *Environment and Planning D: Society and Space*, 15, 19–35.

Smith, D M (1998a) 'Geography and moral philosophy: some common ground', *Ethics, Place and Environment*, 1, 7–34.

Smith, D M (1998b) 'How far should we care? On the spatial scope of beneficence', *Progress in Human Geography*, 22, 15–38.

Smith, D M (1999a) 'Geography, community, and morality', *Environment and Planning A*, 31, 19–35.

Smith, D M (1999b) 'Social justice and the ethics of development in post-apartheid South Africa', *Ethics, Place and Environment*, 2, 157–177.

Smith, D M (2000a) 'Moral progress in human geography: transcending the place of good fortune', *Progress in Human Geography*, 24, 1–18.

Smith, D M (2000b) *Moral Geographies: Ethics in a World of Difference*, Edinburgh: Edinburgh University Press.

Smith, D M (2000c) 'Social justice revisited', *Environment and Planning A*, 32, 1149–1162.

Smith, D M (2002) 'Social justice and the South African city' in Eade, J and Mele, C (eds) (2002) *Urban Studies: Contemporary and Future Perspectives*, Oxford: Blackwell Publishers.

Smith, D M (2003) 'Geographers, ethics and social concern', in Johnston, R J and Williams, M (eds) *A Century of British Geography*, Oxford: Oxford University Press for The British Academy (in press).

Smith, D M (2004) 'Open borders and free population movement: a challenge for liberalism', in Barnett, C and Low, M (eds) *Spaces of Democracy*, London: Sage Publications (in press).

Sterba, J P (1998) *Justice for Here and Now*, Cambridge: Cambridge University Press.

Tuan, Y-F (1986) *The Good Life*, Madison, Wis.: The University of Wisconsin Press.

Tuan, Y-F (1989) *Morality and Imagination: Paradoxes of Progress*, Madison, Wis.: The University of Wisconsin Press.

UNDP (United Nations Development Programme) (1999) *Human Development Report 1999*, New York: Oxford University Press.

Walzer, M (1994) *Thick and Thin: Moral Argument at Home and Abroad*, Notre Dame and London: University of Notre Dame Press.

Young, I M (1990) *Justice and the Politics of Difference*, Princeton, N.J.: Princeton University Press.

11

Deliver us from evil? Prospects for living ethically and acting politically in human geography

Paul Cloke

Introduction

> 'imagine a world of respectful equality, not only of talents or achievements, but of conditions of life and life changes – a world, in short, where the ugly habit of shifting the burden of one's support onto the shoulders of others has disappeared.' (Harvey, 2000, p280)

> 'this is not a discourse *about* ethics, but an ethical form of discourse in its own right, one which takes the task to be to stretch the limits of what it is possible to think, not in the interest of this or that project of enlightenment or reform, but in the interests of an exercise in judgement itself.' (Osborne, 1998, p193)

> 'for I was hungry and you gave me nothing to eat, I was thirsty and you gave me nothing to drink, I was a stranger and you did not invite me in, I needed clothes and you did not clothe me, I was sick and in prison and you did not look after me.' (Matthew, 25: 42–43; *New International Version of the Bible*)

Arguments for ethicality in human geography have been deployed over a relatively long time frame, drawing on a variety of different theoretical, philosophical, ideological and spiritual prompts. David Harvey's contribution represents an extraordinarily seminal and sustained outpouring of historical-geographical materialism, capable of prompting the ethical imagination to a radical consideration of how the world could be a better place. Tom Osborne's sociological account of 'an ethical form of discourse in its own right' represents a rather different portfolio of theoretical explorations in cultural studies, recognising ethical skills, or expertise, with which to expand the imaginative bounds of judgement. The biblical listing of charitable failures indicates the sort of grounds by which the sheep will be separated from the goats, and thereby represents how ethical practice can (variously) be entwined in the pursuit of faith. In this chapter, I want to argue a vision for the future in which each of these strands – the justice of political economy, the intense engagement with judgement in cultural studies and the potential contribution of faith and spirituality – has its place in acknowledging appropriate ethical frames, imaginations and practices for human geography.

At the outset, I want to emphasise what I believe is often a disjuncture between what we say, what we practise and who we are. When I came to Bristol from mid-Wales in 1992 I encountered on-street homeless people for the first time in my everyday life. The everyday sites and sights of homelessness appalled me, even though I had previously read pretty widely about the issues facing homeless people. In particular, my hackles of social justice were raised, prompting questions about what kind of society it was that allowed this very evidently 'wrong' and 'bad' form of injustice to be sustained. I responded by undertaking regular voluntary work in a local night shelter and partially reorientating my research priorities to take up 'the cause' of the homeless. Now I don't tell you this as a naked act of self-aggrandisement, on at least two counts. First, as Nick Blomley (1994) and Noel Castree (1999) amongst others have recorded, there is a rich history of social activism in the human geography academy demonstrating life-changing commitment in some cases, and certainly a commitment which far outweighs mine. Second, I have to tell you that my initial shock of seeing on-street homeless people has subsided, and that my personal response in terms of regular work at the shelter has suffered from a definite sense of fatigue. Mine, then, is definitely not a heroic story. No, I mention my small-scale experience simply because I believe that many of you will have faced, or will do in the future, similar dilemmas about how easy it is to talk and write about human geographies of ethics and justice compared with the difficulties of living out those geographies in our everyday life practices. It is necessary to acknowledge here the argument that there can be a useful division of labour between talking and doing; some are better talkers than doers, and vice versa. Yet it is my firm belief that radical ideas and radical practice should go hand in hand in human geography. In the words of Alison Blunt and Jane Wills (2000) in their discussion of radical ideas and practice:

> 'While there can be no doubt that dissident geographies have had a great impact on the discipline, there remains much more to be done. Inequality and injustice have not disappeared and, in many ways, they remain more pressing than ever. Dissident geographies remain crucially important in attempting to change both the discipline of geography and the world.' (pxi)

It is with this emphasis on the symbiosis of ideas and practice that I have to own up to mixed feelings about the current state of some human geography. The cultural turn has been exciting, and the emphases on difference, discourse, representation and performance have each brought new light to society space and nature, and have reinvigorated discussion about, for example, place and embodiment as well as the interconnectedness of all of these. Why, then, do I have nagging doubts that we may be losing our way a little, and why do I find myself particularly frustrated by our apparent inability to retain a critical political edge in human geography? It almost seems as though as we become theoretically more sophisticated in identifying difference and differentiating identity, so our ability to offer imaginative and practical guidelines for doing something about anything appears to be diminishing. In part, such sentiments reflect fears expressed by Chris Philo (2000) about 'an impulse towards both dematerialising and desocialising human geography' (p44), but in addition, they convey a sense of unfulfilled potential with respect to socio-cultural geography's 'moral turn' (David Smith, 1999). While we now understand some of the subtleties and differences previously plastered over by reductionist and 'tanky' political economies, the resultant emphasis on identity politics seems to have evaded important issues relating, for example, to the interconnectivities between one identify group's freedom and another's oppression, or to the grounds on which relative priority is distributed amongst different forms of social exclusion. For me, a significant part of the envisioning of future human geographies is to develop a more critical understanding of these issues through new readings of moral and ethical geographies.

Moral geographies?

David Smith's excellent essay in this book (Chapter 10) presents an informative cartography of moral terrains in human geography, and brooks no repetition here. However, I want to question whether the 'progress' made over the last decade in unfolding geographies of morality and ethics has presented human geographers with any new, and critical, apparatus with which to 'do something about anything'. Felix Driver (1991) warns that the interest in morality should be less of a return to timeless concerns and more of a reflection of the need to respond to the significant political and intellectual shifts of the times. Could it be that the ensuing response in human geography has more often been motivated by *intellectual* rather than *political* shifts, with a consequent underplaying of the need to connect ideas with practices?

Any such blunt conclusion immediately seems harsh and disrespectful to those in human geography for whom action has been a characteristic geographical practice. It is, however, instructive to return to Chris Philo's (1991) vision in *New Words, New Worlds* for the potential scope of moral geographies. Here he reflects on the geographies of, and in, everyday moralities. Geographies of morality refer to:

> 'the different moral assumptions and supporting arguments that particular peoples in particular places make about "good" and "bad"/"right" and "wrong"/"just" and "unjust"/"worthy" and "unworthy".' (p16)

They reflect the varying scales of assumptions made about the inclusion and exclusion of people from particular social groups and the codes which they live by. Geographies in everyday moralities suggest that issues of space, place, environment, landscape and so on are often built into the very heart of moral arguments and assumptions. Philo also spotlights the potential value of human geographers reflecting on their own morality, in order to identify the impacts of the values brought by geographers to their own work. At their most basic, such reflections identify the blurred moral biases inherent in scientific objectivism, or vague appeals to broad humanism. Some, however, will in Philo's view wish to go further, either by exploring particular forms of moral rootedness (for example in Marxist or Christian concepts of human freedom), or by proceeding:

> 'from the "common moral talk" of the people and places that we study to the deeper moral presuppositions informing the lives of these people and places, and … allowing these revealed moralities to guard how we – as outsiders maybe needing to unlearn our own presuppositions – evaluate what we find occurring here.' (p27)

Many geographers found, and continue to find, this vision really exciting. Surveys of the geographies of, and in, everyday moralities promised the very nuanced and critical readings that many human geographers found lacking in the subject. In one of my own areas of interest, for example – geographies of rurality – there has been an emergent recognition of how rurality is implicated with morality. A recent essay by right-wing think-tanker Roger Scruton (1998) presents an interesting illustration. He describes a contemporary *moral mobility* in Britain, by which people are able to break loose from their traditional codes of conduct, and experiment with lifestyles which were once the privilege of the rich and glamorous. Such moral mobility, Scruton, with Anthony Barnett, argues:

> 'has shaken rural society, since it has removed its self-image: as the repository of changeless values in a world of change. Rural people can no longer attract their children home from the cities with a promise of old fashioned decencies and good homely sentiment. Those who love the pattern and rhythm of rural society must accept the paradox that it is now only by a conscious effort that a sense of rootedness can be revived.' (Barnett and Scruton, 1998, pxvi)

Here, then, is a picture of rurality as a repository of moral values; an amalgam of spatial and moral assumptions. This, however, is a very particular form of moral discernment. In Scruton's argument, the value of the countryside lies precisely in a well-bounded series of 'we-feelings' – in morally prescribed shared values which cohere in a narrowly constructed sense of common destiny, inheritance and continuity. Accordingly, the vision for future countrysides involves opposing the loss of social order, community attachment and environmental stillness, and contesting the social entropy which is seen to lie at the heart of the postmodern condition.

Scruton's moral reading of contemporary rurality itself excludes rural people who are unable or unwilling to share in his 'we-feelings'. These morally prescribed values of the rural render unthinkable problems such as poverty and homelessness in rural spaces, as my own research with Paul Milbourne and Rebekah Widdowfield has sought to establish (Cloke *et al.*, 2000a). It is this very sense of exclusion which has prompted a very different reading of geography and morality in rural areas; a reading which has reflected the marginalisation of 'others' in rural contexts (see Paul Cloke and Jo Little, 1997). French anthropologist Marc Augé (1998) has suggested that we need to be sensitive to two strands of otherness. First, he urges a sensitivity to a *sense of the other*, a sense of what has meaning for others and of that which they elaborate upon. Over the last decade in particular, it is clear that human geographers have been active in this respect. In geographies of the rural, for example, there has been a listening to 'other' voices and a looking through 'other' windows onto the rural world. Such activities have brought an understanding of some of the moral geographies which are instituted among and lived out by people belonging to particular social and identity groups. This trajectory of research has been at once fruitful and problematic. A rich vein of understanding regarding processes of exclusion and marginalisation has been accompanied by well-documented (see, for example, Marcus Doel, 1994) philosophical and methodological problems: the tendency to lock 'others' into the thought-prison of the same; the tendency to illustrate 'otherness' in terms of a series of socio-cultural variables (age, gender, sexuality and the like) often *without* serious commitment to the particular issues and people involved, and *without* a complete sense of the range of 'other' geographies; and the real difficulties in moving beyond 'others of the same' to the 'other of the other', that which is unfamiliar, unexplainable and unrecognisable.

Here, Marc Augé's second strand of sensitivity to otherness seems highly relevant. He also urges a sensitivity to a *sense for the other*. Here I return to my nagging doubts about much of the current interplay between moral geographies and a critical political edge to human geography which incorporates active practice as well as intellectual transformation. In broad terms, I believe that it is easy to detect in human geography an abstract, intellectually fascinated, but often uncommitted sense *of* the other. However, with some significant and notable exceptions, I believe it is far more difficult to discover in contemporary human geography as a whole a sense *for* the other which is emotional, connected and committed. This is due, at least in part, to the academic environment itself. Inevitably the self-serving nature of contemporary research conditions in human geography is conspiring against the development of a sustained sense for the other. Too often, research will inescapably be connected with the professional need to attract research funding, and publication will be about fulfilling the requirements and expectations of an academic career. Moreover, the unwillingness to promote and fund long-term, longitudinal research has created the conditions for 'flip' ethnographies by which researchers too often breeze into and breeze out of research situations, with insufficient commitment to the people and issues concerned. However, such contingent conditions only partly explain the phenomenon. The lack of a sense for the other is grounded in the choices we make about how to live ethically and act politically.

The further possibility for moral and ethical geographies

Having reached such a sweeping conclusion, I should immediately admit that I find two particular reasons for optimism in the search for a prioritised, committed sense for the other in human geography. First, there does seem to be a significant commitment to the process of developing a geographically sensitive ethics, and an ethically sensitive geography. If such a process is to be viewed as a journey, then not only are more human geographers seemingly willing to travel, but also the quality of the guidebooks which accompany such travel has increased sharply in recent years (see for example, David Smith, 2000; and James Proctor and David Smith, 1999) As Iain Hay (1998) has recently commented, these signs of progress are not so much because of the imposition of new ethical codes or guidelines, but more because of the introduction of more flexible prompts for moral contemplation which have stimulated and nurtured moral imaginations in human geography research. Brief mention of four such prompts illustrates how the ethical cross-cuts (sometimes longstanding) political themes in human geography:

1. The acceptance of a need for greater levels of 'normative self-criticality' (Andrew Sayer and Michael Stoper, 1997, p11) amongst human geographers, especially in view of the moral propositions which are unwittingly or unreflectively deployed in the pursuit of human geography. Self-criticality needs to embrace not only the substantive topics of research, but also the practices involved in the doing of human geography.

2. The emerging agreement that moral positions in human geography need to be justified in terms of improving the lives of others, rather than in terms of self-interest or traditional practices (Robert Sack, 1997). There are important implications here for reciprocity between researcher and researched, especially highlighting the need for research to make a practical contribution to the lives of people being studied (Thomas Herman and Doreen Mattingly, 1999).

3. The recognition of interconnections between the symbolic processes of culture and the material processes of politics and economics, leading to exploration of the links between cultural domination and political economic exploitation in defining the problematic, and between identity recognition and socio-economic redistribution in searching for responses to the problematic (see Fraser, 1995).

4. The willingness to take seriously the notion of evil (Yi-Fu Tuan, 1999), both as a significant element in disturbing relationships between people and other people, and between people and nature, and as a consequence of a compartmentalised and disconnected world. The former points us to the destructiveness, cruelty and contempt which can result from uneven power relations, and the latter represents a morally problematic separation between our selves and others.

These prompts, although still the subject of occasionally fierce contestation, seem to suggest the emergence of a more ethically nuanced, if polyvocal, human geography. Moreover, Tuan's discussion of 'evil' introduces a more spiritual dimension and leads me to my second point of optimism.

The possibility for spiritual geographies

'Some of the lost moral certainties of earlier ages need to be recovered, not as fixed and repressive codes, but as carefully crafted anchors to prevent continuing drift in a sea of relativism or "nihilism"' (David Smith, 2000, p214). For many human geographers, the recovery of lost moral certainties will be anathema to the deconstructive relativism which holds a dominant position in the so-called 'cultural turn' (see Ian Cook et al., 2000). For others, the notion of moral certainty will only be found in the theoretical steadfastness of political ideology. However, I want to argue that new readings of moral and ethical geographies can be enhanced significantly by reference to aspects of spirituality, albeit paying strong heed to David Smith's predilection for 'anchor points' rather than repressive behavioural codes. Apart from the motivational experience of faith in my own life (see Paul Cloke, 1994), there seem to me to be both material and philosophical prompts to the inclusion of the spirituality in human geography's discussion of morality, ethics and politics.

First, a considerable proportion of the world's population subscribe to a particular established religion. For example, Patrick Johnstone's (1993) projections for the year 2000 indicate very significant religious adherence world-wide (1800 million Christians, 1300 million Muslims, 800 million Hindu, 700 million Buddhists and so on). Moreover, non-established spiritual activity is on the rise. Michael Brown (1997) suggests that in the USA for example, some 12 million people actively participate in the New Age activities, with another 30 million more peripherally involved. This scale of religious adherence and spiritual involvement inevitably suggests that aspects of spirituality (some perhaps more concerned with social justice than others) will have become intertwined with dominant moral codes in different parts of the world. Thus, for example when Anglo-American geography involves itself with moral rootedness, even using the neo-Kantian idea of 'common moral talk', it seems very likely that the moral precepts of Christian traditions will have found their ways into secular laws, assumptions and expectations. This material presence of what was originally constructed as spiritual morality in what has now become secularised society and government, suggests considerable scope for continuing to understand moral and ethical codes through spiritual lens. It should be added that in the 'secular' society of Britain, for example, a very considerable proportion of voluntary social action which has filled the vacuum created by a retreating welfare state, has been associated with the motivation of a spiritual faith (see David Conradson, 1999). In this case Christian ethics are continuing to have a material impact on action for social justice.

These material presences are connected with philosophical prompts in moral and ethical landscapes. Such prompts have often been construed as extremely negative. As Roger Stump (2000) has pointed out, the greatest negative impact of spirituality on such landscapes stems from obsessive fundamentalism:

> 'The absolute certainty of fundamentalism has important consequences because it precludes the possibility of compromise with others with whom they disagree. Fundamentalists see the conflicts in which they are involved in strictly dualistic terms – as a struggle between good and evil. In their view, the only satisfactory solution to such a struggle is complete victory. To achieve victory, moreover, they presume that they must assert some form of territorial control. Indeed, they believe that they are both entitled to and obliged to wield such control because they alone have access to the truth' (p216).

However, to hold fundamental belief in other spiritually inspired moral codes which reverse the natural order of power – prioritising the weak over the strong, the neighbour over the self, love over hatred and so on – suggests a capacity for the prompting of very different, and socially very positive effects, not least a rediscovery of the necessity for charity in philosophies of citizenship.

As an illustration of the potential philosophical power of spiritual faith on moral and ethical landscapes, I turn briefly to the (re)discovery of Christian principles by two well-known European authors, who approach the legacy of Christian thought from substantially different directions. Gianni Vattimo is a philosopher from Turin. In *Belief* (1999) he argues that the Christian inheritance needs to be emphasised because of its relevance to contemporary culture, which has become what it is because 'it has been "worked" and forged in friendship by the Christian message' (p33). He writes:

> 'I have begun to take Christianity seriously again because I have constructed a philosophy inspired by Neitzsche and Heidegger, and have interpreted my experience in the contemporary world in the light of it; yet, in all probability, I constructed my philosophy because I started with the Christian inheritance, which I have now found again, though, in reality, I had never abandoned it' (p33).

Vattimo's recovery of Christianity is inextricably linked with the philosophical notion of charity. He argues that the guiding thread of the interpretation of Old Testament biblical doctrine by Jesus is 'the new and more profound relation to charity established between God and humanity, and consequently between human beings themselves' (p49). This essential charitable impulse is present in many types of common moral talk, and Vattimo's nihilistic recovery of Christianity represents an interesting route by which to expose the Christian core values of many ethical and moral 'anchors' in Western society.

My second illustration concerns Slavoj Zizek, a social scientist from Ljubljana. In *The Fragile Absolute* he argues that there is a direct lineage of Christianity to Marxism, and that Christianity and Marxism should fight on the same side against what he regards as the onslaught of new spiritualisms. The authentic Christian legacy, he suggests, is far too precious to be left to the 'freaks' of fundamentalism. Zizek's thesis majors on the significance of *agape*, the Christian concept of love as charity expounded in St Paul's biblical letters, which rather than being understood as a spontaneous overflow of generosity, or a self-assertive stance, should, he argues, be viewed

> 'as a self-suppressing *duty* to love neighbours and care for them, as hard *work*, as something to be accomplished through the strenuous effort of fighting and inhibiting one's pathological inclinations' (p100).

Zizek contrasts this agape attitude to the neighbour/other with New Age attitudes which in his view ultimately reduce the neighbour/other to some kind of mirror-image of the self, or to a step along the path of self-realisation, thereby reducing others to external projections of disavowed aspects of the self personality.

Agape, then, is identified as the key intermediary between faith and hope; a very significant set of practices to be worked at. It is an inspired love which enjoins us to 'unplug' from the organic community in which we find ourselves, and to plug into a sense for the other. Agape suspends the social hierarchy. Jesus, for example, clearly regarded those who were viewed socially as the lowest of the low – outcasts, beggars, prostitutes and especially the poor – as founder members of his radically new sense of community. As Zizek argues,

> 'such an "unplugging" as the direct expression of love has nothing whatsoever to do with the escape into an idealised Romantic universe in which all concrete social differences magically disappear' (p127).

Rather, it is 'the active work of love which necessarily leads to the creation of an *alternative* community' (pp129–30).

These two illustrations each involve the recovery of lost moral certainties in the spiritual realm. Vattimo's recovery of Christian charity and Zizek's rediscovery of Christian 'agape' love which engenders a radical reorganisation in ethical attitudes to the social hierarchy, and plugs into a sense for the other, represent important spiritual prompts to the moral and ethical landscapes traversed by human geographers. Their essays of personal experience also suggest that seemingly atheistic explorations in social theory and philosophy can reveal interesting lineage – connections with the spiritual philosophies of Christianity. Although the brief account here hardly scratches the surface of these issues, there certainly seems to be scope for far greater attention to be given by human geographers to spiritual dimensions of love, faith and charity, as well as to the equally important ideas of sin and evil, both as very significant ethical anchors, and as one pathway to a more prioritised and committed sense for the other in geographical thinking and research. My argument here is not that of the proselytiser. Human geographers will approach these issues from very different positions of faith, ideology, agnosticism and pragmatism. Rather, my argument is that the goal for human geography of discovering an emotional, connected and committed sense for the other, may necessitate a prompting of the moral imagination which includes political/ethical/spiritual constellations of issues such as charity and agape, and evil. For further discussion of such constellations, I want to turn briefly to the work of Hannah Arendt.

Hannah Arendt: a recasting of the political?

Craig Calhoun and John McGowan (1997) say this of Hannah Arendt:

> 'Brilliant, demanding, inspiring, original, and sometimes perverse, her writings offer an important resource for theorists who would conceptualise a politics in which questions of meaning, identity and value take centre stage. Arendt frequently frustrates, but her work is indispensable for those who would learn how to take human plurality seriously, how to grasp public life not just as an occasion for choice but also as an opportunity for different human beings to make a world in common, and how to address the problems of not just suboptimal utility but also violence and evil' (p1).

Born in 1906 in Germany, Arendt grew up as part of the Jewish community in Koningsberg. As a teenager she read Kierkegaard, Kant and Jaspers, and at university she fell under the intellectual and personal spell of Heidegger. In 1929, she married the Jewish intellectual and writer Gunther Stern and, in developing severe doubts about Zionism, she became, as John McGowan (1998) notes, 'deeply committed to a pluralist model of polity in which all citizens learn to live amid differences' (p2). Arendt was politically active in Nazi Germany, compiling evidence of anti-semitism, and providing refuge for persecuted

Communists. After a brief period of arrest and detention she fled to Paris, where she met Walter Benjamin, and in 1940 she was married for a second time – to Heinrich Blucher, a non-Jewish German Marxist.

In remarkable circumstances Arendt managed to travel to New York in 1941, taking with her deep insights concerning the experience of statelessness. She quickly learnt English and began to write. *The Origins of Totalitarianism* (1951) brought her academic recognition, and was followed by other essays, notably *The Human Condition* (1958), *Between Past and Future* (1961), *Crises of the Republic* (1972) and *The Life of the Mind* (published posthumously in 1978). However, it was her report on the trial of Adolf Eichmann in 1961 that made Arendt (in)famous. In *Eichmann in Jerusalem: On the Banality of Evil* (1963) she paints Eichmann both as the architect of the Holocaust, and as a completely ordinary man, so enveloped in the task in hand that he lost the capacity to distinguish right from wrong. This elision of the monstrous and the banal prompted heated debate, but encapsulates Arendt's important contribution to the recasting of the political. For the purposes of this paper I want briefly to mention three significant aspects of Arendtian politics.

1 Resisting totalitarianism

For Arendt it was the totalitarian form of rule which set the horizons for the experience of core ethical problems. Her work presents a consistent response to the political evils of the twentieth century in which humanity and human beings were somehow being made superfluous in the pursuit of super-state objectives. Arendt, then, as Kimberley Curtis (1999) explains:

> 'seeks to re-sacralise our feeling for human particularity, to teach us to feel quickened, awed, and pleasured by it through the cultivation of the specific aesthetic sensibility. This sensibility is ethically rooted in, and must be evaluated in relationship to, an analysis of those evils which, in our time, most menace our capacity to form human lives' (p12).

Accordingly, Arendt's emphasis is not only on knowing the worlds of the 'other' so that we can know the 'other', but also on the cultivation of sensibility so as to be able to live in a world which *feels* its suffering and its deprivation, and *experiences* the menace of evil. Meaningfulness is lost by 'enacting oblivion towards others and thus proliferating loneliness' (Curtis, 1999, p153). Meaningfulness is gained by a sense for the other and a responsiveness to the complexity and changing nature of human plurality. In some ways, then, Arendt argues for what Vattimo and Zizek find in charity and agape respectively.

2 Recognising evil

The concept of evil is central to Arendt's analysis of the political failures of society, yet there is considerable debate over the precise formulation of evil in her work (see Stephen Leonard, 1997). Originally she characterised a 'radical evil' as the totalitarian transformation of human nature so as to eliminate the key conditions required to live a *human* life – including spontaneity, individuality and plurality. This 'radical evil' transcends that which can be accounted for by the evil intentions of individuals. It is deep-rooted and perhaps (given Arendt's background in the Jewish community) might embrace some sense of the demonic. Later, as Richard Bernstein (1997) records, Arendt turns from this idea of radical evil to propose the notion of 'extreme' evil capable of overgrowing and laying waste to the world precisely because it spreads rather like a fungus on the surface rather than being deep-rooted or demonic. This revision from 'radical' to 'extreme' takes in Arendt's conclusion that Eichmann's trial demonstrated the 'banality' of evil. She increasingly believed that the capacity to distinguish good from evil presupposes the mental activities of thinking and judging, aided by the voice of conscience. It was precisely these activities which she found lacking in Eichmann. In 'Thinking and Moral Considerations' (1971) she states:

> 'Some years ago, reporting the trial of Eichmann in Jerusalem, I spoke of "the banality of evil" and meant with this no theory of doctrine but something quite fractured, the phenomenon of evil deeds, committed on a gigantic scale, which could not be traced to any particularity of wickedness, pathology, or ideological conviction in the doer, whose only personal distinction was a perhaps extraordinary shallowness. However monstrous the deeds were, the doer was neither monstrous nor demonic, and the only specific characteristic one could detect in his past as well as in his behaviour during the trial and the preceding police examination was something entirely negative: it was not stupidity but a curious, quite authentic inability to think.' (p417).

Arendt's analysis raised a storm of contention, not least because it appeared to some to excuse the monstrous by describing it as banal, and it appeared to reject spiritual dimensions of evil and wickedness. Nevertheless, what Arendt opens up here is both the recognition of the place of evil in imaginations of power and power relations, and the pursuit of what John McGowan (1997) calls 'a polity (constitutions and compacts), ways of acting in concert (performatives in the space of appearances before others) and a phenomenology of relatedness (including the crucial acts of promising and forgiving)' (p263).

3   Action, politics and freedom

Arendt's work crucially emphasised a constellation of three ideas, which for her constituted the basis of acting politically. The first idea is the capacity for action – the ability of initiative, spontaneous activity and innovation to disrupt causal chains of processes and practices. A gloomy acceptance of an inability to change things represents an abrogation of the responsibility to recognise the extent of this capacity for action, as well as a fear that the engagement of this capacity may demand significant and uncomfortable changes in the (self-centred) ways in which we live our lives. The second idea is a politics of doing. As Hanna Fenichel Pitkin (1998) notes:

> 'because we tend to associate initiative and creativity with science, technology and the material world, Arendt stressed doing rather than making, praxis rather than poiesis' (p2).

Again there is a critique here of the frequent human resistance to acknowledging the degree to which our life-patterns reflect what we do – such patterns may not have been originated by our own choosing, but they are often sustained by our doing. While we may not be able to change these life patterns alone, there are strong prospects for a collective politics of undoing and redoing. The third idea is antithetical to contemporary framing of freedom as wrapped up in individual rights to privatise and personalise. Real freedom, for Arendt, represents a collective bringing together of the human capacity for action for the purpose of changing what is wrong in the current shared arrangement.

Each of these ideas has an alternative counterpart: for action read behaviour; for politics read the social; for freedom read necessity. Arendt's recasting of the political, although frustratingly not fully worked through, provides human geographers with provocative and action-orientated markers for developing a connected and committed sense for the other. In the last part of this chapter I want to apply these markers to a more concrete agenda for ethical, and perhaps spiritual, human geographies.

Living ethically, acting politically

Melissa Orlie's (1997) book *Living Ethically, Acting Politically* draws on Foucauldian theory, Arendtian politics and empirical studies of the early seventeenth-century Quaker movement to present something of a manifesto for ethical-political action in the circumstances of contemporary power. She demonstrates how an appreciation for our capacity for spiritual natality can regenerate distinctive senses of freedom, responsibility and ethical-political possibility. Orlie's grounded application of Arendtian ideas offers us a framework for setting out some of the steps which can be taken towards more nuanced and committed ethical-political geographies. I offer these steps as waymarkers rather than an exclusive route; in line with David Smith's notion of 'anchor' points rather than as fixed or repressive codes. Three such waymarkers are presented here.

I Imaginations of power that recognise 'evil'

It is my belief that human geography needs to sponsor imaginations of power that recognise 'evil' in various forms. In the past, there has tended to be a focus on particular loci of power such as capital, class, government policy, individualism and the like. However, we exist amidst historical harm and wrongdoing, and amongst inherited and institutionalised advantage and disadvantage. Our relations with those seemingly like ourselves, and with 'others', are suffused by individual and collective harms, located both in the past and in the present. Clearly, given my own faith-beliefs I want to give due emphasis to demonic and personal forms of evil here, both as invisible powers in the world and as crucial components of the environment of individual behaviour. However, it also seems important to recognise that often we do not *possess* these powers that bring harm or disadvantage to others. Rather we are constituted by and through such powers. This is not to suggest that *malevolent evil* and malicious crime do not remain significant factors in our society and space. Indeed, it is in this form that evil is easiest to agree about and to organise collective resistance to. However, it is also clear that a more *ordinary evil* exists as the product of what Arendt calls 'trespasses': the lack of thought about the unanticipated/ invisible/distant effects our actions may have on others, just because our actions are simply fitting in with the prevailing norms of socio-economic life. As Orlie (1997) explains:

> 'According to Arendt, trespasses inevitably inhere in all human activities because as we locate ourselves in the world we establish new relationships … We can neither undo trespasses ourselves nor prevent them: they occur under circumstances where we did not or could not have known what we were doing … Trespasses are unavoidable because they flow not from our intentions *per se* but from makings and unmakings as they constitute and condition us. We trespass against others when we pursue a living and create a home. Furthermore, at least potentially, or some of the time, we are trespassed against.' (p21)

Such ordinary evil will have important spatiality, since it is often in the spatial 'spreading' of consequences away from the sites of unintended or unthinking actions that everyday evils (such as not having enough to eat or drink, not having a roof over their head, not having clothes to wear, getting sick, imprisoned, excluded and so on) become manifested.

Trespass, then, constitutes thoughtlessness rather than wickedness. In contemporary times, we recognise that we live in the context of organisations which are seemingly organised by no one, yet which cause harm to others in a systematic manner. This recognition can be used to suggest that if no one is responsible for harmful outcomes, then no one is free to change them. The individual conscience can be as sensitive as it likes in such situations, because the individual is deemed to have little or no capacity to make an impact on these ordinary evils. Could it be, then, that systematic power relations are being sustained, and even elabor- ated, by the routinised behaviour of the collectivity of individuals? Individual behaviour may well be conforming to contemporary notions of ethically sound conduct. Contracts are being kept. Behaviour is reasonable and predictable, malicious action is avoided. Yet ordinary evil is not diminished by this seemingly 'ethical' behaviour, and indeed may well be sustained by it. Orlie suggests to us that the predominant political ethos (or 'social rule') of contemporary governance, and the preponderant ways of thinking and activity promoted by it (in Foucault's terms, 'governmentality') are unable to affect a suitable response to the ethical-political issues posed by ordinary evil.

This point can be illustrated powerfully by reference to the issue of homelessness with which I started this paper. I want to claim that homelessness *is* evil. Sometimes it does arise as a result of malevolent or malicious action, but more often it is an effect of more ordinary evils by which individuals, families, landlords, public sector departments, charities and governments are bound together in social relations which produce and reproduce the harmful effects which we construct as homelessness. Accordingly, it is usual for no one but the victims themselves to be held responsible for homelessness. Personal consciences can be held broadly clear, and daily routine behaviour can be regarded as reasonable, ethical and even sympathetic towards homeless people, all *without* any response to the needs of such people. We thereby sustain systemic power relations between the 'homed' and the 'homeless'.

It seems crucial for the future of human geography to explore imaginations of power that recognise both the outcomes of ordered evils *and* the harmful trespasses of more ordinary evils.

2   The crisis of the subject

> 'As subject-citizens incorporate social powers, they engender and elaborate governing effects and become sovereign, individually and collectively, which is to say, they ncreasingly become one and uniform. By this method of popular authorisation, the conventional is made essential and the freely subject product social necessities. As a consequence, competing and conflicting bodies/minds are made governable. Ordinary evil ceases to be a visual problem to the extent that it is ordered.' (Orlie, 1997, p42)

By recognising ordinary evil alongside more ordered evil, and by realising that predominant rationalities constitute us as sometimes thoughtless agents of the governing powers that multiply trespasses, we encounter once again a crisis of the subject. Orlie draws on Foucault to examine the difficulty of forming ourselves as ethical subjects of our actions, and identifies two sets of issues which again seem crucial in envisioning the future of human geography. First, there is the problem of *responsibility*. Too often, it seems, we find that we can neither recognise the harm brought to others by our imbrocation in social rules and their governing ways of representing and constructing the world, nor can we imagine how such harm might be alleviated. The outcome is an often numbing inability and/or unwillingness to grasp responsibility for the social rather than the individual. Second, there is the problem of *freedom*. Our own actions, and those of others can become thwarted by the constrictive patterns of the social, and undermined by the unthinking nature of some social behaviour. In combination, it can be argued that we haven't yet found an effective way of thinking through issues of responsibility and freedom without instinctive reference to an original unified agent of power, whether this be individual or collective. We are still, in Foucault's terms, searching for the head of a headless body politic.

Recognising these problems of responsibility and freedom permits a reorientation of the approach we often take to understanding socio-spatial issues. For example, in the recent work on homelessness in rural areas, carried out by Paul Milbourne and Rebekah Widdowfield and myself, we have recognised a widespread sense of denial that homelessness exists in the countryside (Cloke *et al.* 2000b,c). Even where the issue is tentatively accepted as something more than a figment of the academic imagination, we have encountered immediate attribution of responsibility for rural homelessness to obvious external targets: the government isn't doing enough; the cities should take more responsibility; there needs to be more input from charities and so on. There has been little or no recognition that buying into, or maintaining the traditional moralities embedded in socio-cultural constructs of rural life will result in an imbrication in social rules and governing ways of seeing and doing in rural areas which bring harm to homeless people, of those in poverty. We have detected little by way of imagination about how to alleviate such harm, other than wishing it away to the cities. In this situation, then, the freedom of the self, and the freedom of others, are thereby restricted, and the search remains for some unified agent of power to blame, not least focussing on the victims of homelessness themselves. As Orlie argues:

> 'The predominant political ethos, or 'social rule', of late modern states and the prevalent ways of thinking and acting that it promotes … are ill-suited to the ethical and political dilemmas posed by ordinary evil'. (p12)

In other words, the imaginations of power that we so often deploy in human geography serve to sanction a political ethos which pre-empts the political conditions required to live ethically in the face of ordinary evil. Thus political ethos occasions a crisis of the subject by obstructing the political bodies through which individuals might become more thoughtful agents of the powers which frame their conduct and through which they, in turn, shape the actions of others.

3 Invisible powers

By posing the question of what directions we can follow to go beyond the crisis of the citizen-subject, Orlie (1997) encourages us to recover political enthusiasms for 'invisible powers':

> 'Reconceiving the head of the body politic entails experimenting with the relationships among "body", "mind", and "soul", between corporeality and incorporeality, between visibility and invisibility. In other words, we must explore alternative political theologies as different ways of naming and enlisting invisible powers'. (p63)

These invisible powers can be recognised both outside of us (that is the workings of God and his angels; the intervention of good and evil external spirits and 'ghosts') and within (that is the responses of our souls, our internal spirituality, our ability to communicate with external invisible powers).

Orlie's own study of seventeenth-century Quakerism suggests one such political theology of invisible powers. The Quakers, she argues, held revelation to be a continual possibility. The ability and right to act in new ways, to distance themselves from ordinary concerns and to transfigure everyday life, represented a collaboration between thoughts/words/deeds and invisible powers which opened up a gap between past and future, and (re)created space for different thinking and new actions. In this example, then, the Quakers were seeking after something which was different from what governing powers had made them to be. Chris Philo (1997) notes similar attributes amongst the Shakers of Shaker Lane. The search for the 'something other' here is, however, fuelled by intuitive rather than discursive reasoning; by a *spiritual* perception. Although the Quakers were eventually seen to lose some of the qualities of this search, because of their acceptance of establishment recognition in other spheres, Orlie recognises in them invisible powers, which related to the spiritual realm, and which were crucial in the productivity of individual and collective embodied action, including the challenge to the trespasses of ordinary evil.

Our analysis of contemporary power relations, then, might do well to recognise these spiritual concerns. If political thinking and action work within the limits of ourselves and of our world, then it may be in the spiritual realm that hope lies for transgressing these limits; for allowing the invisible within and without us unsettle the ordinariness of the visible. These spiritual matters can, of course, take different forms. There is room here for deliberation and perhaps discovery of the spiritual associated with the divine, as Orlie's study of the Quakers demonstrates so effectively. Gianni Vattimo's 'charity', and Slavoj Zizek's 'agape' both, for example, suggest a legitimate Christian legacy of allowing the invisible within us to unsettle contemporary attitudes and relationships of self and other. Equally, for some (including, of course, Hannah Arendt) the spiritual need not be conceived as associated with the divine. Either way, human geography may do well to respond to the idea that something within us ('spirit') can and does exceed any particular instantiation of individual conscience and reason. We do, therefore, need to recognise the invisible within us that deals with the invisibles of the world.

Living and acting?

My argument here, then, following Arendt and Orlie, is that ethical and political thinking and action can unleash and enlist those aspects of our spiritual selves that exceed governing forms of individual conscience and public reason. In this way we can reveal, and maybe even hope to address, the impacts of ordinary evil. We cannot substantially change what we are – how and what we have been made to be by history, institutional frames and patterns of social rule, for which no single person can be responsible. However, we can become responsible for who we are – how we live with, and impose on others, the social effects which configure what we appear to be.

Such a recognition has, I believe, important implications for how we adopt political and ethical positions both in and beyond the academy. First, there is a need to recognise appropriate ethical and political practices in amongst the issues we study. A significant element of this search is to look for evidence of 'spirited' political thinking and action, which transgresses the limits of the self. This going-beyond-the-self will not always be good, just or freedom-enabling. Yet in relation to substantive issues, such as that of homelessness for example, is possible to conceive of a going-beyond-the-self in which new forms of selfless responsibility, freedom and resistance are expressed for the benefit and inclusion of homeless people. Such practices may take the form of recognisable collective action, fuelled by ideological, charitable, spiritual or volunteering motives. Or it may be smaller, more individual, more radical, including the resistances of homeless people themselves.

Second, being responsible for who we are also turns the spotlight on ourselves – not being content merely with mapping our ethical terrains as academics, researchers, geographers, are we ready to ask difficult but crucial questions about the importance of invisible powers and the potential for agape in our own being, of which such work is only a part? What 'free actions' do we engage in – for example, by following our inclination to associate only with colleagues/neighbours/friends with whom we readily feel comfortable, and thereby in our making of assumptions about 'others' – which reinforce social rule, and contribute to ordinary evils which may exclude or harm others? Ethical and political action in human geography may require us to contest and transfigure what we are made to be, so as to reveal who we are becoming – not least in order to cultivate a sensibility which permits an ability to live in the world in such a way as to feel its suffering and experience the menace of evil.

Conclusion

'It does seem to me that we are in fact increasingly, maybe more than ever before in human history, jointly bringing about disasters for ourselves and each other, knowing that

> we are doing so, yet somehow unable to stop. More and more the conditions under which we live are the resultants of human activity, and more and more they seem to constrain, cripple, impoverish, and destroy millions of human lives, while we stand by – or rather, sit in front of our television sets or our computers – wringing our hands and blaming each other.' (Pitkin, 1998, p252)

Hanna Fenichel Pitkin's conclusion to her analysis of Arendt's concept of the social is particularly poignant given the academic penchant for sitting in front of a PC, or in front of a class, and metaphorically wringing hands. My argument, inspired by those human geographers who are already way ahead of me on these issues, is that it doesn't have to be this way. We can envision a human geography in which living ethically and acting politically can be essentially intertwined with a sense for the other in a sensitive, committed and active approach to the subject.

Such a human geography would entail a continuing engagement in collective political action against ordered evil. Equally, it necessitates processes and practices which add up to a taking responsibility for what we have been made to be, and for who we are becoming. Taking responsibility will not equate to a simple increase in our agency, for we would still be implicated in distant harms, and disjunctures in will/capacity/desire would remain sources of ethical crisis. Rather, taking responsibility will involve an engagement with the conjunction between individual conduct and invisible powers; an exploration of the participant role of our selves, and others, in the authority of political contexts without authors – in the headless bodies politic.

In practice such a vision will entail:

- being open to plurality, and problematising what we take as given, necessary, ordinary or ordered, both within and without ourselves
- refusing to reinscribe social rule, and assuming responsibility for trespasses by seeking to interrupt rather than repeat them
- forgiving and releasing these trespasses, and promising to redirect how our effects bear upon the future
- understanding the importance of invisible powers, and unleashing aspects of the spiritual which exceed governing forms of individual conscience and public reason.

Is this too idealistic, or a wallowing in pious hope? My concern is that, with notable exceptions, we have begun to lose sight of key aspects of human collectivity in our work: the ability to be organised in such a way as to bring about concerted and effective action; the ability to encourage others to act, particularly those who see no need, or who do not know how to go about it; the ability to recognise real capacities for action and to resist the systematic distortion of issues which prevents us from acting effectively together; and the ability to think as an actor, and not just think about action. My dream is that we can add a critical edge to the political-ethical becoming of human geography by making visible, and responding to, what is ordinarily invisible, silent and outside. Idealistic or not, I prefer this vision to some of the more cynical, and perhaps even hypocritical, alternatives.

Acknowledgements

This chapter is a slightly modified version of a paper which first appeared in *Progress in Human Geography* (2002) Volume 26(5) pp 587–604. It is reproduced by permission of Arnold Publishers. I gratefully acknowledge the really helpful and supportive comments on a previous draft from Sarah Johnsen, Roger Lee, Jon May, Paul Milbourne and Chris Philo.

Bibliography

Arendt, H (1951) *The Origins of Totalitarianism,* San Diego, CA: Harcourt Brace.

Arendt, H (1958) *The Human Condition,* Chicago, IL: University of Chicago Press.

Arendt, H (1961) *Between Past and Future: Eight Exercises in Political Thought,* New York: Penguin Books.

Arendt, H (1963) *Eichmann in Jerusalem: A Report on the Banality of Evil,* New York: Penguin Books.

Arendt, H (1971) 'Thinking and moral considerations: a lecture', *Social Research,* 38, 417–446.

Arendt, H (1972) *Crises of the Republic,* New York: Harcourt Brace.

Arendt, H (1978) *The Life of the Mind,* New York: Harcourt Brace.

Augé, M (1998) *A Sense for the Other* (Trans. A Jacobs) Stanford, CA: Stanford University Press.

Bernstein, R (1997) 'The "banality of evil" reconsidered' in Calhoun C and McGowan J (eds) *Hannah Arendt and the Meaning of Politics,* Minneapolis, MN: University of Minnesota Press.

Barnett, A and Scruton, R (1998) 'Introduction' in Barnett A and Scruton R (eds) *Town and Country,* London: Jonathon Cape.

Blomley, N (1994) 'Activism and the academy', *Environment and Planning D: Society and Space,* 12, 383–385.

Blunt, A and Wills, J (2000) *Dissident Geographies: An Introduction to Radical Ideas and Practice* Harlow: Prentice Hall.

Brown, M (1997) *The Channelling Zone: American Spirituality in an Anxious Age,* Cambridge, MA: Harvard University Press.

Calhoun, C and McGowan, J (1997) 'Introduction: Hannah Arendt and the meaning of politics' in Calhoun, C and McGowan, J (eds) *Hanna Arendt and the Meaning of Politics,* Minneapolis, MN: University of Minnesota Press.

Castree, N (1999) 'Out there? In here? Domesticating critical geography', *Arena* 31, 81–86.

Cloke, P (1994) '(En)culturing political economy: a life in the day of a "rural geographer"' in Cloke, P, Doel, M, Matless, D, Phillips, M and Thrift, N (eds) *Writing the Rural: Five Cultural Geographies,* London: Paul Chapman.

Cloke, P and Little, J (eds) (1997) *Contested Countryside Cultures: Otherness, Marginalisation and Rurality,* London: Routledge.

Cloke, P, Milbourne, P and Widdowfield, R (2000a) 'Homelessness and rurality: "Out of place" in purified space?' *Environment and Planning D: Society and Space,* 18, 715–735.

Cloke, P, Milbourne, P and Widdowfield, R (2000b) 'The hidden and emerging spaces of rural homelessness', *Environment and Planning A,* 32, 77–90.

Cloke, P, Milbourne, P and Widdowfield, R (2000c) 'Partnership and policy networks in rural local governance: homelessness in Taunton', *Public Administration,* 78, 111–134.

Conradson, D (1999) *Voluntary Spaces,* Unpublished Ph.D. thesis, School of Geographical Sciences, University of Bristol.

Cook, I, Crouch, D, Naylor, S and Ryan, J (eds) (2000) *Cultural Turns/Geographical Turns: Perspectives on Cultural Geography,* Harlow: Prentice Hall.

Curtis, K (1999) *Our Sense of the Real: Aesthetic Experience and Arendtian Politics,* Ithaca, NY: Cornell University Press.

Doel, M (1994) 'Deconstruction on the move: from libidinal economy to liminal materialism', *Environment and Planning A,* 26, 1041–1059.

Driver, F (1991) 'Morality, politics, geography: brave new worlds' in Phil C (ed) *New Words New Worlds: Reconceptualising Social and Cultural Geography,* Lampeter: St David's University College.

Fraser, N (1995) 'From redistribution to recognition? Dilemmas of justice in a "post-socialist" age', *New Left Review,* 212, 68–93.

Harvey, D (2000) *Spaces of Hope,* Edinburgh: Edinburgh University Press.

Hay, I (1998) 'Making moral imaginations: research ethics, pedagogy, and professional human geography', *Ethics, Place and Environment,* 1, 55–75.

Herman, T and Mattingley, D (1999) 'Community, justice, and the ethics of research: negotiating reciprocal research relations' in Proctor, J and Smith, D (eds) *Geography and Ethics: Journeys in a Moral Terrain,* London: Routledge.

Johnstone, P (1993) *Operation World,* Carlisle: OM Publishing.

Leonard, S (1997) 'Evil, violence, thinking, judgement: working in the breech of politics' in Calhoun, C and McGowan, J (eds) *Hannah Arendt and the Meaning of Politics,* Minneapolis, MN: University of Minnesota Press.

McGowan, J (1997) 'Must politics be violent? Arendt's Utopian vision' in Calhoun, C and McGowan, J (eds) *Hannah Arendt and the Meaning of Politics,* Minneapolis, MN: University of Minnesota Press.

McGowan, J (1998) *Hannah Arendt: An Introduction,* Minneapolis, MN: University of Minnesota Press.

Orlie, M (1997) *Living Ethically, Acting Politically,* Ithaca, NY: Cornell University Press.

Osborne, T (1998) *Aspects of Enlightenment: Social Theory and the Ethics of Truth,* London: University College Press.

Philo, C (1991) 'De-limiting human geography: new social and cultural perspectives' in Philo, C (ed) *New Words, New Worlds: Reconceptualising Social and Cultural Geography,* Lampeter: St David's University College.

Philo, C (1997) 'Of other rurals?' in Cloke, P and Little, J (eds) *Contested Countryside Cultures: Otherness, Marginalisation and Rurality,* London: Routledge.

Philo, C (2000) 'More words, more worlds: reflections on the "cultural turn" and human geography' in Cook, I, Crouch, D, Naylor, S and Ryan, J (eds) *Cultural Turns/Geographical Turns: Perspectives on Cultural Geography,* Harlow: Prentice Hall.

Pitkin, H F (1998) *The Attack of the Blob: Hannah Arendt's Concept of the Social,* Chicago, IL: University of Chicago Press.

Proctor, J and Smith, D (eds) (1999) *Geography and Ethics: Journeys in a Moral Terrain,* London: Routledge.

Sack, R (1997) *Homo Geographicus: A Framework for Action, Awareness, and Moral Concern,* Baltimore: John Hopkins University Press.

Sayer, R and Storper, M (1997) 'Ethics unbound: for a normative turn in social theory', *Environment and Planning D: Society and Space,* 15, 11–17.

Scruton, R (1998) 'Conserving the past' in Barnett, A and Scruton, R (eds) *Town and Country,* London: Jonathan Cape.

Smith, D (1999) 'Social justice and the ethics of development in post-Apartheid South Africa', *Ethics, Place and Environment,* 2, 157–177.

Smith, D (2000) *Boundaries of Faith: Geographical Perspectives on Religious Fundamentalism,* Oxford: Rowman and Littlefield.

Stump, R (2000a) *Boundaries of Faith,* Oxford: Rowman and Littlefield.

Stump, R (2000b) *Moral Geographies: Ethics in a world of Difference,* Edinburgh: Edinburgh University Press.

Tuan, Y-F (1999) 'Geography and evil: a sketch' in Proctor J and Smith D (eds) *Geography and Ethics: Journeys in a Moral Terrain,* London: Routledge.

Vattimo, G (1999) *Belief* (trans. L D'Isanto and D Webb) Cambridge: Polity Press.

Zizek, S (2000) *The Fragile Absolute,* London: Verso.

12
Activist geographies: building possible worlds

Sue Ruddick

> 'For we have to ask ourselves, here and now, do we wish to join that procession, or don't we? On what terms shall we join that procession?' (Virginia Woolf, *Three Guineas*)

Introduction

When I was first invited to do this chapter I was tempted to write a strident 'call to activism in geography', pointing out the privilege we have as members of academia (both as faculty and students) relative to the rest of the population; listing growing social and economic disparities – the increasing divide within the First world and between First and Third; and exhorting readers to do their 'larger duty' as politically-engaged intellectuals, as critical geographers. In fact, over the past 30 years, as critical geography has become more comfortably ensconced within academia in the West, and as radicalism of a variety of stripes has acquired a certain intellectual *cachet*, poverty, social exclusion and a whole range of new forms of marginalisation – class and otherwise, in both the First and Third World – have grown apace. In the United States, reputedly one of the richest nations in the world, for example, the average CEO now makes *four hundred* times more than the average employee, a tenfold increase from even a decade ago; prison populations are ballooning with young black males; families with children, and in particular single parents, are falling deeper into poverty; on a global scale, the bulk of the world's wealth is now concentrated among around 14% of its population and *two-thirds* of the world is systematically excluded – through immigration barriers, among other things – from the benefits of the latest round of 'globalisation'; and over the past 30 years, the poorer regions of the world such as sub-Saharan Africa and parts of South America, have fallen deeper into poverty by any accepted standard.

But 'activism' responds only momentarily (if at all) to such calls to action. Long-term, committed, political and intellectual engagement requires a different set of conditions to nurture it – the undertow of biography that pulls us towards one issue or another, sustained personal connections that keep us there, a sense of community, the possibility and necessity of making things better for the people and issues we care about, the anticipation of making a different way of life a little more possible, the fear and excitement of pushing boundaries, of challenging and changing the rules about how things are and what should be done. And activism of this nature, and in particular activism that involves sustained intellectual and political engagement *outside* of the academy – the recent activities around the WTO aside – is difficult to come by these days. But it does exist, albeit in fragmented and fractured forms.

For many of us in academia, activism *in any place* has become something of a problem child – a child we feel sometimes vaguely, sometimes passionately attached to; a child nobody wants to dismiss outright; but one paid only intermittent attention, and one which – if the truth be told – most academics are just a little uncomfortable embracing wholeheartedly: a child best left in the care of others. Partly this stems, not from an outright rejection of activism *per se*, but from the conflicted nature of the meanings generally ascribed to the term and the growing difficulties of being politically engaged beyond the confines of our institutions, that at best do not reward this activity, and at worst actively discourage it. Activism remains something of an illegitimate discourse. And yet, activism still takes place, if in spite of these circumstances rather than because of them.

'What does it mean to be an *activist*?' 'What does it mean to be an activist *geographer*?' 'What does it mean to be an activist geographer *here and now*?' – in this place and time, or the many differentiated space–times in which geographers are currently attempting to be activists? I want to address these questions in part by retelling, somewhat selectively, the story of activism in geography as it has been written in (and in relation to) Anglo-American institutions over the past 25 years. But I want to use this history to reflect on how the meaning, content and context of our activism has changed over time and must continue to change.

This in itself is a difficult task. I will not be able to capture or reflect fully the multiple forms that activism takes within and alongside the academy; partly because of the fragmented and fractured nature of people's activities – that they alternate or interweave with academic work in a variety of ways; partly because individuals make their own accommodations as to when, where and how they become activists; and partly because there are significant differences in the contexts within which people act – both in the nature of the academy and the so-called 'outside' world, in different parts of the globe. This chapter, as well, will draw only marginally on situations outside of the Anglo-American world because my own experience and networks remain so substantially within that world. And these difficulties in themselves, mirror a challenge we face: to begin to weave together interconnections in our praxis; between the 'in here' and 'out there' of activism (see Castree, 2000) across neighbourhoods, across countries and between different parts of the world.

But these difficulties aside, I *do* want to suggest ways in which academia as an institution *can* be made more 'activist friendly'; ways in which we *can* channel our activism to continue to fashion an institutional context that sustains, rather than thwarts, its conditions of reproduction; and ways in which we, as activists *can* 'join that procession', on our own terms.

What is activism?

Is it possible to think of such a thing as 'activist geography'? What questions does such a term raise? How might we envision it: what could or should it be?

The term does not appear in past compendiums on the historiography of the discipline, neither the recent *Human Geography* (Agnew, Livingstone and Rogers, 1997), nor the *Dictionary of Human Geography, Second Edition* (Johnston, Gregory, Smith, 1989), nor *New Models in Geography Volumes One and Two* (Peet and Thrift, 1989), nor the *Feminist Glossary of Human Geography* (McDowell and Sharp, 1999). In the most recent *Dictionary of Human Geography*, Castree recalls its historical definition as an activity 'in which (i) research was focused on politically charged questions and solutions and (ii) in which geographers actively involved themselves in the peoples and communities studied', and he notes the recent concern about whether activism takes place inside or outside the academy.

The problematic nature of activist geography, however, begins not in the academy or in geography *per se*, but in the doubled nature of the term itself. The *Compact Edition of the Oxford Dictionary* does not define activism or activist, but:

> Active: 1. a) Opposed to *contemplative or speculative*: Given to outward action. b) Practical as opposed to *theoretical*. 2. Opposed to passive … exerting action upon others …
> 3. Opposed to quiescent or extinct …, existing in action, working, effective having *practical* operation or results.

And the *American Heritage Dictionary of the English Language* provides a definition of the term 'activism' itself: 'activism: The theory, doctrine or practice of assertive often militant action, … used as a means of opposing or supporting a controversial issue, entity or person.'

What the two terms have in common is a necessary implication of engagement, of response to contemporary *issues* of a political and social nature. The conflicting understanding and usage of the terms active and activism, the indeterminacy of their meaning, however, is apparent at the outset: one sets activity in opposition to theory (practical as *opposed* to theoretical) the other makes a necessary *link* between the two, activism *embodying* a theory of action itself.

This *doubled* nature of activism – as praxis – echoes a doubled relationship between theory and practice, between the rational and the extra-rational, and has been the source of much debate and discussion about *activism's proper place* as the generative locus of new conceptual/theoretical production. This has dogged geography and other disciplines in various forms over many years. Twenty years ago, the burning question was whether one should locate the forward momentum of theoretical production – and political change – as emanating from an abstracted reason, in philosophy, in fact (see Althusser, 1971) or the maw of messy human experience (see Thompson, 1978). Debates around the multiple natures of our activism have surfaced in various forms since then. There have been heated discussions about whether activism has specific places of privilege, or whether it can be thought of as occurring along a continuum, embodied in all activity – even the troubled struggles of the subconscious in sleep (Smith, 1996; Pile, 1996). There have been reflections on the public or private nature of our activism – do we continue to privilege masculinist understandings – 'the street', 'the demonstration', over the activities have been traditionally the purview of women, nurturing and sustaining types of involvement (Pratt, 1998)? There have been discussions about whether activism best occurs inside or outside of the academy (Blomley, 1994; Castree, 2000; Bakker, Page and Swyngedouw, 1998).

Those most critical of activism tend to distort its oppositional nature – as practice exclusively *in opposition to* theory. In an era that celebrates nuance, multiplicity and ambiguity, to be an 'activist' can seem, at times, to be one sided and singular. In a discipline that on the whole rewards rational, dispassionate analysis, activism is too often discounted as irrational, earnest, emotive, partial, biased – falsely portrayed – not as the *acknowledgement of bias* at the outset, which directs one towards more critically engaged action, but as the *clouding of proper judgment* by bias – hence resulting in having one's work labeled as 'polemical'. In an institutionalised, intellectual context such as academia, which both reflects and reinforces the division between mental and manual labour, too often activism (or its cousin, practice) is wrongly conceived of as a derivative, an end-product (or worse a by-product) of theorisation, rather than a point of genesis of intellectual growth and development. It is often thought of literally and figuratively as an 'extra-curricular activity', the manual side of the mental-manual split, characterised at its crudest by envelope stuffing, telephone trees, marches, and endless, endless meetings. The thing you do after the teaching and the research and the writing is done.

And yet, as Doreen Massey recently noted, these days we seem to write about activism a *lot* (Massey, 2000). (See, for example, Peck, 1999; Blomley, 1994; Katz, 1998; Berg, Morin and Simonsen, 1998; Bakker, Page and Swynegedou, 1998; Pratt, 1998; Tickell, 1995; Uribe-Ortega, 1998; Pile, 1996; Smith, 1996). We write about transformations inside and outside the academy, our necessary social responsibility, about the proper place of activism, the need to hold our institutions responsible for the ethics of their actions, difficulties in sustaining extra-institutional involvements. The current proliferation of articles on activism betrays larger anxieties, symptomatic both of our desire to be more politically engaged and the continual frustration of that desire, which it seems, can only be momentarily assuaged in the act of writing.

The acknowledgement of activism's dualities, moreover, has led many of us to revisit an expanded, more varied and vibrant understanding of our possible roles as politically committed intellectuals – less committed to an 'either/or' model, and more open to the possibilities of 'both/and'. Models for this abound in the literature that currently inspires geographers. They include those focused on individual acts of engagement in teaching and writing, which suggest that there is nothing easy about attempting a transformative politics even when it is restricted to the written word or contained within the moment-to-moment exchanges in the classroom. Here I am thinking of Kristeva's tripled notion of the dissident, which validates not only political engagements of the rebel who challenges state power, but also the psychoanalyst who challenges the power of religion or writer who challenges thought itself (Kristeva, 1977). Or hooks' rethinking of pedagogical practice and advocating a politics of transgression that builds on the work of Friere (hooks, 1994). Or Monture-Okannee's reflections on the double violence endured by oppressed people when their pain is appropriated and dissected unfeelingly by well-meaning critics, and the contradictory ways women of colour must act to accommodate their own difference in the academy (Monture-Okanne, 1995.) Still others assess the limits and possibilities of sustained action within and outside the academy. Gramsci has provided us long ago with the model of the organic intellectual, engaged in the political struggle of every day life – 'constructor, organiser, permanent persuader' (Gramsci, 1971). Cornel West speaks to the new role of intellectuals as cultural workers – who not only demystify social structures, but make explicit social values and political aims (West, 1987).

My own experience of activism reflects this multiple meaning, although I have tended to split my activism inside and outside of the academy, where others have made the relationship more synthetic. I have been, and continue to be involved in organisations attempting to transform geography within the academy, such as the USG and ICG. And I have taken several 'holidays' from academic life (though not, I might add, from intellectual life) and participated in a variety of movements, such as initiatives in cooperative housing in Montreal, health care collectives, municipal politics, community planning with low income neighborhoods and in strategic planning in downtown Los Angeles (in and against the state, as it were) dealing with issues of homelessness on Skid Row, to name a few. Most often this has involved activism in this doubled sense, making it almost impossible for me to separate out 'intellectual' and 'pragmatic' engagement – one endlessly feeding the other. And in this chapter, it is this understanding of activism that I hope to recuperate – in the ways activism is experienced both inside and outside the academy – and to reflect on how we as geographers are best placed to build bridges between the two, and the rewards and necessities of doing so.

Within the academy

The history of activism within geography could be depicted in part, as a 'long march through the institution' (Mao): one marked by a series of victories and institutional appropriations that have enhanced the acceptability of our engagement in controversial issues around social equity and social justice; one marked by the continual redrawing of the boundaries set on what (and how) we teach, and how, and with whom and for whom we do research – and redrawing of boundaries which circumscribe the nature of our engagements within and beyond the academy.

There have been many milestones in this march over the past 30 years. To name a few, we might include: the formation of the journal *Antipode* in 1969; the *Detroit/Toronto Geographical Expeditions* (1973, 1975) pioneered by Bill Bungee, which pointedly mirrored and parodied the tradition of the 'geographical expedition' as it took students on research field trips to investigate the lives of children in the poorer neighborhoods in that city; the organisation of the *Union of Socialist Geographers* in the early 1970s; the formation of the *IBG Women and Geography Study Group* in the same decade; the establishment of *Gender, Place and Culture*; and the fronting of a range of political, social and cultural issues of note to geographers in the *Environment and Planning* series; the creation of a range of specialty groups within the *Association of American Geographers* to nurture critical interests; the recent formation of the *International Critical Geographers*; the growing inclusion of women and, to a lesser extent, people of colour (still one of the more pernicious divides between those in the academy and those outside of it) in the ranks of students, faculty and tenured faculty; and the changing terrain of acceptable research and teaching.

Read backwards, the success and longevity of these achievements endows them with an aura of certainty. But many forms of activism — those that truly challenge and change the boundaries and the rules of engagement, rather than diffusing and consolidating particular practices — necessarily involve uncertainty and risk. If we examine the history of activism over the past three decades it is the locus of this risk that has shifted.

Through the 1970s, these achievements occurred without institutional sanction and often largely in spite of it. The question of engagement with issues and organisations outside of academia was not as critical during this period. Often geographers came to the discipline to try and make sense of the activities that they were *already* involved in on the outside — and there was no dearth of political activity beyond the academy, whether it be civil rights, the Vietnam war, or later on the rise of municipal progressive political parties, issues of separatism in Ireland and Quebec, union movements in First and Third World venues, or struggles against dictatorships. The task at hand was to bring these issues into the classroom, to make the classroom more relevant and reflective of the range and breadth of political engagements outside and to use academia to help us make sense of the world outside and to sharpen our strategic engagements within it.

At the time, the fact of being largely 'outside the project' of mainstream geography, while contributing to a sense of uncertainty, often allowed for greater experimentation among its participants. In North America, the Union of Socialist Geographers (USG) for example (which I belonged to through the mid 1970s), organised conferences synchronised with the American Association of Geography to allow our members to use institutional funding for the larger conference to piggy back USG meetings. Although theoretical formulations about positionality and a politics of place had not yet graced our literature, there were heated internal debates about where the conference should be held, and the limits and possibilities of remaining in a venue close to but off the premises of the formal conference, to mark our difference, to permit an atmosphere of informality, to break to some extent with competitive modes of production of knowledge. The parallel conference included non-conventional fora, such as large roundtable workshops in which the group could debate or discuss issues in great depth, and unsanctioned publications such as the USG newsletter, which provided an outlet for position papers, announcements about political issues of note, poems, cartoons. In Britain, the Women and Geography Study Group engaged in a similar strategy in relation to the IBG. The results of a series of these engagements produced a collective work titled *Geography and Gender*. This book was not only significant for providing a coherent treatment of contemporary thinking about gender in geography, but also an alternative to competitive forms of production of knowledge.

While contemporary debates sometimes bemoan our lack of activity outside of the academy, these accomplishments are not to be taken lightly. All involve a kind of coming to voice of critical thinking. All expanded the space for critical political engagement, in a whole range of diverse arenas, including the nature of research, methods, teaching styles, equity issues in representation among students and faculty.

Taken in this light, it is important not to downplay the significant advances critical geographers have made in successfully colonising our own discipline. Without appropriate venues to publish the types of research we feel important, or to teach about the issues that are dear to us, activism could not flourish either inside or outside of the academy. It is important not to forget that for nearly two decades, critical geographers were faced continually with challenges to the legitimacy of our concerns about class inequities, racism, sexism, homelessness and the like. 'Yes all well and good', was the standard response 'but is this *really* geography?' We should celebrate the fact that we have won increased freedom (occasional challenges aside) in broadening the definition of *what* is accepted as the purview of geography – the nature of geographical knowledge. Moreover, while these gains reflect the context for geography in Anglo-American institutions, in other countries this battle has yet to be won. Geography departments in South, Central and Latin America, in Japan and Asia, in many countries in Africa, still struggle for the kinds of recognition that critical geographers in the West can now take for granted.

That said, as I will argue below, *how* we produce this knowledge and *who* we produce it with, and most importantly who we produce it *for*, are still significantly circumscribed – increasingly so, perhaps, as our axes of marginalisation and incorporation are shifting. In North America, during the late 1960s and 1970s, for example, while activist geography was largely *outside* the intellectual project of mainstream geography, its adherents remained economically very much *supported* by the institution: housing was cheap, the cost of living and fees were low, students had relatively healthy remuneration as teaching assistants, there was a relative availability of jobs for faculty, lighter teaching loads and less pressure to publish – all these factors left sufficient time for students and faculty to develop critical perspectives. At the same time, sanctions against the substance of people's activities were sometimes dire, involving battles around tenure and around the legitimacy of these endeavours.

By the 1980s and through to the 2000s, however, we face the converse situation. Critical perspectives are sanctioned within Anglo-American geography now, in fact, to be critical has become somewhat trendy. Members of our discipline who might be included as activists now hold positions of esteem within geographies' representative organisations, sit on editorial boards, adjudicated grants, chair departments. Indeed, workshops and research – on what were once considered 'radical issues' – are now supported by healthy funding through government organisations such as the ESRC, SSHRC, NSERC and the like. And with the proliferation of a range of internationally respected journals whose central focus is critical engagements of the discipline, faculty have far less difficulty finding venues that meet the disciplinary standards for peer-reviewed publication.

But increased student indebtedness, tightening of the job market and increased pressures to publish even among postgraduates allow for little experimentation outside of the institutionally sanctioned channels. Nowadays, students at all levels are more strapped for funding and often undertake postgraduate education already saddled with high burdens of indebtedness. The time and freedom to experiment with new forms of pedagogy; to involve oneself in issues both inside and outside the academy; to read broadly to enhance one's critical knowledge base rather than selectively to 'produce a thesis' or book or article – this time is in short supply.

For faculty, moreover, teaching loads have increased substantially, as have expectations to publish, which reduce opportunities for collective activities and force intellectual discourse and discussion into narrow 'product-oriented' encounters, whose measures of success risk being overwhelmed by terms sanctioned by the academy: the foundation of new journals, development of research agendas and the like. And some barriers remain more impervious to challenges than others. We have *appropriated* many of the institutions within academia, allowing critical perspectives a wider acceptance, but we have not *transformed* these institutions in any formal terms, and it is our practices of collaboration instead that have co-exist in an uneasy accommodation with the pressures towards individual authorship and reward for publications. The difficulties in legitimating alternative forms of production of knowledge, in challenging increasingly circumscribed, individualised and competitive modes of production of knowledge, often involves a kind of *perruque* (to borrow from de Certeau) – the colonisation of one activity to perform another under cover. In the main, our success within the formal confines of the discipline has been accompanied by a retreat from these more transgressive forms. We cease to publish as collectives but include all authors' names, or alternate 'first authors' in joint publications to allow for equal recognition in our respective institutions, or provide opportunities for formal papers at conferences to allow participants to engage in workshops and discussion at roundtables and still receive institutional funding.

I don't mean to disparage these strategies: activism in any venue can only be sustained over the long term if it somehow nourishes and sustains its adherents, and academia is no exception. Transgression, particularly in the production of knowledge, remains a risky business. And if we decide to put our energies into new forms of intellectual production or pedagogy, we still need to be mindful of the larger picture: *Who ultimately benefits* from these activities in the long term? If the workshops, the reading groups, the symposia serve *only* to hone our critical intellectual capacity and ultimately *only* further our careers, this is sad news indeed. In spite of this danger, however, I think it is critical that we develop venues that reframe the rules of intellectual engagement, make them less individualistic and competitive: it is not possible to develop an image of an alternative world unless we experience this world in some form (however fleeting or compromised) in our own day-to-day practice.

There have been other gains within the academy. Curricula have expanded to reflect issues of equity and social responsibility (largely fuelled by the exponential growth of geographers' publications on these subjects); women are increasingly represented in the ranks of geographers as students, postgraduates and faculty, and assuming high levels of responsibility within academic institutions and the representative institutions of our discipline although we still need to make greater strides in including people of colour, lesbians and gays, people from the Third World and disabled geographers. This move towards inclusivity should not be understood as an attempt simply to change the face of the discipline for its own sake. It is, rather, a strategy to enhance the network of connections that tie us to places, issues and people beyond the academy – to enhance our wider frame of reference. To allow 'others' in, who can harness the resources of the institution for social change. To tie our institutional resources more tightly to those whose hearts and minds are bound up in, and connected to, the lifeworlds of those who are truly excluded.

This move towards inclusivity is all the more important when we take stock of the casualties resulting from our success. One, I believe, is that the opportunities to think *beyond* the limits of the academy or to collaborate in creative ways, are becoming increasingly limited, even as the possibilities for thinking critically *within it* (albeit in very specific ways) are expanding. While the substantive concerns of the discipline have grown more critical, the formal criteria that sustain it have grown more conservative, making activism outside of the academy a more difficult prospect than it was in the past.

But it is this disjuncture between 'inside' and 'outside' that has given rise to debates that becoming focused around the '*proper place of politics*' rather than the '*proper politics of place*' – that is to say, a concern with *where* political activity takes place (as if this is the singular signifier of its relevance), rather than *what* political activity occurs in any given place and how it becomes connected with other similarly or dissimilarly located actions.

Activism in the academy is sometimes dismissed as irrelevant to events in the 'outside world' (in spite of its demonstrated importance to making connections with that outside world). Activism beyond the academy is sometimes treated with scepticism, diminished in its significance against the imagined futures that accompanied struggles for social change in the 1970s, each of them crushed under the weight of the 'burden of revolution'. The real question should be not whether activism 'inside' or 'outside' the academy is more valid, but how we can begin to forge more active connections within *and* beyond the academy – how to make both more possible.

One way of retrieving ourselves from this impasse, is to think of these different contexts in terms of Gramscian notions of the 'war of movement' and 'war of position', each requiring different kinds of engagement: the former suggesting a frontal assault on the power of the institutions of the state and the latter a need to build new forms of state life.

The history of the last three decades suggests that the nature of institutional and extra-institutional conditions in Anglo-American countries are diametrically opposed to one another. Within the academy we are engaged in a war of movement: we are now relatively established within the discipline and able to chip away at the representational structures and mandates of our institutions – at least for some issues, though others, like ablism and heterosexism continue to be 'outside the project' (see Chouinard and Grant, 1995; Christopherson, 1989.) Outside of the academy we currently need to engage in a war of position, helping to sustain organisations that are under attack with neo-liberal cutbacks and nurture new ones that respond to the new ways in which people are marginalised or excluded by reconfigurations of the state.

Here, our role not simply as activists but as geographers comes into play. What does geography as a discipline bring to our understanding of activism – for if we are *activist* geographers, we are also activist *geographers*? It is by now almost commonplace in our understanding that space plays an unequivocally central role in people's oppression. But 30 years ago, the co-constitutive dimensions of spatiality had yet to be understood. In the 1960s for instance, Foucault recalls a period when space and time/geography and history were counterposed: space was deemed reactionary and capitalist; time – or history – becoming revolutionary. Insurgent geographers of the 1970s were hard pressed to rethink master narratives in terms of their spatiality – except perhaps on the grand scale of development and underdevelopment, or the exclusions that wrought ghetto's (development studies aside) – and mapping inequity, though a powerful tool, was something of an additional manifestation, was still considered very much an end product of larger processes. Perhaps caught within the anti-spatial traditions of Western Marxism (see Soja, 1989) scholars considered the spatial dimensions of inequity provided an additional 'proof', but only in specific instances were they considered to provide additional explanatory power (spatial fix, development/underdevelopment, the necessary unevenness of capital).

Now space is 'on the agenda' as never before. Geography brings to activism an understanding of space, that is nuanced, complex, multi-layered, entangled. Without repeating the historiography of a discipline, work now abounds on all fronts – from the 'great strategies of geopolitics to the little tactics of the habitat' (Foucault) – on the role of space in social struggles, in the formation of social identities, in the multiple and multi-scalar articulations of power. Geographers are drawing in creative ways on the works of many theorists from outside the discipline, whose interest in power has drawn them to an exploration of space. And theorists outside the discipline are also turning to geography.

As our understanding of space has become more complex, more nuanced, more insightful, so too have socio-spatial relations and articulations of power become more tangled and difficult to discern, analyse and organise in response to. And our strategies around activism must become more complex and nuanced as a result, taking into account the multiple scales at which our social life is constructed and the myriad ways that we are not only torn apart, but can join together.

How can we do this and, more importantly, exhortations aside, why should we do it? Activism is difficult, not rewarded much by institution. In fact, although we may think of activism as occurring along all moments of a continuum, these moments are nevertheless unequally rewarded. Publishing takes precedence over political engagement. And political engagement is best done (or rather most tolerated) in forms of institutional service within the discipline, so long as it remains at a comfortable distance from life on our own campuses, outside of our cities. We often seem oblivious to the fact that quite outside the realm of teaching and research, our own universities have much influence: as a employers of a wide range of sectors, as real-estate owners; as pension fund holders, as municipal actors. And of all of these activities, the act of building institutional and organisational movements outside of academia, in concert with local, regional and transnational organisations and NGOs, is the least rewarded.

This form of activism requires a temporal engagement that does not fit the one-to-three year cycle of grantsmanship. It sits uneasily with the 'tyranny of the new' within academia that demands fresh conceptual contributions every year. It rails against the singularity of intellectual production that works against collaborative political activity. These pressures, in fact, can encourage a form of engagement that pilfers movements for their ideas, analyses, insights, while offering precious little return – yet another variation on the theme of getting a bit of the 'other'. Activism is often a moment of creation, the invention of new practices – the bricolage of old ones, pulled together out of the necessity of the moment – academics often, at best, are able simply to name these practices and, in doing so, make them readable and hopefully reproducible.

Activism requires academics – as political intellectuals – to cross boundaries of privilege and confront their personal stake in an issue, and the ways they are positioned differently from members of the organisations they work with. The abstracted allegiance of academics may well enable them to think dispassionately about strategies over the long term, but may make it more difficult for them to see the necessary messy, imperfect, compromises that are required by coalition building or in order to keep political constituencies engaged.

And yet in spite of these difficulties, activism occurs. We continue to push boundaries along all points of the continuum. We attempt to deepen intellectual conversations and engagements by incorporating non-academic styles of writing and authorship, or by researching politically challenging and academically unconventional topics. And we continue to publish in popular venues to reach a non-academic audience (though this is time away from publishing rewarded by our departments); we continue to present testimony at hearings and commissions; we continue to work with community and union groups and others.

Activist geographers continue to work with unions, farm workers, homeless people, prison populations, high schools, around issues of racism, classism, ablism, sexism, heterosexism, postcolonialism, imperialism, and many other forms of oppression, precisely because of the deep personal and long-term connections that draw people to particular activities and communities. Ruth Gilmore's work with prison populations, Bennett Harrison's work with unions, David Slater's work with Third World NGOs, Jan Monk's work with women's organisations and NGOs in both the Third and First World, Audrey Kobayashi's work against racism, Nick Blomley's work with neighborhoods on the eastside of Vancouver, Don Mitchell's work with high school teachers, Linda Peake's work with the women of Red Thread in Guyana, to name a few – all of these locate their centre of gravity outside of the academy, in ways that harness individual energies and institutional resources for the service of a wider populace, and all speak to these kinds of commitment.

Geographers become activists not solely as a call to biography, responding to issues and people that have touched them through their lives, but also because it is intellectually engaging and challenging in the fullest sense. Far from its representation as the manual form of mental labour, far from its depiction as the by-product of theory, activism can become a generative locus of new ways of thinking about the world and being in the world.

Activism – when it involves mounting a challenge to particular structures of power – requires the simultaneous engagement of multiple layers of interpretations, analysis and meaning, from the psycho-dynamics of leadership and styles of negotiation, to the reading of the complexity of political conjunctures traversed by many 'outside forces' which permit or disallow a range of tactics, to the understanding of long-term institutional and economic processes. Activism calls upon the full range of our critical sensibilities.

So what can we do to enhance activism within and outside the academy? While acknowledging that activism exists along a continuum, we need to increase the possibilities for certain kinds of activism within academia. We need to encourage funding possibilities for scholars who work with outside organisations – this is already happening with some funding sources, in response to intense lobbying by both scholars and NGOs, that now require partnerships as prerequisites for funding; we need to continue to expand our critical sensibilities about what it means to 'work with outside organisations and groups' and ask ourselves the difficult question: 'in the balance, am I working with them to help further their goals, or are they working with me to help further mine?''. If the latter is the case, think long and hard about how to redress this balance. We need to fight for greater recognition of policy-relevant work within our institutions. And we need to change the face of academia and bring new faces into academia to break down the still strong social divides that exist between those inside and those outside. In many of our institutions we are in sufficient numbers and in significant places of power to begin to push for these kinds of changes.

We cannot write ourselves over these hurdles, or across the divides that separate us from allies in institutions whose struggles and histories are embedded in different contexts, both inside and outside of academia. Words alone will not suffice.

Bibliography

Althusser, L (1971) *Lenin and Philosophy and Other Essays*, New York: Monthly Review Press.

Bakker, K, Page, B and Swyngedouw, E (1998) 'Lost and found in the posts: addressing critical human Geography. Letter 2. Reply from the Oxford Group', *Environment and Planning D: Society and Space*, 16(3), 262–264.

Berg, L, Morn, K and Simonsen, K (1998) 'Lost and found in the posts: addressing critical human Geography. Letter I. Impressions of the Conference', *Environment and Planning D: Society and Space*, 16(3), 258–262.

Berg, L (1998) 'Lost and found in the posts: addressing critical human Geography. Letter 5. Round 2', *Environment and Planning D: Society and Space*, 16(3), 268–271.

Blomley, N (1994) 'Editorial: Activism and the academy', *Environment and Planning D: Society and Space*, Vol. 12, 383–385.

Castree, N (2000) 'Professionalisation, activism and the university: whither "critical geography"?', *Environment and Planning A*, 32, 6, 955–970.

Chouinard, V and Grant, A (1995) 'On being not even anywhere near "the project": ways of putting ourselves in the picture", *Antipode*, 27:2, 137–166.

Christopherson, S (1989) 'On being outside the project', *Antipode*, 21:3, 83–89.

Gramsci, A (1971) *Selections from the Prison Notebooks*, edited and translated by Quintin Hoare and Geoffrey Nowell Smith, New York: International Publishers.

hooks, b (1994) *Teaching to Transgress*, New York and London: Routledge

Katz, C (1998) 'Lost and found in the posts: addressing critical human Geography. Introduction', *Environment and Planning D: Society and Space*, 16(3), 257–278.

Kristeva, J (1997) 'A new type of Intellectual: The Dissident' in Moi, T (ed.) *The Kristeva Reader*, New York: Columbia University Press.

Massey, D (2000) 'Editorial: Practising political relevance', *Transactions: Institute of British Geography*, NS 25, 131–133.

Monture, P A (1995) 'Ka-Nin-Geh-Heh-Gah-E-Sa-Nonh-Yah-Gah' in The Chilly Collective (eds) *Breaking Anonymity: The Chilly Climate for Women*, Waterloo: Wilfred Laurier Press.

Monture-Okanee, P A (1995) 'Introduction. Surviving the Contradictions: Personal Notes on Academia' in The Chilly Collective (eds) *Breaking Anonymity: The Chilly Climate for Women*, Waterloo: Wilfred Laurier Press.

Peck, J (1999) 'Editorial: Grey geography?', *Transactions: Institute of British Geography*, NS 24, 13 1–135.

Pile, S (1996) 'Space and the politics of Sleep', *Environment and Planning D: Society and Space*, 14, 1996, 503–504.

Pratt, G (1998) 'Lost and found in the posts: addressing critical human geography', *Environment and Planning D: Society and Space*, 16(3), 257–8; 264–5.

Smith, N (1996) 'Rethinking Sleep', *Environment and Planning D: Society and Space*, 14, 505–506.

Soja, E (1989) *Post-Modern Geographies*, London and New York: Verso.

Thompson, E P (1978) *The Poverty of Theory and Other Essays*, New York: Monthly Review Press.

Tickell, A (1995) 'Reflections on "Activism and the academy"' *Environment and Planning D: Society and Space*, Volume 13, 23, 5–237.

Uribe-Ortega, G (1998) 'Lost and found in the posts: addressing critical human Geography. Letter 4. Moving Past the Posts', *Environment and Planning D: Society and Space*, 16(3), 265–7.

Uribe-Ortega, G (1998) 'Lost and found in the posts: addressing critical human Geography. Letter 6. Second Reply from Mexico', *Environment and Planning D: Society and Space*, 16(3), 271–2.

West, C (1987) 'The Dilemma of the Black Intellectual', *Critical Quarterly*, 29.4 (Winter 1987): 39–52.

Index

Note: page numbers in *italics* refer to information contained in tables, page numbers in **bold** refer to figures.